𝔗𝔥𝔢 𝔖𝔲𝔫𝔡𝔞𝔶 𝔗𝔢𝔩𝔢𝔤𝔯𝔞𝔭𝔥

Guide to
Commuterland
Country life within reach of London

The Sunday Telegraph

Guide to
Commuterland
Country life within reach of London

Caroline McGhie

AURUM PRESS

AURUM PRESS

First published in 1992 by Good Books.

This updated and extended edition published
2000 by Aurum Press Ltd, 25 Bedford Avenue,
London WC1B 3AT

A catalogue record for this book is available
from the British Library

ISBN 1 85410 691 0

2003
5   4   3   2

Edited by Jane Hutchings
Produced by Norfolk Wordfarm Ltd
Cover illustration by Chris Gilvan-Cartwright
Line drawings by Vincent Design

Rail travel information by Barry Doe

Printed and bound in Wales by Creative Print
and Design Group

Contents

Introduction

What London dinner party is complete without its stock-in-trade conversation about the quality of life? The questions are always the same. What point is there in slaving round-the-clock at the office if our precious leisure hours have to be spent drumming our heels in urban parks and shopping malls? What point is there in sitting daily in traffic jams if the local schools are inadequate, the air quality too poor and the garden too small for the lifestyle we feel we deserve? How can we introduce more pleasure into our lives, and reduce the stress? How and when should we make the leap?

It has been calculated that many of us spend up to a third of our lives wondering whether or not to make radical changes – to uproot, gear-up, move along, or (and this is the latest phrase) opt for voluntary simplicity. The yearning to swap dirty pavements for honest mud, ghetto-blasters for birdsong, is one of the most basic urges. Now, as the property market surges and house prices in London make homeowners cash-rich, the magic carpet of Commuterland beckons once more as the quickest and easiest means of escape.

Couples who have reached pivotal points in their lives are especially prone to restlessness. Older couples whose children have left home inevitably feel tempted to adjust their lifestyles. Alone together at last! Perhaps a flat in town and a cottage in the country might be the answer? Younger couples with new prams in the hallway find themselves wondering if they want their children hip and streetwise or ruddy-cheeked and nature-loving. But where should they move to? What can they afford? Where would they fit in?

It is extraordinary how often people will buy a house without researching the area they are moving to. The result is that the longed-for move out of the city can end up as quick and ill-considered as an unwanted pregnancy. A single expedition to the country, a stroll around a pretty village on a sunny day, and they're ready for a lifetime of commuting.

What to watch for

Be quite certain about whether you want to live in the country, or whether you would be happier living in a town with the country a short drive away. If you want people close by, shops within walking distance, roads that are well-lit at night, then the deep countryside is not for you. Look at the towns.

What are your primary needs? Proximity to a good school, supermarket, fashion and foodie shops? Isolation, great walks, big views, village life?

If village life is what you want, find out how the village of your choice works socially. Are you prepared to put time into keeping the cogs of the village turning? Do you want to belong to a local painting/choir/bridge group?

Make sure you have allowed for inflation, interest rate rises and house market fluctuations in your house-price-plus-season-ticket calculation (and mounting school fees if they are part of the package).

Remember that villages with cohesive centres and period houses will have the highest prices. You can be quite sure that wherever a modern developer has been too heavy-handed the prices will be lower. Areas hit hardest in the slump were those which lacked architectural distinction.

Beware taking on too much land unless you really have the time to garden it or can afford to pay someone to do it for you.

Such ill-considered plunges are simply too much of a temptation to fate. The reality is that a manageable commute coupled with a genuinely enhanced lifestyle is possible only after careful consideration of a wide range of factors, some of them far from simple. You may never find exactly what you want, but you have to be happy with the compromise.

For full-time commuters the first consideration is the length and convenience of the rail journey. Decide which London terminus you want to arrive at. If you work in the City, for instance, London Bridge and Liverpool Street win hands down over Paddington or Victoria.

The conventional wisdom is that the journeys which sandwich the main commute (home to station, London terminus to place of work) are best kept down to 15 minutes each. The maximum sensible number of changes en route is two. Each extra change increases the likelihood of missed connections or other unplanned delays. Psychologists say that the stress in commuting is largely due to the suppression of our "fight or flight" response when we feel trapped and helpless in just this sort of situation

As far as the main commute is concerned, most people find that 90 minutes is the maximum tolerable limit – a time-band which has an inevitable influence on property prices. Longer commutes may be considered by those – an increasing number – who can work from home for part of the week.

It is no good consulting a map to estimate your likely journey time – the rail networks make a nonsense of geography. You will find throughout this book that stopping services from stations closer to London may take longer to get into the city than faster trains from places further out. Speed is not the only factor, however. Frequency of service is just as important. If you miss your train, how long will you have to wait for the next one? This is especially important if you need to work flexible hours and you don't want to turn into an office clock-watcher.

The purpose of this book is to do as much as possible of the initial homework for you. It follows the railway lines out of London in all directions and describes villages within reach of each station. It tries to encapsulate the character of each town and village, the landscape that surrounds it, the quality of schools and communications, journey times to London, the range of available property and what it costs. The detail is not comprehensive, but it should be enough to give you a clear idea of where to look – and where to avoid.

Caroline McGhie
North Norfolk
March 2000

Acknowledgments

This book is the result of team effort, put together by dedicated researchers who have talked to estate agents, parish clerks, town and county councils up and down the country in order to update the original text. Sophie Butler worked on East Anglia, Charlotte Williamson on the Midlands, Lu Hersey on the West, with Emma Stanford taking the lion's share of the South and East and Harriot Lane Fox casting an expert eye over Kent.

Crucial information about season tickets, journey times and frequency of trains has been prepared by the public transport travel consultant Barry Doe, who sifted all the timetables and fares manuals of all the rail companies crossed by the guide. His knowledge is encyclopaedic. I turned to the School League Tables to pick out the highest-performing schools in each area, both state and private, checking them against *The Daily Telegraph Schools Guide*, edited by John Clare. There are many more good schools in the areas but we were only able to mention those with the best results.

Useful sources of further information include local government websites, the *Shire County Guides* (Shire Publications Ltd), and *The Villages of Britain* series (Countryside Books),

which are marvellous repositories of oral history prepared by the Women's Institute.

Supreme efforts have been made to achieve factual accuracy in a world where perceptions of people and places vary, and where the pace of physical change in our towns and villages is now extremely rapid. We are grateful to all those people who have shared their local knowledge with us to make this book as useful as it is.

I would like to thank the editor of *The Sunday Telegraph*, Dominic Lawson, for having faith in the idea, Jane Hutchings for being such a good editor and my husband, Richard Girling, for embracing the project.

This edition is dedicated to my late father, Brian Hodges, who was a commuter on the Kintbury and Oxford lines for many years.

Notes on rail travel information and schools

Some explanation of the rail travel information given for each station is necessary. (For more detailed information, consult the *National Rail Timetable*.)

Journey time

This is the time taken by the **fastest** train from London in a normal off-peak hour. Any significant differences between peak and off-peak services are indicated.

Peak trains

Except where indicated, this represents the number of **through** trains per hour arriving at the London terminus between 0730 and 0930. (A margin has been allowed to take account of trains arriving within a few minutes either side of these times.) Note that there may well be a greater overall frequency offered by changing en route. Some detail on this is offered where the difference is significant. For example, Reading West has 1 through peak train per hour from Paddington, but 5 per hour by changing at Reading.

Off-peak trains

Except where indicated, this is the total number of (non-overtaken) **through** trains to the London terminus in a normal off-peak hour. Where there is no off-peak through service, but one exists locally, details are given about alternatives by changing. Note that even where an off-peak service exists there may well be a greater overall frequency offered by changing, as for the peak hour, above.

Season tickets

The price quoted is for the **Standard Class Annual**. The cost of a weekly season is obtained by dividing the annual rate by 40. A monthly season is the weekly rate x 3.84. These are the only rates available – which means that, for example, a season for six months is charged at six times the monthly rate with no further discount. However, it is possible to buy any season ticket for any length of time above a month, in odd days, at pro rata the monthly rate. **First Class** season tickets, where available, are 1.5 times the standard rate.

Out-of-town commuters can pay a supplement to incorporate a Travelcard with their annual season ticket.

This offers unlimited travel on trains, Underground and buses in Greater London. The annual supplement is only around £380 (£570 first class) which is good value as they normally cost £1416 standard class.

At most stations, an annual season ticket (with or without Travelcard) automatically becomes a 'Gold Card', entitling the holder to a third off off-peak rail fares for any journey in London and the South East area. Prices are correct as for the fares increase of 9 January 2000.

Season tickets are valid to any appropriate London terminus. For example, tickets from Brighton cover not only the services shown to Victoria or London Bridge, but also to Cannon Street, Blackfriars, Waterloo and Charing Cross by changing at London Bridge. Similarly, tickets from stations on the Bristol/Paddington line are also valid to Waterloo via Staines. Seasons issued for stations between Bedford and St Albans to Kings Cross Thameslink and from stations south of the Thames to London Bridge can now be obtained to allow travel across London on Thameslink services without extra charge – but not, of course, on the Underground, for which a Travelcard remains necessary.

Note that some stations now have dual prices for seasons. This means that one season is available on all services, and the new, cheaper, option is for just one of the operators (usually the slower or less-frequent). Note that season tickets are often available at higher prices from nearby stations on different lines. For example, in this book the quoted annual from Uckfield is £2200, but a version for £2720 also allows use from Haywards Heath to London. It is worth bearing this in mind if a place has a slender service yet a nearby station on a different line offers optional extras.

Charing Cross/Waterloo (East)

All trains to Charing Cross stop at Waterloo (East), and most trains also serve London Bridge. In the peak hours on these lines there are also additional trains into Cannon Street.

Rail maps

The maps are schematic route diagrams only, and are not to scale.

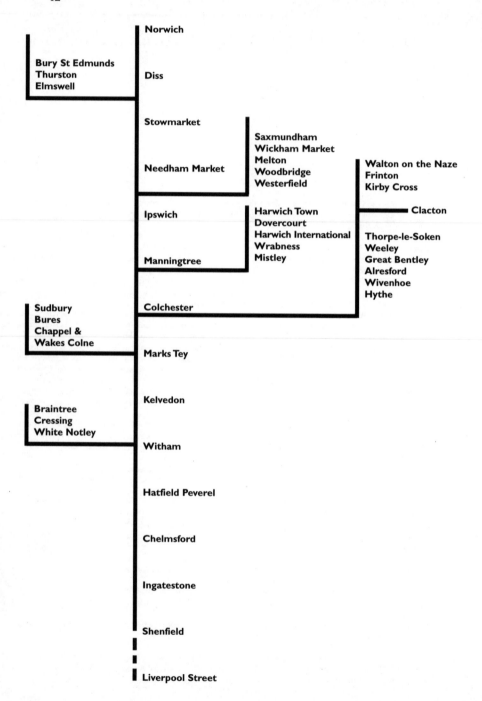

Norwich

Bury St Edmunds
Thurston
Elmswell

Diss

Stowmarket

Saxmundham
Wickham Market
Melton
Woodbridge
Westerfield

Walton on the Naze
Frinton
Kirby Cross

Needham Market

Ipswich

Harwich Town
Dovercourt
Harwich International
Wrabness
Mistley

Clacton

Manningtree

Thorpe-le-Soken
Weeley
Great Bentley
Alresford
Wivenhoe
Hythe

Sudbury
Bures
Chappel &
Wakes Colne

Colchester

Marks Tey

Kelvedon

Braintree
Cressing
White Notley

Witham

Hatfield Peverel

Chelmsford

Ingatestone

Shenfield

Liverpool Street

Liverpool Street ➡ Norwich

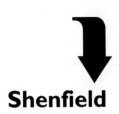

Shenfield

Shenfield is a mutated village but nonetheless the greengrocer and butcher know you by name. There are three parts to it: the village itself, with bread-and-butter Victorian and Thirties streets; Hutton Mount, where avenues of huge double-garaged detached houses priced at £400,000 to £850,000 peep out from between the trees; and Hutton proper, which is strictly Sixties, congested but more affordable. It is on London's doorstep, just outside the M25, with the result that the station car park is so crowded that parking creeps up the side roads.

Journey: 21 min
Season: £1920
Peak: 9 per hr
Off-peak: 7 per hr

Ingatestone

This is a village with small-town pretensions and well over 3,000 inhabitants, many of them East Enders who have moved up and out. Its best features are a collection of 19th-century almshouses and the High Street, which is on a reassuringly human scale. A three-bedroom semi-detached will cost £125,000 upwards; a five-bedroom house in a smart address like Charity Drive, £500,000. One of its greatest attractions is the European School, to which parents send their children from all over Essex. Many of the passengers drive south to avoid the parking problems at Chelmsford, though they lose with one hand what they gain with the other because it is more difficult to get a seat at Ingatestone.

Journey: 28 min
Season: £2064
Peak: 3 per hr
Off-peak: 1 per hr

Chelmsford

Chelmsford has just billowed with new developments. Broomfield and Links Drive are the right side of the railway tracks, Boarded Barns the wrong side. A lot of investment has been made in shopping. There are several out-of-town superstores including Tesco and Sainsbury, two malls – High Chelmer and The Meadows – while the antiques and secondhand market continues to draw the bargain-hunters. The brilliant grammar schools are a magnet to those disillusioned with London state schools. A family house in a leafy street will cost £200,000 to £275,000. The sur-

Journey: 28 min
Season: £2288
Peak: 8 per hr
Off-peak: 5 per hr

Danbury is a commuter village but not posh. It's not a don't-touch-me-place. Everyone and his grandmother goes there on Sundays for a walk

rounding countryside, despite its savaging from developers, still contains some wonderful surprises. The station lays claim to being the busiest in the country, funnelling 15,000 people each morning into London. Extra trains start here, rather than further up the line, in an attempt to provide more seats.

Close in on the east flank of the town is **Sandon**, a village distinguished by its remarkable Turkey Oak, one of the best outside Kew, which throws a tent of leaves over the entire village green. Two-bedroom cottages just off the green cost around £100,000, while a five-bedroom Georgian house would fetch £350,000. Modern four-bedroom houses are £185,000. The village is very much a dormitory, protected by the A12 bypass – though the roar of the traffic is still audible in some of the houses. The excellent comprehensive school has a large sixth form and draws children from further afield, including Maldon and South Woodham Ferrers.

A little further out is **Danbury**, larger than most people's concept of the archetypal village and on the busy A414. It has its own shops and pubs, some of them 16th-century, and the common, woods and lakes are big attractions. A period house with four bedrooms would cost £250,000 at least. "It's a commuter village but not posh. It's not a don't-touch-me place. Everyone and his grandmother goes there on Sundays for a walk," was how one local pundit described it. The heather and bracken of Danbury and Lingwood Commons (National Trust) provide one of the few known breeding grounds for the Rosy Marbled Moth. Blake's Wood also offers 100 acres of hornbeam and chestnut coppice carpeted with bluebells in the spring. **Little Baddow**, scarcely separated from Danbury, is much more snooty. It has a post-office-cum-grocer, a lovely cricket pitch in the woods and huge six-bedroom houses on The Ridge that sell for £350,000 to £1m.

Another classic commuter village is **Stock**, with its cluttered narrow streets, pond and village green, though it suffers from the traffic on the B1007. It has recently lost its butcher and greengrocer but has its own wine store, post office, general store, newsagent, fish shop and antique shops, and a wealth of societies from flower arranging to drama and the British Legion. There are some staunch churchgoers. Opinions of village life vary. One who moved away after five years describes it thus: "I never got to know anyone. They were all at work. It is well-to-do, overpriced, snobby. People tend to talk about things that don't mean anything, like the weather or Lady So-and-So's hat." A Tudor house with a quarter of an acre on the main road would cost £300,000; a three-bedroom modern semi around £140,000.

To the west of Chelmsford is a whole clutch of picturesque villages. **Writtle** is close enough to be a suburb, with 16th- and 17th-century houses costing up to £275,000. Its green and duck pond are the envy of the

House style in East Anglia

This is a region where stonelessness has led to resourcefulness. Without stone with which to build, early residents turned to timber and plaster, and later brought in the first Flemish bricks as ballast in returning wool boats. Hand-made bricks can still be bought at Bulmer in Suffolk.

It was to timber, though, that the early builders on the Essex marshes turned, round the horizontal mudflats and sea wall walks of the Blackwater estuary. Here you find modest white weatherboarded cottages like land-locked boats or beach-huts that have strayed on to solid ground. The cleft oak boards are laid with the seasoned bark-edge to the outside of the building in order to give the walls maximum protection from the elements.

Once the lovely pastoral landscape of Suffolk unfolds, it reveals some of the best medieval houses

in the country, built upon the early profits of the wool trade at a time when this was one of the richest and most densely populated regions of the country.

Streets full of drunken timbered houses, their first-floor jetties projecting over the street, built long before the chimney or the water closet had even been thought of, are the survivors of a veritable building boom. They are now fiercely guarded by the Suffolk Preservation Society, whose headquarters is among the silvery timbered buildings of Lavenham.

Suffolk also offers a wonderful architectural palette of colours – distinctive buffs, creams, yellows and pinks. Old manor houses with many gables have often had their wattle and daub walls plastered and colour-washed. Others have distinctive pargeting – the plaster raised into patterns of foliage or figures to make the walls resemble skilfully iced cakes.

county. Highlands Park, a picture of beautiful decay, stands fenced off with its grounds open to the public. It provides the setting for the annual Chelmsford Spectacular, when people take their own deckchairs to hear classical music and watch synchronised fireworks displays.

Nearby is a collection of hamlets, linked to Chelmsford by an intermittent bus service, where four-to-five-bedroom houses cost anything from £200,000 to £400,000. **Mashbury** is without a pub or shop or jumble sales, but remarkable for its togetherness. **Good Easter** has one of the oldest barns in the county and a village green with a pump on it. **High Easter** is the prettiest, with a general store, a post office and a restaurant. **Chignall Smealy** and **Chignall St James** have plenty of timbered houses but seem to lack a social or geographical focus. **Pleshey**, on the other hand, is particularly sought after because of its thatched cottages, church and motte-and-bailey castle.

Hatfield Peverel

Commuterland in the lee of the A12. Good-neighbourliness shows itself in the form of Neighbourhood Watch and a wine club set up by bibulous incomers. A cottage on the green in **Hatfield Peverel** would start at £300,000, though a small two-bedroom house might be had for £85,000. New home lovers should watch for a new Countryside Properties development of 45,000 houses called Beaulieu Park between Hatfield Peverel and Chelmsford. A Grade II listed period farmhouse with a small plot of land at **Great Leighs**, a good six-mile drive from the station, might cost around £350,000.

Journey: 42 min
Season: £2460
Peak: 3 per hr
Off-peak: 1 per hr

Witham

Journey: 39 min
Season: £2576
Peak: 7 per hr
Off-peak: 4 per hr

The smart set don't live in **Witham** itself, which has become a town that people shop in (no large department store) or pass through on their way to the station. Dorothy L. Sayers was not so proud, however. She lived and wrote in Newland Street and a little plaque is there to prove it. The town still serves as the social hub for the surrounding villages which feed commuters on to the fast main line train services to Liverpool Street. Car parking spaces are plentiful.

The conservationist lobby is strong, with old stalwarts belonging to the Witham and Countryside Society; culture vultures join the Witham Operatic and Dramatic Society. The whole of the 18th- and 19th-century High Street has been designated a conservation area. Apart from the Bramston Sports Centre, there is little for the young. The nearest cinema is miles away in Colchester or Chelmsford. In the Seventies the town was identified as a London overspill, which is why it now contains five modern estates. Old two-bedroom terrace houses cost £85,000. New first-time-buyer properties are priced similarly at £85,000 too.

The surrounding villages are significantly more expensive, with three-bedroom period houses in the £300,000 range. Scarcely separated from Witham itself is **Chipping Hill**, with the Woolpack Inn, a triangular green and a manor house. The view from here was described by Horace Walpole in 1749 as "sweet meadows falling down a hill and rising again on the other side of the prettiest winding stream you ever saw". **Wickham Bishops**, set on a hill a couple of miles out, looks down its nose at the others. **Great Braxted** is slightly cheaper, as is **Great Totham**, which is further from the station. The yachting fraternity flock to **Tollesbury**, 12 miles away, where there is a large modern marina on a creek of the Blackwater.

Branch line to **Braintree** via **White Notley** and **Cressing**

From Braintree
Journey: 64 min
Season: £2652
Peak: 2 per hr
Off-peak: 1 per hr

The through train service to Liverpool Street on this line was introduced in 1990 as a result of vigorous lobbying by the Witham and Braintree Rail Users Association. People still tend to take the shuttle into Witham and wait five minutes for a fast connection. The snag is that the last through train to Braintree leaves Liverpool Street at 8.30pm, which makes London theatre trips arduous. It is possible to catch a 10.32pm to Witham and change.

Few commuters use **White Notley**. The station is kept open because there is a level crossing here, manned by human hand until very recently but now automatic. **Cressing** is another walk-to-the-station village. The station is no more than a country halt with a platform and shelter. The village has 1,400 inhabitants, three pubs, a general store, newsagent, butcher, post office and hairdresser. It also has its own primary school, though the nearest secondary schools are in Braintree. A three-bedroom bungalow could be bought for at least £120,000. Old Cressing, part of which is a conservation area, is scissored from new Cressing by the main road. As one parish councillor put it, "Nobody would ever describe it as quaint, or even picturesque, but it is a good working village." **Braintree** is the birthplace of the Crittall window and about as pretty – definitely not a first choice for those seeking views from the sitting-room window. Yet there are whole estates built on the outskirts which are full of former Londoners, happy to swap the East End for a slower pace of life, better schools and no traffic jams. Property prices vary from £80,000 for a three-bedroom semi to £160,000 for a four-bedroom detached house, and £150,000 for a thatched cottage with three bedrooms in a third of an acre.

Traditional Essex weatherboard house

Continuation of main line
Kelvedon

Kelvedon is sought after for its strong village heartbeat. St Peter's church and the Kelvedon Players organise endless activities including children's groups and an annual pantomime between them. Once people have settled here they rarely move out. A three-bedroom period cottage with a long rear garden will cost £160,000. An Edwardian family house with five bedrooms, swimming pool, tennis court and three-and-a-half-acres would sell for around £600,000. **Feering**, less than two miles away, is almost umbilically linked. It has a new community centre and village school, an art club, a village orchestra and choir, a WI flower arranging club, bowls, badminton, scouts, guides. The villages share a cricket club. On May Day the pubs stay open all day while the village green throbs with dancers. Newcomers quickly become assimilated. A pink-painted 16th-century cottage with four bedrooms and two bathrooms can be bought for £240,000.

Journey: 48 min
Season: £2588
Peak: 3 per hr
Off-peak: 1 per hr

Marks Tey

Journey: 47 min
Season: £2664
Peak: 3 per hr
Off-peak: 2 per hr

All the Teys, **Marks Tey**, **Little Tey** and **Great Tey**, are within a 10-minute drive of this or Colchester station. Parking at both is difficult. Marks Tey has large Seventies estates where you can buy a two-bedroom house for £60,000 or a four-bedroom detached for £120,000. Little Tey, next door, is also a grazing ground for first- and second-time buyers. Great Tey is a little more remote, with its own village shop, post office and village hall. **Coggeshall**, a couple of miles from this and Kelvedon station, is more seductive, wonderfully medieval, with old lace-making traditions and a much-loved inn called The Woolpack. It has a regular Thursday market which sells everything from buttons and WI jam to fruit and vegetables. Another feather in its cap is Paycocke's House (National Trust), one of the most famous Tudor houses in the country. A period four-bedroom terrace house might cost £150,000 to £160,000.

Branch line to **Sudbury** via **Chappel & Wakes Colne** and **Bures**

No through trains.
Trains to Marks
Tey: 1 per hr
Journey: 76 min*
Season: £2952
*From Sudbury

Villagers living down this branch line would be just as likely to drive in and catch one of the more frequent trains from Colchester. **Chappel** and **Wakes Colne** are two villages sewn together by a vast and spectacular Victorian viaduct. The river Stour, crossed by a small bridge, marks the line which slices up **Bures** between Essex and Suffolk. It therefore has two of everything, from parish clerks downwards. The cricket club and green are picturesque – matches are watched by the sheep kept by the vicar in the field next door. There is conspicuous wealth here, and some weekend

Thatched cricket
pavilion, Bures

cottages. The odd pop musician sweeps through in his Rolls Royce. A little two-bedroom Victorian cottage costs £60,000; a detached three-bed-

room house on a modern development will fetch £80,000 or more, while a four-bedroom house in half an acre might reach £180,000.

Sudbury's irresistible charms compensate for the inconvenience of the journey for the brave few who commute from here. The jumble of historic cottages, churches and grander gabled houses, Gainsborough's birthplace among them, sit in the arm of the River Stour, cushioned by water meadows. The market square is filled with stalls on Thursdays and Saturdays. The Sudbury Dramatic Society raised money to establish The Quay Theatre, which is also the home of the Sudbury Light Operatic Society, the cinema and the jazz club. Down towards the water meadows there are the tennis club, the rowing club and the cricket club. The Kingfisher Leisure Pool provides a dash of Disneyland with flume rides, a wave machine and giant bouncing rubber balls.

Cricket matches are watched by the sheep kept by the vicar in the field next door

A few commuters choose to live in the town and walk to the station, or even drive to Marks Tey or Colchester. You might get a little one-bedroom cottage for around £46,000, or a three-bedroom house standing in its own garden for £139,000. Five-bedroom Victorian houses in large gardens on the outskirts can be bought for £180,000 to £200,000. Stear clear of the Great Cornard, originally a London overspill zone and still stigmatised as such.

Most people opt for the villages. **Long Melford**, three-and-a-half miles out, is one of the most admired in the county with an achingly lovely long main street (hence the name of the village) which eventually erupts on to the green and a cathedral-sized church. No wonder it was used as the backdrop to the television series *Lovejoy*. The Hall is National Trust. The Green is one of *the* addresses. A four-bedroom house with beams, peg-tile roof and an inglenook fireplace would cost £230,000, though you can get a two-bedroom Grade II listed cottage for £70,000. The village has its own school, post office, grocery stores, butcher and baker. It crawls with antique dealers and American tourists in the summer.

A film-set village with 300 listed buildings

Lavenham, four miles from Sudbury, is another film-set medieval village, with restaurants, dried flower and teddy bear shops, 300 listed buildings and the home of the Suffolk Preservation Society. "A place caught in time" is how one resident describes it – but unfortunately it is beyond the

10-mile belt round Colchester and therefore hard for regular commuters to reach at the end of a long day. **Cavendish** on the River Stour is another with a village green, antique shops and restaurants, but think hard about the journey before you look at it. A converted barn with two bedrooms will cost £120,000.

Continuation of main line
Colchester

Journey: 45 min
Season: £2808
Peak: 7 per hr
Off-peak: 6 per hr

People have time for **Colchester**, which is the oldest town in Britain, with a show-stopping Norman castle built on the foundations of a Roman Temple. The medieval alleyways in the old quarter harbour specialist shops such as a teddy bear shop, while the two pedestrianised shopping centres serve up all the usual chain stores. Three-bedroom terrace houses in town cost £67,000 to £76,000. A five-bedroom period semi with a generous garden in one of the best areas such as Lexden will cost £300,000 to £350,000. There are any number of societies including archaeological, jazz and folk and choral. It has two theatres – the Mercury, which is a repertory company, and St Mary's Arts Centre, in a converted church, which puts on a mix of concerts and shows. There is also a cinema with six screens. Colchester Leisure World is an impressive new multi-sports stadium. Annual events include summer concerts in the park and the rather bizarre Oyster Feast in October, at which assorted media figures are invited to gorge themselves.

The Colchester bag is brimming with goodies. The Colnes (see Chappel & Wakes Colne, page 18) are handsome but not glamorous. **Earls Colne**, two miles away, is the biggest and is distinguished for having a gas supply – no dreaded oil tank lurking in the garden. It is self-contained, with a supermarket, restaurants, banks and individual shops in the period High Street. There are a few modern one-off executive houses which fetch from £250,000. A three-bedroom, part-tiled, part-thatched cottage will fetch £175,000. **White Colne** is merely a ribbon settlement along the main A604 to Earls Colne. It has no shop, but properties along the main road come considerably cheaper – possibly 20% less than those on quieter roads. **Colne Engaine** is the most desirable of this group. It has a classic village green framed with period houses, a village shop, a pub, a church and a primary school. You need around £60,000 for a two-bedroom

Stoke-by-Nayland is where the poetry begins and timber-frame houses colour the landscape

cottage but over £150,000 to start looking for a family house here.

Eight Ash Green is also highly prized. The A1124 cuts through the centre, skirting the green and the little houses that circle it. It has a village store, a primary school, a church and a petrol station *and* a gas supply. It has a mix of houses, from ex-local authority selling from £65,000, to small peg-tiled timbered cottages at £100,000 to £200,000; or you might get a four-bedroom house in half an acre for just under £200,000. **Fordham**, on the River Colne, is rather more dislocated. It does a kind of vanishing act half way through the main street, then gives you a second helping as you turn the bend. Children travel up to 20 miles to Colchester Royal Grammar School (boys) or The County High (girls) if they can get a place.

The Horkesleys are not greatly loved, though you could pick up a cottage in **Little Horkesley** for £175,000. **Stoke-by-Nayland**, however, eight miles from Colchester, is where the poetry begins and drunken timber-frame houses splashed with Suffolk pink wash begin to colour the landscape. It is set high on a ridge over the Stour, with a church that commands a giddy view of Constable country in all directions. **Boxford**, a couple of miles further out, is as pretty and quieter.

Branch line to **Clacton** or **Walton** on the Naze via **Hythe, Wivenhoe, Alresford, Great Bentley, Weeley, Thorpe-le-Soken, Kirby Cross** and **Frinton**

Wivenhoe is subject to commuter clotting. It is a little quayside town which grows lumps of commuter cars each day, left there by those who want to avoid the stressful drive into Colchester (which can take 45 minutes). Parking space is so precious that the public car park, which is meant for shoppers only, is locked between 6am and 8.30am. Local councillors have even considered buying houses to knock them down, simply to create more parking spaces.

The village is gradually metamorphosing from a working port where the oyster catch was all important, to a boating village with craft shops that attract local artists and writers. The pubs bulge with students at certain times of year and parties of foreign students at others, brought in by Essex University, based in the tower blocks in Wivenhoe Park. It is distinct from Colchester five miles away, cushioned by green fields which are fiercely defended from development. Old shipyards are being turned into new houses and prices vary from £130,000 for a two-bedroom flat to

From Clacton
Journey: 82 min*
Season: £3164
Peak: 2 per hr
Off-peak: 1 per hr
* Clacton, Thorpe-
· le-Soken and
Wivenhoe only.
Other stations
change at
Colchester, except
for 1 peak-hr
service from
Walton on the
Naze.

£200,000 for a quayside house. The ferry to Rowhedge (once rowed by an elderly man who smoked a pipe) now operates only in the summer. Detached period houses on the quay cost over £100,000. Smaller three-bedroom Victorian terrace houses come in under £85,000. It has an infant and a primary school, and local societies including the Gilbert and Sullivan Society, the Wivenhoe Players and the Pantomime Group. There is also an annual regatta. The new Colne Barrier controls the tidal flow south of town in order to protect homes from flooding during surges.

Great Bentley is chiefly notable for the extraordinary size of its village green. At 45 acres it swallows the cricket green, two football pitches and the annual gymkhana – and the houses on it are the ones to aim for. Something with three bedrooms off the green might cost £100,000. There is a baker, a general store that sells everything from second-hand fire engines to candles, a primary school and allotments for residents only.

Clacton may one day find itself a conservation area. It epitomises the pre-war seaside resort, where those with fond memories of holidays in bed-and-breakfasts and days on the pier might choose to buy their final bungalow and take up a round of golf on Sundays. The average three-bedroom semi costs £70,000; a two-up-two-down £50,000. Described by some as being full of "East Enders-made-good driving their Range Rovers".

My dear, if you live in **Frinton**, you have arrived. That is to say that you have certainly distanced yourself from that frightful candyfloss and razzmatazz in Clacton. The old railway level-crossing gates are the heavenly portals to Frinton. Outside is where the modern estates are put, and it isn't Frinton proper. For Frinton is *very* proper. There are no pubs, and the beach is free of ice-cream sellers. It is genteel, with a strong church-going community. It also has its commuters who use the direct trains to Liverpool Street. Solicitors, doctors, dentists and accountants are attracted to the cavernous houses, servants' quarters and tennis courts included, worth over £250,000, that sit in swathes of garden in The Avenues. There is no problem buying olive oil here. Connaught Avenue, with its designer clothes shops, jewellers and delicatessens, is known as the Bond Street of Essex. The local clubs and societies cover three foolscap pages, but it is bridge evenings that make the world go round, coupled with the Frinton Arts and Music Society, the annual tennis tournament and the 18-hole links.

You cannot be lonely in Kirby-le-Soken. You need only weed your front garden and you could spend all day talking to passers-by

You get sand as fine but house prices considerably cheaper in **Walton on the Naze**. A three-bedroom semi on the outskirts could take £70,000 off you. There are regulation seaside resort chip shops, safe bathing, fresh lobster to be bought in the summertime and a pier, but the main attractions are the sheltered inlets behind The Naze where the yacht club is. The salt-ings and mudflats, designated as a Site of Special Scientific Interest, are a staging post for flocks of migrating birds and there are monthly guided walks.

Kirby-le-Soken, two miles away, is sought after because of its proxim-ity to Frinton. It was originally threaded on to a single long main street, in the Essex tradition, but has since sprung bungaloid growths around it. One village shop has closed, leaving one remaining and two pubs. Everybody knows everybody in this village. Cottage windows are papered with posters flagging local events, and gardens are regularly thrown open to the public for good causes. Weed your front garden here and you could spend all day talking to passers-by.

Continuation of main line
Manningtree

This station is often preferred to Colchester because it is marginally easier to park the car (though nothing is free) and easier to get a seat. **Manningtree** town itself has a charming frontage on to the Stour, known as the Walls, where homeowners think their houses are worth over £170,000, though they can tend to stick at that price. Legoland-style exec-utive houses have leeched on to it. Visitors to the port are struck by the swans and sailing barges. The social life is mixed – old skippers and com-muters drink together in the pubs – and the Manningtree Society and Stour Music Society add a cultural note.

Journey: 54 min
Season: £3132
Peak: 4 per hr
Off-peak: 3 per hr

East Bergholt is one of the set-piece villages in this area, sprawly but prime commuter territory, where houses go for up to 20% more than sim-ilar ones nearby. Constable wrote of it in 1776: "I even love every stile and stump and every lane in the village." He painted it enough times, and the cottage he used as a studio is still there – as is Willy Lott's cottage, which he made famous by painting. It doesn't seethe with tourists quite as much as other local sightseeing spots. A late Georgian house with three bedrooms might sell for £175,000. A modern four- or five-bedroom detached house that would sell for £120,000 in Ipswich would fetch at least £15,000 more here. Houses at **Flatford Mill**, the hamlet nearby, are sim-ilarly fought over. The mill, which was owned by Constable's father and painted by the man himself, attracts so many vis-itors that there are now one-way lanes.

Flatford Mill, which was owned by Constable's father, attracts so many visitors that there are now one-way lanes

Dedham is positively stockbroker now. In spite of the paralysing tourist influx in the summer, it is a place that people still dream of moving to. Sir Alfred Munnings's home, Castle House, where his paintings are on display, lies just to the south. Those who live in the High Street are martyrs to the tourists who make parking and shopping impossible. Vendors tend to think their houses are worth up to £100,000 more than comparable houses in other villages – it has the much admired Elizabethan Free Grammar School as well as historical cachet. One resident of 17 years remembers how quiet it used to be. "It looks beautiful at eight o'clock at night when nobody is here." Her commuting husband used to park in a field to catch the train at Manningtree. Now he will wait three hours to get on a later train that allows him a seat.

Branch line to **Harwich Town** via **Mistley, Wrabness, Harwich International** and **Dovercourt**

Journey: 80 min
(from Harwich
Town)
Season: £3168
Peak: 1 per hr
Off-peak: 1 per hr
changing at
Manningtree

While Manningtree benefits from the stops made by fast trains coming through from Harwich and Norwich, the small stops out along the tidal estuary towards Harwich do not. Properties are scattered and isolated along this out-of-the-way bit of coastline, and the journey, which usually involves a change at Manningtree, is slow (around 95 minutes) but spectacular.

Continuation of main line

Ipswich

Journey: 61 min
(all); 67 min (GER)
Season: £3720 (all);
£3140 (GER)
Peak: 5 per hr
Off-peak: 4 per hr
(all); 2 per hr
(GER)

Ipswich itself is described as a town of convenience, good for shopping. There is a theatre and a live rock venue. Two-bedroom terrace houses to the east, near the well-respected Northgate comprehensive, can be bought for around £55,000; three-bedroom semis for £80,000 and detached houses for £150,000 to £350,000. The prices rise when you get close to a park, especially Christchurch Park where the private schools are. Here a substantial family house will cost £150,000 to £175,000. An old rectory in a dishevelled state in a nearby village might be expected to cost £300,000. Restored, with 20 acres of meadowland and a range of outbuildings, the price will rise to £500,000.

The Shotley Peninsula, in the tongue of land just below Ipswich, is where the naturalists and yachting types gather. It has the River Orwell to one side, the Stour to the other and oozing mudflats between that attract wildfowl and waders. **Stutton** is the popular village here, on the Alton Reservoir which is the sailing centre. **Shotley Gate** at the tip provides a vantage point from which to watch the ships ploughing in and out of Harwich.

The price of houses in Kersey depends on how desperate people are to buy their fantasy

To the west of Ipswich is **Hadleigh**, a classic period market town untouched by the deadening hand of the huge supermarket chains. Eight miles out, it is a model collection of medieval and Georgian houses, and provides everything that a small town should, from wine bars and interior designers to banks and solicitors. But the young complain of feeling stifled. A small two-bedroom Tudor cottage here would cost £85,000 to £95,000; a large Georgian town house £220,000. Just two miles beyond it is **Kersey**, where the price of the houses depends on how desperate people are to buy their fantasy. The hillside, running steeply down to a watersplash and up again, is stacked with remarkable lichen-cloaked half-timbered houses, built 500 years ago on the profits of the cloth industry. A three-bedroom detached 19th-century house in two acres would sell for £230,000.

Continuing east you have to beware the flight-path of the low-flying jets that come screaming out of RAF Wattisham.

To the east is **Woodbridge**, one of the most sought-after towns in this part of Suffolk. It has its own station and has a new direct service once-a-day into Liverpool Street – members of the new commuter club here pay

Schools in Suffolk

One of the honeypots is Ipswich, which has two star private schools, Ipswich School for both sexes and Ipswich High for girls. Another is Bury St Edmunds (now more accessible by train) which has Culford independent school, and two comprehensives, King Edward VI and St Benedict's Catholic voluntary-aided co-educational school. Woodbridge (also more accessible) has a pair of independent schools in Framlingham and Woodbridge, as well as the comprehensive Thomas Mills High. For girls another school with good results is St Felix at Southwold overlooking the Blyth estuary.

for their tickets monthly by direct debit. High-ranking, high-salaried types buy up the 16th-century houses round this old port on the Deben estuary. It is serious boating and foody country. You can buy a three-bedroom terrace close to the ancient weatherboarded tide-mill and old quayside buildings in the town itself from £90,000 with on-road parking. Or you could spend over £500,000 on a period house with six bedrooms and exposed beams. It also has its own highly respected co-educational school (Woodbridge School) and a prep. Prices have been rising fast here.

Branch line to **Saxmundham** via **Westerfield, Woodbridge, Melton,** and **Wickham Market**

No through trains off-peak.
Trains to Ipswich: 1 every 2 hrs.
Journey: 105 min (from Saxmundham)
Season: £4336
Peak: 1 through train; 1 changing
Off-peak: 1 every 2 hrs changing at Ipswich

Much of this remarkable coast is just too far for daily commuters. But a new direct early morning service into London will make it appeal to home-workers who only need to make weekly or bi-weekly visits to the capital. There is just one train out at breakfast and one tea-time train home. Otherwise you have to change at Ipswich. Late stragglers should be aware that the last train out of Ipswich is at 22.02pm.

Those who can't afford **Woodbridge** (see Ipswich) might consider **Little** and **Great Bealings** where a two-bedroom cottage can be bought for £75,000, or **Grundisburgh** (pronounced Grundsbra), which is popular with families because it has a good primary school, or **Ufford**, which is very pretty and unspoilt. **Wickham Market** is also an unpretentious little town with a market square fringed with white-fronted Georgian houses. An end-of-terrace two-bedroom cottage recently sold for £52,000.

Or you could journey on to **Saxmundham** and head for **Aldeburgh** – described by E.M. Forster as "a bleak little place, not beautiful". Most people find it enchanting (fresh fish to be bought off the boats on the beach every morning) and many like to retire or take second homes there, intending to commute during the summer months only. Prices vary from £120,000 for a three-bedroom cottage in the town centre to £250,000 for a four-bedroom semi with a garden and garage. The internationally renowned music festival is held down the road at **Snape**. There are the huge seaside holiday villas at Tudoresque **Thorpeness** that sell for £90,000 to £200,000.

Beyond the Sizewell power station, which is not everyone's idea of a scenic embellishment, you come to the villages of **Westleton** and **Middleton**. These are hugely popular with escapees from the City who want to don Barbours, wellies

Suffolk half-timber and thatch cottage

and tweed hats and visit the wonderful vanishing cliffs at Dunwich (National Trust) or the Royal Society for the Protection of Birds reserve at Minsmere. Westleton has a village green and duck pond to go with its Suffolk thatch, colour wash and wattle-and-daub cottages. You could get a three-bedroom end-of-terrace for £55,000 but it would need a lot of renovation. **Yoxford** is worth thinking about, too. A converted village shop with five bedrooms could be bought for £220,000. **Peasenhall** is also pretty, and **Framlingham** provides the nearest classic country town, with a market square and old castle at its heart, though it is rather too far for commuters.

Continuation of main line
Needham Market

Needham Market has plenty of old houses, some with Georgian facades, and a wondrous 15th-century chapel with a roof that sent the art historian Nikolaus Pevsner into orbit. He described it as "a whole church with nave, aisles and clerestory seemingly in the air". Buyers are drawn to the villages to the west that bask in the reflected glow of nearby Lavenham. **Hitcham** has the crucial ingredients of shop and a densely-packed parish calendar, but the property prices are a fraction lower than those around Stowmarket. **Bildeston** has all the black and cream wickerwork architecture of a village built on the profits of the medieval clothing industry, and one of the most perfect rows of cottages running off the square. It also has restaurants and a doctor's surgery. To the east of Needham Market the houses have much humbler origins.

Journey: 82 min
Season: £4048
Peak: 1 through train; 2 per hr changing at Ipswich
Off-peak: 1 every 2 hrs changing at Ipswich

Stowmarket

Stowmarket has a strategic position just on the lip of the Suffolk prairie. Beyond the A45 all the last dimples in the countryside have been ironed flat, and the trees and hedges unpicked from a landscape which blazes yellow with rape in the summer. Little two-up-two-downs cost £45,000; modern three-bedroom detached houses £85,000. **Haughley**, however, is pretty enough to have been colonised by commuters to Bury or Ipswich. It combines new developments on the outskirts with an intimate old village street and a green with a large parish coal-house on it, built in 1861. It also has shops, restaurants, and a strong interest in organic farming (this is where the Soil Association experiments with pesticide-free crops). **Wetherden** has not been developed quite so much, and its preoccupations are firmly agricultural and horsey. Newmarket is not that far away, and point-to-points are regular and well attended. A three-bedroom thatched cottage in either village could be expected to cost £150,000.

Journey: 75 min
Season: £3960
Peak: 3 per hr
Off-peak: 1 per hr

Branch line to **Bury St Edmunds** via **Elmswell** and **Thurston**

Journey: 110 min
(from Bury St
Edmunds)

Season: £4228 (also
valid into Kings
Cross via
Cambridge)

Peak: 1 through
train; 1 per hr
changing at
Ipswich or
Cambridge (into
Kings Cross)

Off-peak: 1 every 2
hrs changing at
Ipswich or
Cambridge

This area is not nearly as popular with London commuters as that served by the fast electric trains to Diss. Both **Elmswell** and **Thurston** are earmarked for expansion by the local authority.

Bury St Edmunds could be forgiven for regarding itself as the capital of East Anglia. As atmospheric as Norwich, Cambridge or King's Lynn, it sits right at the heart of the region on the conjunction of the A45, A143 and A134. On the rail network it stands on the watershed, suspended 28 miles from Cambridge and Ipswich. People travel west via Cambridge, east via Ipswich. A new breakfast train direct to London each day and home again in the evening makes things easier. Georgian and medieval houses crowd the centre, and in summer the tourists flock in to see the abbey ruins. The covered market opens on Wednesdays and Saturdays. British Sugar has made it the base for one of its major production plants. West Suffolk Hospital is also there, and so is the Greene King brewery. Victorian terrace houses stand in appropriately named streets – Queens Road, Kings Road, Albert Crescent and so on. Two-bedroom versions start at around £70,000. Something more lavish at an address like Home Farm Lane will cost over £170,000.

Most people prefer the more undulating landscape to the south of the Fens

Three miles to the north is **Culford**, best known for its mixed day and boarding public school. Four-bedroom modern estate houses sell at £125,000. To the north-west you rapidly enter the Fens, and most people tend to prefer the more undulating landscape to the south.

Fornham St Martin on the northern edge, has recently been relieved by a bypass. Four-bedroom houses skirting the Fornham Park golf course sell at over £130,000. **Fornham All Saints** is an older village altogether, centred around the church and village green. Its golf course, the Lark Valley, is owned by businessman Eddie Shah. Four-bedroom houses here might fetch £130,000.

To the south is **Horringer** (once known as Horningsheath) with a set-piece church and green beside the entrance to Ickworth House (National Trust). The green is framed by neat cottages in plastered timber, flintwork and white brick that sell in an instant. Or there is **Cockfield**, an extraordinary cluster of hamlets, each with its own green, where a five-bedroom period house with three reception rooms might sell for £240,000. A mile away is **Great Green**, where you have village cricket on summer Sunday afternoons and four-bedroom period houses selling at £175,000.

Continuation of main line

Diss

Diss is extremely popular with commuters because the trains whistle through to London. During the property boom of the late Eighties the town expanded, a few computer companies moved in and prices went up. It currently has a population of around 7,500, and still has a weekly Friday market, though it no longer includes livestock. It has an indoor swimming pool, squash and tennis courts, and an 18-hole golf course but no cinema. In the town itself (which has mains gas) the most desirable streets include Mount Street, but also Denmark Street and Friends Road, where older Georgian houses mix with Fifties properties. A period semi with three bedrooms might sell for £100,000; a four-bedroom detached with large garden £125,000, and a good barn conversion with three to four bedrooms £250,000.

Journey: 87 min
Season: £4200
Peak: 2 per hr
Off-peak: 1 per hr

Georgian farmhouse, south Norfolk

Dickleburgh, three miles to the north, has its own village stores, post office, doctor's surgery and primary school, and has been bypassed. Or you could look west to **Redgrave**, which has a village green, post office and pub. Much closer to Diss is **Palgrave**, which has a preponderance of artists, including a cartoonist, who live in the plastered and thatched cottages and regularly show their work. It has a post office-cum-shop, a green and a primary school. Locals complain that the school is cramped Victorian, but it cannot expand because it is built on common land. The only pub closed several years ago and the bar in the village hall is open only occasionally. Houses on the new David Wilson Homes development sell at over £150,000 for four to five bedrooms.

South-west is **Mellis**, a tiny scattered village with the most extraordinarily large 1,400-acre green. It has a pub, but no post office or shop, and the most talked-about feature is the common. The Suffolk Wildlife Trust likes to delay the hay-cutting in order to allow the wild flowers to reseed, but some villagers worry that so much dried grass represents a fire hazard. The green is bisected by the main railway line which can be noisy, depending which way the wind is blowing. Children attend the primary school here, then go to secondary school in Eye which also has a sixth-form college.

Schools in Norfolk

In Norfolk the widest choice is in Norwich. Schools here include the two strong independents, Norwich School for boys and Norwich High for girls, as well as the Roman Catholic voluntary-aided comprehensive Notre Dame High School.

A particularly interesting school in Norfolk is the grant-maintained Wymondham College, Europe's largest mixed state boarding school (tuition is free, and the cost of boarding lower than at any comparable private school) – not to be confused with Wymondham High comprehensive, which also does very well.

Gresham's, at Holt near the North Norfolk coast, is the dominant co-educational independent school in the area, admitting both day pupils and boarders.

For a very lively village life it would be better to look east to **Hoxne** (rhymes with oxen) which is set around the village green with an outstanding half-timbered priory with herringbone brickwork. It has its modern ribbon development, a primary school and very good secondary school. The clubs and societies vary from the Ramblers to Hoxne Players, and there is a weekly youth club for teenagers that throws the occasional disco. The village has one pub, a shop and a petrol pump. Country dancing around the maypole is a must, as is the Harvest Breakfast on the green in the autumn. This comes a fortnight after the rousing Harvest Festival and Harvest Lunch. A small terrace house here could be had for around £65,000. Something bigger with three bedrooms would start at £75,000.

Eye, four miles south, is a typical sleepy Suffolk town on the River Dove, with a pharmacy, butcher, greengrocer, fabric shop, bank and post office, an old castle and a new business park on the old airfield. Though it is no longer a borough, it still has its mayor and deputy mayor. It attracts lots of London commuters and buzzes with societies. These include the Gardening Club, the Eye Theatre, the Eye Bach Choir. There was once a ladies' cricket team called The Eye Catchers. It has a primary school and a small hospital that caters mainly for the elderly. Gardening is competitive – residents throw their gardens open to the public. Church fund-raising activities are frequent and impressive. A four-bedroom thatched cottage with a separate annexe at **Yaxley**, two miles away, would hit the market with a price tag of around £160,000. New four-bedroom houses cost £169,000.

Norwich

Few people commute this far, though the new half-hourly service to London makes it much easier. The attractions of **Norwich** are strong, especially with the Broads and the Norfolk beaches just a car drive away. The hospital and the University of East Anglia swell the ranks of the middle-class professionals. The city retains a strong sense of history with the old castle, huge tented market and vibrant shopping centre at its heart, where street buskers, students and wealthy shoppers mix. To be near enough to the station you need to look to the south-west, in an area known as The Golden Triangle, where you could pay up to £220,000 for a double-fronted Victorian villa, though there are plenty of cheaper Victorian terrace houses to be had, too. On a modern estate you could buy a detached four-bedroom house for £100,000 to £125,000.

Journey:	100 min
Season:	£4400
Peak:	3 per hr
Off-peak:	2 per hr

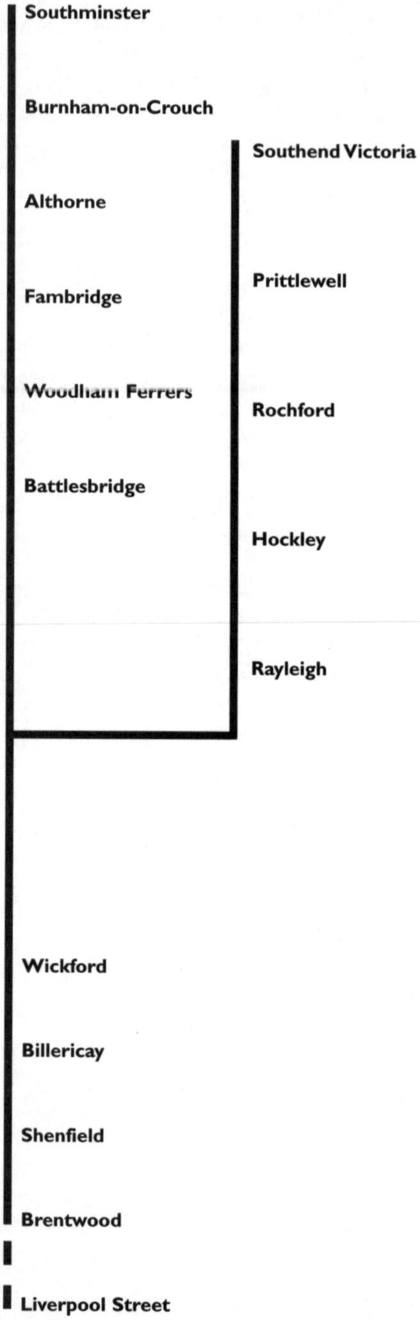

Southminster

Burnham-on-Crouch

Southend Victoria

Althorne

Prittlewell

Fambridge

Woodham Ferrers

Rochford

Battlesbridge

Hockley

Rayleigh

Wickford

Billericay

Shenfield

Brentwood

Liverpool Street

Liverpool Street ➡ Southend

Brentwood

People are fond of **Brentwood** because of its traditional high street with independent shops and its convenient position. It is right on Junction 28 of the M25, yet within walking distance of fields, woods and the lakes of Thorndon Park. It exudes a sense of wealth, even among the young. Ford, Mobil and British Telecom have a strong presence as employers; Ford once owned a lot of property which has now been sold off. Modern estates have been grafted on to gracious Victorian terraces and Thirties culs-de-sacs. In The Homesteads, for instance, mansion-sized houses are packed as tight as country cottages to create a feeling of village intimacy. A four-bedroom property here would cost £275,000 to £325,000. Brentwood's adult population empties into London every weekday, though many of them opt to catch the train at Shenfield.

Journey: 34 min
Season: £1760
Peak: 7 per hr
Off-peak: 6 per hr

Shenfield

On London's perimeter, just beyond the M25, Shenfield offers busy suburban life with a villagey feel and fast and frequent trains to London. For main entry, see **Liverpool Street to Norwich** line (page 13).

Journey: 21 min
Season: £1920
Peak: 9 per hr
Off-peak: 7 per hr

Billericay

Billericay is quiet, respectable and genteel. House prices are not as high as at Shenfield or Brentwood, but they are higher than at Chelmsford. The town is close enough to the open countryside to attract a steady drift of people from London's East End. A private golf course has been built on the Chelmsford side. To park your car in the station car park you have to strike up a close relationship with the car park attendant, or join a waiting list which is a year long. And remember, there are between 3,000 and 4,000 season ticket holders to compete with.

Journey: 30 min
Season: £2104
Peak: 8 per hr
Off-peak: 3 per hr

Wickford

Journey: 35 min
Season: £2324
Peak: 8 per hr
Off-peak: 3 per hr

People who live in **Wickford** consider themselves superior to those who live in Basildon but inferior to those from Rayleigh. Commuters pour in from the Dengie peninsula to catch the fast trains here, rather than take the slower service on the Southminster branch line. Some of the trains stop at Stratford, where people can switch painlessly to the London Underground or Docklands Light Railway. The town is a tumour of Sixties estates built on to the village of Shotgate, with green belt on three sides. You could spend £100,000 on a new three-bedroom semi, or well over £120,000 on a house with four bedrooms. Housing estates are popular. On the Wick housing development, 3,000 houses (of a projected total of 4,000) have been completed, selling at £100,000 to £120,000 for three to four bedrooms.

Branch line to **Southminster** via **Battlesbridge**, **Woodham Ferrers**, **Fambridge**, **Althorne** and **Burnham-on-Crouch**

Journey: 80 min
(63 min peak) from Southminster
Season: £2588
Peak: 2 per hr
Off-peak: 1 per hr

South Woodham Ferrers is almost other-worldly, epitomising all that the Essex Design Guide had to say about the use of traditional materials and regional styles. Building began in 1976, which makes it one of the more recent attempts to create a planned new town instead of a rash of new developments. Banks are made to look like barns. Everything has steep pitched roofs and eaves, and the William de Ferrers school doubles as a public library and the hall for the amateur dramatics society. Planning regulations are fierce. You need permission for double glazing, and satellite dishes are frowned upon. The Round Table and other similar organisations are strong in a place where people were once all newcomers together, forging links for the first time. The town has grown up now though, and a place once entirely inhabited by thirty-somethings who were all relatively well-off and wrinkle-free, now has much more of a mix of ages and income brackets. One-bedroom houses start at £50,000, four-bedroom detached houses at £110,000. The Marsh Farm Country Park offers 320 acres of reclaimed marshland in which to walk the dog. The shopping development offers retail therapy.

At **Fambridge** you enter yachting country. It has a post office and a general store and is encircled by new estates. A modern three-bedroom semi costs £85,000 to £90,000. **Althorne** is a tiny hamlet, half-a-mile from its station on the river. It is mostly modern, with a post office and a pub. A semi there costs £68,000 upwards, a bungalow from £110,000 and a detached house £150,000 to £300,000. It is **Burnham-on-Crouch**, however, which is the real yachting capital of the Dengie peninsula, known as the pearl or the Cowes of the east coast. Burnham Week attracts hundred of yachts and thousands of visitors every year. The town has a mix

> Burnham-on-Crouch is known as the pearl or the Cowes of the east coast

of Victorian, Georgian and classic Essex weatherboarded cottages, and a huge modern complex of flats built on the quay, popular with weekenders who want long lonely walks. Those overlooking the river start at £160,000; the smallest flats go for £60,000–£70,000. An older two-bedroom cottage might be had for £65,000.

Southminster suddenly seems remote at the end of the line, and house prices dip accordingly. It is a close farming community on the very edge of the marshes that stretch timelessly off into the North Sea. A three-bedroom semi here would cost £70,000. A grander house on the outskirts with a paddock would be upwards of £200,000. Southminster has its own primary school, cricket and football teams and choral society. **Tillingham**, to the north, is the archetypal Essex village with weatherboarded cottages, a green, a church and a pub. A two-bedroom cottage in a terrace starts at £60,000; a four-bedroom detached house in an acre would cost over £200,000. Still within reach of

Southminster station is **Bradwell-on-Sea**. It has a good collection of cottages, and Bradwell Lodge, a Georgian house near the Blackwater, with internal decorations by Robert Adam. Its church, St-Peter's-on-the-Wall, is one of the earliest in England, built in 654, though only the nave remains. You can walk 12 miles along the sea wall without meeting a soul. Close by is a marina and bird reserve, but the area is stigmatised by the presence of the nuclear power station.

Riverside apartments, Burnham-on-Crouch

Continuation of main line
Rayleigh

Journey: 40 min
Season: £2428
Peak: 6 per hr
Off-peak: 3 per hr

This is where the large local Sainsbury is situated and where people from many of the surrounding towns come to do their shopping. **Rayleigh** mushroomed in the Thirties, and considers itself upmarket of Basildon and Wickford. A modern three-bedroom semi costs £90,000 to £95,000. The nearby village of **Hullbridge** once had the dubious honour of being dubbed by *The Sun* as the sexiest place in England. The reasons given were no more exciting than its high per capita birthrate and a local councillor's claim that the place is so boring that people have nothing better to do than stay at home and make babies. The village should be valued more for the fact that it sits on the Crouch Estuary. You can walk along the sea wall to Battlesbridge, where you can enjoy one of the few slivers of Essex landscape which have remained unsullied by modern pressures.

Hockley

Journey: 45 min
Season: £2420
Peak: 6 per hr
Off-peak: 3 per hr

The Southend area was developed in the 1890s, and the further you come inland from the tip, the more modern it becomes. **Hockley** and **Hawkwell**, roughly six miles inland, have mostly Sixties and Seventies houses. Hockley Woods is the place for Sunday walks along the bridleways, with drinks at The Bull afterwards. Lakeside and Bluewater provide the all-singing all-dancing shopping experiences in this part of the world.

Rochford

Journey: 48 min
Season: £2420
Peak: 6 per hr
Off-peak: 3 per hr

Rochford is a plain town with a square surrounded by banks and specialist shops, including an arts and crafts shop, a tea and coffee shop, and a watch repairer. The market is held here every Tuesday. Hall Road is the smart address. The houses here have huge gardens running down to the golf course, and you'll need over £500,000 to buy. The town tends to feel overshadowed by Southend. It has a lake popular with anglers on Sundays. The choice of shops has improved with the opening of a new Lakeside shopping centre off the M25 at Thurrock. **Ashingdon**, three miles away, has higher property prices. A modern one-bedroom flat can be had for

"I'll tell you how bad Prittlewell used to be," says one commuter. "I sent a bottle of wine to the station manager just because my train was on time. Then 77 consecutive journeys were 10 minutes late"

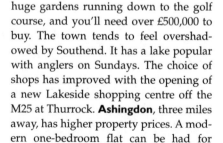

£43,000, while four-bedroom houses can cost over £125,000. It has a pub, a few shops, and it sits in a patch of rural Essex that is trying to keep urbanisation at bay.

Prittlewell

Prittlewell is a restrained northern suburb of Southend where two- to three-bedroom semis cost around £53,000. People who travel this line have seen the service improve dramatically. "I'll tell you how bad it used to be," says one commuter. "I sent a bottle of wine to the station manager just because my train was on time. Then 77 consecutive journeys were 10 minutes late."

Journey: 52 min
Season: £2420
Peak: 6 per hr
Off-peak: 3 per hr

Southend Victoria

Good grammar schools, sea air, reasonable house prices and a frequent service to Fenchurch Street and Liverpool Street make **Southend** a tempting choice. For main entry see Southend on the **Fenchurch Street to Shoeburyness** line (page 41). Most people prefer to use that line because the journey is quicker.

Journey: 55 min
Season: £2440
Peak: 6 per hr
Off-peak: 3 per hr

Shoeburyness

Thorpe Bay

Southend East

Southend Central

Westcliff-on-Sea

Chalkwell

Leigh-on-Sea

Benfleet

Pitsea

Basildon

Laindon

West Horndon

Fenchurch Street

Fenchurch Street
➡ Shoeburyness

For stations to Fenchurch Street there is a 25% discount (approx) on a season ticket for trains arriving in London before 0715 or after 0915 Monday–Friday. There is no restriction on the return leg or in either direction at weekends.

West Horndon

Classic between-the-wars and post-war suburbia has sprouted at **West Horndon** because of the sheer convenience of the rail service, though it somehow remains rural and most of the Thirties bungalows have 150ft gardens, many of them backing on to fields. The station attracts commuters along the A128 from Brentwood who find it easier to drive south and catch the train here rather than tangle with the traffic in Brentwood or Basildon. A three-bedroom bungalow sells for around £95,000; a detached one for around £160,000 to £170,000.

Journey: 29 min
Season: £1400
Peak: 4 per hr
Off-peak: 2 per hr

Laindon

Laindon station has the advantage of an extra platform. A number of services start from here, and its commuters are guaranteed a seat. The downmarket area is known locally as Alcatraz, where three-bedroom terrace houses cost around £40,000. The better area is Langdon Hills, within a few minutes' walk of the station, where modern detached houses sell for about £150,000 to £200,000.

Journey: 34 min
Season: £1840
Peak: 7 per hr
Off-peak: 2 per hr

Basildon

Basildon has virtually swallowed up **Laindon** and **Pitsea**. As one of a clutch of new towns planned after World War II to absorb people and industry from London, it exists as a kind of joke to people who once thought we could be weaned away from commuting. The planners decided people could live and work in the same place – industrial development was zoned to the north of the town – and for this reason it was built without a station. They finally had to bow to pressure and build one in the Seventies. The town's phenomenal rate of growth has not been without its problems. Older residents have felt increasingly uneasy about walking alone at night, and sometimes Basildon has to be heavily policed. Against that, the centre has been given a multi-million-pound makeover, together with a millennium glass bell tower opened by the Queen. You could buy a four-bedroom executive's house-with-garage for £130,000 to £180,000.

Journey: 33 min
Season: £1840
Peak: 6 per hr
Off-peak: 4 per hr

Pitsea

Journey: 41 min
Season: £1996
Peak: 5 per hr
Off-peak: 4 per hr

Pitsea is rather more friendly than Basildon proper, with a defined centre and an open-air market in the sea of ex-council housing. A three-bedroom terrace house can be found for £55,000, an ex-council one-bedroom flat for £26,000. Pitsea Mount offers some of the best private housing very close to the station, with four-bedroom detached houses costing £130,000.

Benfleet

Journey: 39 min
Season: £2200
Peak: 9 per hr
Off-peak: 4 per hr

The Southend Rail Travellers Association says this is one of the busiest stations on the entire line, serving a huge catchment area swollen with Sixties development. **Benfleet** itself is little more than ribbon development along the A130, and it is hard to find anything you could define as a centre. Little weatherboarded cottages can be bought for £65,000, detached executive houses with four or five bedrooms for £140,000 to £300,000.

Leigh blends a certain eccentricity (of the take-the-tricycle-rather-than-the-bus kind) with airs and graces

The station also attracts commuters from **Canvey Island**, which is really the scrag end of Essex. So much of it lies below sea level that houses tend to offer views of the sea wall or of oil refineries. Property is cheap. You can get a little one-bedroom bungalow for £55,000 to £65,000, or a three-bedroom semi for around £80,000. Traffic in and out of the island strangles the only two roads linking it to the mainland. Peter de Savary's plans to build 4,300 houses, accompanied by a new station just south of Benfleet, have now been shelved.

Leigh-on-Sea

Journey: 44 min
Season: £2220
Peak: 9 per hr
Off-peak: 4 per hr

Leigh blends a certain eccentricity (of the take-the-tricycle-rather-than-the bus kind) with airs and graces, and is more sought-after than its neighbours. The old town in particular is worth just going to see, since it retains its historical integrity as a working fishing village. You can watch the boats landing their catches, and the cockle sheds are well stocked. The two- or three-bedroom terrace cottages rarely come on the market and are quickly snapped up, for £90,000 or more, when they do.

Birdwatchers are treated to endless sightings of migratory birds that stop off at Two Tree Island, a stretch of saltmarsh that was once a refuse dump. Hadleigh Country Park offers 100 acres of grazed downland with birds, butterflies and urbanised wildlife. Many of the larger Victorian houses have been filleted into flats. Something with one bedroom might sell at £50,000, two bedrooms at £60,000. Unconverted Twenties and Thirties houses up on the cliffs go for over £180,000.

Chalkwell

The Chalkwell Hall estate is extremely popular, being south of the London Road, close to the Fenchurch Street line and the bracing breezes from the seafront. Large detached Victorian houses with four bedrooms cost over £200,000.

Journey: 47 min
Season: £2220
Peak: 8 per hr
Off-peak: 4 per hr

Westcliff-on-Sea

Westcliff is a dignified old Victorian lady of a town which has managed to fend off the encroaching seaside tat. Sadly, however, her densely layered streets of 19th-century houses, many of them now converted into flats, tend to be jammed with cars that can't find anywhere to park. Average prices of flats range from around £35,000 for one bedroom to £45,000 or £50,000 for two. The Cliff Gardens run all the way along the cliffs to Southend.

Journey: 49 min
Season: £2320
Peak: 8 per hr
Off-peak: 4 per hr

Southend Central

Southend has spent the last few decades adjusting to the death of the Great British Holiday, while simultaneously adapting itself as a London dormitory. It remains popular with day-trippers and bank holiday week-enders, and hasn't lost the brash, kiss-me-quick, ice-cream and candyfloss feel of the Fifties. Strolling along the Prom is still a popular Sunday morning pastime. Its efforts in the late 18th and 19th centuries to rival the elegance of other seaside resorts such as Brighton have endowed it with some fine buildings, including the Royal Terrace. The one-and-a-quarter mile pier, which miraculously survived a fire in 1976 and being cut by a boat 10 years later, is being restored, and a large roller-coaster called The Swine is being created to provide a sister attraction.

Journey: 52 min
Season: £2320
Peak: 8 per hr
Off-peak: 4 per hr

Westcliff is a dignified old Victorian lady of a town which has fended off the seaside tat

The Access credit-card company and the administrators of VAT are both large local employers. The shopping centre is

Even those who live on the fringe-of-the-fringe say they live in Thorpe Bay

now pedestrianised, though it is outdone in choice of shops by Basildon and the huge Lakeside development at Thurrock. Southend has its own airport with flights to the Channel Islands and permission is being sought for a combined train and air super terminal for business travellers. The sailing fraternity is strong. There are seven yacht clubs either side of Southend, in the stretch between **Thorpe Bay** and **Leigh Old Town**.

Average house prices run from £60,000 for a two-bedroom house, £75,000 for a three-bedroom semi and well over £100,000 for one in a better area.

Southend East

Journey: 54 min
Season: £2320
Peak: 8 per hr
Off-peak: 4 per hr

This is the area known as **Southchurch**. A great web of residential streets extends from Southend Central to Thorpe Bay, stitched together by a long main road of shops and offices. A three-bedroom semi on one of the nicest roads – Southchurch Boulevard or Arlington Road, for example – will cost over £90,000. In less popular streets the price drops to around £70,000. Two- or three-bedroom terrace houses sell for around £65,000 to £70,000.

Thorpe Bay

Journey: 58 min
Season: £2400
Peak: 8 per hr
Off-peak: 4 per hr

Thorpe Bay is the most expensive part of Southend, and even those who live on the fringe-of-the-fringe say they live there. Detached houses with four to five bedrooms, built early this century, sell for £200,000. Those on the seafront might go for anything from £400,000 to £500,000. The private golf club and Conservative politics feature large on the social circuit, which is fuelled with new money and is anxious to dissociate itself from anything too down-market. There is only one pub. The place excites envy in its neighbours, as described by one local cricketer with typical Essex bluntness, "When you played against Thorpe Bay, you bowled at the batsman, not the wicket."

Shoeburyness

Journey: 63 min
Season: £2400
Peak: 8 per hr
Off-peak: 4 per hr

With its sprawling council estates and industrial zones, **Shoeburyness** has little to offer other than cheapness. A three-bedroom house can be had for around £80,000. It also has a beach which is good for windsurfing, sailing and jet skiing. There are a few flats right on the beach that sell for around

£80,000, but the marginally more salubrious part lies to the north and it is possible to buy a good house in the £240,000 range. Seafront property, Southend

Barling nearby offers a profound contrast with one foot still firmly planted in the past. Among the 300-year old cottages, it is also possible to buy a detached Twenties bungalow needing complete renovation for £220,000. A period house with a paddock in this area would cost at least £500,000. Alternatively there is **Great Wakering**, with its church, pubs and shops. A two-bedroom Grade II listed mid-terrace here would cost £75,000; a three-bedroom house with a long rear garden over £85,000.

Schools in Essex

The choice of high-peforming grammar, ex-grammar and opted-out comprehensives in Essex makes it attractive to ambitious parents with young families who cannot afford to use the private sector. Be warned, however, that some of the best schools have five times too many applicants for the number of places. Entrance requirements are stiff.

Many of the schools appear in clusters. Southend, for instance, has Southend Boys' High, Southend Girls' High, both traditional grammar schools, as well as two good state schools, Westcliff High for boys and Westcliff High for girls. Brentwood independent schools are Brentwood and Peniel Academy (non-selective). The good comprehensives include St Martin's, Brentwood County High and the Ursuline ex-grammar opted-out comprehensive girls' convent. Not far away is the Anglo-European at Ingatestone, an opted-out comprehensive which promotes the International Baccalaureate.

Chelmsford has the grant-maintained County High School for Girls and the boys' equivalent, King Edward VI Grammar School, which has choral links with the cathedral. New Hall is the nearby girls' day and boarding school.

Colchester has the grant-maintained Grammar County High School for Girls and Colchester Royal Grammar for boys – a descendant of the ancient town school established in 1206. Choices here also include St Benedict's Roman Catholic and Philip Morant grant-maintained co-educational schools.

Other places with strong schools are Hornchurch, which has The Campion boys' Catholic voluntary-aided comprehensive; Loughton, which has the Davenant Foundation grant-maintained co-educational school; Saffron Walden with its County High; Hockley, which has Greensward College comprehensive; and Woodford Green, which has the girls' grammar, Woodford County High.

Pitsea

Stanford-le-Hope

East Tilbury

Tilbury Town

Grays

Fenchurch Street

Fenchurch Street
➡ Pitsea (via Tilbury)

Grays

Grays was built in two surges – one in the late 19th century and one in the Thirties – and is now one of the busiest commercial centres in this part of Essex. The most sedate area to live is **North Grays**, where the roads are filled with large Thirties houses. The four-bedroom detached variety would cost between £110,000 and £135,000. **North Stifford** is another popular part, with the remnants of the old village still intact (blink and you miss it). A 15th-century cottage with two bedrooms could sell for around £145,000. The vast Lakeside shopping centre at Thurrock, two or three miles away, offering the largest concentration of shopping in Europe, a Mississippi steamer restaurant and 11-screen cinema, is challenging shoppers' loyalty to Basildon and Southend. It has also spawned the new Bannatynes Leisure Centre. Grays itself is a good shopping centre with small outlets of the big chains. Nearby is the site of the Chafford Hundred development, where a whole new town of 5,000 new houses is being built on the old chalk pits beside the M25 and the Dartford Tunnel. It has a rich mix of one-bedroom flats for £45,000 to £60,000 up to four-bedroom houses selling for around £150,000 to £220,000, with maisonettes, semis and terrace housing between. It also has its own new main line rail station into Fenchurch Street via Upminster (just under 35 minutes); schools are already in place and more housing is to come.

Journey:	35 min
Season:	£1400
Peak:	6 per hr
Off-peak:	4 per hr

> Tilbury bears all the warts and eyesores that the 20th century could have thrown at it

Tilbury Town

Tilbury itself bears all the warts and eyesores that the 20th century could have thrown at it. When the ships coming up the Thames got so big that they couldn't squeeze up to London any more, Tilbury developed a dock complex so huge that it can be seen for miles around. Housing is very council-orientated and cheap. Many former council tenants have bought their properties and an ex-council house with three bedrooms now costs

Journey:	39 min
Season:	£1696
Peak:	5 per hr
Off-peak:	2 per hr

around £50,000. The Tilbury loop line has abandoned the use of first class carriages since the operator found there was little call for them. **Tilbury Riverside** burgeoned on the back of the new boat-trains to Europe in the 1850s, but now the only ferry that ploughs in and out is for Gravesend and it has long since lost its own station.

East Tilbury

Journey: 45 min
Season: £1996
Peak: 5 per hr
Off-peak: 2 per hr

There are strangely rural, forgotten-about pockets in this town that has no bus service. Around quiet corners you come suddenly upon dirt tracks that open up long walks beside the Thames. The Bata shoe company was started here by Czechoslovakians who built their own distinctive Thirties flat-roofed houses, schools and cinema, now much admired and designated a conservation area. The factory is still open but many of the houses have been sold on the open market. The old Bata office block has been converted into flats. A second-hand three-bedroom terrace house here costs about £60,000, but you can also buy the ubiquitous four-bedroom detached house for about £70,000 to £75,000. The Lakeside shopping centre at Thurrock has sucked much of the retail energy from these nearby areas. Modernisation came late to this line but the old timber platform in the station has now been replaced, and the manually operated level crossing gates now work automatically.

It's called the Misery Line. I can honestly say I haven't come into work for a whole week ever without a problem

"It's called the Misery Line. I can honestly say I haven't come into work for a whole week ever without a problem," said one commuter a few years ago. British Rail, however, spent a great deal of money on track and signalling improvements before LTS Rail took over. The overcrowding on the line – it carries 165,000 passengers a week – is caused by an inexorable growth in housing and the rail service has to scamper to keep up.

Stanford-le-Hope

Journey: 49 min
Season: £1996
Peak: 5 per hr
Off-peak: 2 per hr

There are a few late 19th-century streets near the station but otherwise most of **Stanford-Le-Hope** is an eruption of low-cost Sixties housing that engulfed **Corringham** and **Coryton** as far as the big oil refineries on the edge of the Thames. Three-bedroom semis are priced at about £75,000 to £120,000, standard four-bedroom detached houses at £90,000, with the most expensive in the range selling for about £120,000 to £220,000. From here people might prefer to travel by rail up to **Pitsea** and change to the main line into Fenchurch Street, rather than take the slow and indirect route through **Tilbury**.

Pitsea

Pitsea is to Basildon what Jonah was to the whale – something to be swallowed whole. It has slipped into the open jaws of the new town's sprawl, council housing and all. For main entry, see **Fenchurch Street to Shoeburyness** line (page 40)

Journey: 41 min
Season: £1996
Peak: 5 per hr
Off-peak: 4 per hr

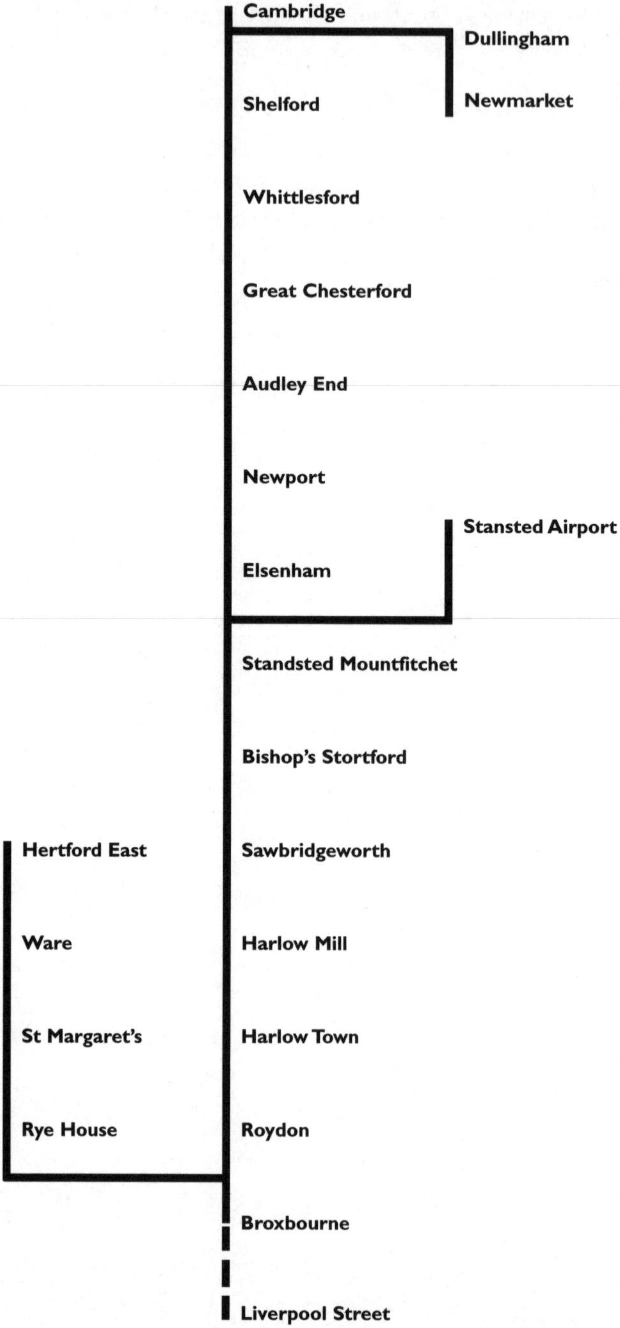

Cambridge

Dullingham

Shelford

Newmarket

Whittlesford

Great Chesterford

Audley End

Newport

Stansted Airport

Elsenham

Standsted Mountfitchet

Bishop's Stortford

Hertford East

Sawbridgeworth

Ware

Harlow Mill

St Margaret's

Harlow Town

Rye House

Roydon

Broxbourne

Liverpool Street

Liverpool Street
➡ Cambridge

Broxbourne

The railway came to **Broxbourne** in 1840. Victorian houses immediately started going up around the station, and it has been commuter country ever since. To the south of it is a soothing pocket of countryside where the New River lazes across the meadows. Other relics of the rural past, including Broxbourne Woods, have been retained by conversion into parkland. The Lea Valley Regional Park runs for 23 miles from Bromley-by-Bow through Broxbourne to Ware, making Broxbourne a handy resort for boating and holiday chalets – the newly refurbished leisure pool competes for people's affections with the Grundy Park Leisure Centre. Detached houses on the more residential western side of the town can sell for up to £300,000. Smaller three-bedroom houses to the east fetch between £110,000 and £140,000. There is a vast out-of-town Marks & Spencer and Tesco development at Cheshunt to the south. Cheshunt also has a golf course.

Broxbourne doesn't stop before **Hoddesdon** begins, though the atmosphere becomes rather more industrial. Hoddesdon is tightly bound by the green belt and it has a proper town centre with 17th-century buildings set around the old clock tower – an area busy with stalls on market day. Houses on the west and south sides are more desirable, being removed from the more industrial east. In the mix of Victorian, Thirties and Sixties houses you could buy a three-bedroom semi for £100,000 to £140,000. Larger houses, such as those in the privacy of College Road, sell for around £250,000.

Journey: 24 min
Season: £1660
Peak: 8 per hr
Off-peak: 4 per hr

Fork to **Hertford East** via **Rye House, St Margaret's** and **Ware**

Rye House sits on the northern edge of Hoddesdon, on the finger of the Lea Valley Regional Park where the remains of the old Rye House gatehouse still stand. There was once a thriving nursery garden industry here. In the Thirties, says the local council, the Lea Valley had "the world's largest accumulation of glasshouses". Between 1968 and 1971 much of the old nursery land was surrendered to housing, thus creating what is now

Journey: 43 min
(29 min peak)
Season: £1720
Peak: 2 per hr
Off-peak: 2 per hr

known as the Hundred Acre Estate, attached to the north side of Hoddesdon. Here you can buy a basic terrace house for £100,000; a three-bedroom semi for £125,000. The 1999 addition is Rye House Village, 140 houses built beside the station, where a two-bedroom flat can cost £72,500 and a three-bedroom detached house £137,000. Elsewhere in Rye House, property tends to be fairly cheap. The relative modesty of the houses here is ironic when you remember that there was once a plan to make Rye House into a kind of genteel pleasure garden. The plans were buried when Sir Giles Gilbert Scott's huge power station arrived. Today a new combined-cycle gas turbine power station does the job. Entertainments at Rye House Stadium include go-karting, speedway and greyhound racing.

St Margaret's

Journey: 46 min (31 min peak)
Season: £1832
Peak: 2 per hr
Off-peak: 2 per hr

The village here is **Stanstead St Margaret's**, divided from **Stanstead Abbots** by the River Lea, though sharing a vicar. A bypass has reduced the amount of through-traffic from 19,000 vehicles a day to 9,000. It is a fast-growing village with new houses going up all the time. There are two pubs, one of which used to be called the House Up A Tree (it had a tree house to which people used to take their pints in the summer). It is now called The Crown. The old malt industry lingers like a ghost. Disused cowls and chutes litter the skyline, and the smell of it still hangs over the terraced cottages and modern estates in Stanstead Abbots. There are some small shops and a post office on this side of the river, with playing fields and sports club just outside at St Margaretsbury. Stanstead Abbots has a voluntary-aided primary school attached to the church. Most of the older children attend secondary schools in Hertford or North Hoddesdon. The Stansteads have a marina with narrowboats, and cruisers for hire. Property prices are slightly higher than those in Hoddesdon.

Ware

Journey: 50 min (35 min peak)
Season: £1992
Peak: 2 per hr
Off-peak: 2 per hr

People say that this is where the chimneypots stop and the countryside begins. **Ware** is a good old market town which hasn't been spoilt. The main local employer is Glaxo, with a factory which has all the grandeur of a country house set in parkland by the river. Beyond it lies what the estate agents like to call the "golden box" – a group of handsome villages in a landscape which, despite its proximity to London, preserves a feeling of real remoteness. The town has a strong sense of history. In developing new sites it has dug up Roman remains. Bodies from the Black Death were shipped out along the River Lea for burial outside London. What Hertfordshire sent in return was water – channelled to the East End by way of the New River, a canal built in the early 17th century. Much of the town's wealth was created by the malting industry, and many of the old maltings have been converted into flats, mini-Docklands style. You can buy a one-bedroom flat on the water for £80,000; a three-bedroom apartment with parking for £110,000 to £140,000. It is a very charming place to live. The narrowboats still come past, there is a chandlery on the quayside, and there are some very pretty walks along the river-bank. These allow you to view the

18th-century riverfront gazebos, Ware

extraordinarily delicate old gazebos behind the houses in the High Street, where the gardens run down to the river.

The town centre also contains quite a few mews houses, developed from the old stables and courtyards behind the High Street. Four-bedroom town houses with paved courtyards at the back cost £230,000. There are some smart modern houses closer to the golf course on the south side of the town, where something with four bedrooms and a double garage would fetch £230,000 to £350,000. The town has lots of clubs and societies, which show themselves off once a year during Ware Week. Leisure revolves around the swimming pools, cricket on the Old Hertfordians ground, Hertford Rugby Club at Hoe Lane, and Ware Football Club. For major shopping, however, most people prefer Hertford.

The villages are in a quite different price zone. Footballers, pop stars and television personalities lurk down these country lanes, and you could easily pay up to £600,000 for an ex-farmhouse with acreage. **Great Amwell** is both the most expensive and the prettiest, with the New River draped in willows. Here it widens to a pool with two islands in it. These hold monuments to the New River's creator, the engineer Sir Hugh Myddleton, and floodlit concerts are sometimes given from them in the summer. Two miles away are the imposing buildings of Haileybury College. A period house with five bedrooms and two acres in Great Amwell could easily cost £600,000, though at the other end of the scale you might find a little two-up-two-down in need of modernisation for £75,000. The village has an annual flower show and every so often it opens its gardens to the public.

To the east is **Hunsdon**. Its timbered and weatherboarded cottages, village school and friendly atmosphere all contribute to its great appeal. Saturday coffee mornings are a regular event in the village hall, and there are societies for toddlers, tennis players and the elderly. Small Victorian cottages cost around £110,000. Three-bedroom cottages can be expected to cost at least £150,000, and farmhouse-sized properties between £300,000 and £400,000. New houses have been built in small handfuls for those at managing director level, priced at over £300,000 for five bedrooms.

In the precious northern belt are villages like **Standon** and **Puckeridge** in the Rib Valley. Standon is favourite, with its wide curving High Street, timber-frame houses and village school. St Edmund's Roman Catholic College is a few miles to the west. Property prices are similar to those in Hunsdon. Puckeridge has a twisting High Street and more the feel of a small town about it, with Sixties and Seventies developments tacked on. More new development has followed as a result of the expansion of Stansted Airport. An older two-bedroom terrace here would cost £100,000; a new four-bedroom house £180,000. The Puckeridge and Thurlow hunt rides out from Brent Pelham nearby.

Braughing is a film-set village built at the confluence of the River Quin with the Rib. The approach to it is by way of a ford that occasionally floods. Doug White is a superb local butcher who makes special Braughing sausages (the recipe is secret). The colour-washed cottages have often been used as backdrops to television feature films, and some have superb pargeting. The smallest cottage here would cost around £110,000, with prices rising to about £600,000 for the larger period houses.

Hertford East

Journey: 55 min (41 min peak)
Season: £2056*
Peak: 2 per hr
Off-peak: 2 per hr
*Also valid from Hertford North.

Hertford is a charming, self-sufficient country town with a conservation area at its heart and good road and rail links to London. For main entry see **Moorgate/Kings Cross to Stevenage** line (page 90).

Continuation of main line

Roydon

Journey: 40 min
Season: £1788
Peak: 2 per hr
Off-peak: 1 per hr

Roydon is quite a commuter haven, being handsome enough to have a conservation booklet written about it, but not chocolate boxy. Some of the houses are genuinely Georgian; others have false Georgian fronts. The village revolves around the church, the green and the High Street, which has many listed buildings. The school still thrives and, though the butcher has gone, there is a bakery, chemist, part-time doctor's surgery, an Italian restaurant and hairdresser. Historical relics include village stocks and lock-up. Roydon has a flower festival every other year; the tennis court is well-used, the Roydon Players can be relied upon for local drama and the conservation society for fending off too much new development. There are some five-bedroom houses with large gardens that sell for £250,000 to

£400,000; a period house with 13 acres and a swimming pool will cost £550,000 at the very least.

Harlow Town

It has to be said that many people hate **Harlow** in spite of its parks and Henry Moore sculptures (most of which are now so valuable that they have had to be put away in museums). The New Town was created in 1947, to the masterplan of Sir Frederick Gibberd, as a series of four large residential zones in a rural setting, each with its own infrastructure. The population jumped from 4,000 to over 80,000, mostly as a result of London overspill, and the influx continues as another 3,500 houses go up at Church Langley on the east side of town. A two-bedroom terrace house here will cost over £80,000 and a five-bedroom detached house £200,000. Harlow has a good shopping centre at Broad Walk, its own nightclub, bingo hall and the Playhouse theatre. There is a sports centre, and Harlow Pool has a trimnasium, solarium and dance studio. The newest canine night spot is the Greyhound Stadium. Two large industrial estates on the edge of the town accommodate, among others, Beecham and Longman.

Journey: 31 min
Season: £2100
Peak: 6 per hr
Off-peak: 4 per hr

Harlow Mill

This is the station for some of Harlow's smarter parts – Mark Hall North, for instance, where a three-bedroom house costs £90,000. **Harlow Old Town** is very popular because of the older period properties it contains, together with good little shops including two bakers. A house here is likely to cost 10% to 20% more than its nearest equivalent in the New Town. There are many pretty villages to the east. At **Fyfield** or **Moreton**, for example, you could buy a Victorian terrace cottage for £100,000, or a discreet country house with six bedrooms and 11 acres for £600,000. People who live in this area are not famous for their liking of Harlow and are more likely to nip south and use the Central Line from Epping.

Journey: 47 min
Season: £2148
Peak: 2 per hr
Off-peak: 1 per hr

Sawbridgeworth

Sawbridgeworth is a low-rise town set in the fields and woods between Harlow and Bishop's Stortford, and – though at this point you are in Hertfordshire – this is where you begin to see the distinct local building styles of Essex: steep tiled gables and dormers, overhanging upper storeys, timber and weatherboarding. The town has two primary schools and enough shops for day-to-day needs, including bakers and butchers. There are all the usual societies, plus a lacemakers' group, the

Journey: 37 min
Season: £2260
Peak: 2 per hr
Off-peak: 3 per hr

Sawbridgeworth Musical Youth Theatre and the Old Malt House Music Society. In a strange reversal of trends, the old cinema has been turned into a Catholic Church. Horse-riding is popular with local children. Flats by the river overlooking the marina are popular with commuters who also benefit from being little more than five miles from Stansted Airport. Two-bedrooms cost £95,000, three-bedrooms £115,950. Older three-bedroom semis can be bought for £145,000.

Bishop's Stortford

Journey: 36 min
Season: £2396
Peak: 6 per hr
Off-peak: 5 per hr

Bishop's Stortford is a wealthy little market town surrounded by very pretty villages. Aircraft coming in and out of Stansted Airport fly around it to avoid causing any distress to those who live here. It has a good shopping centre, with a Sainsbury, a Tesco and a discreet old department store. A market is still held on most Thursdays on the twisting main street. The town buzzes with activities, including both operatic and amateur dramatic societies. The H20 disco and a couple of wine bars cater for ravers.

The older, more attractive buildings are in North Street, Windhill and the Old High Street. It is possible to buy a two-bedroom house in Bishop's Stortford for as little as £80,000, but a three-bedroom semi would take you to £95,000 and you should expect to pay £150,000 to £200,000 for a four-bedroom detached. The better side of town is the north-west corner. The private boys' school, Bishop's Stortford College, is here, and the houses are large and secluded. Prices range between £200,000 and £300,000. There is an equestrian centre at Hallingbury Hall, Little Hallingbury, and stables at Thorley. A substantial country house with nine bedrooms and 10 acres on the edge of town might cost £500,000.

To the west, on the Hertfordshire-Essex borders, are the Hadhams. **Much Hadham** is probably the smartest village in the area. Its fashionable status derives from the fact that the Bishop of London once took up residence here, and subsequent bishops kept the palace going for centuries. It has a charming mix of Elizabethan cottages, 18th-century town houses and Victorian almshouses, and the blacksmith's forge has only recently become part of a crafts museum. As in any village, the sizes and prices of the houses span a very wide range. The 18th-century four-bedroom town houses with walled gardens can be bought for £350,000. A five-bedroom barn conversion was sold recently at **Little Hadham** for £595,000.

Further north are the Pelhams. **Stocking Pelham** is a particularly pretty village where a good country house with three acres could easily reach £500,000.

To the south-east is **Hatfield Broad Oak**, built on the edge of Hatfield Forest – more than 1,000 acres of National Trust woodland donated by the Puckeridge and Essex hunts. It is a handsome old village full of Georgian buildings. There is some post-war development south and east of the High

Street. Hatfield Broad Oak has a post-office-cum-general store, a butcher and wet fish shop, and a silversmith. Time does not stand still, however: the former craft shop now sells computers. The influx of commuters and working wives who are out of the village during the day, and so shop elsewhere, is making life difficult for the shopkeepers. Barrington Hall, a grand country house set in parkland, is now the office of a perfume company. You do get the occasional stray aircraft overhead, but for the most part they disturb other villages such as Great Hallingbury.

Stansted Mountfitchet

The expansion of **Stansted** Airport cannot but have a huge effect on the area surrounding it. The new passenger terminal opened in spring 1991, and the airport is growing steadily towards its predicted passenger total of 15 million a year. New airport-related housing developments are going up in four earmarked zones. A four-bedroom converted barn in the area will cost £415,000. One of the nicest villages within striking distance of the railway station is **Manuden** – a tiny one-and-a-half street village on the River Stort with some very pretty jettied timber-frame houses. A three-bedroom detached bungalow might cost around £150,000; a four-bedroom, thatched 16th-century cottage would be likely to fetch £285,000 to £350,000.

Journey:	48 min
Season:	£2456
Peak:	3 per hr
Off-peak:	2 per hr

Branch line to **Stansted Airport**

As parking is plentiful beside Norman Foster's spectacular **Stansted Airport** terminal, and the trains into London are swift, commuters are increasingly tempted to use this station now. This and the M11 brings the land of windmills within easy reach.

Journey:	41 min
Season:	£2520
Peak:	4 per hr
Off-peak:	4 per hr

Continuation of main line
Elsenham

Elsenham offers a good view of the air traffic in and out of Stansted but strangely it is little affected by the noise. Its two most prominent features are a village pump in a domed octagonal well-house, and Elsenham Hall, a late Georgian red-brick mansion by the church. The village has seen a lot of new development in the last 10 years, and the range of property types and prices is large, from £60,000 for a three-bedroom flat to over £200,000 for a modern estate house and £325,000 for a four-bedroom period house on the outskirts. Shops include a post office, a newsagent, a supermarket, a hairdresser and

Journey:	54 min
Season:	£2520
Peak:	2 per hr
Off-peak:	1 per hr

a chip shop. Bishop's Stortford is nearby for major shopping. It is a very horsey kind of a village, with plenty of activities, including the WI, a gardening club, allotment association, cricket, football and keep fit clubs. The eponymous jam factory is not as huge as you would expect.

Ugley just to the north does not deserve its name, and **Quendon**, too, is very pretty. The big house, Quendon Park, is surrounded by a wooded deer park and has a good William and Mary south front. A five-bedroom Georgian farmhouse with outbuildings recently sold for £395,000.

To the north-east on the young River Chelmer is **Thaxted**, an impressive old town with a guildhall that broods over the open market place and an old windmill at the end of Fishmarket Street, which has been restored as a museum. The church, with 181ft spire and medieval roofs, is one of the finest in Essex. Thaxted's problem is that it lies beneath the flight path to Stansted Airport, though people are so attached to it that they don't seem to mind. Many of them move house within the village, and some Londoners have second homes here. A two-bedroom terrace house will cost around £100,000; a three-bedroom detached house £140,000.

Newport

Journey: 57 min
Season: £2608
Peak: 2 per hr
Off-peak: 1 per hr

Newport has always been more expensive than the neighbouring town of Saffron Walden, to which it long ago lost its market. It has a fine main street of gracious houses, all within easy reach of the station and the M11. A two-bedroom Grade II listed cottage would be snapped up overnight for £120,000. An added attraction is Newport Grammar School for boys – an ex-grammar but still highly respected.

Rickling Green has a picture-book green with a cricket pitch overlooked by a pub called The Cricketers

Essex begins to get pricey here, with a collection of very pretty villages. South-west of the station are **Clavering**, with its cluster of cottages around the church, and **Rickling Green**. The latter has a picture-book green with a cricket pitch appropriately overlooked by a pub called The Cricketers (owned by the parents of the television naked chef Jamie Oliver). Two-bedroom thatched cottages sell for £130,000 to £180,000, large country houses with land for £450,000 to £1m.

Only a mile from the station to the west is **Wicken Bonhunt**, very small and exclusive, where a five-bedroom bungalow will cost around £400,000. Another mile brings you to **Arkesden**, by a little stream called Wicken Water. Thatched cottages spread themselves around a green, and there is a good 16th-century hall and 13th- to 14th-century church. A three-bedroom thatched cottage would be likely to fetch over £200,000.

On the east side is **Widdington**, also very small and expensive, a hill-top village with cottages around the green and larger houses hidden in the lanes. A four-bedroom detached house would cost around £300,000; a small lath-and-plaster cottage around £120,000. **Debden** is another thatched village on the way to nowhere but it does have a community shop. A four-bedroom cottage with very little land in the centre of the village will cost £200,000.

Audley End

There is little more at **Audley End** than the station itself. The town it serves is **Saffron Walden**, which is one of the few places in this extremely wealthy part of the country where the less-well-off and the young can afford to buy. The town has a handsome market place with narrow medieval rows running off it, small specialist shops, a Waitrose and a branch of Eaden Lilley department store. It is a stronghold of conservationists who want to protect the charming streets of timber-frame houses. The huge common, once used for grazing cattle and medieval tournaments, now serves as a fairground and recreation area. Its most puzzling feature is a rare turf maze – archaeologists still don't understand its purpose. The schools are a draw for many of the families who come to live here. There are quite a few inexpensive modern estates. A one-bedroom flat will cost around £40,000; a four-bedroom detached Georgian-style house up to £400,000. The town can be rather touristy in summer.

Journey: 57 min	
Season: £2648	
Peak: 4 per hr	
Off-peak: 2 per hr	

The villages nearby are beyond the reach of most local young couples. At **Wendons Ambo** one of the (very few) four-bedroom modern houses would be likely to fetch around £250,000. The more substantial five-bedroom, three-reception room houses built in the Sixties would sell for £300,000. The lane to the church has some particularly appealing cottages. **Littlebury** nearby is also expensive, with a good collection of lath-and-plaster cottages beside the miniature River Cam near the site of an Iron Age camp. A 150-year-old two-up-two-down will cost £80,000; a converted barn would be likely to fetch well over £350,000.

On the east side of Audley End is **Wimbish** – little more than a smattering of houses through the lanes. The presence of an army barracks pulls the prices down. **Hempstead**, Dick Turpin's birthplace, is very popular though the road to it is winding and slow.

Finchingfield is much photographed because of the beautiful juxtaposition of church, pond and cottages, not to mention its windmill and Elizabethan big house. A four-bedroom period house with a garden could be bought for around £270,000.

Great Chesterford

Journey: 65 min
Season: £2740
Peak: 2 per hr
Off-peak: 1 per hr

Little and **Great Chesterford** are both extremely prestigious, having a very popular primary school and being close enough to attract people working in Cambridge. The River Cam tiptoes through both, and in Great Chesterford it is overlooked by a large watermill converted into flats. The village has a family grocer, a post-office-cum-shop, and some very stylish early houses, one of which has some spectacular pargeting. A four-bedroom period terrace house will cost £190,000. **Hadstock**, to the east, is a pretty village with thatched cottages around a green, but it is less expensive. A four-bedroom period cottage on the green will sell for £230,000.

Whittlesford

Journey: 65 min
Season: £2808
Peak: 4 per hr
Off-peak: 2 per hr

Whittlesford, ideally situated close to Cambridge and the M11, is quite a sizeable village and prices are higher than neighbouring **Duxford**. Most people know Duxford for its airfield (well to the west), which houses part of the collection of the Imperial War Museum. In addition to the permanent display of historic aircraft there are flying displays and pleasure flights in the summer. There are some nice old pubs and some thatched cottages, though these have been rather swamped by the new estates and bungalows. A two-bedroom detached bungalow will cost around £95,000; a three-bedroom detached house £115,000.

Sawston has an image-problem caused by the large council estates by which it is surrounded. What draws many people to it, however, is the presence of a Cambridge Village College (see page 60). Small one-bedroom houses cost around £65,000; three-bedroom semis £85,000; new three- and four-bedroom houses £110,000.

Shelford

Journey: 74 min
Season: £2884
Peak: 2 per hr
Off-peak: 1 per hr

Great Shelford and **Little Shelford**, with **Stapleford** into which they merge at the base of the Gog Magog Hills, all ooze prosperity. This is where the Cambridge wealthy – businessmen and London commuters rather than academics – choose to make their homes. The houses are large and secluded, with parks and other green open spaces to enhance the feeling of spaciousness. There are plenty of shops. Period houses in Great Shelford's Mingle Lane and Gog Magog Way, which leads to the Gog Magog Golf Club, are thought to have particular appeal. A seven-bedroom house in 10 acres recently sold for just under £2m. You don't *have* to be rich to live here, however. There is a development close to the station which has two-bedroom starter homes at £85,000. Sawston Village College, one of the much-admired Cambridge Village Colleges (see page 60) is the local secondary school.

Cambridge

The property market in **Cambridge** has a mind of its own, being heavily influenced by the constant comings and goings of university academics and the staff of the high-tech industries that have thrived in the university's shadow. During the Eighties the explosion of scientific, medical and agricultural companies based on university research became known as the Cambridge Phenomenon – and predictably it delivered an upward thrust to local house prices. The boom continues as people continue to pour in to work in the area. So tight is the green-belt girth now of this beautiful but quite tiny city, that an entirely new settlement called **Cambourne** is being built to the west. Prairie fields are being turned gradually into 3,000 houses, with a 50-acre business park, two primary schools and a heavy environmental spin (ponds and trees and walks are high on the agenda). Small three-bedroom houses sell at £125,000, larger versions at £250,000.

Journey: 76 min*
Season: £3012 (also valid into Kings Cross)

Peak: 4 per hr
Off-peak: 2 per hr
*For faster trains see Kings Cross to Grantham page 75.

To the north of Cambridge lie the Science Park and the stark flat landscape of the Fens. It is the south, therefore, that most people prefer. The station is here, and so are the better schools, including The Perse co-educational private school. The area closest to the station, around Tennyson Road, is popular with professional couples. Two-bedroom Victorian terraces in this area cost £120,000. On the other side of the tracks they cost £100,000. Larger four-bedroom Victorian houses in the station area will cost around £130,000. The Kite, so-called because of its diamond-shape, is another favoured address,

The Cambridge Phenomenon predictably delivered an upward thrust to local house prices

close to the shopping centre. A two-bedroom Victorian house here would cost around £100,000. Alternatively, to the west there is Newnham – an old-established residential area where a typical bay-fronted three-bedroom Victorian house would cost £230,000. One of the highest prices reached in Cambridge recently came attached to a pair of Japanese-style houses linked to a swimming pool and gym, set in two acres of woodlands in Newnham, valued at £1.55m.

The most expensive, exclusive and attractive village in the area has to be **Grantchester**, two miles to the south. Rupert Brooke lived here as a student at the Old Vicarage, now occupied by Jeffrey Archer. Brooke's best-remembered lines, "Stands the Church clock at ten to three?/And is there honey still for tea?", are a reference to his time in Grantchester. The village's many attractions include walks along the Cam, the old tea-rooms which students punt out to, and pretty cottages that sell for enormous sums. You could possibly get a small two-bedroom Victorian terrace for £170,000; but a favoured five-bedroom house with a large garden is likely to fetch £500,000 to £1m.

Madingley has stunning views to the spires of Cambridge

To the west of Cambridge is **Comberton**. This is a good village for families since it contains one of the highly-regarded Cambridge Village Colleges. A handful of these were built to embody the ideas of Henry Morris, chief education officer at Cambridge from 1922 to 1954. He believed that secondary schools could be run like small colleges, serving several villages while at the same time fulfilling their cultural needs and providing adult education. Property and prices in the villages (excluding Grantchester) tend to be more family-friendly than in Cambridge itself.

Due west of Cambridge is **Madingley** – worth looking at because of the stunning views to the spires and towers of Cambridge, seen against the backdrop of the Gog Magog hills. Much of the village is owned by the university, and the hall is now a hostel for graduates. Prices are probably up to 10% lower than Grantchester's.

The countryside in the north looks markedly less friendly but lower prices are increasingly attracting those who want big roomy houses. **Histon**, having long been the base of the Chivers jam-making enterprise, is almost a small town now, with shops, sub-branches of banks, building

Schools in Cambridgeshire

Educational excellence in Cambridgeshire is centred on Cambridge itself. High-flying state schools include the Village College comprehensives such as Bottisham, Swavesey, Cottenham, Sawston, Comberton, Impington, Linton, and Melbourn, from which children can go on to sixth-form studies centres. In the private sector there is The Leys for both sexes, The Perse independent school for boys (girls in the sixth), Perse Girls', St John's College for both sexes, and St Mary's Roman Catholic day and boarding school for girls. Those who live at St Ives or St Neots often look to Kimbolton in Huntingdon, a co-educational independent day school (with some boarding), which was once a grammar.

societies and garages. Its main attraction is its proximity to **Impington**, which has a Village College designed in the early Thirties by Walter Gropius and Max Fry. It is also close to **Girton**, home not only of Girton College but also of Girton Golf Club. A two-bedroom house here will cost £100,000.

In the east, on the edge of The Fens, which can sometimes look like the edge of the world, are **Swaffham Bulbeck** and **Swaffham Prior**. They are eight miles from Cambridge, but worth considering if you want to escape the academic atmosphere which affects some of the other villages. Both are remarkably unspoiled and have some charming period cottages. At Swaffham Prior (where the poet Edwin Muir once lived) you could buy a three-bedroom cottage in need of modernisation with half an acre for

£145,000; a five-bedroom Victorian house with an acre for £250,000 to £300,000.

The A14 is an important dividing line in the east. Anything to the south of it, where the countryside starts to ripple again, will command a higher price. **Fulbourn** serves as a Cambridge suburb, with new developments encroaching on the older houses and thatched cottages. There is a range of shops, a primary school and a mill which occasionally opens to the public. Nearby is Fulbourn Fen, an educational nature reserve. The old Victorian asylum is being turned into a nursing college. A three-bedroom semi on a new estate will cost £100,000; a four-bedroom detached house with two bathrooms around £180,000 to £220,000; a four-bedroom period house over £250,000.

The line beyond here to **King's Lynn** was electrified in 1993. For villages close to stations on the Kings Cross to King's Lynn line via Cambridge and Ely, see page 75.

Branch line to **Bury St Edmunds** via **Dullingham**

Dullingham is quite remote, probably suited to two-car families, and it stands out as expensive in an otherwise low-priced area. It is very pretty, with thatch-and-clunch cottages, an old farm and stables, and a village green. There are two new small developments, one of maisonettes overlooking the heath, priced at over £100,000. Tesco provides a coach service into **Newmarket**. This is the place to live if you are a fancier of horseflesh. The town lives and breathes racing. The chalk downland is peppered with stud farms, shelter belts and exercise areas, with the National Stud at Newmarket Heath. Strings of horses can be seen each day trailing through the town to the horsewalks on to the gallops. There are two racecourses – the Rowley Mile (currently being given a makeover) and the July. A large house with stabling and acreage could cost anything from £400,000 to £1m. The co-educational Japanese Boarding School, Shi-Tenoji, is nearby. **Kennett** is also remote – a very quiet Fenside village that feels a little stranded between Cambridge and Suffolk. It has no shops, but there is a primary school. At secondary age children must take the bus to Soham Village College eight miles away. The single street has some period houses, flint and half-timbering. At the end of it is the grave of a gypsy boy who was hanged for stealing sheep. He died at least 200 years ago but the grave always has flowers on it. A family-sized house here could be bought for £150,000. For **Bury St Edmunds**, see branch line from Colchester, page 28.

No through trains. Trains to Cambridge 1 per hr.
Journey: 75 min (from Newmarket)
Season: £3064

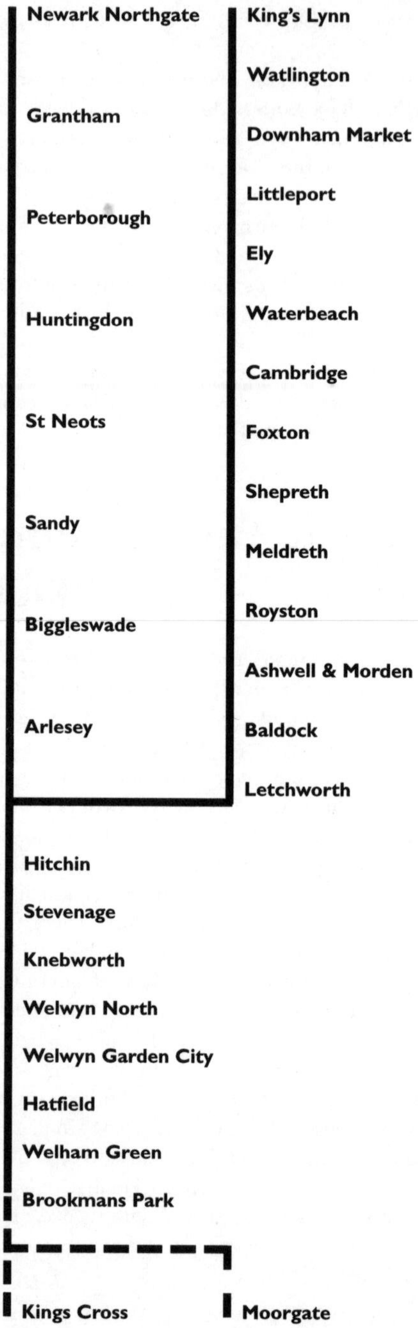

Newark Northgate

King's Lynn

Watlington

Grantham

Downham Market

Littleport

Peterborough

Ely

Huntingdon

Waterbeach

Cambridge

St Neots

Foxton

Shepreth

Sandy

Meldreth

Royston

Biggleswade

Ashwell & Morden

Arlesey

Baldock

Letchworth

Hitchin

Stevenage

Knebworth

Welwyn North

Welwyn Garden City

Hatfield

Welham Green

Brookmans Park

Kings Cross

Moorgate

Kings Cross ➡ Grantham

Brookmans Park

This is the world of personalised number plates and golf courses, the playground to **Potters Bar**. Large expensive houses, some of them sealed behind tall hedges, have been built between lakes and woodlands in the grounds of two long-demolished country houses, called Brookmans and Gobions. The railway arrived in 1926, and suburbia gradually ate up the surrounding fields. A four-bedroom house in more exclusive **Brookmans Park** can be bought for £300,000, though prices run into millions with ease. Moffats Farm is thought once to have been the home of Dr Thomas Muffett, author of the nursery rhyme *Little Miss Muffet.*

To Moorgate
Journey: 36 min
Season: £1536
Peak: 3 per hr
Off-peak: 3 per hr

Welham Green

Welham Green is definitely a step down from Brookmans Park. The village offers a mix of private developments and council estates built around a centre with a green, shops and a garage. A three-bedroom detached house could be bought for £180,000 – possibly 50% cheaper than an equivalent house in Brookmans Park. There is a commemorative stone to the Italian balloonist Vincenzo Lunardi, who made the first balloon ascent outside France in the 1780s. He landed here to let his dog and cat out of the basket because they were feeling sick.

To Moorgate
Journey: 38 min
Season: £1700
Peak: 3 per hr
Off-peak: 3 per hr

Hatfield

Hatfield is probably the dreariest of the new towns in this area, though the council is valiantly building up the new business park on the old British Aerospace site, and has introduced elements of American town life to the scene. The Galleria shopping mall has a superstore, a nine-screen cinema and a drive-in McDonald's. Exercise is made easy at the swimming pool and new leisure centre – the pool has the largest hyperbolic paraboloid roof in Europe. Hatfield's advantages lie in its strategic position – being close to the A1, the M25, and only a wingbeat from Kings Cross by train – and in offering lower house prices than surrounding areas. Its greatest

To Kings Cross
Journey: 21 min
Season: £1864
Peak: 2 per hr
Off-peak: 2 per hr

To Moorgate
Journey: 41 min
Season: £1864
Peak: 3 per hr
Off peak: 3 per hr

public attraction is Hatfield House, built by Robert Cecil at the top of the hill. It is open to visitors and numbers among its many distinctions the fact that it was one of the first houses to be lit by "Edison-Swan electric incandescent light bulbs", patented in 1879.

Most people prefer the red-brick houses of Old Hatfield to the Thirties-style, bypass variegated houses and shopping parades of the 1948 New Town. A cottage with two bedrooms in Old Hatfield would be likely to cost around £100,000, though a flat of similar size would be slightly cheaper at £80,000. A three- or four-bedroom detached house will cost from £90,000 upwards but won't have a large garden. Two of the best areas are The Ryde, which has detached houses and bungalows, and Ellenbrook, where there is a mix of Thirties semis and detached houses. The lowest price for something with three bedrooms here would be £160,000. In New Hatfield the starting price for a four-bedroom detached house is around £185,000, rising to around £250,000.

Welwyn Garden City

To Kings Cross
Journey: 25 min
Season: £2056
Peak: 4 per hr
Off-peak: 2 per hr

To Moorgate
Journey: 47 min
Season: £2056
Peak: 3 per hr
Off-peak: 3 per hr

Ebenezer Howard, with his chief architect Louis de Soissons, designed **Welwyn Garden City** as a sustainable town with its own employment zones, but the lure of the commute was not resisted for long. Early residents in the Twenties had to wade through the builders' mud in their Wellington boots to get to the station, and changed into their city shoes on the train. The fusion of garden and city still remains very attractive, and the original cottagey houses behind perfectly-clipped hedges are very much sought after. Many have been kept on a ball-and-chain by 99-year or

"Executive" home, Wheathampstead

999-year council leases (inherited from the Welwyn Garden Company), but freeholds are now available. The utilitarian planning means that there is very little sense of one street being more up-market than any other. The wide main shopping boulevards now look strangely dated, and local shops and businesses tend to feel they have lost out to the bustle and variety of St Albans and Stevenage. There is, however, a John Lewis department store, and the Howard Centre close to the station has added greatly to the shopping scene. Sports enthusiasts are catered for by the Gosling Sports Stadium and two 18-hole golf courses.

The best side of the town is the west, where a three-bedroom semi with a garage in a quiet tree-lined road could cost £180,000 to £200,000. It is possible, however, to buy a two-bedroom house for £135,000 to £170,000. The town is still evolving – large new private estates have gone up at the Panshanger aerodrome. A three-bedroom semi on a new private estate will cost around £175,000.

There is some very pretty, rolling wooded countryside around Welwyn Garden City, and those who prefer an older village could look at **Wheathampstead** to the west. As you approach the charming High Street from the direction of St Albans you pass a small quay on the River Lea, where people stop to chat or sit and fish. On one side of the road is a 400-year-old pub, The Bull. On the other is a converted water mill which now contains a butcher and a silversmith. The village has two primary schools, from which children move on to secondary schools in Harpenden and St Albans. There is a library, four churches of different denominations, and lots of clubs and societies, including wine-making and archery clubs, cricket and tennis. You could pay well over £120,000 for a modernised Victorian cottage. Nearby is Brocket Hall, where Lady Caroline Lamb once emerged naked from a soup tureen and where more recently Lord Brocket ran a glitzy hotel and conference centre. In 1996 it appeared on the market with a price tag of £15m when its owner was imprisoned for insurance fraud. The Hall still hosts conferences and has been redecorated.

Old Welwyn, just to the north of Welwyn Garden City, is so much more refined and mature than its neighbour. It has a mix of houses from one-bedroom cottages with small courtyard gardens, priced at around £85,000, to larger three-bedroom cottages fronting the road at £158,000. On the edge, away from the shops in the main street, is the executive development Danesbury Park where a four-bedroom house will cost £325,000.

Welwyn North

The village best served by this station is **Digswell**, which consists of large detached houses with secluded gardens sewn into the lanes behind high hedges – some of them dominated by the huge viaduct built to carry the Great Northern Railway over the valley. It has the advantage of being close to a main line station yet only two miles from Welwyn Garden City. Houses tend to be sold very discreetly, and are not cheap. You would need to spend £335,000 for a four-bedroom bungalow. A small but pretty lake is

Journey: 28 min
Season: £2088
Peak: 3 per hr
Off-peak: 2 per hr

maintained by the Digswell Lake Society. **Tewin** is another wooded dormitory, but the sale of the village by the Cowper estate in 1919 led to its rapid expansion, with large new estates leeching on. The Upper Green is still used for tennis, cricket and football matches. A three-bedroom modernised cottage on the green would cost £200,000; larger four- and five-bedroom detached houses in large gardens fetch around £385,000. The tomb of Ann Grimston in the parish church fascinates visitors and locals alike. Before her death in 1713 she had scoffed that the after-life was as likely as a tree growing through her grave. The tomb is now a macabre tangle of root and branch.

The **Ayots** to the west, like Digswell, are very exclusive: **Ayot St Peter**, perched on a hilltop, and **Ayot St Lawrence**, with its narrow lanes enclosed between hedgebanks. The latter also has a popular old pub, the Brocket Arms, a post office and George Bernard Shaw's house, the late-Victorian Shaw's Corner, where he lived until his death in 1950. The house, which has Shaw's writing hut at the bottom of the garden, is in the hands of the National Trust. The village's most prominent landmark, however, is the extraordinary neo-classical parish church, seen like an 18th-century folly across a meadow. House prices are higher than those in Tewin. Two-bedroom cottages cost £220,000, flats in the converted manor house start at £550,000, and one large house in the area is rumoured to have sold for £14m recently.

Knebworth

Journey: 32 min
Season: £2280
Peak: 3 per hr
Off-peak: 2 per hr

As is the case with most towns and villages in this area, there is an old and a new **Knebworth**. Old Knebworth grew up around the big house and parkland. The newer part was built around the railway station, which arrived at the turn of the century. Lutyens tried his hand with some cottages in Deard's End Lane and Park Lane, and he also produced a golf clubhouse and the remarkable church of St Martin. Knebworth retains a village atmosphere and has a library and village school as well as a co-op store. It is hugely popular with commuters, many of whom never escape from the sound of the trains. Because the railway line runs right through the middle, many of the older, quainter cottages back straight on to it. A two-bedroom cottage in this position costs £125,000 to £135,000. In Deard's End Lane, a Lutyens house will cost around £600,000. There are plenty of local activities and clubs, including cricket, amateur dramatics and old-time dancing, and there is an annual summer fête. This is aside from the rock festivals at Knebworth House.

Commuters at Knebworth nurture a huge grapevine, planted when the station opened, with its roots in the platform. At one time the station master harvested up to 55lb of grapes from it and made five or six gallons of wine.

Many people prefer the atmosphere of the smaller, more rural villages such as **Datchworth** to the east, where the community spirit remains strong and anyone who falls ill, or who can't fetch the children from school, soon finds their needs catered for. Pony paddocks abound. There are several riding stables in the area. It has general stores and a much-loved sports pavilion where badminton and squash are played, with a rugby field behind it. There is a mix of property, from two-bedroom cottages needing a bit of work which sell at around £185,000 to the kind of place that comes with an acre of ground, tennis court and price-tag of around £450,000. The village is spread between a web of greens. The harsher realities of life in the past are recalled at Datchworth Green in the centre, where the children's swings and summer tennis and cricket matches are overlooked by the old whipping post.

Stevenage

Stevenage offers something like safety-net housing for people who can't afford Hertfordshire's plusher towns and villages. Huge new estates are now zoned west of the A1 and in the north-east of town. It isn't attractive, but the prices are low by comparison and the train service is excellent. The station is served not only by the Cambridge and Peterborough commuter services but also by the InterCity 125s on the East Coast line into Kings Cross, and Moorgate trains on the Cuffley loop (see page 89). The New Town developments, colour-coded on old maps, have streets fancifully named after famous explorers, cathedrals, inventors, cricketers and so on, but in reality they offer little more than the uniformity of the three-bedroom mid- and end-terrace. Most are designed according to what is called the Radburn principle, which means that motorists and pedestrians are kept well apart.

To Kings Cross	
Journey:	19 min
Season:	£2468
Peak:	5 per hr
Off-peak:	4 per hr

To Moorgate	
Journey:	59 min
Season:	£2468
Peak:	2 per hr
Off-peak:	1 per hr

The beauty of the large modern shopping centre is that it is genuinely traffic-free. The various neighbourhoods, including the industrial area, are joined to each other, and to the centre, by cycleway, a cleverly designed miniature road network which at peak periods takes up to 1,100 people per hour on their way to and from school or work. There is also a horse and pony route around the town, though it is not nearly as extensive as the cycle network. The shopping centre offers excellent choice, with all the major chain stores as well as a large range of retail warehouses such as B&Q and Homebase and the Forum shopping centre. At Poplars there is a giant Sainsbury superstore. The covered market under the town centre multi-storey car park is open three days a week, and the stalls for the outdoor market go up on Wednesdays and Saturdays.

Stevenage is very strong on computers and technology, both in the businesses it attracts to its huge industrial parks – most recently GlaxoWellcome Medicines – and in its educational facilities. The College

Distinctive late
Victorian cottage,
Old Stevenage

of Further Education prides itself on its computer and technology courses, supported by the Stevenage Business Initiative. Leisure facilities are lavish, too, with a huge leisure centre-cum-theatre and exhibition hall. There are three 18-hole golf courses – a municipal one in Stevenage itself, and one each at Knebworth and Graveley. The place for Sunday walks is Fairlands Valley Park, where there is a sailing and fishing lake, a boating lake and a bandstand for open-air concerts.

The Old Town, "Hilton" in E.M. Forster's *Howards End*, is greatly cherished, and property prices are proportionately higher. A two-bedroom cottage would cost around £85,000; a three-bedroom cottage more than £110,000. On Stevenage's margins are some sedate, tree-lined roads that attract the middle-class professionals – Rectory Lane and Granby Road, for example, where a detached house with four or five bedrooms and a large garden may cost upwards of £300,000.

There is also a leap in house prices between the New Town and the villages that surround it. **Benington** in the east, for example, has a picture-postcard village green and timbered cottages, and is very sought after – though it does also have its share of new developments and local authority housing. An older house with five bedrooms would take you into the £250,000 range.

Walkern is much busier, with a main street that takes quite a lot of traffic. New estates have sprung up around the old dovecote and pond, and by the chequer-brick Manor Farm. A two-bedroom period cottage will cost around £80,000.

Aston is also popular and much closer to Stevenage, though it is a little hemmed in by Stevenage and has had its own struggle to restrict development – the field in the village centre has been fiercely defended. Most of the new housing is kept to small developments in culs-de-sacs. A large four-bedroom detached would cost £230,000.

House style in Hertfordshire

In Hertfordshire you find an essentially modest county, now marbled with stockbroker enclaves and new towns. The prettiest cottages tend to be small and unassuming. Geologically the county sits on the rim of a saucer of chalk filled with clay and knuckles of flint. Without stone, early builders had to make use of timber from the local forests. Every town has a handful of timber-framed buildings, though in Hitchin these were hidden behind brick facades when brick superseded timber as the fashionable material to use. There are also some charming cottages built of clunch, a sort of chalk stone, some of the best of which can be seen at Ashwell. The county has also borrowed from its neighbours – some weatherboarding from Essex, some yellowy brick from Cambridgeshire and Bedfordshire.

Hitchin

Hitchin has managed to retain its character better than some of the surrounding towns. Parts of the centre still remain in a medieval time-warp – the Market Place, the lanes leading off it to the cathedral-size St Mary's church and the River Hiz. Tilehouse Street, now relieved of much of its through traffic, remains just as medieval England must have known it; and Bancroft was once admired as one of the best urban streets in England. It is a classic small market town, once famous for straw-plaiting, surrounded by popular commuter villages. The shopping centre is good enough with a large traditional market, bars and restaurants. Prices have been rising fast here in the last three years. In the town itself a five-bedroom town house in Tilehouse Street has recently sold for £330,000, though it had only a small garden and no off-street parking. Larger three-bedroom semis on the south side of the town can be bought for around £135,000. The Avenue, Wymondley Road and Benslow Lane are quiet leafy roads only 15 minutes' walk from the station, and contain some rather grand houses. Large Victorian and Edwardian houses in The Avenue tend to sell for up to £600,000.

| Journey: 29 min |
| Season: £2520 |
| Peak: 5 per hr |
| Off-peak: 4 per hr |

The villages of **Gosmore** and **Charlton** to the south are very close to Hitchin and therefore desirable. Gosmore has a green and some pretty old houses. You could spend anything from £150,000 for a tiny two-bedroom cottage to over £200,000 for a three-bedroom period house. To the west, **Pirton** also scores because it isn't linear like many of the other villages in the area, but has a good, compact round shape which somehow affects the social dynamics and makes it a more convivial place to live. It is a little cheaper than Gosmore. A Victorian three-bedroom semi will cost around £180,000.

Great Wymondley and **Little Wymondley**, to the east, also loom in the Hitchin firmament, the irony being that Little Wymondley is by far the larger of the two. Great Wymondley is little more than an untidy cross-roads with a few cottages, a pub, and the humps of a medieval castle. A bypass has relieved Little Wymondley of traffic, causing house prices to rise. A two-bedroom period cottage will now cost £100,000.

St Ippollits (sometimes just called Ippollits, and spelled in a variety of different ways) is a rather pretty hilltop village with smartly painted timbered houses and a dominating church which gives the village its name. Unfortunately it is threatened by vast new housing estates – new four-bedroom executive homes cost £220,000 to £280,000. Commuters from St Ippollitts and the Wymondleys also have the option of travelling from Stevenage, where car-parking is easier.

 Fork to Cambridge and King's Lynn Letchworth

Journey: 34 min (25 min peak)
Season: £2600
Peak: 3 per hr
Off-peak: 2 per hr

You need to make sure your face fits in **Letchworth**. This was the first garden city, and the dream is still intact, as wholesome as a Hovis advertisement. To those who come from elsewhere to live – and to the groups of Japanese architects who come to gawp at it in summer – it can seem strange indeed. Ebenezer Howard's social experiment attracts a distinct type of middle-class teetotaller, full of good intentions and disposed to vegetarianism. It was a pretty dry town and until recently it had only one pub. Once upon a time there was just the Skittles Inn, which sold only lemonade and ginger beer, but this has been turned into The Settlement community centre. Pleasant evenings are spent in patchwork groups, making friendly quilts, or in other activities whose fruits are apt to appear at craft fairs. The beauty of all this is that it is quite safe to roam the streets at night. The town has belatedly got itself a three-screen cinema complex, a new supermarket, sports and leisure centre.

The sought-after properties are the original garden city houses, which have a rural calm about them. The cottages in Nevells Road, Icknield Way and Wilbury

 Outsiders think the people in Letchworth are crazy. It is very tight-knit socially, artistic, and rather like a commune

Road are worth just going to look at. An original garden city house with four bedrooms would cost around £350,000 (Sollershott West and East, and The Broadway have good examples), while a two-bedroom Victorian terrace cottage could be bought for £100,000.

"Outsiders think the people in Letchworth are crazy. It is very tight-knit socially, artistic and rather like a commune," said one who is now devoted to the town and wouldn't live anywhere else. It can afford to be particularly proud of its schools. Not only does it have two well-known public schools, St Francis College for Girls and St Christopher's for boys and girls (the latter known for its relaxed approach and amazing vegetable gardens), but it also has two well-respected comprehensives, Highfield and Fernhill. The town is still growing, and properties on the new estates tend to be much cheaper than in the Garden City proper. A three-bedroom detached house on the Lordship Farm estate, for instance, will cost £85,000; a four-bedroom house on the Manor Park estate £135,000.

Of the villages close by, **Norton** has a haphazard charm, a good pub and a common that offers 63 acres of woodland and deer. It also has the local leisure centre. **Willian** is little more than a hamlet, made endearing by its duck pond and some very old houses, but property in both these villages rarely comes on the market.

Baldock

Baldock is a classic small market town, with an old coaching history and a much admired wide main street. People enjoy living here, and like to protect the place from further development. After years of wrangling a bypass has finally been laid to siphon traffic out of the centre. The main asset for shoppers is a vast and impressive Tesco superstore in a converted neo-classical hosiery factory which once also enjoyed a brief life as a film studio. Initially the smaller, traditional High Street shops suffered both from the competition of Tesco and the shopping centres in Stevenage and Cambridge, but they seem to be recovering now. The town does still muster a butcher and a baker, plus plenty of solicitors and estate agents, antique shops and a steak house.

Journey: 37 min
(28 min peak)
Season: £2628
Peak: 2 per hr
Off-peak: 2 per hr

Almost anywhere in Baldock is nice to live. There are streets of timber-frame and colour-wash, Georgian and Victorian houses and some modest modern estates. Even the council estates are arranged in well-kept, tree-lined avenues. A two-bedroom mid-terrace Victorian cottage will cost around £80,000; a Georgian house with four bedrooms £250,000 to £300,000. Baldock is just within range of people who work in Cambridge (20 miles), and this is reflected in the property prices. It is also attractive for its secondary school. Knight's Templar Comprehensive has a high reputation for academic achievement and is the preferred choice of many parents who could afford to have their children educated privately.

Ashwell & Morden

Journey: 53 min (33 min peak)
Season: £2744
Peak: 2 per hr
Off-peak: 1 per hr

The station is too far outside the village to walk, so parking spaces are keenly contested. Waiting to be picked up is no great hardship, though, since there is a comfortable country pub right opposite the station. **Ashwell** is a commuter dormitory which manages to retain a ferociously active village social life. There is a playgroup, a babysitting circle, a stage school and a dance school, and every year the Ashwell Show grows less like a village flower show and more like a county horse show. It really is

People expect their houses to sell at a premium in Ashwell, so you have to be ready for this when you go house-hunting

the chic village to live in this rather flat countryside. The attraction lies in its sense of complete self-containment and in the preservation of its architecture. Timber-framed cottages, some cob, are followed by dignified Georgian town houses. It has a pretty church in clunch and flint, and a primary school that is not only highly thought of educationally but is also a social engine to the village. It has a bakery, three pubs, a pharmacy, a doc-

tor's surgery, a dentist, a weaver and a potter. There is also the Ashwell Village Museum, housed in an ancient timber-frame cottage and entirely run by volunteers. People expect their houses to sell at a premium in Ashwell, so you have to be ready for this when you go house-hunting. A two-up-two-down here might cost £105,000 to £110,000 – 10% more than it would fetch a few miles away in Royston. A four-bedroom cottage will cost £350,000.

Kelshall sits in the foothills of the Chilterns, open to views right across the prairies of Bedfordshire and Cambridgeshire. It is an extremely well kept and close-knit village. A two-bedroom cottage will fetch around £90,000; a four-bedroom detached house around £300,000. **Therfield** is another proud old Chilterns village whose agricultural heritage goes back a very long way, as the long barrows on Therfield Heath testify. A two-bedroom period cottage will cost £200,000; a four-bedroom house around £300,000.

Royston

Journey: 45 min (34 min peak)
Season: £2836
Peak: 2 per hr
Off-peak: 2 per hr

Royston has recovered successfully from the recession and new shops have opened up during the Nineties. It sits on the borders of Hertfordshire and Cambridgeshire, so people have the choice of two education systems. It offers cheap housing and convenience. In addition to the railway line it also has easy access to the A10, M25, A1 and M11. Traditionally the south side of town is thought to be better than the north, where some of the housing estates have been built at a very high density – and where a new Tesco has opened. Property prices start at £70,000 for a two-bedroom Victorian cottage and £90,000 for a three-bedroom semi to £120,000. The modern houses tend to be cheaper than the older Victorian and Edwardian ones which offer more room. The heath, which has a golf course on it, is the place to walk and ride.

The surrounding countryside offers a wide choice of villages. **Barley**, to the south-east, is a no-frills village with a strong local community, pretty walks and an all-purpose village shop. The Barley Players put on summer and Christmas shows, and there is a good local riding school. Its greatest assets are an early Tudor restored town house, used for village activities and harvest suppers, and a small village cage or lock-up, which remains as a curiosity. A two-bedroom cottage will cost £115,000 or more. Barley's position on the chalk toes of the Chilterns accounts for the villagers' historic nickname, "the little men from the hills".

Three-bedroomed
period cottage,
near Royston

Barkway is rather more elegant, with a wonderful array of timber-framed and Georgian brick houses. One of these with four bedrooms and parking on the main street will cost over £200,000. A two-bedroom cottage will cost over £80,000 but these are few and far between. Barkway still has a good village school where the numbers are increasing. **Bassingbourn**, to the north, also has an impressive main street lined with period houses. The nearby army barracks does not affect house prices. A five-bedroom detached house with four reception rooms will cost over £200,000.

Meldreth

This was once serious fruit-growing country but **Meldreth** now has only one commercial orchard left with a farm shop attached. It has a small green, and beneath a spreading chestnut tree are the old village stocks and a whipping post. It is an enormously welcoming village, though it is rather scattered. The primary school is well regarded, as is the nearby Melbourn College for 11- to 16-year-olds. Leisure opportunities include tennis,

Journey: 61 min	
Season: £2964	
Peak: 2 per hr	
Off-peak: 1 per hr	

croquet and football. Village people may also use the riding stables attached to the Meldreth Manor School which is run by Scope. The village contains a mix of old thatched cottages and new developments, though much of the newer housing seems very uniform. Semis sell for around £80,000; four-bedroom detached houses for £300,000.

Melbourn is across the fields. Its attractions include two restaurants and a very strong community spirit. Property prices are similar to those found in Meldreth.

Shepreth

Journey: 64 min
Season: £2944
Peak: 2 per hr
Off-peak: 1 per hr

The feature of **Shepreth** village centre is a stream with two old mills on its banks. There are some pretty thatched cottages and several modern closes built in the late Sixties and Seventies. The village has a shop-cum-post-office, a Montessori school and two trout farms. The houses tend to be larger than those in Meldreth – those backing on to open fields in Frog End are probably the best. Two-bedroom cottages start at around £80,000 while four-bedroom detached houses cost around £200,000 upwards. Annual village events include a horticultural show, harvest festival and the Shepreth festival of arts and crafts. Several artists live in the area. One of the results is an art-bus which serves as a mobile studio for children and adults. It is a horsey area, including even a few driving carriages.

Foxton

Journey: 67 min
Season: £2968
Peak: 2 per hr
Off-peak: 1 per hr

Foxton is attractive and quiet, with a pretty but tiny green and some good timber-frame houses in the long main street. The village has two churches, a shop-cum-post-office, a pub and a green which stretches for three-quarters of a mile. There are all the usual societies for women, toddlers and the elderly, plus the formidable Foxton Gardeners Association which organises a regular September show. The village is best known to outsiders for being the subject of a highly-praised historical book, *The Common Stream*, by local author Rowland Parker, published in 1975. Foxton tends to be rather sought-after because of the railway station and its proximity to Cambridge. Prices are similar to those in Shepreth.

Barrington nearby has a huge set-piece green with thatched cottages on one side and a fine church on the other. The Cambridge factor is a significant influence on prices. A four- to five-bedroom house on the green cannot be bought for less than £350,000. There are some modern developments discreetly tucked away in culs-de-sacs, where four-bedroom detached houses sell for around £250,000 to £300,000. An acre or two of land, however, could put the price up. Clunch, the chalk-stone used so extensively in local building, was quarried nearby.

Cambridge

Puffed up by its own commercial success, and by its academic fire-power, **Cambridge** now has very high house prices to match. For main entry see **Liverpool Street to Cambridge** line (page 59).

Most London services from the following stations go to Kings Cross. At peak times there is a limited direct service to Liverpool Street, otherwise passengers for Liverpool Street must change at Cambridge.

Journey: 45 min
(56 min peak)
Season: £3012*
Peak: 2 per hr
Off-peak: 3 per hr
*Season tickets from Cambridge and stations to King's Lynn are valid to Liverpool Street and Kings Cross.

Waterbeach

The trains out of **Waterbeach** in the morning are full of children on their way to school in Cambridge or Ely. The village does have its own primary school, attached to the community centre. Here you can also take evening classes, or join the Waterbeach Players or the brass band. Waterbeach has an army barracks, a post office, hardware store, grocer, cobbler, fish-and-chip shop, butchers and bakers, and several pubs. There is a Tesco three miles away at **Milton**. The Waterbeach Feast, a procession of floats and stalls, is held every June, when the local women traditionally have always made frumenty – boiled wheat in a thick, sweet milk-and-sugar sauce with raisins. The best houses are the classic Cambridge brick houses around the village green, which have a preservation order on them. A two-bedroom version recently sold for £90,000. A three-bedroom semi in Waterbeach is likely to cost around £100,000.

Journey: 53 min
(66 min peak)
Season: £3028
Peak: 1 per hr
(plus 1 per hr to Liverpool Street)
Off-peak: 1 per hr

Cottenham, also on the edge of the Fens close to Waterbeach station, has a Village College and some useful shops in its favour, but it has expanded rather brutally. Its population has doubled in only 20 years. A three-bedroom Victorian terrace will cost £100,000 to £115,000, better value than in nearby Histon.

Ely

Ely had remained aloof, cut off from Cambridge by the Fens for so long that the Eighties property boom arrived as something of a shock. Older residents were heard to claim that they hadn't let anyone from outside the area cross their threshold in 30 years. Now, however, it has become an immensely popular alternative to the hothouse of Cambridge. There are also a few London commuters, and some Londoners with second homes. A house with a view of Ely's remarkable 11th-century cathedral is usually thought more desirable than a home in one of the villages. It is a very small, compact city with a tiny High Street, though it does have both a

Journey: 62 min
(75 min peak)
Season: £3088
Peak: 2 per hr
(plus 1 per hr to Liverpool Street)
Off-peak: 1 per hr

Tesco and a Sainsbury. Georgian houses sit quite happily alongside Thirties semis, and there are no distinct up-market areas. A renovated Grade II listed town house with four bedrooms can be expected to cost £200,000. There are dramatic and choral societies for those inspired by the theatrical Fen landscapes. King's School is situated close to the cathedral. Some people are also attracted to the area by thoughts of the Good Life – the cottage with a productive vegetable garden, a few ducks and a goat. Villages to the south, such as **Witchford**, **Sutton**, **Haddenham** and **Stretham**, are the most sought-after. You should expect to pay around £50,000 for a two-bedroom semi; around £190,000 for a four-bedroom detached.

Littleport

Journey: 69 min (83 min peak)
Season: £3220
Peak: 1 per hr (plus 1 per hr to Liverpool Street)
Off-peak: 1 per hr

Littleport is a thriving little town on this huge horizontal landscape, with some beautiful old houses as well as plenty of new estates. The thatched electrical shop is an attractive local curiosity. A four-bedroom timber-frame house on a small plot will cost around £190,000. Littleport has a new leisure and sports centre and Littleport Village College provides evening classes. It has plenty of day-to-day shops, including a wonderful bakery, a butcher and fishmonger, and a clothes shop. "The best thing about living here is that there are such beautiful sunsets, flooding across acres and acres of open sky," says one local resident. Some of the older people are keenly superstitious and fond of weather-prediction: grasshoppers in a ditch mean foul weather for Thursday week.

The best thing about living here is that there are such beautiful sunsets, flooding across acres and acres of open sky

Downham Market

Journey: 78 min (92 min peak)
Season: £3452
Peak: 1 per hr (plus 1 per hr to Liverpool Street)
Off-peak: 1 per hr

Downham Market is popular with people who are taking early retirement. Estate agents say that nine out of ten people looking for properties here are about to stop work. It is a pleasant Norfolk town with plenty of shops, a good high school, a floodlit football ground, a swimming pool, and an industrial estate on the outskirts. It used to be an inland port but today the river, contained in its high banks, is a thing to walk beside rather than a busy thoroughfare for imports and exports. This is the kind of place where you can leave your car unlocked all day, and where you don't have to queue in the supermarket. A two-bedroom turn-of-the-century terrace house will cost around £50,000; a three-bedroom semi with a garage £65,000.

Watlington

This is a village that has been straitjacketed with new development but has now protected itself with a thick layer of green belt. It has a couple of shops, a primary school and a doctor's surgery. It is slightly cheaper than Downham Market – a two-bedroom terrace house would cost around £45,000. A small farmhouse out on the Fens could be bought for £275,000.

Journey: 83 min
(98 min peak)
Season: £3520
Peak: 1 per hr
(plus 1 per hr to Liverpool Street)
Off-peak: 1 per hr

King's Lynn

The old port of **King's Lynn** has a definite appeal for birdwatchers, who can be seen in their anoraks and Wellington boots scanning the sky with their binoculars. The marshes and mudflats of the Wash are a great attraction for waterfowl and waders. The riverside is a favourite spot for watching the fishermen come in, though Fisher Fleet, the fisherman's quarter, can get a little smelly. Architecturally, much of the stuffing was knocked out of King's Lynn as old buildings were replaced by housing estates. The conservationists now have a firm grip on what is left – a historic legacy which includes the merchants' houses of Nelson Street, Queen Street and King Street – most of which are now used as offices. The King's Lynn Arts Centre has a gallery and theatre, and in the summer there is a music and arts festival, usually attended by one of the Royals (Sandringham is only eight miles away). It has the biggest shopping centre for miles around. Among the older properties you could pick up a three-bedroom semi for £65,000. Even a good period three-bedroom town house will probably not exceed £100,000.

Journey: 93 min
(105 min peak)
Season: £3668
Peak: 1 per hr
(plus 1 per hr to Liverpool Street)
Off-peak: 1 per hr

200-year-old
brick-and-flint
farmhouse,
Downham Market

Continuation of main line from Hitchin

Arlesey

Journey: 34 min
Season: £2700
Peak: 2 per hr
Off-peak: 1 per hr

You are on to the Bedfordshire plains here, where the low, sprawly, yellow-brick villages can seem monotonous and unimaginative after the variety of Hertfordshire. **Arlesey** itself might be short on charm but lays claim to being the longest linear village in the country, with a High Street of Victorian brick houses, many of which have been extended at the back to provide bathrooms and kitchens. A four-bedroom detached house will cost around £110,000. Traditionally the town has had two social fixtures in the year – the Agricultural Show and the Wives' Pram Race. Its immediate neighbour, **Stotfold**, is a similar large village dominated by the local yellow brick, and has a similar mix of Victorian and modern housing at similar prices. Stotfold has the additional advantage of having a secondary school, being close to the A1M, and offering the choice of whisking down the motorway for the better train service from Stevenage. Letchworth and Baldock are also nearby.

    Shillington is another large, though rather more rural village of yellow brick with the occasional timber-frame house and an intimate gathering of 17th-century houses around the hilltop church of All Saints, an impressive local landmark. Closer to Arlesey is **Henlow**, where prices are slightly increased by the proximity of RAF Henlow. This is the village where sports and showbiz personalities come to revitalise at the Henlow Grange Health Farm. Henlow has a few shops and pubs and good sports facilities. County cricket is sometimes played at The Pyghtles. Other villages worth looking at in this catchment are **Meppershall**, **Lower Stondon** and **Clifton**.

Biggleswade

Journey: 37 min
Season: £2764
Peak: 2 per hr
Off-peak: 2 per hr

Biggleswade has a population of around 14,500 and is very much a dormitory for Cambridge and Bedford as well as for London. It is a town of yellow brick houses and market-gardening set on the River Ivel. Greene King had a brewery here, which may explain why there are so many pubs. There is a busy market on Saturdays. Shops are enjoying a £7m town centre makeover, yet people still tend to go to Cambridge for major purchases. Proximity to the A1 (where there is a new Sainsbury) means that Stevenage is also easily accessible. One of the more highly regarded streets is London Road, where large four-bedroom houses can be bought for £150,000 upwards. It is a busy road, however, and seems to have less appeal for incomers than it does for people moving locally.

    Those in search of the rural idyll must go west to **Ickwell Green**, whose village green has a cricket club and a maypole on it and is fringed with colour-washed, brick and tiled cottages. Houses for sale here are as rare as hen's teeth and agents are wary about quoting prices because they are all so individual.

The RSPB has its headquarters at Sandy Lodge, and there are some pleasant woodland walks

Old Warden is even more picturesque, having been preserved in aspic by the Shuttleworth Estate. The cottages are thatched, with gingerbread trimmings and chimneypots, and very few of them ever reach the open market. But its very presence is a magnet to the area, attracting people to the neighbouring villages. The Shuttleworth Collection of historic aircraft is a major attraction to visitors, especially on flying days.

Northill, the third village in the cluster, is not quite so rarefied. The occasional modern house has crept in beside the older cottages around the pub and the duckpond. A two-bedroom thatched semi will cost around £75,000. There are stables in the area and it is fairly horsey.

Potton, to the north-east, is the size of a small town, with a population of over 5,000. Its market square is much admired, though the only way to live in it would be to buy a flat over one of the shops. The likely price for a two-bedroom cottage is £60,000. Otherwise property in the town tends to be cheaper than Biggleswade or Sandy (see below). It is the headquarters of the eponymous Potton company, makers of neo-Tudor self-build home kits.

Sandy

Sandy is plain as can be, an old Bedfordshire village that acquired a station and then sponged up overspilling Londoners into its large council estates and yellow-brick streets. It is perhaps a shade cheaper than Biggleswade. The Royal Society for the Protection of Birds has its headquarters outside the town at Sandy Lodge, and there are some pleasant woodland walks. Two of the more expensive places to live are the large Victorian houses along Bedford Road, which can be a little noisy because of proximity to the A1, and the modern houses on the river-front at Mill Lane. The average price of a two-bedroom house in Sandy is £50,000. Two huge new housing estates, Ivel Park and Dapifer Drive, offer modern family houses.

| Journey: 42 min |
| Season: £2764 |
| Peak: 2 per hr |
| Off-peak: 1 per hr |

Beeston, on the southern edge of Sandy, is divided by the A1, and quite a few properties are blighted by it. Nevertheless, the conservation area with the green, old thatched cottages and blacksmith's forge offers pleasant relief from some of the other, drearier villages in the area. **Tempsford**, to the north, is also spliced by the A1. Its wartime aerodrome was used by the Special Operations Executive to drop secret agents into occupied France, and it was from here that the bandleader Glen Miller took off for his final flight.

St Neots

Journey: 47 min (34 min peak)

Season: £2960

Peak: 3 per hr

Off-peak: 2 per hr

St Neots is considerably prettier than many of the towns in the area – larger, too, with a population of 27,000 or more. Yet it has the atmosphere of a backwater. The rather fine market square was badly hit by the early-Nineties recession, but has now sprung back to life. Even so, the shopping centre still pales beside the glamour of nearby Cambridge. Teenagers at a loose end in the evenings can end up hanging around the market square. Cricket and rugby are played on the huge 160-acre common. There are three golf courses and there is an operatic society called the St Neots Players which puts on productions at the Priory Centre. There is also an annexe of Huntingdon Technical College.

The River Ouse contributes both colour and charm. There is a rowing club and two marinas. People come to St Neots to mess about in boats and to fish, or to walk the Ouse Valley Trail. Some of the nicest places to live are close to the river. **Eaton Ford**, for example, was once a riverside village in its own right. It has now been absorbed by the town and offers some of the most expensive housing. The period architecture, combined with the St Neots Golf Club and the river meadows, have pushed the price of a three-bedroom semi here up to £80,000. A four-bedroom detached house will sell for around £150,000 to £180,000.

Also popular is Old St Neots, in the area around the market square and shops, with walks in the woods of Priory Park. A two-bedroom house with a garden will cost about £80,000. Slightly cheaper is **Eaton Socon**, another former village drawn into the St Neots fold, where houses tend to be

Semi-detached thatched cottage, Bedfordshire

arranged in terraces. A four-bedroom detached house could be bought for between around £140,000 to £160,000. It has the advantage of being on the A1, convenient for commuting to Stevenage or Hatfield, and it is competitively priced. Less popular is **Eynesbury**, where the council estates have mushroomed over the years, prices are low and new private estates are now appearing.

People looking for a village home tend to head eastwards, where the countryside starts to undulate a little – though property prices also begin to rise as you get closer to Cambridge. **Great Gransden**, **Little Gransden** and **Waresley** have pretty Elizabethan thatched cottages and are particularly popular with professional couples. A three-bedroom semi in one of these villages would fetch around £120,000. **Eltisley** is slightly cheaper – pretty but not quite so special, with an extraordinarily large village green and a lovely thatched cricket pavilion which is used for meetings as well as cricket matches. The village has a pub and a popular primary school that also serves other villages nearby, and a thriving youth club. There are some small new housing estates popular with young families, and there are some bungalows for the elderly. A three-bedroom detached house would cost more than the equivalent in St Neots but less than in the Gransdens.

To the north-west is Grafham Water, a huge man-made reservoir that draws people from miles around for walking, water-skiing, windsurfing and other watersports. **Perry** was a village that had little to say for itself before Grafham Water was made, but prices are now similar to those in Eaton Ford. One possible drawback of living near open water is that midges can be a problem in the summer.

Huntingdon

Most people will probably prefer the neighbouring villages to **Huntingdon** itself, though the old county town is not unattractive. Oliver Cromwell lived here, and the old school which both he and Samuel Pepys once attended has been turned into a Cromwell Museum. House-price booms have brought quite a few Londoners in search of cheaper housing, so there is a well-established body of commuters. Since 1991 the town has spawned 700 new houses a year under what is called the Huntingdon Scheme for expansion. The truth is, however, that people tend to spend their lives trying to move *out* of this area rather than in. The cheapest housing is found among the ex-council houses. The better addresses are in Hartford and Sapley, where the period properties add a touch of class to the newer developments and bungalows. A modern house with four bedrooms in either area will cost around £120,000.

Across the remarkable 14th-century bridge in **Godmanchester**, the tone is raised by some pretty, pastel-coloured 16th, 17th and 18th-century

Journey: 56 min	
(45 min peak)	
Season: £3140	
Peak: 3 per hr	
Off-peak: 2 per hr	

houses, and by pleasant walks along the Great Ouse to Portholme Great Meadow, which is ablaze with wild flowers in spring. Much of Godmanchester is a designated conservation area, and there are some particularly fine houses in Post Street, Earning Street and the Causeway, where some of the gardens run down to the river. A modern five-bedroom house here is likely to fetch £120,000, while a five-bedroom period house with a garden on the river will push the price towards the £700,000 mark. Not far to the west is **Brampton**, where Pepys lived and where the Brampton racecourse is. It still retains its village green, though there have been a lot of new developments. The RAF station here is nothing to worry about – its function is purely administrative. The proximity of Grafham Water makes it a popular village for water-sports enthusiasts.

St Ives, five miles to the east, also has more charm than Huntingdon, with a pot-pourri of building styles along the quay and a smattering of pubs and restaurants. The centre is a conservation area, and the thread-work of alleyways between Market Hill and the riverside is particularly intriguing. It grew up on the site of a large Easter Fair, and is the St Ives of the nursery rhyme.

Close to it, nudging the Fens, are some of the most desirable villages in the area. **Hemingford Abbots**, formerly part of the Ramsey Abbey estate, seduces everyone with its thatched cottages and lovely walks. It is full of successful local businessmen and young couples attracted like moths to the Cambridge lamplight – all waxed jackets, Land Rovers and labradors. "You know if someone comes from Hemingford Abbots because they talk down to you," says one local resident. "There is a lot of pride in the village. If there is an art exhibition in the area, it will always be held in Hemingford Abbots." For the young, there are two-up-two-down courtyard houses selling for £90,000. The wealthier aim for the small urban palaces in Common Lane. Some of these have river frontages and might sell for around £2m. The walks are idyllic, along footpaths that cross the meadows to Houghton Mill. This is an early Ouse watermill, in a beautiful setting that gets rather touristy in the summer. Those with less money might look next door in **Hemingford Grey**, which is the poor relation living off the Hemingford name. There are many more family-sized houses here. A four-bedroom modern house would cost around £150,000 to £200,000.

Houghton and **Wyton**, linked by a main street, are also cheaper because they are that much further from the A1. The High Street has a small tea-room, a supermarket and a delicatessen. The housing market offers a mix of old and new. A four-bedroom modern estate house will cost around £135,000; a five-bedroom period house up to £500,000. To the north is **Woodhurst**, a perfect example of a ring village. Some of the four-bedroom houses on new developments will cost £150,000 to £250,000. Due north of Huntingdon are **Little** and **Great Stukeley** (where former prime minister John Major lives), which offer a reasonable mix of old and new houses, council estates and chalet bungalows. A modern house with four bedrooms and a plot of land in Great Stukeley is likely to cost around £225,000. A four-bedroom period family house can be bought for £250,000.

Peterborough

The tower of the Norman cathedral, which contains the tomb of Catherine of Aragon, is just about the only thing of beauty in **Peterborough**. It is visible from almost anywhere in the city and is illuminated at night. What the city lacks in aesthetics, however, it might be said to gain in purpose-built leisure facilities – cathedrals of contemporary life. The Queensgate shopping centre's malls and squares, in marble, glass and steel, are air-conditioned, American-style. There is a 13-screen cinema, an ice-rink, a rowing and canoeing centre, an indoor cricket stadium and three golf courses. The city is ringed with fast roads and bypasses, making life easy for drivers and pedestrians, too. The Key Theatre, opened in 1973, keeps the culture vultures happy with everything from opera and ballet to Christmas panto. And the Lady Lodge Arts Centre, in an old farmhouse at Orton Goldhay, puts a crafty-vegetarian spin on photography, music and the theatre.

Journey: 44 min*
with dual season;
65 min peak, 71
min off-peak with
WAGN season
Season: £4376 (all);
£3168 (WAGN)
Peak: 4 per hr with
both options
Off-peak: 3 per hr
fast; 2 per hr
(WAGN)
* Peterborough is
now the fastest
commuting service
to London at
104mph average,
but only with the
higher priced
season.

Those interested in new housing should trawl the streets of the new £500m satellite town to the south called **Hamptons**, with homes for 13,000 people and a separate shopping centre, where four-bedroom houses cost £90,000 to £150,000. Otherwise househunting becomes a question of working your way around the various Ortons. **Orton Goldhay** has shoals of ex-council terrace properties. At **Orton Malborne** there are more private houses in the mix, but prices remain similar. A three-bedroom semi will cost around £50,000; a three-bedroom detached £55,000. Prices rise sharply in the sumptuous, newly-built estates of **Orton Wistow**, where a family-sized modern house can start at £150,000. Similar properties can also be found in **Werrington** and **Gunthorpe**, both of which still retain a core of older housing, too.

The tower of the Norman cathedral is just about the only thing of beauty in Peterborough

Much of central Peterborough is to be avoided, especially the repetitive drab of the older terraces. **Westown** is one of the more popular inner areas, where three-bedroom semis with gardens sell at around £50,000. For real one-upmanship, there are the houses in Thorpe Park Road, Thorpe Road and Westwood Road, where Thirties houses in voluminous gardens

There are no hedgerows, no trees and no hills.
But it grows on you

sell at anything over £210,000 to the city's doctors, dentists and solicitors. The less wealthy middle-classes find themselves in **Longthorpe** and **Netherton**, where there is a range of older houses. A three-bedroom thatched cottage recently sold for £100,000.

To the east of Peterborough is the stark Fenland. Those who are interested will find it expertly interpreted at the Wildfowl and Wetlands Centre at Peakirk. Most people find it too glum, and head determinedly for the undulating landscape and stone villages to the west. For those who are undeterred, however, **Whittlesey** in the east is set right in the Fens. Just to the south of it is King's Dyke, designed to introduce a sharp kink into the network of navigable waterways and so limit the size of vessels passing between the Rivers Nene and Ouse. The village has a brickworks but is still dwarfed by the huge flatness that surrounds it. A two-bedroom detached bungalow might cost £60,000; an older three-bedroom bay-fronted semi £55,000. **Thorney**, slightly further north, was kept intact as an estate village throughout the 19th century and so has a greater sense of history. The rather mock-Jacobean water tower adds a flourish to the skyline. An older three-bedroom semi here will cost £50,000.

The villages to the south of Peterborough are also somewhat lacking in visual appeal. **Yaxley**, being so close to the A1, offers the convenience of an easy commute to the towns both north and south. Technically it is a village, though it has all the amenities and proliferating housing estates of a small town. Nearby RAF Alconbury is no longer used as a base by the Americans and is ear-marked for new development. The old part of Yaxley is the most sought after – particularly the thatched cottages that skirt the village green with the old village pump in the centre. Run-of-the-mill three-bedroom semis fetch around £54,000; two-bedroom period cottages £65,000. The countryside around is not for those who want conventional beauty. "There are no hedgerows, no trees and no hills. But it grows on you," said one resident who had been converted. Large tracts of it between Yaxley and Fletton, including an old brick pit, are to be swallowed by the new Hamptons township.

Villages to the west of the A1 tend to feel a little cut off by it. Crossing is difficult because of the traffic, and it is a known accident blackspot. It is now being turned into a three-lane highway, which means that the traffic noise will be brought that much closer to villages such as **Folksworth**, **Haddon** and **Stilton**.

North and west of Peterborough are the best areas to look. **Market Deeping** and its satellites **Deeping St James** and **Deeping Gate** ("Deeping" refers to the deep meadows on the banks of the River Welland), are a major attraction. Market Deeping is an attractive old town with wide streets, some old stone houses and pubs, and with good old-fashioned butchers and bakers mixed in between the antique shops. It has its own leisure centre, library and health centre, and an industrial zone including such light industries as fireplace manufacturers and double-glazing specialists. There are two

The poet John Clare is buried in the churchyard at Helpston, and there is a memorial to him at the crossroads

primary schools and a good comprehensive. The eight-mile drive to Peterborough station is only a matter of minutes along the A15. An older stone house with three bedrooms will cost £80,000 upwards depending on how much land comes with it. A three-bedroom semi will fetch considerably more than its counterpart in Peterborough. A four-bedroom detached house with a garage on a modern estate would cost around £130,000.

The stone villages in the Deepings corridor are all desirable and have been protected from over-development. They include **Maxey**, **Barnack**, **Ufford** and **Helpston**, the last being where the poet John Clare lived in the 19th century, and where he wrote his poems about the agricultural changes he saw going on around him. He is buried in the churchyard, and there is a memorial to him at the crossroads. A large cottage with four bedrooms might cost £170,000 in any of these villages, or slightly more if it is thatched.

Due west of Peterborough you find a similar kind of charm in villages such as **Wansford**. The village has a combined post office and shop serving a population of about 450. A beautiful stone packhorse bridge links the two halves across the River Nene. The Fitzwilliam Hunt meets outside the Haycock Hotel, an old coaching inn, on Boxing Day or New Year's Day. Close by is **Elton**. It has some good 17th-century houses, with Elton Hall just to the south and a lock on the Nene just to the west. A three-bedroom stone cottage in Elton might cost £160,000. All these villages benefit from being close to Stamford, which is a pretty medieval town and a very good antidote to Peterborough.

Grantham

A solid band of commuters, many of whom arrived in **Grantham** on the crest of the last housing boom, still solemnly take the London train each day. In the boom of the Eighties, around 80% of the people looking for houses in and around the town came from outside the area. During the early-Nineties slump around 90% of the buyers were local. Now there is a return of the outside buyer or "virtual commuter" – those who need only to make occasional visits to London. What everyone knows about Grantham is that Lady Thatcher was born here, in North Parade. Not quite so many people remember that Sir Isaac Newton was born here, too.

Journey: 63 min
Season: £5004
Peak: 2 per hr
Off-peak: 1 per hr

Early 20th-century farmhouse, Grantham area

Thatcher was educated at Kesteven and Grantham Girls' School, which is still doing for girls what Kings does for boys. The town also has an associated college of Nottingham Trent University offering courses in building, business studies, engineering and general studies. Leisure is high on the agenda, in the form of the £8.5m Meres Leisure Centre and £4m athletics and football stadium. There are golf courses at Belton Park, Belton Woods and Stoke Rochford, and good fishing on the River Witham.

Grantham still has a smattering of ancient houses in Castlegate and Church Street, plus the celebrated Angel and Royal Hotel. But much of it now consists of new development. At the lower end of the market, two-bedroom period town houses start at £40,000. Four-bedroom detached houses cost between £90,000 and £100,000. The best roads to live in are probably those leading out towards the villages of Manthorpe and Belton. Large detached houses set well back from the road can be bought now for £150,000.

Everyone remembers Margaret Thatcher, but Sir Isaac Newton was born here too

The limestone hills around Grantham contain some pretty stone villages, particularly in the west. **Barrowby**, for instance, stands high enough to afford good views across the Vale of Belvoir. A four-bedroom family-sized stone house here might cost £140,000. **Denton** is another handsome stone village which used to be part of the Welby estate. Denton Reservoir nearby is popular with anglers, and has some pretty pathways along its banks. There is some modern housing in the mix, and a small council estate. You could expect to pay £140,000 for a four-bedroom period house with a garage; £60,000 for a semi.

Closer to Grantham is **Harlaxton**, which is sufficiently attractive to have been designated a conservation area and hasn't been abused by unimaginative modern development. It owes much of its style to the Gregory family, who built the eye-catching manor house in the early 19th century, plus some of the Regency-style houses in the village. A pretty country cottage with four bedrooms might cost £150,000.

Perhaps two of the most exclusive villages are **Manthorpe** and **Belton** to the north, sandwiched by Belton Hall and its magnificent park, now in the hands of the National Trust. Little ever comes up for sale in Belton, but if you were lucky you could expect to pay £150,000 for something with four bedrooms.

Newark Northgate

This proud town, a Royalist stronghold in the Civil War, does its best to ignore the great snake of the River Trent which slithers past, encased inside high banks to stop it flooding. The lovely cobblestoned market place is major feature, though the old 14th-century draper's shop, which is supposed to be one of the oldest domestic buildings in the Midlands, is now occupied by a building society. The annual diary in **Newark** is full of antiques fairs – at least six are held each year. A three-bedroom terrace house in a good road will cost £45,000; a five-bedroom family house in a village nearby £150,000 to £200,000.

Journey: 75 min
Season: £5416
Peak: 2 per hr
Off-peak: 1 per hr

Stevenage

Watton-at-Stone

Hertford North

Bayford

Cuffley

Moorgate

Moorgate ➡ Stevenage

Cuffley

Cuffley is prime commuter country, much of it built in stockbroker Tudor style on what was once a wooded hillside. Though the character of the houses is intensely suburban, the village is still surrounded by proper farmland. Some of the large bungalows in their ample gardens have had new houses squeezed in beside them. Others, most oddly, have been converted into houses by having extra storeys added on top. There is no council housing to speak of. Two-bedroom flats can be bought for around £100,000; four-bedroom semis around £180,000. In the Ridgeway, mansions backing on to woodland can cost well over £500,000.

Journey: 37 min
Season: £1256
Peak: 5 per hr
Off-peak: 3 per hr

The village has quite a high proportion of elderly residents, though young families are moving in and the place has a robust spirit. A vociferous group of conservationists opposed the building of a golf course on nearby farmland. The village has enough shops to provide practically two of everything. It also has a new saddlery and its own primary school. Older children go to Potters Bar or Goff's Oak. Leisure activities include the Cuffley Players and an operatic society, plus football club, rugby club, cricket and bowls. There is a tennis club, but it has a two-year waiting list. People ride here, too, though the shortage of bridlepaths means that they have to take to the roads. The Round Table is a force to be reckoned with.

Bayford

Bayford is significantly more rural than Cuffley. It is set quietly in the heart of the Broxbourne woods, which are full of footpaths and bridleways, and is not so overburdened with modern development. The older Georgian houses have a pleasing presence as a result. The village is rather spread out. It has both a pond and an open space which it treats as a green. There is a cricket field with a new cricket pavilion built with Lottery money. There is a pub, the Baker's Arms, but no post office or shop, and most people stock up from Waitrose or Tesco in Hertford. The village has its own mixed infants and junior school, but older children must go to Hertford. Every two years villagers open their gardens to the public, with the admission charges going towards local amenities.

Journey: 42 min
Season: £1748
Peak: 2 per hr
Off-peak: 3 per hr

There is little point harbouring any ambition to live here unless you're looking in the £200,000 to £500,000 bracket

Together with its neighbours – **Brickendon, Little Berkhamsted, Epping Green** and **Bayfordbury** – Bayford exudes wealth and charm, and there is little point harbouring any ambition to live here unless you're looking in the £200,000 to £500,000 bracket. A four-bedroom family house wallowing in 20 acres recently sold for £1m. Brickendon is little more than a tiny hamlet set around a green, half a mile's walk from Bayford. Little Berkhamsted is delightfully wooded and has some lovely weatherboarded cottages opposite the church. Bayfordbury is perhaps not so exclusive since it has the B158 running through it.

Hertford North

Journey: 47 min
Season: £2056 (also valid at Hertford East)
Peak: 5 per hr
Off-peak: 3 per hr

Hertford is a surprisingly small, old-fashioned county town, protected by a quilt of green belt at the junction of the Rivers Beane, Lea and Mimram. It is possible to take a boat south to the sea from here by negotiating a series of locks. Much of the town centre is a conservation area, charmingly provincial considering its proximity to London. Family firms still thrive alongside all the antique shops and there is a Saturday street market. The cattle market has fallen prey to property developers and been turned into flats. There is a county court, county hospital and all the other public buildings you would expect of an administrative centre, the 1939 County Hall on its hilltop being the most ostentatious.

The Round Table has a strong presence and organises the annual carnival. Other prominent social groups include the Company of Players, based at the Little Theatre, the Dramatic and Operatic Society, which organises the annual theatre week. There are also choral and art societies, and a symphony orchestra. There is quite a sporting fraternity, too, with a cricket club, canoe club, Hertford Football Club, the Old Hertfordians Rugby Club, and fishing in streams made famous by Izaak Walton in *The Compleat Angler*.

Hertford is generally more expensive than other nearby towns, partly because of its status as county town. Commuters have a good choice of routes into London. The Moorgate/Kings Cross trains from Hertford North provide easy changes to the London Underground at Finsbury Park or Highbury & Islington. Or, if you prefer, there are trains to Liverpool Street from Hertford East (page 52), which connect with the Underground at Seven Sisters

People are often so fixated on Bengeo that they will consider living nowhere else

and Tottenham Hale. So many people scuttle through the short cuts con-
verging on Hertford North station in the morning that there is a prescribed
route known locally as the Commuter Trail. Not many of them live in the
area immediately behind the station, which is dominated by council
estates, but there are plenty of good streets within walking distance.

Period country
house in
Hertfordshire

At the cheaper end of the market, modern town houses can be bought
for around £120,000. For middle-range, three- and four-bedroom houses
with generous gardens you should look in the Fordwich area. Here you
will find semis at around £175,000 to £200,000; detached houses around
£250,000. For more extravagant housing see High Molewood and Great
Molewood, where large detached houses and chalet bungalows are spread
along unmade private roads surrounded by woodland. Five bedrooms,
two bathrooms and four reception rooms in Thirties architectural style
might cost £350,000 to £400,000.

The smartest suburb to the north is **Bengeo**. People moving to
Hertford are often so completely fixated on Bengeo that they will consider living nowhere else, so to a certain extent house prices here are reces-
sion-proofed. It has a parade of shops and two boutiques – one for chic
brides and the other for chic babies. A six-bedroom house in an acre or two
of garden will cost well over £500,000.

However great the appeal of Bengeo for commuters, it is the south side
of town which locals consider to be the more desirable. The large Victorian
and Edwardian houses of Queen's Road and Highfield Road, enlivened by

the occasional architectural curio, sell at around £240,000 for four bedrooms.

In the centre of Hertford, upwardly mobile young couples are attracted to the riverside, where terrace cottages were originally built for mill or malt workers. In the last decade Folly Island has been mercilessly gentrified, regardless of the shortage of parking places, and tiny two-bedroom houses with small gardens now cost around £115,000 to £120,000. The second bedroom tends only to be cot-sized, so those with growing families have to think of moving on.

Outside Hertford, Hertingfordbury is probably one of the most exclusive villages in the area

Outside Hertford, **Hertingfordbury** is probably one of the most exclusive villages in the area. The thriller writer Frederick Forsyth has a house here. The village has no more than 20-odd houses with a cricket pitch and two pubs, a church and a bridge over the Mimram. Its quaintness easily sends house prices through the £600,000 barrier.

Watton-at-Stone

Journey: 52 min
Season: £2224
Peak: 2 per hr
Off-peak: 1 per hr

Watton-at-Stone is daubing its pretty face with new development. The main street is where the older properties are – yellow and red-brick houses, jettied timber and plaster. But most of the rest of the village is new, and building has been more or less constant throughout the last decade, even during the recession. A two-bedroom house, without garage, on a modern estate might cost around £125,000; a four-bedroom, modern detached house around £190,000. One of the more recent development plans has been to convert an old salmon-smoking factory into flats. The village combines the best of both worlds by being intensely rural (and horsey), and yet close enough to London for theatre and other trips. There is cricket, football and – a most unusual asset – tennis on floodlit courts; plus three pubs – one of which has the old pudding stone outside from which the village derives its name – a flower club and other village societies. It also has the Heath Mount private infant and junior schools. This is one of the villages to benefit from Lottery funding for a new village hall. The spring which gave the village the other half of its name ("wat", meaning watery) and which gave it brief prominence as a popular spa, dried up long ago. But a hedgerow near the station is supposed to be one of the most ancient in Hertfordshire.

One of the pubs has the old pudding stone outside from which the village derived its name

Stevenage

The new town offers affordable housing in an otherwise expensive county. The old town is the Hilton of E.M. Forster's *Howards End*. For the main entry, see **Kings Cross to Grantham** line (page 67).

Journey: 59 min*
Season: £2468
Peak: 2 per hr
Off-peak: 1 per hr
*See also Kings Cross to Grantham.

Leicester

Market Harborough

Kettering

Wellingborough

Bedford

Flitwick

Harlington

Leagrave

Luton

Luton Airport Parkway

Harpenden

St Albans

St Pancras   Kings Cross Thameslink

Kings Cross Thameslink and St Pancras
➡ Bedford and Leicester

Thameslink services operate from Bedford and stations south, calling at Kings Cross Thameslink, Farringdon, City Thameslink, Blackfriars and London Bridge. Season ticket prices quoted are valid to Kings Cross Thameslink, St Pancras and the above stations to London Bridge at no extra cost (but not on the Underground).

St Albans

Forget the villages around **St Albans**. The attractions of the town itself, with its medieval centre focused around the cathedral, are such that it has become one of the smartest places to live north of London. Georgian and Edwardian town houses snuggle against quaint old cottages and 15th-century coaching inns. In the cramped but charming streets in the town centre conservation area you could buy a two-up-two-down cottage for around £135,000 to £140,000.

Journey: 19 min	
Season: £2080	
Peak: 8 per hr	
Off-peak: 4 per hr	

St Albans has excellent communications. It lies roughly equidistant from the M1 and A1, and only a few miles from the M25. The train journey into London is so fast that, in terms of time, it's hardly further from the City than Clapham. In the last decade some of the country's biggest accountancy firms have moved here, including Price Waterhouse, Deloitte and Touche and KPMG.

The shopping centre feels reassuringly traditional. There are old-fashioned individual shops, antique shops, and a mews where hand-crafted goods are sold. It has three theatres – the Albans Arena, the Maltings and the Abbey Theatre, where the formidable local dramatics society, The Company of Ten, performs. There are also frequent concerts and recitals in the cathedral.

Schools are another of St Albans's particular attractions. The local state schools have good reputations, and there are private schools for those who want them (see page 96).

The really stylish 15th-, 16th- and 17th-century houses are on Fishpool Street, the old London-Holyhead Road, where a Grade II listed two-bedroom cottage will sell for £190,000. The main residential area is Marshalswick. Three-bedroom semis here cost £170,000 to £250,000. Large detached houses in Marshal's Drive, with tennis courts, come with price-tags in the region of £650,000. Marshalswick has its own small shops, library and free car park. Further out of St Albans you will find roads of semi-detached houses where a three-bedroom home will cost in the range of £180,000 to £220,000.

For more modern, executive-style houses, the eastern corridor towards Hatfield, around the Hatfield Road, is the place to look. Three-bedroom semis sell for around £175,000 upwards; four- to five-bedroom detached houses will break £350,000.

Villages in the St Albans catchment include **Chiswell Green** – home of the Royal National Rose Society – **London Colney** and **Shenley**. These are fairly popular with commuters, and look reasonably pleasant at first glance. Locals tend to look down their noses at these areas, however, because of the volume of ex-council housing.

Harpenden

Journey: 24 min
Season: £2320
Peak: 7 per hr
Off-peak: 4 per hr

Harpenden is, if such a thing is possible, even smarter then St Albans. It has two cricket clubs, two leisure centres and a covered swimming pool. People have to travel to St Albans or London for professional theatre, though the local amateur dramatics and operatic societies regularly entertain at the civic hall. It has a Sainsbury, and plenty of boutiques, gift and speciality shops in the centre of the village. The green runs right through the centre, providing a perfect spot to sit and watch the world go by in summer. Schools for all age ranges – both private and state-run – have a particularly high reputation.

Schools in Hertfordshire

Hertfordshire is stuffed with good schools. But be aware that many which call themselves comprehensives actually run a selective entry system.

Watford's schools are within reach of people living near Chorleywood. Watford Boy's Grammar and its girls' counterpart are grant-maintained comprehensives with strong academic records. Both are heavily over-subscribed.

Harpenden also has two strong schools – St George's voluntary-aided co-educational comprehensive, which takes some boarders, and Roundwood Park co-educational grant-maintained school for boys and girls.

Bishop's Stortford has a good private school in Bishop's Stortford College and three good comprehensives – Bishop's Stortford High, The Hertfordshire and Essex High, and St Mary's Catholic School.

Rich pickings can be had in St Albans, not only with the high-performing St Albans Girls' comprehensive but also a matching pair of independent schools – St Albans School for boys (with girls in the sixth form), and St Albans High for girls. Two more worth mentioning include the private St Columba's College for boys and Loreto Roman Catholic Girls comprehensive.

Other good comprehensives can be found in Potters Bar, Hemel Hempstead, Hitchin, Sawbridgeworth and Welwyn Garden City. Strong private schools include Berkhamsted Collegiate in Berkhamsted, Haberdashers' Aske's for boys and for girls in Borehamwood; Haileybury in Hertford and St Francis College in Letchworth.

16th-century town
house, St Albans

Some of the most desirable properties are those close to the two golf courses or to the East and West Commons (though The Avenues might consider itself a cut above them). East Common has its own golf course; West Common is more purely residential. In the area of the Commons you could pay £150,000 for a two-bedroom terrace; up to £600,000 for a large family house. Properties span various architectural periods from Tudor right through to the present day, and many of them have large gardens with the occasional tennis court and swimming pool. The odd family house with a dozen bedrooms will sell for over £1m. Those with shallower pockets could find a two-bedroom terrace away from the Commons at around £135,000.

There are some extremely pretty villages within reach, any of which might have been lifted straight from the pages of *Country Life* or *Horse and Hound*. **Redbourn**, five miles away, is a large village with a population of over 5,000, centred around a classic common and picture-book High Street. Small shops and a post office provide for day-to-day needs, and there is an infant and junior school. However, it lies too close to the M1 for its own good – the roar of the cars can be heard. A three-bedroom cottage with half an acre will cost £325,000, while a five-bedroom house in two acres will cost £675,000. Hunt through the jumble of older cottages in the High Street to find something smaller and cheaper. For **Wheathampstead** see **Kings Cross to Grantham** line (page 63).

Kimpton to the north-east also has an attractive High Street with small shops and has good walks nearby in Gustard Wood. Commuters rub shoulders with long-established locals. Prices are slightly lower than in nearby Wheathampstead. There are plenty of terrace cottages, but a four-bedroom period house in one and a quarter acres will cost £420,000. There is a village infant and junior school.

Flamstead, due west, is popular for its charm and active village social life. A thick blanket of green belt gives it a very rural atmosphere, and in the Flamstead Society it has an influential local history group. Newcomers are welcomed as long as they are willing to fit in, though not if they charge around trying to change things. Many of the older-established residents are allotment holders, and the garden show is an important annual event. For the amusement of the young there is a football ground and tennis courts. Small shops include a good butcher and a post-office-cum-green-grocer. The village has its own junior school, and there are two old pubs which attract customers from miles around. The cottages are a picturesque mix of brick and flint. A two-bedroom example will cost around £130,000-plus; a larger, 17th-century three-bedroom house £160,000-plus.

Luton Airport Parkway

Journey: 30 min
Season: £2440
Peak: 5 per hr
Off-peak: 4 per hr

Generous and easy parking arrangements make Luton Airport an attractive alternative to catching the train from Luton proper – anything to avoid stressful early morning traffic jams. For Luton main entry see below.

Luton

Journey: 24 min
Season: £2440
Peak: 7 per hr
Off-peak: 6 per hr

Luton spreads its mess of modern housing estates, industrial complexes and shopping streets with little grace. It does still have some industrial pride, however, with major local employers including Vauxhall, Electrolux, Whitbread and London Luton Airport. Shopping is unfussy and run-of-the mill, and includes an Arndale Centre. There is a nine-screen cinema, three recreation centres, two swimming pools and the new Luton University. Luton Town Football Club plays at Kenilworth Road.

There are a few odd enclaves for those who prefer period homes. Along and just off the Old Bedford Road, about half a mile from the centre, are some 19th-century villas which have been so lavishly restored that some of them have two or even three bathrooms. A four-bedroom home here will cost between £150,000 and £300,000, depending on how much has been spent on it. Throughout the town there are plenty of detached Thirties houses selling at over £90,000 for three bedrooms; up to £200,000 for four bedrooms or more.

Kensworth, to the south-west, is a popular commuter village. Cottages line the main road, with a recreation ground and village hall to provide the community focal points. You might get a tiny two-bedroom cottage for as little as £65,000, but the sky's the limit for the large farmhouses in the area. The village has a post office, two general stores, a newsagent, a flower shop and its own infant and junior school. There is also some retirement housing.

Timber-frame cottages, Dunstable

To the east and south-east of Luton, just over the border into Hertfordshire, are the small villages of **Breachwood Green**, **Bendish** and **Peter's Green**. Bendish is probably the most stylish, being very tiny with old period cottages. A three-bedroom cottage in half an acre will set you back by £310,000 here, while a five-bedroom house in two acres will cost £600,000. Prices at Peter's Green are similar, though the place is so small that you could drive right through before you realised you'd reached it. Prices drop by about 15% at Breachwood Green. The village lies directly under the flight path to Luton Airport, and the ex-council properties put choosy buyers off.

Leagrave

Leagrave is hardly distinct from Luton. It has its own small precinct of shopping streets, but otherwise can be considered part of the town. In the centre of Leagrave, two- and three-bedroom pre-war terrace houses sell for between £55,000 and £65,000. On the outskirts you find the occasional new development where two-bed terraces start at around £65,000.

Journey: 35 min	
Season: £2440	
Peak: 4 per hr	
Off-peak: 4 per hr	

Dunstable, two miles west at the threshold of the Dunstable Downs, is far more captivating. The old town centre is dotted with timber-framed buildings, old coaching inns (Dunstable was an important coaching stop on Watling Street), and some attractive Victorian terraces. It is full of small designer-shops, good for birthday presents, though for mundane household purchases most people go into Luton. State schools include middle schools and an upper school which also provides adult evening classes. All have good reputations. Dunstable has its own sports centre and swimming pool, and a nightclub. The Downs, too, provide plenty of leisure opportunities. They provide the landscape for a golf club, Whipsnade Wild Animal Park, and form a favourite haunt for hang-gliders and kite-fliers. Victorian terrace homes with two or three bedrooms fetch around £65,000 to £70,000. A two- or three-bedroom semi on a modern estate would cost around £75,000; a three- or four-bedroom detached house from £150,000 upwards.

Also in the Luton catchment area is **Houghton Regis** – a former village of about two miles square, not quite swallowed up by encroaching development. Modern estates and Thirties semis make up the bulk of the property stock, with prices hovering at £75,000 to £80,000 for three bedrooms. At its heart it has some small quality shops around Bedford Square.

Harlington

Journey: 41 min
Season: £2480
Peak: 5 per hr
Off-peak: 4 per hr

Harlington, on the very tip of the Chiltern Hills, has an attractive core of timber-framed houses and thatched cottages grouped around the church. They are in a conservation area, and anything with two bedrooms will cost at least £90,000. On the outskirts are two estates built around 25 years ago. Three-bedroom semis are priced at around £110,000 to £115,000; four-bedroom detached houses at £150,000 upwards. A few local shops and a post office serve a population of approximately 2,300. There is a good infants school, an upper school and a sixth-form college. The nearest middle school is at Toddington (see below), a few miles to the south-west. There is quite a strong sporting tradition in the village.

Toddington, which lies just off the M1, is much larger – really a town with a population of about 10,000 and a range of shops and schools. There are a few elegant houses around the green, and some intriguing old pubs. Toddington Manor is thought once to have been the home of Henrietta Wentworth, mistress of the Duke of Monmouth. The town has grown paunchy with new development. Property prices are slightly lower than Harlington's, with three-bedroom semis at around £110,000 upwards.

Prettier villages in the Harlington area include **Tingrith** and **Milton Bryan**. Both these are hamlets of no more than 40 picture-postcard cottages each, plus the occasional Georgian farmhouse. There are no shops or schools, and both appeal to the better-heeled sort of commuter. Cottages start at around £120,000; family-sized period houses fetch between £200,000 and £500,000.

Flitwick

Little is left of old **Flitwick**, which was just a cluster of timber-framed houses and brick cottages. New development in the last 20 years has entirely changed its character. Much of the new building has been for the benefit of commuters, whose trains come thundering straight through the centre of the town. Apart from the railway, the most noticeable central landmark now is a huge branch of Tesco. Flitwick has three lower schools and one middle school; upper-school children have to travel to Ampthill (see below). For those with surplus energy there is a sports centre with a dance studio, swimming pool and squash courts.

Journey: 45 min
Season: £2480
Peak: 7 per hr
Off-peak: 4 per hr

Prices in the modern estates range from £80,000 to £100,000 for a three-bedroom semi; over £160,000 for a four-bedroom detached house. To the east of the town are some turn-of-the-century houses backing on to Flitwick Wood and open countryside. These cost around £155,000 with four bedrooms.

Ampthill, a small Georgian market town with a population of around 6,000, makes Flitwick look like an ugly sister. Its piituresque centre is set around a market square, dotted with antique and other small specialist shops. It also has a supermarket, schools for children of all ages, and a handsome park of around 150 acres. It is believed that Catherine of Aragon once lived here and received visits from Henry VIII. A small two- or three-bed cottage costs around £80,000 to £120,000; a character Georgian town house between £180,000 and £200,000.

Ex-Duke of Bedford cottages, Steppingley

Steppingley, a tiny village a mile to the west of Flitwick, has a little more than 40 Duke of Bedford peg-tiled estate cottages, a cricket club, pub and a good restaurant. The atmosphere is upmarket and horsey. Prices for two- to three-bedrrom cottages are in the region of £150,000 to £200,000. A four-bedroom detached period house will fetch between £300,000 and £600,000. Out of the village along one of the lanes you could expect to pay up to £500,000 for a Georgian farmhouse with a bit of land.

Bedford

Journey: 33 min
Season: £2480
Peak: 7 per hr
Off-peak: 4 per hr

Though still a market town, **Bedford** has to a certain extent allowed its individuality to become submerged by its own commercial success. Modern office blocks have appeared in the historic centre. Multi-national companies located here include Unilever. The Harpur Centre – a modern shopping mall – is complemented by quality small shops along the High Street, plus big-name stores and several supermarkets. The Bunyan Centre is the place for most sports, and there are two swimming pools including the Oasis "beach pool". The Civic Theatre provides a forum for amateur dramatics, but is upstaged as a venue by the Corn Exchange. The Aspects leisure centre has a nightclub, two restaurants, a bowling alley and multi-screen cinema.

Along the embankment by the River Ouse, where people stroll and sit in summer to watch the waterfowl, are some large, tree-shaded Victorian houses – probably the nicest properties in the town. One of these with five to seven bedrooms would cost over £400,000. There are also some pur-pose-built flats in the same area. The smallest one-bedroom apartment starts at £40,000. A three-bedroom Victorian terrace house nearby would cost £75,000; a three- to four-bedroom semi up to £100,000. For the rest of the town general rule is that the houses are more modern the further out you go, but prices do not vary much. You can expect to pay around £85,000 for a three-bedroom semi; £100,000 for a three-bedroom detached.

Schools in Bedfordshire

Bedford's strongest suit is its independent sector schools which include Bedford High and Dame Alice Harpur for girls, and Bedford and Bedford Modern for boys. These schools take pupils from a large catchment area, who have to be bussed in daily.

Most of the sought-after villages in the flat countryside around Bedford are to the north. **Oakley**, just over four miles to the north-west, has in its High Street some old brick farmworkers' cottages that once belonged to the Duke of Bedford's estate. You would pay from around £85,000 for one of these with two bedrooms and a long garden. There is also a good deal of modern development where you would pay about £90,000 for a three-bedroom semi; from £125,000 for a four-bedroom detached. Youngish families mix with the small number of commuters. Village social life revolves around the village hall, cricket and football teams, the gardening club and the two pubs. There is a village store, a post office, primary and middle schools.

Bromham, on the Ouse three miles north-west of Bedford, is a large village with a population of 5,000. Many of the local families have lived here for generations. The limestone cottages in the village centre are surrounded by modern housing, and building is still going on. There are two shops, one with a post office, a soft-furnishings shop, hairdresser, plus a lower school. Bromham House, an old manor house, is now a hospital for the mentally handicapped, the local windmill is restored and open to the public. The town holds an annual apple day. Property prices in Bromham are similar to those in Oakley.

Biddenham, due west of Bedford, is the favourite village for London commuters. It is so close to the town (the station is but a brisk 15-minute walk), yet it feels deliciously remote and is set around a classic village green. All this makes it one of the most expensive villages in the area. Properties range from 17th-century thatched cottages to imposing Thirties houses, plus a few modern developments built with managing directors in mind. Prices range from £80,000 for a one- or two-bedroom cottage to £500,000 for a substantial family house. A development of 300 houses has been built with a shop, a cricket field, tennis courts and a community centre as part of the package. Four-bedroom houses here cost £210,000. There is a cricket club and tennis club. The village hall is packed at parish council meetings, and everyone gets involved in local events, including an annual summer show. The area's conservation issues are policed by the Biddenham Society.

There are a few small sporting estates in the Bedford area. One with three houses, 500 acres and fishing rights will cost around £2m.

Wellingborough

Wellingborough is so plain it defies description yet the improved train service is bringing in new life blood in the form of commuters. It has a good range of major chain stores, several supermarkets including a Sainsbury and a new Tesco, and a modern shopping mall, the Swansgate Centre. Schooling is adequate, with three state secondary schools and one private school, Wellingborough School for boys. A night out in Wellingborough used to mean going to a pub, but the town now also has a theatre called The Castle, an arts complex and a leisure centre.

Journey: 49 min
Season: £4112
Peak: 3 per hr
Off-peak: 2 per hr

The town has a mix of Victorian terrace houses, smart newish developments and some not-so-nice council estates. Developments around the railway station are popular as starter homes. A two-bedroom quad (a quarter of a house split into four) will cost £35,000; a three-bedroom semi

Red-brick and stone cottage, Wellingborough

£50,000; a four-bedroom detached just over £90,000. There are some pleasant older properties in Northampton Road, where you could expect to pay over £75,000 for a three-bedroom period house. For Victoriana look in Hatton Park where houses cost £100,000 to £250,000. A four-bedroom modern detached house on one of the better develop-ments – the Gleneagles Estate, for instance – would cost between £90,000 and £130,000.

Rushden, a few miles to the east, is about one third the size of Wellingborough and rather less attractive, with some charmless early Seventies architecture and an extra dollop of houses planned which might simply add to the anywhere-land feel. The consolation for house-buyers is some reasonably-priced Victorian terraces, ranging from around £30,000 to £50,000 for two or three bedrooms. A four-bedroom detached modern house will cost over £75,000. Shopping is adequate: there is a Safeway on the edge of town and a Budgens within. The main source of local pride is the sports centre and the splash-leisure pool. There is no cin-ema since the old picture house was converted into a theatre for amateur dramatics and bingo. Rushden was the birthplace of H.E. Bates, who used Rushden Hall – one of the few historic buildings surviving in the town – as the model for Evensfield in *Love For Lydia*.

A favourite state school is Ferrers School in **Higham Ferrers**, four-and-a-half miles to the east of Wellingborough. The village has now become a town, hardly separated from Rushden, with an attractive High Street lined with period stone properties and new developments fanning out on either side. A four-bedroom stone house here will cost over £160,000. A rambling five-bedroom terrace on the market square might cost as much as £250,000. Some of the villages close to it are worth looking at, too. **Wymington** has a good mix of stone and thatch, with a spread of old farmhouses down the lanes, and **Podington** has a quality of timeless-ness that is very attractive. You could find a period three-bedroom stone house for around £70,000.

Wollaston, about seven minutes' drive due south of Wellingborough, is centred around a cluster of old cottages, with modern developments, an industrial estate and council housing on the outskirts. The makers of Doc

Martens have their headquarters here. It has small shops, a post office and its own primary and secondary schools. The conservation watchdogs of the Wollaston Society have enjoyed some triumphs, including the arrival in 1985 of a bypass to take the strain off the A509. Property prices start at £55,000 for a three-bedroom semi; £90,000 for a four-bedroom detached; and £100,000 for a 17th-century stone cottage. A four-bedroom, double-garaged, detached stone house overlooking the fields might cost £185,000 but would be a rare find.

Grendon is a pretty village consisting of 18th-century cottages gathered around the church

For real village atmosphere, however, you should head south to **Grendon**, about five miles from Wellingborough. This pretty village consists of 18th-century cottages gathered around the church, with some Victorian terraces and a few individual modern properties. Villagers get by with one post office/general-store and a good primary school. There is a limited bus service. The population of over 500 includes some commuters, and some elderly residents in bungalows. Village life centres around the Church Social Committee, Village Hall Committee, the WI, scouts, guides and cricket team. There is an annual church fête and periodic fund-raising ventures which attract considerable support. Expect to pay at least £100,000 for a period cottage; upwards of £55,000 for a two-bed Victorian terrace.

East of Wellingborough is **Raunds** – a small town not to everyone's taste, with a 14th-century manor house and Victorian buildings surrounded by modern estates. Its tightly-knit community of about 8,000 is served by two supermarkets, a post office and smaller shops. Little terrace houses can be bought for £32,000; three-bedroom Victorian semis for £50,000 to £65,000; and modern three-bedroom detached houses for £55,000 upwards.

Also on this side of Wellingborough are **Great** and **Little Addington**. Both are cottagey with some modern development on the wings – mainly four-bedroom detached houses. If your idea of village life includes a post office run from someone's back room, and an infrequent bus service, these are the places for you. The two villages share a vicar, a playing field and WI, though there is still a certain amount of friendly rivalry which brings people out in summer and winter for inter-village sporting contests. Another highlight of the social calendar is the annual horticultural society show. There is a youth club, a Church of England primary school and a playgroup for tots, of which there are a fair number – a third of the popula-

Green wellies, Land Rovers and waxed jackets are common currency in the Addingtons

tion in Great Addington is under 16. You would have to pay around £115,000 for a three-bedroom stone cottage, possibly thatched; around £120,000 for a modern four-bedroom detached. A five-bedroom stone country house with an acre of land could cost up to £250,000. The area is so seriously horsey that estate agents say that anything with a pony paddock is bound to sell. Green wellies, Land Rovers and waxed jackets are common currency here.

Kettering

Journey: 57 min
Season: £4368
Peak: 4 per hr
Off-peak: 2 per hr

Kettering is a no-nonsense East Midlands market town, well supplied with leisure opportunities and good shopping. All the big-name stores are here, including Tesco, Sainsbury and Marks and Spencer, and the modern Newland Shopping Centre is useful if not actually inspiring. There is a leisure centre and the 180-acre Wicksteed Park is not far away with its fairground/theme park. Those addicted to more sedentary pleasures will be pleased to hear that there is a 10-screen cinema.

The town has a few old Georgian terraces in the centre, larger Victorian houses forming a ring around them, and two modern estates on the outskirts. You might pick up a two-bedroom Victorian terrace for £36,000, or a three-bedroom Victorian house with original features and a good garden for around £60,000.

The countryside here at last begins to pick itself up off the Bedfordshire plains. It is a mellow, slightly rolling, farmland landscape which draws people from Kettering out into frankly villagey little market towns that surround it. Look at **Rothwell** and **Desborough** to the north, and **Burton Latimer** to the south. All have Victorian market places, small shops and their own primary and secondary schools. Property prices are similar to those in Kettering. Rothwell is particularly pretty and has a gem of an Elizabethan market hall. The centre is a designated conservation area, and it has the benefit of a state secondary school, Montsaye, with a very good academic record. A two-up-two-down terrace will cost £40,000; a three-bedroom terrace £45,000; a three-bedroom semi £50,000 to £55,000; a four-bedroom detached £100,000 to £120,000.

People grow very fond of Market Harborough, home of the first liberty bodice

One of the more notable smaller villages is **Geddington**, four miles north of Kettering, with a population of around 1,200. A medieval bridge crosses the River Ise here, with a forested hillside providing an attractive green backdrop. It has three pubs, a village hall, two shops, a post office and a primary school. Its heart is a cluster of old cottages, though new housing has forced itself in and there are some Victorian terraces, too. For a two-bedroom terrace house or a small cottage you would have to pay upwards of £50,000. Closer to Kettering on the north side is the tiny village of **Weekley**. There are possibly no more than 150 people living here altogether, many of them from old farming families, some of them elderly (the old vicarage is now a home for the elderly). There is a post office/general store which serves cream teas but no school – and no pub either, though the village social club is the place to go for an evening drink and Jessica's tea-shop is the coffee-morning hot spot. The social club is also the venue for sports club meetings. The village hall, too, rings with the sound of cup on saucer during its frequent coffee mornings. Weekley is a quiet, compact, well-heeled and tight-knit village where a cottage – should you be lucky enough to find one for sale – would cost around £90,000.

Market Harborough

People grow very fond of **Market Harborough**, home of the first liberty bodice, with its distinctive half-timbered Old Grammar School on stilts in the centre, now used for public functions. The population is a manageable 17,000. Georgian offices and shops are still in place in the town centre, and the office blocks of large local employers such as Golden Wonder crisps manage not to be too intrusive. Other companies in the town include Harper Tungsten Batteries and GVC Plastics, and there is a large industrial park on the outskirts. The new St Mary's Place shopping centre in the old cattle market has a Sainsbury and indoor market. There is a leisure centre and swimming pool, a 100-seat theatre large enough for local productions, but no cinema.

Journey: 69 min
Season: £4828
Peak: 3 per hr
Off-peak: 2 per hr

Some of the nicest properties are the large Victorian villas along the Northampton Road, where three-bedroom houses start at £100,000. There are also some rather gracious tree-lined avenues in which mature Thirties semis and detached houses are likely to cost £130,000 to £150,000. Victoria Avenue, actually a cul-de-sac, and Lubenham Hill, are both popular.

North of Market Harborough you enter the wide-open, rolling coun-

Schools in Leicestershire, Rutland and Peterborough

Leicester itself has the Beauchamp School, a co-educational comprehensive with a reputation for being liberal and achieving good results, and two independent schools – Leicester Grammar for boys and the High School for girls. The Leicester Islamic Academy and the English Martyrs Roman Catholic comprehensive also do well in the school league tables. Other dominant public schools in the area include Uppingham, the boys' boarding school (with sixth form girls), Oakham, which takes day boys and girls, and Wellingborough, which is co-educational day and boarding.

tryside of the Welland Valley, where villages of thatch and stone are connected by unhurried roads. This is serious hunting country – Quorn territory. Life in The Langtons – **Church Langton, Tur Langton, West Langton, East Langton** and **Thorpe Langton** – revolves around horses and farming. Church Langton is the largest of this idyllic clutch of villages and West Langton the smallest, though they are all really little more than hamlets, clusters of stone and thatched cottages. All except West Langton have a pub. Church Langton has the only primary school. Prices vary according to how much land comes with the house and how good the views are, but you could reckon on paying over £100,000 for a three-bedroom stone cottage; up to £300,000 for four bedrooms and an acre of land on a hilltop.

Another gem is **Foxton**. It lies about two-and-a-half miles north-west of Market Harborough on the Grand Union Canal. Its famous series of locks – 10 altogether in two flights rising through 75ft – and the remains of an inclined-plane boat-lift are a great attraction to tourists in the summer. The village itself is pretty, too, with old stone and thatched cottages and only a few ex-council houses. Swingbridge Street is possibly the nicest. The population is a friendly mix of young families, commuters and farmers. There is a shop, village hall, infant and junior schools and three pubs. A three-bedroom detached cottage will cost £150,000, rising to around £250,00 if it has an acre or two of land. Ex-council houses fetch around £70,000 to £80,000. It is worth noting that in the villages to the north of Market Harborough you can still find old manor houses which make very compact, manageable homes. For six or seven bedrooms, a few acres of land and stabling, you would pay around £500,000.

Close to Foxton is **Gumley**, a tiny one-street village on a hill. There is a pub but no shop or school. Many of the villagers own horses and have farming interests. Property rarely comes on the market, but if you were lucky you might buy a two-bedroom Victorian brick cottage for £95,000, or a modern four-bedroom house for £200,000.

Leicester

Journey: 69 min
Season: £5444
Peak: 4 per hr
Off-peak: 4 per hr

This gutsy, modern Midlands city is not likely to woo the heart of too many London commuters though it is very conveniently placed close to the M69, the M6 and the M1. Its prosperity was built on hosiery, then on the mass production of boots and shoes, and more recently on engineering and computing. Though it was badly hit by the recession the city has cleverly married public and private spending to good effect, making sustainability a central theme. There is a student population, for both Leicester and De Montfort universities are here, and there is also a very high percentage of non-white residents. This is the land of steam, antique and agricultural fairs, but also now a land of many cultures, where the Caribbean

Festival in August attracts 30,000 people and the Hindu celebrations of Diwali and Navratri eclipse those anywhere else in Europe. Leisure here means sport. For participants the city has bowling rinks, BMX cycle tracks, tennis courts, cricket and football pitches, swimming pools and leisure centres. For spectators there are Leicester City FC, Leicestershire County Cricket Club and the indomitable Tigers – Leicester Rugby Football Club.

To the east is classic hunting country, where the Fernie hunt borders with the Quorn

Highfields, the red light district that has been cleaned up, is generally avoided. So are some of the ugly council estates, though these offer cheap housing – three-bedroom semis at £36,000. Just to the south of the city is the comparative comfort of **Stoneygate**, where there are large Victorian and Edwardian villas, some of which have been converted into flats. A three-bedroom Victorian house here will cost £95,000; a four-bedroom detached £160,000. Prices are similar in **Oadby**, which also has its share of older streets and a gentle mix of new housing.

There are some very pretty villages to te north-west in the Charnwood Forest and to the north-east along the Wreake valley, though perhaps some of the most unspoilt stone villages lie slightly out of reach towards Oakham. To the east is classic hunting country, where the Fernie hunt borders with the Quorn. **Hoby** in the Wreake valley is particularly charming. In this and any of the villages close by, a four-bedroom detached period house might cost £150,000 to £250,000, while the smaller two-bedroom variety will cost £80,000 to £90,000. In the Charnwood Forest you come close to the coal-mining areas of Coalville and Mountsorrel, but the forest itself is completely unspoilt and fiercely protected. Prices of small cottages in **Quorn** are similar to those in the Wreake Valley, but large period properties with six to eight bedrooms and a swag of land can reach £650,000.

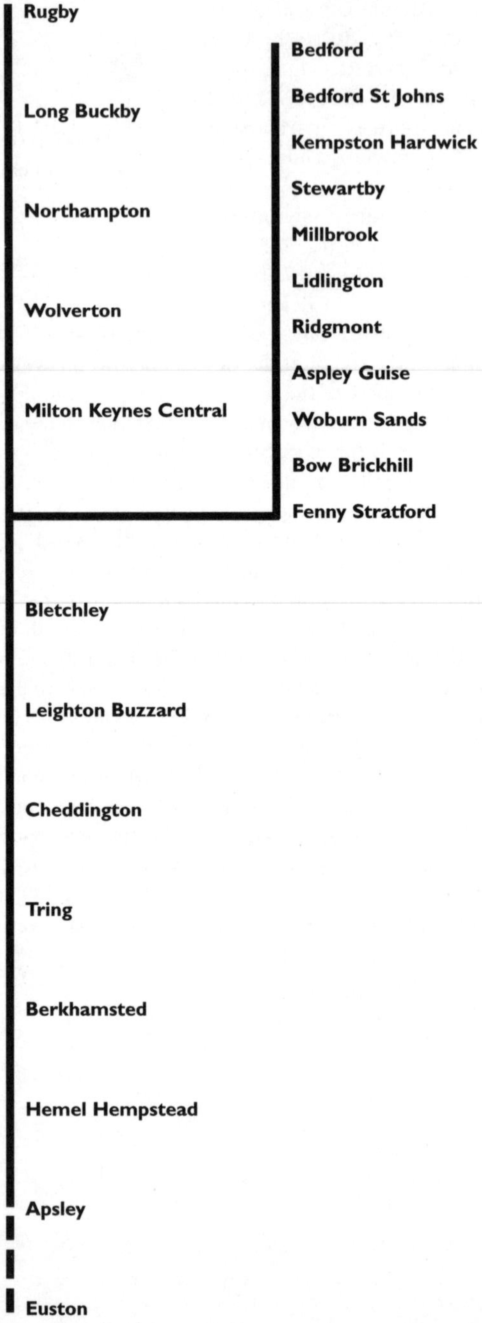

Rugby

Bedford

Bedford St Johns

Long Buckby

Kempston Hardwick

Stewartby

Northampton

Millbrook

Lidlington

Wolverton

Ridgmont

Aspley Guise

Milton Keynes Central

Woburn Sands

Bow Brickhill

Fenny Stratford

Bletchley

Leighton Buzzard

Cheddington

Tring

Berkhamsted

Hemel Hempstead

Apsley

Euston

Euston
➡ Rugby (via Northampton) ⬇

Apsley

Apsley is mostly Victorian, with three-bedroom terraces priced at around £130,000. The area has been allowed to breathe again now that it has a bypass. It is well liked because the houses are within walking distance of the station, and it has a sense of identity. **Boxmoor** is also worth looking at as a refuge from the modernity of Hemel Hempstead, to which it is now annexed. It still has a few little canalside cottages. You can buy older two- or three-bedroom cottages for around £140,000, or spend £160,000 on a smart modern house with four bedrooms. Sunday afternoon walks might take you close to Watford to Cassiobury Park beside the Grand Union Canal, which leads into Whippendell Woods – 200 acres of beech, oak and hornbeam.

Journey: 29 min
Season: £2220
Peak: 2 per hr
Off-peak: 2 per hr

Bovingdon, to the south-west, is another antidote to Hemel Hempstead. The centre still has a village feel to it, with a green and a good medieval hall house. House prices are 10% higher than in Hemel Hempstead, though there has been a lot of modern development. The market, held on Saturdays on the site of the old Bovingdon airfield, has more than 500 stalls, selling everything from home-made pies to hand-sewn clothes. "To tell you the truth, Bovingdon is a bit of a nothing place but people who live there think they live in a village," is how one local cynic described it.

Hemel Hempstead

Hemel Hempstead may not be to everyone's taste, just pre-dating Stevenage as a New Town, but it is very conveniently placed. The M1 and M25 both pass very close to it, the train to London takes less than half an hour, and Heathrow is but 40 minutes away by car. It also still has rough Hertfordshire meadows on three sides of it. After all, the idea which underpinned the New Town concept was that people could combine the pleasures of town and country, and escape the overcrowded conditions of London. In 1994 the centre was pedestrianised, making life easier for the footsoldiers of shopping. The town also has a shopping centre, sports centre, a ski slope, concerts at the Pavilion and an eight-screen Odeon. The

Journey: 25 min
Season: £2224
Peak: 4 per hr
Off-peak: 4 per hr

Potten End borders on beautiful National Trust land that stretches along the spine of the Chilterns from Ivinghoe Beacon to Berkhamsted

old town grew up around the Norman church, with Regency and Victorian villas springing up along Marlowes to take advantage of the distant views to the Chilterns. A two-bedroom cottage in the old town will cost £118,000.

To the east you come to **Leverstock Green**, where the housing is mostly post-Fifties. A four-bedroom home would cost between £260,000 and £280,000. There are also some very large houses set in one-acre plots that fetch over £300,000. Ex-local authority housing tends to sell for a good deal less than private housing, so a two-bedroom house might be had for over £60,000.

The New Town has a brash shopping centre with all the chain stores anyone could need. Large companies located here include Kodak and British Telecom. The British Standards Institute also has its offices in Hemel Hempstead.

Potten End, to the north-west, is a dispersed Chiltern village with a green, a pond and the Red Lion pub. It borders on beautiful National Trust land that stretches along the spine of the Chilterns from Ivinghoe Beacon to Berkhamsted. You can buy a Thirties detached house with a tile-hung bay window in a quiet suburban road for around £250,000. Old cottages, however, are thin on the ground. A substantial house with five bedrooms and an acre of garden might fetch £475,000.

Chipperfield is expensive, too, though the centre has long-since been ribboned with developments built to accommodate fugitives from Watford. It is redeemed by its wooded common webbed with footpaths, and by the old village centre where the green is faced by an inn, the church and some little brick cottages. A four-bedroom detached house (most of the houses are this size or larger) would cost £330,000.

Berkhamsted

Journey: 29 min
Season: £2344
Peak: 4 per hr
Off-peak: 4 per hr

Berkhamsted is a prosperous old market town wedged in the valley bottom, with the railway and canal running through some of the best countryside close to London. An antiques market is held on Fridays, a general market on Saturdays, and a flower-seller in the High Street provides constant charm and colour. The old castle, where Chaucer was clerk of works, is now little more than a few fingers of flint but an increasing source of wonder to historians who have been studying fresh excavations. People are attracted by the thickly wooded common, towpath walks along the Grand Union Canal, and Berkhamsted Collegiate School, which includes Graham Greene among its alumni. On the steep valley slopes to the south are shoals of Victorian and Edwardian houses with large gardens, while the centre of town is packed with Victorian terraces. You can get a double-fronted, bay-windowed, two-bedroom 19th-century house for £150,000 to £175,000. Canalside flats right in the centre sell for around £100,000 for two bedrooms. Detached houses built in the Sixties and Seventies hover at £200,000. The large, individually designed, secluded houses in private roads run extravagantly over £600,000.

The Rothschild Zoological Museum is full of stuffed bears and other exotics – unsurprisingly for a family who used to drive around in traps drawn by zebras

A bypass came to the rescue in 1993, removing much of the traffic from the centre. The busy shopping centre has all the chain stores, a Café Uno in the Victorian town hall, lots of restaurants and two fitness centres. There is a sports centre, and a golf course on Berkhamsted Common, the rest of which is mostly owned by the National Trust.

Little Gaddesden, to the north, is very desirable, perched on a ridge 600ft up in the Chiltern Hills. Most of the large houses and cottages face directly on to the beechwoods and heathland of the vast Ashridge Estate, which is classified as an Area of Outstanding Natural Beauty. Physically the village is strung out in a linear settlement pattern; socially it is rather cliquey. You would pay £125,000 to £150,000 for a small two-bedroom cottage. There is a Church of England primary school, a church half a mile outside the village, and a village hall that hosts all the usual coffee mornings and clubs. The big house has been converted into a college which specialises in management courses. In nearby **Ashridge**, which is a discreet enclave of Twenties and Thirties houses with stockbroker-appeal, something with five bedrooms and three-quarters of an acre will cost over £750,000; a two-bedroom cottage £275,000.

Close by is **Aldbury**, a film-set village of thatched and timber-framed cottages that cluster round a large pond with stocks and whipping post. Even the smallest cottage here costs at least £125,000 and will usually sell by word of mouth. There is a general store and post office, a crafts shop, a pub called the Greyhound and a country club hotel with a golf course. Sightseers come to admire its good looks.

Tring

Tring station is one-and-a-half miles outside the town in a hamlet called **Tring Station**. The Rothschilds lived at Tring Park, and their stamp is everywhere. They gave open spaces, provided cottages, and in 1905 built the stockbroker-style, half-timbered Rose & Crown Inn. The Walter Rothschild Zoological Museum, full of stuffed bears, sloths and other exotics, is typi-

Journey: 42 min	
Season: £2500	
Peak: 4 per hr	
Off-peak: 2 per hr	

Three-bedroomed
cottage, near Tring

cally eccentric – the family used to drive around in traps drawn by zebras. Today Tring performs the dual role of commuter dormitory and market town. One defining feature has been sadly lost now that the thrice yearly sheep auctions have stopped.

There are plenty of Victorian houses and new estates. A two-bedroom flat might cost £75,000; a two-bedroom Victorian cottage £100,000; a three-bedroom semi £100,000 to £140,000; a four-bedroom detached £230,000. Tring does have a shopping centre, though people tend to use Aylesbury, Hemel Hempstead or Milton Keynes for more serious shopping. The Tring Nature Reserve's four reservoirs (used to store water in the 18th century) attract flocks of wintering ducks.

Two-and-a-half miles further north of Tring Station is **Ivinghoe** – a pretty village close to Ivinghoe Beacon from which you can gaze across to the chalkhill white lion of Whipsnade Wild Animal Park. The centre of the village makes a pretty picture out of the older houses sitting sleepily on two sides of the green and the handsome watermill.

Cheddington

Journey: 47 min
Season: £2552
Peak: 3 per hr
Off-peak: 2 per hr

Cheddington is a quiet little village, best known for the fact that the Great Train Robbery took place at the railway bridge just outside. A farm with around 400 acres of dairy meadows could be expected to cost £1.1m. Prices are similar to Tring's and slightly higher than Leighton Buzzard's. You could buy a four-bedroom detached house for around £165,000 upwards; a three-bedroom turn-of-the-century cottage for £110,000 upwards.

Leighton Buzzard

Journey: 40 min
Season: £2592
Peak: 4 per hr
Off-peak: 4 per hr

Leighton Buzzard has swallowed whole the smaller town of **Linslade** on the west of the River Ouzel, which is actually where the station is. It is prime commuter-land. Leighton Buzzard proper is an old market town with drunken timber and brick buildings, and a twice-weekly market. The main street is in the process of being pedestrianised. The smartest roads to live in are Plantation Road (known as Bedfordshire's most beautiful mile) and Heath Road, studded with trees and a mix of Victorian and modern houses. Prices range between £70,000 for a two-bedroom terrace to

£500,000 for a large family house. You can find older two-bedroom terrace houses for £65,000 in other parts of the town, but the standard price for a modern four-bedroom detached is £140,000. The town is well-padded in green belt.

Between 1912 and 1914, the suffragette Sylvia Pankhurst and her mother lived at Stewkley in a 16th-century cottage

Around the station in Linslade, which is more leafy than Leighton Buzzard itself, are Victorian terraces where two-bedroom houses sell for around £70,000, and three- to four-bedroom houses for around £145,000. There are two large modern estates, Bideford Green and Knaves Hill, built 20 years ago. Three-bedroom semis here cost around £75,000; three-bedroom detached around £90,000; four-bedroom houses around £120,000.

Soulbury, two miles west, is one of the best examples of an open field village in north Buckinghamshire, and its proximity to the station makes it a favourite with commuters. The half-timbered and thatched houses around the green and church overlook the Ouzel valley. Other cottages are spread out between fields which are embroidered with footpaths, and there are a few modern properties at the village margin. You need a car to live here, there is no shop, post office or bus service, though there is a clubroom for the use of local societies. Houses rarely come on the market, and when they do they are expensive. A period two-bedroom cottage would fetch from £76,000; a four-bedroom detached around £160,000 to £170,000.

Further west in the Vale of Aylesbury is **Stewkley** – possibly the longest village in England, stretching a mile either side of St Michael's, its remarkably fine Norman church. Between 1912 and 1914 the suffragette Sylvia Pankhurst and her mother lived here in a 16th-century cottage. The village has a reputation for being rather superior and closed to outsiders whom it decides do not belong. A substantial five-bedroom house would cost over £300,000; an ex-council house with three bedrooms £122,000.

For a less rarefied atmosphere you could look southwards to **Wing**, a busy, no-frills village with several shops including one general store with a post office, two hairdressers, a fish and chip shop and two doctor's surgeries. Ascott House, bought by the Rothschilds in 1874, is close by, and village employment and activities have tended to revolve around the estate. Apart from the black-and-white estate cottages, there are rows of turn-of-the-century brick terrace cottages, plus the occasional thatched house and the usual modern estates lying on the fringe. A two-up-two-down Victorian terrace might cost £70,000; a three-bedroom detached £120,000; four-bedroom £150,000.

The village has junior and secondary schools, several football teams and an adult education centre (upholstery classes are particularly popular). The large green has footpaths and swings. The drawback is that the village is beginning to feel hemmed in by Milton Keynes and Leighton

Buzzard. It is also used as a rat-run by commuters dashing for the Leighton Buzzard trains, though talk of a bypass continues.

One of the most beautiful villages in the area is **Mentmore** – a charming collection of mock-Tudor houses on top of a hill in old Rothschild country. The large village green is ringed with lime trees and offers breathtaking views in every direction. The big house is Mentmore Towers which caused a furore in 1974 when it was offered to the government and turned down. The contents were sold, important works of art went out of the country, and the house was bought by the Maharishi Foundation. In 1999 it came on the market again with an elastic price tag of £10m to £15m which dropped to £3m to £5m and it is now back in the hands of a private individual. A modest two-bedroom cottage on the crest of the hill in Mentmore village would cost over £80,000; a country house with a few acres up to £1m.

Bletchley

Journey: 47 min
Season: £2600
Peak: 4 per hr
Off-peak: 4 per hr

Bletchley is the largest of the three towns gobbled up by Milton Keynes and is home to Bletchley Park, the wartime code-breaking centre, which is now open to the public on alternate weekends. The town has a good shopping centre and an open-air general market is held three times a week. "The funny thing about it is that at the heart of it you will find a 16th-century thatched cottage with an acre of garden selling for around £160,000," says one local estate agent. "Where else can you find an acre of garden in the centre of town?" The rest of Bletchley has been developed in waves, reflecting the repeated housing booms of the 19th and 20th century. You start with the thatched cottages, then come the grids of Victorian terraces selling for between £65,000 and £70,000, then the classic double bay-fronted Thirties houses, built by Tranfield, some of which still have their sunburst stained glass.

Nearly 40% of the town is council housing, which is why it tends to be looked down upon by some of its neighbours. The ex-council houses offer good value, however, with large three-bedroom semis selling for around £65,000 to £70,000. In the last building wave are the houses of the Eighties boom – typical mix-and match styles, with one-bedroom flats, small and large houses all mixed up together. A one-bedroom house costs just over £40,000; a four-bedroom detached with a garage over £90,000.

Padbury, to the west, is the classic chocolate-box village with half-timbered and thatched cottages, and a green swathed in leafy trees. The farms around were once owned by All Souls' College, Oxford. It has a butcher and a part-time post office in the garage, but the grocery stores have gone. There are tennis courts, a sports field and pavilion, and a village hall. Despite all this, old villagers complain that it is not the village it used to be, there has been such an influx of commuters and weekenders. Among the attractions for incomers is a highly-regarded local school for five- to nine-year-olds. People will wait years to get a house in Padbury, and pay over £120,000 for a small semi-detached thatched cottage.

Adstock is slightly closer to Bletchley. Its timber, brick and thatched cottages built along narrow lanes give it a feeling of cosiness and compactness, and there is a popular local pub, the Thatched Inn. A four-bedroom cottage with exposed beams and inglenook fireplace might sell for £200,000.

For a vibrant village life, try **Thornborough**. This is a long, thin village with a church, pub and green (with pond), which is the scene of a great number of village events. There are fêtes, a donkey derby and a sports day, followed by a barbecue in the evening. There are two football clubs and a cricket team which plays in the evenings as well as at weekends, and a gardening society which has helped with the local landscaping. The primary school takes children up to eight years old, and the shop doubles as a post office. When it rains the stream across the road swells and people come out to paddle. There are also ducks, which are none too fussy about where they lay their eggs. Some of the drakes have been known to end up in village freezers. A circular five-mile walk round Thornborough watermill and the old canal is a favourite Sunday afternoon stroll. A five-bedroom detached house might cost £200,000; a three-bedroom 18th-century stone-and-slate cottage £180,000.

Branch line to **Bedford** via **Fenny Stratford, Bow Brickhill, Woburn Sands, Aspley Guise, Ridgmont, Lidlington, Millbrook, Stewartby, Kempston Hardwick** and **Bedford St Johns**

This is the only remaining section of the old Oxford-Cambridge line and locals call it the Noddy Train because it is small and it rattles. The line is only 17 miles long but is extremely busy since it serves villages that lack good local bus services and is heavily used by children on the school-run to Bedford. Commuters can change at Bedford for either St Pancras or King's Cross Thameslink. Or they can go to Bletchley and change for Euston, which is most people's preferred choice. None of the stations along the line have car parks, nor are they manned. Information is tannoyed from Bletchley to the individual platforms, and tickets are bought from the guard on the train. Season tickets to Euston, St Pancras or Kings Cross Thameslink are available from Bletchley or Bedford.

People living in the eastern suburbs of Milton Keynes (see ahead) tend to use the first two stations, **Fenny Stratford** and **Bow Brickhill**, rather

No through trains.
Journey: 65 min (from Aspley Guise)
Season: £2480 (via Bletchley – £2848 for additional use via Bedford)
Frequency: 1 per hr Bedford and Bletchley

House style in the South Midlands

The least attractive part of the region is Bedfordshire, blanketed in clay which has been made into huge quantities of yellow and orangey-red bricks over the years. Industrial farming has done its worst, and the clay-clogged hedgeless fields only rarely erupt into pretty village scenes or pleasing countryside.

Northamptonshire has long been under-rated by London commuters, though it is peppered with lovely limestone houses. Near Collyweston the houses are roofed in stone slates, with gabled bay windows and double stone chimney-stacks. The stone turns pale and grey as you travel eastwards. Pantiles for the roofs were brought from eastern ports up the rivers Welland, Nene and Ouse.

than drive to Milton Keynes Central. Fenny Stratford is mainly Victorian, and you would have to pay over £60,000 for a three-bedroom house here. Bow Brickhill sprawls along a steep hillside reputed to have been a favourite haunt of Dick Turpin. Old woodland has been cleared to make way for golf courses. It is an old village, with a beautician and a pub, but lies on a very busy road. Property is varied, from two-up-two-downs selling at around £60,000, to four-bedroom Sixties houses at around £150,000.

Woburn Sands has its own distinct identity, with a small High Street for day-to-day needs, and wonderful walks within five minutes of the centre in the Duke of Bedford's woodlands. There are a couple of dress shops, several restaurants, wet fish shop, butcher, doctor's surgery and medical centre, tennis courts, a cricket ground and a lower and middle school. You could buy a small turn-of-the-century house for £80,000 to £120,000, but a four- or five-bedroom Victorian house would be likely to fetch £300,000. Local activities include football teams, bowls and village fairs. **Aspley Heath** (within reach of Woburn Sands station) is where people from Woburn Sands aspire to move, since it has spacious houses set in large gardens with good views. It is known locally as millionaires' row and it would be hard to find anything here for less than £250,000.

Woburn itself (also within reach of Woburn Sands station) is a beautifully preserved Georgian town, best known for its proximity to Woburn Abbey and popularity with golfers. It has a wine bar, antiques shop and restaurant. Very few houses are freehold since most are tied to the estate, but the occasional four-bedroom modern house might come on the market for around £125,000; or you might find an ex-council three-bedroom semi for around £75,000. It does get cluttered in summer with tourists visiting the Abbey and its Wild Animal Kingdom.

For a sedate, select and expensive village, you would look at **Aspley Guise**. Middle-class Victorians regarded it as an "inland Bournemouth", but modern estate agents like to describe it as "the Darling Buds of May of Milton Keynes". It is very traditional. People smile and say good morning to each other, and they bother to keep the village tidy. There is a shop, post office, hairdresser and hotel, and the railway station is tiny. People pay a lot to live here and then stay a long time. A two-bedroom Victorian terrace would cost over £90,000; a four-bedroom house between £200,000 and

£300,000. People hunt and fish and go to church. The finest house in the village is Aspley House, believed to have been built by an assistant to Sir Christopher Wren, or perhaps even by Wren himself.

Eversholt (within reach of Aspley Guise), on the other side of the Woburn Estate, is typical of the Duke of Bedford's estate in that the rows of cottages have no front doors. It is said that the Duchess didn't like to see people gossiping. A rectory with five or six bedrooms and four acres might cost over £335,000.

Ridgmont is a typical Bedfordshire estate village with cottages built in two styles. There are two-up-two-downs with leaded lights that might sell for £90,000; and three-bedroom terraces, built in distinctive red brick in the late 19th century, which might sell for £110,000. Motorway noise can be a problem.

Lidlington is another estate village where the Duke of Bedford sought to muzzle the gossips by building houses without front doors. It has a post office, general store, butcher, two pubs and a nursery school. Property prices are similar to those in **Millbrook**, which is little more than an old hamlet built for farm workers, with a pub and a golf course. The wooded valley near the church is supposed to have inspired Bunyan's Valley of the Shadow of Death in *Pilgrim's Progress*. A two-bedroom cottage might be bought for £90,000; the odd four-bedroom modern house, built to plug the gaps, might fetch up to £170,000. Watch out for cars going at break-neck speed – the lanes are sometimes used as a proving ground by car manufacturers.

Stewartby is dominated by its brickworks, which emits fumes the locals say they cannot smell. It was built as a model village in the Twenties by the Stewart family, owners of the brickworks, as a gesture of concern for their employees. The village was extended in the Thirties and Fifties, and a worked-out quarry was flooded to create a lake for watersports within a landscaped country park. A three-bedroom semi here would sell for around £65,000; a two-bedroom house for £50,000. **Kempston Hardwick**, the next station along the line, is given mainly to light industry and has very little housing.

At **Bedford St Johns** you have reached a suburb of Bedford and the nursery slopes of the local housing market. Here first-timers can start out with a three-bedroom Victorian terrace at £65,000, or a semi at £80,000 to £100,000. For Bedford itself, see page 102.

Continuation of main line
Milton Keynes Central

The train service to **Milton Keynes** station is so good that it has a vast catchment area stretching all the way to **Daventry** (see Northampton, page 124). It has some of the newest rolling stock, a better record for punc-

Journey: 34 min
Season: £2856
Peak: 6 per hr
Off-peak: 4-7 per hr

California style
home, Milton
Keynes

tuality than other lines, and the trains run so frequently that you hardly need bother with the timetable. Parking, however, is fairly chaotic, with vehicles silting up the side roads rather than paying for the privilege of the multi-storey car park.

To enjoy Milton Keynes properly, you need to think American. The grid pattern of wide boulevards in the centre, with one of the largest covered shopping malls in the country, and the sea of car-parking, can make you feel as if the whole world has been turned into a supermarket. This impression will be all the stronger when a new £100m shopping centre opens. But the place is thoughtfully planned and very convenient. The 22,000-acre site, which includes Bletchley, Stony Stratford, Wolverton and 13 old villages, was conceived as a New Town in 1967 and was scheduled to contain a population of 250,000.

Housing is arranged in segments, with a mix of starter homes, three- and four-bedroom houses and retirement flats in each one, ensuring a full range of age groups and incomes. There is a large number of commuters, but many people are employed locally, too – numerous major companies, including Abbey National, Mercedes, Argos and Mobil, have moved here. The Open University gives it academic prowess, and the £19.6m lottery-funded theatre and art gallery creates a cultural life. Because the town is so young, the population is young with it.

Milton Keynes prides itself on offering cheaper housing combined with a fast commute to couples who cannot afford to live in London but who want to maintain their jobs in the capital. English Partnership is selling plots for people to build their own new homes on, priced at £80,000 to £180,000. Much emphasis in the design of new housing has been put on energy-saving. Not all the housing is new, however. There are still places where you can find old thatched cottages (and new thatched houses, too, for that matter).

The sports centres are as new and ambitious as you would expect. The Stantonbury Campus offers indoor and outdoor leisure on a large scale. For watersports there is Willen Lake, and winter sports enthusiasts will soon have a £60m ski-scape. Old fields have been retained to give green lungs to the town and provide playgrounds. The Great Ouse skirts the northern edge, as do the Ouzel and the Grand Union Canal which has canal boats slipping slowly along it. There are also several man-made lakes providing habitats for wildlife. North of the city centre is Linford Wood, a remnant of an ancient forest now laced with footpaths, bridle-ways, picnic sites and two wildlife reserves.

Areas are considered upmarket or downmarket according to how closely together the houses are built, and how spacious they are. Perhaps one of the most desirable is **Woughton-on-the-Green**, where the plots are large, houses are traditionally built, and the cheapest four-bedroom detached house would cost over £200,000. The **Bancroft Park** area is distinctive because the houses are built around a cleft in the landscape where an old ruin has been used to create a park. A three-storey terrace town house here would cost around £100,000. **Willen** is also popular because it has a lake and a sense of space. Many of the houses have been built by the owners themselves, and one of these might now sell for around £300,000 (though the standard price for a four-bedroom house here would be less, at £250,000). In a typical mixed estate like **Bradwell**, a two-bedroom late Victorian cottage would cost £70,000; a two-bedroom new house slightly less.

Village people try to get to know new people, but the big problem is that many of them are mortgaged so heavily that they are both working and we don't see a great deal of them

One of the nicest villages to the north is **Weston Underwood**, built in greyish Cotswold stone (it lies in the northern part of the same ridge of oolite that gives the Cotswolds its character) and dating mostly from the 17th and 18th centuries. Ten miles further into Northamptonshire, the stone starts to turn red. Weston Underwood is entered through stone gates topped with pineapples. It remained in the ownership of the Throckmorton family until the 1920s, when it was sold. A small, three-bedroom stone cottage for sale would be a rare find, and would fetch over £150,000. The green, overlooked by the house once occupied by the poet William Cowper, is decorated with trees, seats and roses, and is the place to buy cream teas during August. There is a small zoological garden which specialises in exotic birds.

There are a few new houses but villagers fight tooth-and-nail against development. Their cause is helped by the watermeadows around the Ouse, which make much of it unsuitable for building anyway. Community spirit is strong, and is expressed through the fruit, vegetable and flower shows, and the playgroup. Local agriculture concentrates on cereals, but rape and flax are also grown. There are walks through the woods at Salcey Forest. "Village people try to get to know new people, but the big problem is that many of them are mortgaged so heavily that they are both working and we don't see a great deal of them," says one of the older inhabitants.

The local shopping centre is at **Olney** – popular because it is as traditional as Newport Pagnell (see ahead), but more rural. Property prices therefore tend to run at five to 10% higher. In the market square is the red-brick William Cowper museum, occupying another house in which the poet once lived with his friend Mary Unwin, who looked after him during his lapses into insanity. The town is famous for its pancake race, run every Shrove Tuesday from the market place to the church. The winning house-wife gets a silver cup and a kiss from the verger.

Ravenstone, three miles west, is as pretty, expensive and exclusive as Weston Underwood. It has a shop-cum-post office and a village green sprouting stone houses. **Stoke Goldington** is the biggest in this clutch of villages, with new housing stitched in between the old. Another hand-some stone village is **Emberton**, with 170 acres of country park and lakes along the River Ouse. Houses in all of these villages sell so easily that the owners often dispose of them privately. This entire belt is very convenient for railway users, and only a short drive from the M1.

Two-and-a-half miles north-west of Milton Keynes is **Castlethorpe**. This is an attractive stone village peppered with modern houses, but it is affected by the railway line running through it. A two- to three-bedroom cot-tage might cost £100,000; a four-bedroom detached house around £140,000.

North-east is **Newport Pagnell**, on the Rivers Ouse and Lovat. It has changed over the years from a lace-making town to an industrial and com-mercial one. But it has managed not to become forbidding, and new mod-ern buildings are sandwiched quietly between the old Georgian houses. The cinema has been turned into a shopping arcade. A two-bedroom house in a Victorian terrace in the centre of town will cost around £70,000. The most popular road is Lakes Lane, where the houses back on to the common. A three-bedroom semi here will cost around £90,000. There are also some huge six-bedroom houses that could fetch up to £300,000. Green Park is the most popular of the new estates. A modern four-bedroom detached house with a double garage will cost over £140,000.

People living in the villages to the north of Milton Keynes might use Wolverton station as an alternative to Milton Keynes Central.

Wolverton

Journey: 57 min
Season: £2656
Peak: 2 per hr
Off-peak: 2 per hr

Stony Stratford is now part of Milton Keynes, but still retains many orig-inal 18th-century buildings. As a quaint old market town, with a market square just off the High Street, it has quite a different character to the modernity which has swallowed it. The George Hotel presents a wobbly, black-and-white profile among the bakers, butchers and building societies that surround it. Note that there are no superstores here. A Twenties semi with three bedrooms might cost £125,000, but a good Georgian house (one of a pair) would cost £120,000. A detached one would fetch £220,000.

Wolverton has the local station and is packed with Victorian terraces, some of them reminiscent of *Coronation Street*. A two- to three-bedroom house here would cost over £80,000 – more than 10% less than the equivalent house in Stony Stratford. Three bedrooms would push the price up. A period end-of-terrace three-storey town house would cost £295,000.

To the west of Milton Keynes is **Upper Weald**, a hamlet of brick and stone. There are no shops, but you might find a small period two-bedroom cottage for £80,000 to £100,000. Another worth mentioning is **Wicken**, for its stone houses, church and superb hotel with a Japanese restaurant. A 300-year-old stone house might cost just under £170,000. Watch out for **Deanshanger**, which has a chemical factory that pumps out red smoke every day and turns the pigeons pink.

Further afield, on a hilltop in unspoilt countryside, is **Buckingham**, a typical market town where the stalls still appear on Tuesdays and Saturdays. It remains a pleasure to walk through its steep narrow streets and admire the old inns and almshouses. You might be able to buy a Victorian detached house with four bedrooms and a large garden for £220,000. There are a few modern estates on the edge of town, of which the most popular is Page Hill. The average price of a four-bedroom detached house here is £160,000. The town is very close to Stowe public school, once the home of the Dukes of Buckingham. The gardens, studded with follies by Vanbrugh, Kent and Gibbs, now belong to the National Trust.

Northampton

It has to be said that **Northampton** is an unprepossessing town with a rugged commercial and light industrial bustle. Historically its prosperity came from the manufacture of boots and shoes, but in recent years it has widely diversified. There is a large brewing industry (the British headquarters of Carlsberg-Tetley), Barclaycard and Avon cosmetics have a substantial presence, and more companies are moving in all the time. The 13th-century market square, in which an open-air market is still held, claims to be the largest in England. The Grosvenor Centre is a huge shopping mall with all the chain stores, while Peacock Place has the slightly more upmarket specialists. Schools include the highly-regarded private Northampton High for Girls.

Journey: 55 min
Season: £3076
Peak: 3 per hr
Off-peak: 4 per hr

Northampton has developed over the years in a series of concentric circles. The Victorian workers' terrace houses at the centre can be picked up for £60,000 and £70,000. In the next band come the more dignified, tree-lined streets of larger Edwardian terraces and semis, selling for between £50,000 and £70,000. Next come the Twenties and Thirties semis, all pebble-dash and bay-windows, with prices from around £70,000. To the north of the town these are rimmed by an arc of Seventies estates, where prices range between £70,000 and £80,000. The suburbs to the east contain the bulk of the new town development, and those to the south have the most modern estates. A detached four-bedroom house here might cost just

Contrasting
terrace houses,
Northants

under £120,000. This area is also closest to the M1 (Junction 15).

Northamptonshire has never been as fashionable as other counties north of London – people think of it as rather plain. There is little in the way of black-and-white building, and the villages close to Northampton tend to be built of dark brown ironstone with roofs of slate rather than thatch. To the north-west you will find some cottages built of cob (clay or earth bonded with straw), which require careful maintenance. When cob is whitewashed it often looks much like stone.

To the north-east, heading towards Kettering and Oundle, you break into a belt of bleached limestone. Being closer to East Anglia, the houses here will sometimes be thatched in Norfolk reed. Or they may have Collyweston slates – which are not slate at all, but slivers of very dense, light-coloured limestone.

Due west is **Daventry**, another small market town that has kept its head. It was once a coaching stop on the road to Holyhead and is in the throes of becoming an international railfreight terminal with links to Europe through the Channel Tunnel. Commuters have long been attracted to it, not only from London but also from Birmingham and Coventry, drawn by the M40 extension. There are plenty of no-frills Sixties estates, where prices are five to 10% lower than they are in Northampton.

Just to the south-west of Daventry is the village of **Badby**, where the 700-year-old woods are famous for bluebells and beeches. The Knightley Way footpath, which runs for 12 miles to Greens-Norton, touches the western edge of the woods, which are a designated Site of Special Scientific Interest. The village itself is built in stone and slate, though there is the occasional thatched roof. The local thatched pub, The Windmill, is one of three buildings in the village which date from before 1500. There is a post office and a general store, a primary school and a village hall where the Brownies, Guides, WI and horticultural society meet. Within a mile you can climb to the highest point in Northamptonshire, Arbury Hill, whence you can see the Malvern Hills. A mile or two in the other direction is the sizeable village of **Weedon Bec**, which has the frustrating disadvantage of having the railway running through it without a station to compensate. It has a similar range of housing and prices to Long Buckby (see ahead), the next stop down the line.

Harpole is closer to Northampton, and only just off the M1 at Junction 16. A vicarage-sized house here might cost between £250,000 and £300,000, though you might pick up a little Victorian terrace house for £60,000. Just down the road, on the south bank of the River Nene, is **Kislingbury** – a pretty stone village with some thatched roofs, relatively unspoilt though there is some new housing. A two-bedroom period house might sell for £65,000; country houses with a couple of acres will reach £500,000.

If you want town life but find Northampton itself too depressing, then you might consider looking south to **Towcester**. It isn't as pretty as

Schools in Warwickshire, Northamptonshire and Peterborough

Rugby has the public school which gave its name to the game. It now takes both girls and boys, boarding and day. It is not to be confused with Rugby High, the academically excellent grant-maintained grammar school for girls which is down the road in Bilton.

Warwickshire has two other high spots, Stratford-upon-Avon and Warwick (both within reach of Leamington Spa station), each with a matching pair of high performing independent schools. Stratford-upon-Avon has the Stratford-upon-Avon Grammar for girls and King Edward VI for boys, while Warwick has King's High for girls and Warwick School for boys, as well as Myton comprehensive as a good local state school.

In Northamptonshire, Northampton itself has a good choice of public and private. The state schools include Guilsborough, Northampton for boys, and Prince William; the non-selective schools include

Bosworth Tutorial college and Quinton House; the independent schools include Northampton High for girls and Northamptonshire Grammar for both boys and girls.

Oundle has the independent day and boarding Oundle School for boys and girls, and the Prince William co-educational comprehensive, to which children are bussed from all over the region. There are good comprehensives to be found in The Ferrers at Rushden and Bishop Stopford at Kettering.

Because of the cathedral, King's school in Peterborough manages to be a kind of hybrid – a grant-maintained co-educational comprehensive with a good academic record and boarding facilities for choristers.

Venture into Lincolnshire and you find a host of high performing grammar schools in Grantham and Lincoln and most of the towns throughout the area.

Buckingham and it has a large belt of new housing on one flank – a new four-bedroom house can be expected to cost £175,000. The central focal points are the square and Town Hall. Towcester racecourse and Silverstone circuit are nearby. Off the main street, two- to three-bedroom Victorian terrace houses sell for £70,000, and there are a few large detached Victorian houses that fetch between £210,000 and £220,000.

Roade, due south of Northampton, is perhaps plainer still, offering a mix of traditional Northamptonshire stone, Victorian terraces and Sixties estates. It is popular with London commuters because they have a choice of station – Northampton or Milton Keynes – or they could opt to take the car down the M1. Property prices are slightly higher than Northampton's.

East of Northampton you could look at **Earls Barton**, which has a church with a remarkable Saxon tower, thought to be the finest in the country. Built of plaster in four tiers, it has inaccessible doorways on the second tier. The village has blown up into a small town. It has a new shoe factory, opened in 1987, and a shoe museum. The fact that it is a whisker away from the A45 makes it very convenient for people working in

Northampton or **Wellingborough** (see page 103), where there is the boys' public school. A small Victorian terrace house would sell for over £70,000; a detached house with four bedrooms would fetch £90,000 to £120,000.

Long Buckby

Journey: 86 min
Season: £3184
Peak: 1 per hr
Off-peak: 1 per hr

Having grown up around the railway, canal and A5, the attraction of **Long Buckby** is good communications rather than charm. With a strong Victorian core and a plethora of Seventies estates, it stretches for one-and-a-half miles and contains a population of more than 5,000. A four-bedroom detached estate house might cost £135,000, but something grander in a landscaped garden could reach £220,000. An old rectory in the area would cost at least another £100,000. The cheapest houses are Victorian cottages selling for around £65,000.

Rugby

Journey: 56 min (75 min Silverlink)
Season: £4856 (all); £3200 Silverlink
Peak: 3 per hr
Virgin; 1 per hr Silverlink
Off-peak: 2-4 per hr all; 2 per hr Silverlink

Rugby has never attracted architectural plaudits but it has managed to develop a certain vigour in the last few years and at night it buzzes with restaurants, nightclubs and bars. The old industrial base has been replaced with a more commercial one. Commuters should be aware that Railtrack is committed to spending £2.5m on improving the station. Rugby is best known for the boys' public school, used as a model for *Tom Brown's Schooldays*, where the eponymous ball game began in 1823 and whose former pupils include Rupert Brooke and Matthew Arnold. A Rugby Football Visitor Centre has opened opposite the school and Gilberts rugby football manufacturers are still going strong.

Small houses for first-time buyers in the centre of town sell at between £50,000 and £55,000. There is also cheap property in the **Brownsover** area. If you can overcome the stigma attached to it, you could buy a two-bedroom semi for £55,000 or a new detached house for £80,000. The more upmarket areas are **Hillmorton** and **Bilton**, where you could find a dignified three-bedroom semi for £80,000, or a larger detached house with four or five bedrooms for £120,000. In Bawnmore Road, Bilton, property becomes more expensive, rising to £250,000. In Hillmorton Road, Hillmorton, there are some very substantial houses built in the Twenties, some very close to the town centre, for which you could pay up to £120,000.

Living to the south of Rugby is thought to be slightly better than living to the north. Its most salubrious suburb is **Dunchurch**, a village two miles from the centre which has a dozen black-and-white timbered houses, as well as large detached new four-bedroom houses which sell for around £200,000. There are also some period two-up-two-down cottages that fetch around £75,000. Second best is **Clifton upon Dunsmore**, to the north, which again has a villagey feel to it, though the houses tend to be smaller. A two-bedroom terrace cottage will cost £60,000 to £70,000.

For a proper village you need to look south-east to **Ashby St Ledgers**, one of the last good Northamptonshire thatch-and-stone villages before the more industrial Midlands takes over. It is remarkable in that it was an estate village, built by Lord Wimbourne in 1912 and designed by Lutyens. Development was so tightly controlled that there are only 44 hous-es in all – the tradition was that two new houses were built every time the lord of the manor died. There is an old barn on the green that serves as the village hall. Since the Wimbournes left, the village has changed hands three times. There is a

In Ashby St Ledgers the tradition was that two new houses were built every time the lord of the manor died

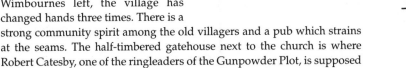

strong community spirit among the old villagers and a pub which strains at the seams. The half-timbered gatehouse next to the church is where Robert Catesby, one of the ringleaders of the Gunpowder Plot, is supposed to have met the other conspirators. Houses rarely come on the market, but you could expect to pay at least £20,000 above local market values for the privilege of living here.

Birdingbury, south-west of Rugby, is another sought-after village. It has only about 150 houses, most of which are now occupied by commuters rather than the agricultural workers for whom they were built. Houses tend to be a bit more expensive because it is so close to **Leamington Spa** (see page 145). A two-bedroom period cottage might cost around £125,000. The River Leam meanders through the village, and there is a fishing club. There is a post office and a village store but no pub, though villagers tend to use the Birdingbury Men's Club for meetings. Cricket and football are played at Marton, a mile away. There are too few young people in Birdingbury itself to make up full teams. The nearest school is at **Leamington Hastings**.

Sheer convenience makes **Kilsby** and **Barby** commuter habitats. Both are beside Junction 17 on the M1, and close to Rugby. Kilsby is unremark-able but has a supply of four-bedroom modern detached houses selling for around £138,000. Some are more lavish, built in stone with five bedrooms and selling for around £195,000. Barby is smaller, with a stronger sense of village about it, and has a few old cob houses among the 19th-century and modern brick. A four-bedroom detached house here might sell for around £135,000. There are a few shops, a village hall, a school, and a claim to fame in that the MacLaren baby buggy was designed here in the Sixties by Owen MacLaren.

Aylesbury

Stoke Mandeville

Wendover

Great Missenden

Amersham

Chalfont & Latimer

Chorleywood

Marylebone

Marylebone
➡ Aylesbury (via Chorleywood)

Chorleywood

The Victorian development of the railways created **Chorleywood** by making the lovely Chess Valley accessible from London. The M25 has done its best to make it inaccessible from anywhere. In theory it is possible to get to Heathrow in 15 minutes. In practice the motorway is often blocked but locals have fought off plans to widen it for the moment because it would be disruptive and might encourage yet more cars. Commuters tend to clog the lanes with their parking and leave the car park (£1.50 per day) empty. Nevertheless, people enjoy the large common with its nine-hole golf course and the wonderful views across the valley – so much so that they are willing to pay £200,000 for a two-bedroom cottage, or over £500,000 for a four-bedroom detached period house in what is known as the station estate, a ring of Victorian and Edwardian houses built to take advantage of the first rail link with London. Berks Hill, South Road, Haddon Road and Hillside Road are all highly prized. Then comes a ring of Thirties and Fifties houses, then an outer ring of Seventies and Eighties houses. In Chalfont Lane, where large properties are set in a couple of acres, prices run from around £500,000 to £1.5m. There are a few small flats from £78,000 – a price which in Watford would buy a two-bedroom house – but first-time buyers in Chorleywood are young City types who can afford to start at £100,000. Whatever the price-range, the emphasis is on individuality, very rarely are two houses exactly the same.

Journey: 25 min (includes Metropolitan Line to Baker Street)
Season: £1620*
Peak: 6 per hr
Off-peak: 4 per hr
*Travelcard includes all Greater London Underground, trains and buses.

Parents bemoan the passing of the schools into Hertfordshire control as this has taken them out of the grammar school system

In addition to the easy half-hour journey into London, Chorleywood offers a lively community which makes good use of the public and club tennis courts, football and cricket pitches. The district beyond the village centre is very scattered. Houses trail up either side of the valley, leaving the shops in the bottom. This is inconvenient for elderly pedestrians, though there is a bus service which shuttles from one side to the other. Big shopping is done in Amersham, Northwood and Beaconsfield, and at the three-times-weekly market in Watford. Parents bemoan the demise of the grammar school system in Hertfordshire, nevertheless local schools retain a very high standard and reputation.

Chalfont & Latimer

Journey: 29 min (includes Metropolitan Line to Baker Street)

Season: £1740*

Peak: 6 per hr

Off-peak: 4 per hr

*Travelcard includes all Greater London Underground, trains and buses.

Little Chalfont is a mini-town with a station, a strip of shops, three restaurants, a library and a number of very expensive houses in large grounds. "Too spread out to be matey," said one resident. **Latimer** is much prettier, with timbered cottages around a triangular green, but a two-bedroom cottage will cost at least £400,000. "It's the schools you see – the state schools are as good as the private," says one agent. The River Chess, flowing past Latimer House, offers trout fishing. **Chenies**, equally picturesque, was a typically feudal village owned by the Dukes of Bedford for 400 years until 1954. Be prepared to pay £250,000 in either village for even the smallest cottage. A couple of miles north-west of the station is **Ley Hill**, a particularly lively and friendly spot with golf and cricket on the common, a couple of nice old pubs and an infant and junior school. There are lots of local activities, including a flower club and a dog club. The wooded countryside which surrounds all these villages attracts hearty backpackers who come to enjoy the spectacular walks.

Amersham

Journey: 33 min (includes Metropolitan Line to Baker Street)

Season: £2080*

Peak: 6 per hr

Off-peak: 4 per hr

*Travelcard includes all Greater London Underground, trains and buses.

The old town of **Amersham** is anchored by a 17th-century market hall. The High Street, lanes and little courtyards offer a picturesque variety of architectural styles from timber-framed houses to Georgian brick, sometimes just facades on much older buildings. A plethora of old pubs recalls the town's history as a staging post on the coach road from London to Aylesbury, and traffic still comes to a halt in September when the annual charter fair is held. The smallest period cottage will cost from £150,000, with substantial houses up to £1m. The new part of the town, Amersham-on-the-Hill, was developed in the Twenties when the Metropolitan Railway Company brought City merchants and West End traders from Aldgate and Baker Street. As the last stop on the Underground, Amersham was considered the end of commuterland until motorways made more distant villages accessible. The more modern housing includes ex-council flats from £75,000, three-bedroom semis from £150,000, and four-bedroom family houses at £250,000. There are cricket, football and hockey clubs, a swimming pool, a film society, an arts club and several riding stables and pony clubs. People often move here to take advantage of the local grammar schools – Dr Challoner's for boys in Amersham, and Dr Challoner's High for girls in Little Chalfont. **Chesham Bois** (the name derives from the Boyes family, owners of the manor in 1276, rather than the surrounding woods) feels itself to be set apart from the rest. It has a village school, a well-managed common and a powerful community heartbeat. The houses stand well apart from each other, some in an acre of land. Prices range between £500,000 and £1m.

Chesham, only a short drive away, is also on the Metropolitan line. The town is beguiling, cupped by the Chiltern Hills and brushed by the River Chess which flows through attended by a riverside walk through beechwoods, past watercress beds and a trout farm. The shopping is good, with standard supermarkets and multiple stores, but also speciality shops including a saddler, French baker and music shop. The new Sainsbury brought with it the Elgiva Arts Centre as lucrative planning gain. Many of the shops front ancient buildings, some half-timbered 16th-century, others brick and plaster.

Great Missenden

The narrow main street lined with houses and shops from the 15th to 19th centuries gives **Great Missenden** an intimate air and makes it an attractive small centre within easy reach of central London. It is also just a short stroll from the surrounding woods. High Street shops provide for day-to-day needs, and street performers liven up the shopping experience. Apart from

Journey:	39 min
Season:	£2020
Peak:	4 per hr
Off-peak:	2 per hr

a private tennis club there is little entertainment for the young. "No youth club, no cinema, no transport. If you are under drinking age, forget it," said one. Roald Dahl is buried in the cemetery, and there is talk of turning the old NatWest building into a museum dedicated to him. A few born-and-bred residents live in the centre, where 19th-century cottage conversions with two or three bedrooms cost between £250,000 and £300,000. There is a good deal of later development within walking distance of the centre. Prices

The Lee has some of the grandest houses ever set round a tiny village green

range from £195,000 for a three-bedroom semi to £275,000 for a newly-built three-bedroom detached. There are also some handsome Edwardian houses set in mature grounds at around £400,000 to £500,000. For a Thirties four-bedroom house in a couple of acres you might expect to pay £400,000.

The surrounding villages have a pecking order headed by **The Lee**, a secluded community in the leafy uplands above Great Missenden. It has some of the grandest houses ever set around a tiny village green, and a picturesque pub. The rambling manor was for many years owned by the Liberty family, who did much to preserve the village. It is a conservation area so new development is frowned upon. There is "a little new money, but they keep the properties as they should". The area is favoured by captains of industry, writers and actors distinguished enough to need shelter from the public gaze. There is nothing under £295,000 here, and the average is £500,000 for a four-bedroom cottage.

Next in line is **Lee Common** (these villages are sometimes satirically nicknamed Lee Posh and Lee Common) separated from Lee by the Liberty Estate parkland where village shows and fêtes take place. The houses tend to be smaller, built for workers on the Liberty Estate, but it benefits from having a village shop and local primary school. A four-bedroom, semi-detached 19th-century cottage would cost around £350,000. For Thirties houses overlooking green-belt farmland, look at **South Heath**. It has a sub-post office-cum-stores, and a likely price-tag of £300,000 for a four-bedroom detached.

Wendover

Journey: 45 min
Season: £2256
Peak: 4 per hr
Off-peak: 2 per hr

The beautiful National Trust countryside of the Chilterns attracts a lot of walkers to **Wendover**. The tables outside the bistro cafés make a picturesque setting for a refreshment stop. Part of the Icknield Way, Europe's oldest highway, runs through the broad High Street, which is cobbled and tree-lined and offers lively shops, restaurants, banks, a post office, and a library. There are many period houses, from Georgian all the way back to the enchanting thatch-and-timber row of Coldharbour Cottages, said to have been a gift from Henry VIII to Anne Boleyn. Infilling has been carefully done and blends well with the mature buildings. A two-bedroom cottage costs around £150,000. Three-bedroom Victorian terrace houses are in the region of £165,000. There is a first, middle and secondary school in the town and three golf courses in the neighbourhood, plus tennis, bowls and squash clubs, church societies and handsome old inns to gather in. Yet the town safeguards privacy by being too big for everyone to know everyone else's business.

At the turn of the century **Weston Turville**, north-west of Wendover, was breeding Aylesbury ducks for the London market and making straw plait for the Luton hat industry. Its older properties are on the eastern edge of the village, but they are well outnumbered by the modern developments. Family houses range from three-bedroom semis at £135,000 to four-bedroom detached houses at £175,000 or more. There is a convenient post office and small parade of shops, several pubs, tennis courts and golf and squash clubs. The village has a combined first and middle school; older children travel to the grammar and secondary schools in Wendover or Aylesbury. The Wendover bypass has turned the village into a bit of an A40–A41 short-cut.

Stoke Mandeville

Stoke Mandeville now is little more than a suburb of Aylesbury. It has a general store, several pubs and a combined first and middle school, but is largely dominated by the world-famous hospital and a lot of Thirties houses. These sell from £140,000 for a three-bedroom semi to £160,000 to £220,000 for a four-bedroom detached house in ample grounds.

Journey: 49 min
Season: £2256
Peak: 4 per hr
Off-peak: 2 per hr

Aylesbury

Commercial development has overshadowed a good deal of **Aylesbury's** ancient past. Its heart was cut out in the Sixties to make way for office blocks, and large council estates were built on the north side to accommodate London overspill. As if that wasn't enough, the town has now been instructed to increase its population by one third again. Despite the inconvenience of having to drive into town and try to park – commuters prefer to live in the surrounding villages. Farmhouses are the popular choice – there is no equivalent of the Surrey stockbroker house here. For those who want something more modern, a three-bedroom semi goes for £135,000, a two-bedroom mid-terrace for £80,000, a studio flat for £35,000. Aylesbury Grammar School for boys and High School for girls, and Sir Henry Floyd Grammar School have excellent reputations; and there is an unusually good selection of hospitals in the area. It also has a big shopping mall, six-cinema complex, a swimming pool, and the county museum with a special Roald Dahl exhibition.

Journey: 53 min*
Season: £2500
Peak: 4 per hr
Off-peak: 2 per hr
*Some services go via Princes Risborough.

The future of Dinton Hall, where Cromwell's sword was once kept, has been a local hot potato for years

Most of the surrounding villages have had their share of new developments, but **Bishopstone** is still rural in nature in spite of the busy roads. A timber-framed farmhouse costs around £400,000. **Dinton** is blissfully peaceful and still has buildings made of witchert (the Saxon word for white earth), proper grass verges and no street lamps at night. The future of Dinton Hall, where Cromwell's sword was once kept, has been a local hot potato for years – at one time it was to become a hotel with two golf courses – but it is now safely in private hands again.

To the north-west of Aylesbury, **Quainton** has all the ingredients of the chocolate-box rural idyll – pretty thatched cottages, a broad village green and a ruined medieval market cross, a restored windmill and a group of 17th-century almshouses with dormers and Dutch gables. Discriminating buyers will pay a premium to live here (it is in the catchment of Aylesbury Grammar). Prices range from £100,000 for a two-bedroom cottage to £200,000 upwards for a modern four-bedroom detached. It is a horsey area.

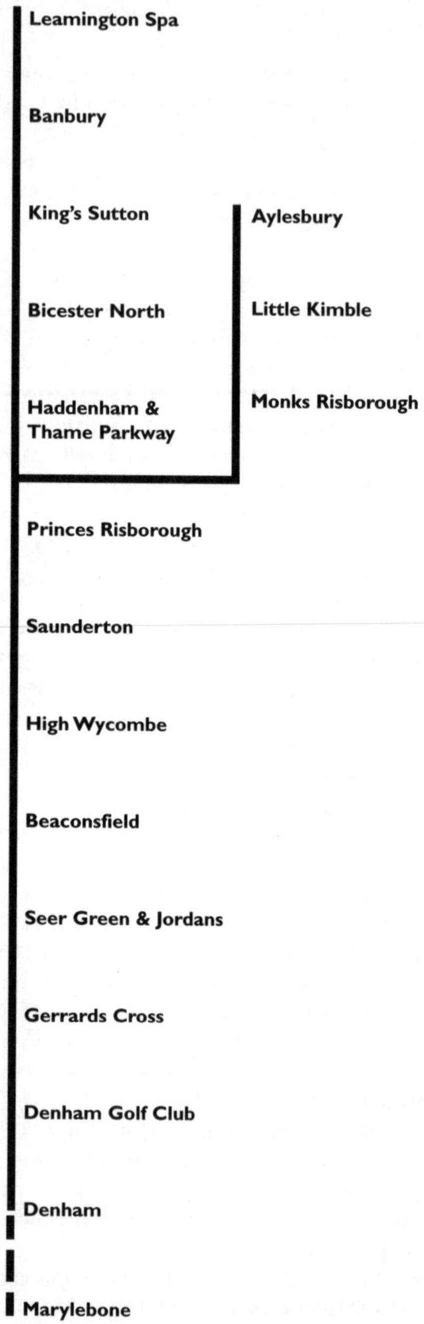

Leamington Spa

Banbury

King's Sutton   **Aylesbury**

Bicester North   **Little Kimble**

Haddenham &
Thame Parkway   **Monks Risborough**

Princes Risborough

Saunderton

High Wycombe

Beaconsfield

Seer Green & Jordans

Gerrards Cross

Denham Golf Club

Denham

Marylebone

Marylebone
➡ Leamington Spa

Denham and Denham Golf Club

If **Denham** had come straight out of the scenery department of the old Denham studios it couldn't be more picturesque. Only 18 miles from London, it is a patch of rural peace – village hall, small green and a stream winding past wisteria-clad old brick. It would be perfect but for the pub visitors whose motors clog the lanes, accounting for the village's sobriquet as "the prettiest car park in Buckinghamshire". Several of the houses are well hidden behind high walls and wooded gardens, so the area is perfect ambassadorial territory, and a retreat for distinguished performers in both courtroom proper and courtroom drama. A three-bedroom semi will command £250,000. Larger houses go for £1.75m up to £5m. The other Denhams – **Higher**, **New** and **Denham Green** – are simply a few streets of Thirties semis and bungalows, and Fifties houses. Denham Golf Club is little more than a railway halt for the club.

From Denham	From Denham Golf Club
Journey: 21 min	Journey: 28 min
Season: £1516	Season: £1576
Peak: 3 per hr	Peak: 2 per hr
Off-peak: 2 per hr	Off-peak: 1 per hr

A retreat for distinguished performers in both courtroom proper and courtroom drama

Gerrards Cross

Because of its easy access to London by rail and road – M40, M25 and M4 all within spitting distance – the area around **Gerrards Cross** has the reputation of being one of the most expensive in the country. Definitely not for the first-time buyer, this is classic stockbroker belt with tree-lined roads and grand Victorian and Edwardian houses in half an acre or so for £700,000 to £1m. There are some modern infills but these, too, are big and luxurious. Five-bedroom detached houses go for £450,000 to £650,000. First-time buyers have to buy flats above shops. There are some modern infills but these, too, are big and luxurious. Five-bedroom detached houses go for £450,000 to £650,000. The population of commuters takes off

Gerrards Cross
Journey: 21 min
Season: £1700
Peak: 5 per hr
Off-peak: 3 per hr

early, leaving the centre to its small-town trading, and the common to dog-walkers treading the paths once haunted by highwaymen. Properties south-east of the town should be visited several times in different parts of the day – noise from the motorways can be a problem in some roads. Golf and tennis are the main sports. Both private and secondary schools have high standards and are well liked.

Jordans is distinguished for the peculiarly English problem of cricket balls flying into gardens close to the cricket ground

South of Gerrards Cross is the neat and tidy village of **Fulmer**, with its little green, pub, infant school, and well-kept gardens. Small, two-bedroom mid-19th-century cottages cost from £220,000 to £300,000. Further west is **Hedgerley**, which has two shops and pub and manages to feel rather remote. The lanes are lined with three- to four-bedroom detached houses with large gardens, selling at around £600,000. Lots of walks can be had from the back door here.

Seer Green & Jordans

Journey: 30 min
Season: £1900
Peak: 2 per hr
Off-peak: 2 per hr

Part 16th-century property, Beaconsfield

Seer Green hasn't a lot to say for itself. Its old rural character has been changed by the station and the modern estate sitting in the middle. A two-bedroom cottage will cost £150,000. Its neighbours are more famous. **Penn**, to the west, is a long straggling village with a green surrounded by Georgian houses and 17th-century cottages in timber or brick. Views over the surrounding beechwoods are magnificent. William Penn lived here, a leading light in the Quaker Society of Friends. In the neighbouring village,

Jordans, the Quaker connection continues with a barn built with timbers from the *Mayflower*. Recently the village hit the headlines because of the peculiarly English problem of cricket balls flying into gardens close to the cricket ground. This is *the* place to live in the area. Houses range in date from the 16th century to the 1940s, and are at a premium. A four-bedroom detached which would sell for £550,000 in Beaconsfield (the next stop along the line), will command £650,000 here. Hopeful buyers need to be in the know to hear about a sale. Estate agents count themselves lucky to get hold of a property here. The charming village centre was designed by Fred Rowntree in 1919, with gabled brick houses set well back from a central green planted with silver birch and poplar. There is the bonus of a good primary school.

Beaconsfield

Beaconsfield has a dual personality and a dual population. The old town grew at the crossroads of the coaching routes to Windsor and Oxford, and is centred on a broad square and a pleasant green. Local people house-hunt in the old town for 17th- and 18th-century cottages, priced at £220,000 for a two-up-two-down terrace. Commuters, and the many incomers who have arrived as a result of the several company relocations, prefer the convenience of the new town which has developed near the station since the 1920s. The average cost of a three-bedroom detached house is £225,000 to £280,000. Typical buyers are middle managers and young City strivers who move on up the scale to houses costing £5m to £10m. A good private school and state schools with high reputations add to the attractions, but what used to be a strong community spirit is struggling to stay alive. It revives most energetically on 10 May for the annual fair. Old town shops include delis and boutiques, which draw visitors who come to see Bekonscot, the model village and railway.

Journey: 27 min	
Season: £1960	
Peak: 5 per hr	
Off-peak: 3 per hr	

High Wycombe

High Wycombe has left behind the wool and furniture industries upon which it was founded in order to embrace modern industries which include paper-making, engineering and new high-tech companies. The result is a myriad of housing from large Victorian piles to Thirties semis and modern houses which fan out on either side of the valley. But the feeling is that it became overblown in the Eighties and that a "knock-down rather than expand" policy is a better one. One- and two-bedroom maisonettes start at £50,000, and there are plenty of starter homes for first-time buyers in the £60,000 bracket. At the upper end of the scale a four-bedroom detached will cost £250,000. The smart places to be are on the

Journey: 29 min	
Season: £2200	
Peak: 5 per hr	
Off-peak: 4 per hr	

Schools in Buckinghamshire

If they can afford the house prices, London parents in search of better state education will often find themselves looking at Buckinghamshire, which still retains its grammar schools. Remember, though, that they are highly selective.

Aylesbury has Aylesbury Grammar for boys and Aylesbury High for girls, as well as Sir Henry Floyd for both sexes. High Wycombe has a whole clutch of good schools – Wycombe High for girls, the Royal Grammar School, a grant-maintained day school for boys (with some boarding), John Hampden High for boys, and Wycombe Abbey girls' school, which occupies a Gothic mansion set in 160 acres.

Beaconsfield has Beaconsfield High, a grant-maintained grammar school for girls, and Amersham has one grammar for each sex – Dr Challoner's for boys and Dr Challoner's High for girls. At Marlow, the proximity of the Thames has encouraged Sir William Borlase's voluntary controlled co-educational grammar to develop a strong rowing tradition. Other high-performing schools include Burnham Grammar, Langley Grammar and St Bernard's, a voluntary-aided Roman Catholic grammar in Slough; Chesham High in Chesham; and the boys' public school, Stowe (girls in the sixth), at Buckingham.

fringes of the town in **Downley**, **Booker** and **Loudwater**. There is a variety of schools with excellent reputations – Wycombe High for girls, John Hampden and the Royal Grammar for boys, plus the famous Wycombe Abbey public school for girls. A new arts complex was opened in 1993 with a theatre, but otherwise entertainment is thin.

Sought-after villages are to the west and include **Lane End**, which has a pretty, cottagey High Street with a pond, and **Beacon's Bottom**, little more than a blink-and-you-miss-it hamlet where 18th-century brick-and-flint houses start at £160,000 for two bedrooms. Both villages have basic shops and post office, and a range of modern housing from £50,000 for one-bedroom cottages to £250,000 for a family detached. Farms and smallholdings in this area can run into millions of pounds.

Saunderton

Journey: 52 min (37 min peak)
Season: £2364
Peak: 2 per hr
Off-peak: 1 per hr

Though **Saunderton** itself is not much more than a station surrounded by small housing estates, it is the most convenient station for some of the prettiest villages in the area. To the west in an area of outstanding natural beauty is **Bledlow**. A compact collection of thatched cottages with a few modern arrivals, it dozes beneath Wain Hill, site of one of the two huge turf-cut crosses in the county. No further building is allowed at present because of its conservation status. There is a village hall and a pub but no post office or shop. Young residents take their children a mile down the road to Longwick junior or to secondary school in Princes Risborough. Nearby **Lacey Green** is a sprawling village with a school, and an ancient windmill run by The Chiltern Society. Life is convivial and centres around the two pubs and busy village hall. A lot of new housing overshadows the few cottages, and the whole area is less cottagey than you might expect. If you can find something small with two bedrooms it will cost £125,000. Many houses are large, detached and swimming in ample grounds. A restored period four-bedroom house would cost £750,000. The window dressing to look for is the superb view over the Vale of Aylesbury. Unlike other areas, where houses in outlying districts cost more than they do in town centres, prices in the villages here vary little from those in Princes Risborough.

Princes Risborough

A pleasant market town with the relaxed feel of an overgrown village, **Princes Risborough** has a semi-pedestrianised High Street with a small market house in the centre. It is an attractive place to shop and stroll. But it is abandoned for the city each day by at least half its population.

Journey: 40 min
Season: £2444
Peak: 3 per hr
Off-peak: 3 per hr

Human-scale architecture is here in plenty – no large modern estates but a few mellow 16th- and 17th-century houses set along little roads and culs-de-sacs. There are some Victorian terraces, not always in the best locations but costing from £80,000. Thirties to Seventies detached family houses cost from £180,000 to £225,000 for four bedrooms. Local schools take children through from toddler to late-teenage, and

Converted barn, near Princes Risborough

local clubs include tennis and bowls. The most prestigious area is **Whiteleaf**, right on the flank of the Chilterns. It has a few cottages and a pub and a whole regiment of expensive houses with large grounds and paddocks, for which you should expect to pay at least £350,000. These tend to be owned by business people who are members of the local golf and cricket clubs.

Line to **Aylesbury**
Monks Risborough

No longer separated from Princes Risborough but rather a suburb of it, **Monks Risborough** has a few relics of its medieval past and some pretty cottages, but now consists mainly of Sixties and Seventies semis and a plenty of bungalows which attract retired people. An estate bungalow costs around £95,000; a roomy three-bedroom semi around £105,000.

Journey: 61 min
(53 min peak)
Season: £2500
Peak: 1 per hr
Off peak: 1 per hr

Little Kimble

Journey: 65 min (56 min peak)
Season: £2500
Peak: 1 per hr
Off-peak: Occasional (1 every 2 hrs changing at Princes Risborough)

Many of the villages in this area sprawl rather than huddle, and **Little Kimble** is typical. Its straggling lanes contain a mix of properties from a few listed 17th- and 18th-century cottages to 1900s and modern houses. The station house itself is a private dwelling. Prices for average-sized houses are around 10% above those in Princes Risborough, but there are also a few at around £500,000 with large grounds and paddocks (Kimble races is an annual event). Although there is no focal point there are a couple of pubs, a post office-cum-store and a village hall. With only 900 people on the electoral roll, most locals would be able to call "I spy strangers" when prospective buyers come knocking. Local activities include the WI and a horticultural society which knows where to look for the rare wild orchids which bloom on the old rifle range. There is also a branch of the British Legion. Walks in the area take in Chequers and Ellesborough church, where successive prime ministers have offered the occasional photo opportunity.

In Little Kimble, the horticultural society knows where to look for wild orchids

Aylesbury

Journey: 53 min*
Season: £2500
Peak: 4 per hr
Off-peak: 2 per hr
*Some service go via Princes Risborough.

Commuters prefer to live in the surrounding villages rather than **Aylesbury** itself, though it provides a useful shopping centre. For main entry see **Marylebone to Aylesbury** line (page 133).

Continuation of main line
Haddenham & Thame Parkway

Journey: 46 min
Season: £2464
Peak: 3 per hr
Off-peak: 2 per hr

Whichever way you look at it **Haddenham** is a pretty big village or a big, pretty village, now split into two, the old and the new. The Sheerstock estate of two-, three-, four- and five-bedroom houses, priced from £140,000 to £180,000, is the new. The southern end is the old, where the green and duck pond make an acknowledged beauty spot popular with television crews filming *Inspector Morse* and Agatha Christie. Here and there are walls made of witchert (the Saxon word for white earth) topped rather surprisingly with Spanish tiles, enclosing little lanes leading to attractive Georgian and Victorian houses. The three-bedroom cottages cost around £150,000. This is a great place for people to retire to, and within the past couple of decades the streets have been pedalled by a clutch of titled residents known locally as the five bicycling knights. Otherwise social life is divided into an energetic squash-playing set who live on the new side and the old Haddenham agricultural and arts set, with new people forming the social sandwich filling. Lots of residents commute to London on the M40. There are plenty of local sports, arts and activity clubs, and a village hall where it all happens.

Haddenham is an acknowledged beauty spot popular with television crews filming Inspector Morse and Agatha Christie

Thame is distinguished by an unusually wide High Street, which the annual fair turns into a medieval parade ground against a backdrop of houses from the 15th century to the present. There are plenty of three- and four-bedroom houses at around £105,000 to £350,000 – many with rooms let to students from Rycote Wood agricultural college. It has three primary schools and good sporting facilities, including football, rugby, squash and snooker, and a sports and arts centre. Some commuters prefer to drive to Princes Risborough for the better choice of early and late trains into London.

West of the A418 between Thame and Aylesbury are three sought-after villages. **Cuddington**, which has a history of being elected best-kept village in Buckinghamshire, has a green and lots of old thatch. Two-bedroom cottages start at £230,000. **Chearsley** has a green, pub, shop and church, but no longer a school. There is a pretty set of thatched cottages and prices are high. **Long Crendon** is considered to be the *crème de la crème* of the area. Once the centre of the needle-making industry, it has a picturesque High Street running off the market square, an attractive green, a primary school and several inviting pubs. It is the sort of place that everyone dreams of calling home, and properties here attract a 10 to 20% price premium. The majority of people who live here work in Oxford.

Bicester North

Bicester has a long history and a famous hunt dating back to the 1700s. But despite an old market square (triangle, rather) and some 16th-century gabled houses, it stopped being a period piece when the army depot, now one of the largest in the country, was established in 1941. The town is mainly regarded as a modern, cheapish provider of very large housing estates with a new edge-of-town factory-outlet shopping centre. One-bed-

Journey: 57 min	
Season: £2808	
Peak: 4 per hr	
Off-peak: 2 per hr	

room starter homes are priced at around £60,000; two-bedroom houses around £75,000.

Villages to the west of Bicester – Steeple Aston (see page 173) and the **Bartons (Middle and Steeple)** – have recently returned to rural tranquillity following the decommissioning of the USAF base at Upper Heyford, but now fear that large quantities of new housing will fill the gap. Meanwhile the stone-built village of **Kirtlington**, where Christopher Wren's father is buried, has retained is popularity because of its polo park and stud farm. It has a village green with a pond, a post office stores, a couple of pubs and a junior school. New developments here are stone-built to blend with the older houses. The larger four-bedroom detached properties cost £200,000 to £270,000. Small houses start at £80,000. An 18th-century cottage with two bedrooms would fetch £100,000 to £125,000. "People move here and don't move out again," says one local.

Villages north of Bicester are good value. For the price of a three-bed-room house closer to Oxford you will get four bedrooms in **Stratton Audley** – Stratton meaning enclosure on a Roman road, and Audley from the family which built the 14th-century moated castle. It is a tiny village where the houses group around the central green but fears are mounting that the buffer which keeps it separate from Bicester – the land owned by RAF Bicester – will be sold off and redeveloped. For £220,000 you could buy a substantial four-bedroom stone period house. Prices are the same in **Stoke Lyne**, a similarly quiet Chiltern village set in undulating countryside.

Just over the county border is **Marsh Gibbon**, with houses built of local stone rather than the brick and timber more usual in Buckinghamshire. A sprinkling of low-cost housing has been built here for sale to local families. The result is a busy little place with a village pond, a primary school and a younger than average age profile. A three-bedroom detached house might be found for £150,000.

Launton, back in Oxfordshire, is growing rapidly into a dormitory of Bicester, though the intervening railway and bypass will prevent its being swallowed completely. It has a mix of old and young in both population and property. There are quite a few modern bungalows and new estates where a two-bedroom semi would cost around £95,000. Young children go the local primary. Their older brothers and sisters attend secondary school or sixth form college in Bicester.

King's Sutton

Journey: 76 min	
Season: £3132	
Peak: 1 per hr	
Off-peak: 1 per hr	

A few London commuters travel regularly from **King's Sutton**. Others prefer to drive to Bicester, which has a more frequent service. The majority of local residents work in Banbury or Oxford. Apart from the village green, which is dotted with thatched cottages and l8th-century stone houses, the property mix is almost exactly 50% old stone houses, 50% council brick, which residents say makes for a good community. They take advantage of the opportunities to get together through the Playing Fields Association, the small tennis club and three churches. The local baker who called three times a week to bake fresh loaves for the village has been stymied by Eurobureaucracy but there are still three village shops, one with a post office, and four pubs. Children go to the local primary school, then to Middleton Cheney Secondary. The local hunt meets nearby and, despite the fact that several farms and barns have been sold off for conversion, there is still a farming presence. A Georgian five-bedroom house with a staff bungalow and paddock costs £350,000; a two-bedroom bungalow with a garden £160,000.

Local stone, ex-weaver's cottage, Deddington

Neighbouring **Charlton** is a one-street village with a popular pub. Pleasant stone houses cost from £120,000 for a small two-bedroom cottage. **Aynho** has pretty cottages, too, plus one or two Georgian houses priced at around £350,000 for four bedrooms. It has a shop but no village green. Both Aynho and **Souldern** have been badly affected by noise from the M40, but those who don't mind say the A41 was bad enough anyway. There are some big properties around here, hidden away in a couple of acres, and for £350,000 you could find something quite special.

Deddington, a couple of miles south-west of King's Sutton, was equal in importance to Banbury until the canals and railways bypassed it. It is officially a town, but its atmosphere is villagey. Houses and small shops gather around the spacious market place. Side roads lead off, lined with honey-coloured stone houses and cottages, many of them Grade II listed. A busy social life revolves around the primary school, the church, a variety of clubs from football, bowls and badminton to yoga and nature conservation, and there are more than a hundred cottage businesses. Residents work locally as surveyors, accountants and solicitors, and the area is also popular with pilots flying from Heathrow and Birmingham. "They put a pin in the map between the two and seem to hit Deddington," says one local. Commuters have tended to drive to Milton Keynes, half an hour's train journey from London, but now that the Banbury line is so much better they don't need to. Otherwise the M40 is close enough for convenience and has unclogged the A423 between Oxford and Banbury. Prices range from £100,000 for a two-bedroom Victorian brick cottage to £150,000 for a Grade II listed 17th-century cottage of similar size.

Banbury

Journey: 76 min
Season: £3132*
Peak: 3 per hr
Off-peak: 2 per hr
* Also valid to
Paddington

Banbury has spent a lot of time burying its past in order to make way for a bright new future which is now bursting upon it, complete with a new shopping centre, new industries and improved rail links. House prices shot up to Oxford and Home Counties levels when the M40 was agreed, fell back in the recession and have returned to high levels again. The new commercial business parks and light industry lie to the east and they have brought increased housing demand. The older part of the town is late Victorian or early Edwardian, but most properties are post-war. Small semis sell at £85,000, but on the more prestigious western side large Sixties houses in well laid out gardens command £350,000. Parking at the station is easy enough.

The M40 has also had a mixed effect on the villages within five miles of Banbury. To the north-west, **Warmington**, which is very picturesque, **Shotteswell** and **Mollington** have all been adversely affected by noise; but **Wroxton**, a charming village with winding lanes, thatched cottages, grassy verges and a duck pond, has been made more accessible without suffering any serious damage. Just off the A422 to Stratford-upon-Avon (handy for a shot of Shakespeare), it preserves its tranquillity and yet is only a few minutes' drive from the motorway. It has a school and a couple of pubs but no shop – people nip over to Horley or do their main supermarket shopping in Banbury. A small semi-detached stone-and-thatch cottage with two bedrooms will cost about £130,000; a three-bedroom detached house £150,000 or more; a four-bedroom detached £200,000.

On the whole, though, commuting professionals tend to prefer **Bloxham**, to the south-west, with the result that prices here are slightly higher than in neighbouring villages. There are several 16th- and 17th-century examples built in the local ironstone and buried down pretty lanes. The village has a parade of shops, a public school and a good girls' school. A couple of small estates of modern houses have brought more cars which clog the centre.

To the west, **Shenington**, too, is a popular and pretty village, full of lovely old golden stone houses. The presence of a rubbish tip not far away does deter some househunters, although most residents feel it isn't a problem. There is also a neighbouring airfield where noisy go-karting is held, but this happens only a few times a year. The pub has seats outside on the verge of the green, and the primary school is a high-flyer. The charming cottages nearby fetch around £160,000 for three bedrooms, while larger five-bedroom houses go for around £240,000.

Sibford Ferris, a little further south, has delightful mullioned houses with broad grass verges and a mellow blend of stone and thatch. It also has a village shop and post office and a well-respected Quaker school. Two-bedroom cottages start at £99,000. The average price for a four-bedroom period house is £250,000 to £350,000. A large seven- or eight-bedroom Queen Anne or Georgian house with stables and three or four acres will weigh in at 15% more.

Leamington Spa

The journey to Leamington Spa is much quicker than it was a few years ago, making it a viable commuter's haunt. In the past the people who chose to live in this spacious spa town, with its Georgian and Victorian houses and attractive riverside walks, often came because of the development of light industry between Leamington and Warwick. The delightful Royal Pump Rooms, where rich and poor once took baths and needle showers, have been restored as an arts centre, and the town now teems with designer boutiques. One of the nicest parts of the town is the tree-lined Beverley Road, offering a mix of Fifties and Sixties detached houses which sell from around £130,000, unmodernised, up to £250,000, restored. Northumberland Road is the most prestigious street, in which the minimum price for a good-sized Victorian or Edwardian house is £250,000, rising to £500,000 for the best.

Journey: 95 min
Season: £3368*
Peak: 2 per hr
Off-peak: 1 per hr
*Also valid to Paddington.

Those who are willing to drive across five miles of farming landscape to Leamington station settle in **Harbury**, a lively village with a good community of mixed ages and a cosy, clustered centre near the church, with frills of modern housing around it. Small modern houses start at £80,000; larger period cottages go for £300,000.

The presence of a rubbish tip not far away does deter some househunters

Neighbouring **Bishop's Itchington** is known in estate agency terms as Harbury's poor relation – a two-bedroom terrace here goes for £65,000; a detached house for £150,000.

Bishop's Tachbrook has a small chatty post office stores and a little row of shops, but the few thatched houses are well outnumbered by Sixties and Seventies red-brick estates. A two-bedroom terrace house will cost in the region of £68,000; a detached family house with four or five bedrooms will be priced around £150,000. The higher prices in this area reflect the bonus of easy access to the extended M40, which tends to attract young professionals.

146

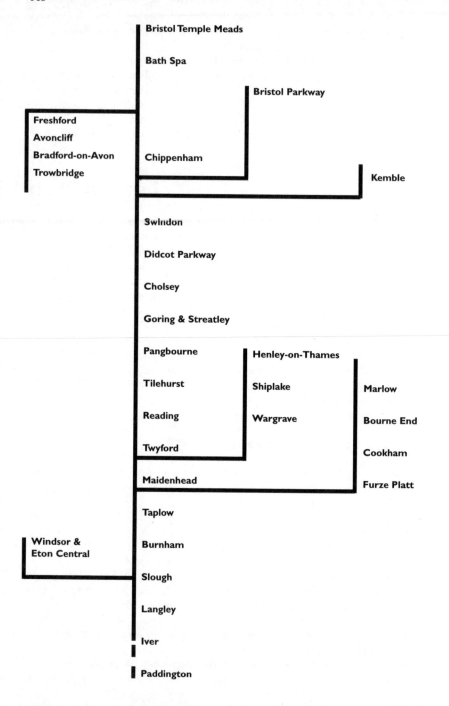

Bristol Temple Meads

Bath Spa

Bristol Parkway

Freshford
Avoncliff
Bradford-on-Avon
Trowbridge

Chippenham

Kemble

Swindon

Didcot Parkway

Cholsey

Goring & Streatley

Pangbourne

Henley-on-Thames

Tilehurst

Shiplake

Marlow

Reading

Wargrave

Bourne End

Twyford

Cookham

Maidenhead

Furze Platt

Taplow

Windsor &
Eton Central

Burnham

Slough

Langley

Iver

Paddington

Paddington
➡ Reading and Bristol

Iver

This is a lovely village of 16th- and 17-century cottages clustered around the church, with tree-covered lanes around, and Iver Heath nearby. The train service is rather infrequent for somewhere so close to London – so people often use Slough. A country cottage with three bedrooms and a small garden will cost £110,000 to £150,000, rising with the amount of land. There are one or two blocks of exclusive flats where you will pay around £85,000 to £100,000 for two bedrooms.

Journey: 27 min
Season: £1412
Peak: 3 per hr
Off-peak: 2 per hr

Langley

Langley is really an extension of Slough, with lots of new housing developments. At its heart is a very popular 15th-century pub called the Red Lion, a Norman church and a rare 17th-century church library. The 17th-century almshouses provided a monastic touch. Houses range from £100,000 for a three-bedroom semi on a new estate to £180,000 for a four-bedroom detached.

Journey: 30 min
Season: £1536
Peak: 4 per hr
Off-peak: 2 per hr

Slough

The huge trading estate – supposedly the largest in Europe – is the backbone to **Slough**, but it doesn't make it pretty to look at. Efforts have been made to improve the quality of life. The use of security cameras in the centre at night has created the conditions for nightlife to thrive. The twin peaks of shopping are contained in the Observatory and the Queensmere shopping malls, while The Village has the specialist shops. There is also a leisure centre and a sports centre, a 10-screen cinema and an ice-rink. It is a great mix of council housing and private modern estates. Windsor Meadows is particularly sought-after by airline staff because it is ideal for the M4 and Heathrow. A one-bedroom studio starts at around £45,000. On the whole, Slough vies with Reading to provide the cheapest properties in Berkshire. A small Victorian two-bedroom terrace would cost £85,000 to £98,000; a larger four-storey town house might fetch £150,000. The large Asian population has settled in certain areas, particularly Chalvey. The

Journey: 16 min
Season: £1648
Peak: 6 per hr
Off-peak: 6 per hr

train service to Paddington is astonishingly good with at least one fast non-stopping train an hour, and a handful of stopping ones. The station has a pavilioned roof reminiscent of a French château, and there is good parking.

The thing to watch out for in this area is how close you are to a Heathrow flight path. **Colnbrook**, a village two miles to the east, is affected by low-flying planes, but you can pick up a listed, detached four-bedroom house in a quarter of an acre for £140,000. At the bot-

Modern estate houses, south Buckinghamshire

tom end of the market, you could get a studio flat for £42,000 to £50,000. Two miles north, the landscape becomes suddenly rural and a village like **Stoke Poges** feels very out-of-the-way. The poet Thomas Gray is supposed to have written his famous *Elegy* in the garden graveyard to St Giles Church, where he is buried. Stoke Poges is a cheaper version of Gerrards Cross, with a small parade of shops and a population peppered with both elderly and young stockbroker types. You might pay £250,000 for a four-bedroom period house in one of its tree-lined avenues. At the lower end of the market you could buy a three-bedroom house on one of the small Sixties estates for £110,000 to £150,000. It's the kind of place where a decade or more ago you could have built a new house in your garden and still have had an acre to spare. Sunday afternoon walks are taken at Langley Park and Black Park.

➡ Branch line to **Windsor & Eton Central**

No through trains. Change at Slough. Journey: 32 min Season: £1872 (£1928 if also valid at Windsor & Eton Riverside) Peak: 3 per hr Off-peak: 2 per hr

Windsor is a smart town at the foot of Windsor Castle with Windsor Great Park at its back door. Eton is dminated by the boys' public school. For main entry see Windsor & Eton Riverside on the **Waterloo to Reading** line (page 193).

Continuation of main line

Burnham

Burnham has quite a few modern shops but still manages to cling on to some of its 15th- and 16th-century charm. The centre is quaint and busy with a cobbler, butcher and baker. Just off the main street, a 17th-century black-and-white beamed house might be had for less than £220,000. North Burnham is the place to be. It leads to Burnham Beeches with its huge pollarded beeches and winding lanes – a 600-acre remnant of a forest which once covered the Chilterns. Here a house with five bedrooms in an acre of land will cost £400,000 to £500,000. The area attracts successful stockbrokers, bankers and the odd television presenter.

Journey: 25 min
Season: £1760
Peak: 4 per hr
Off-peak: 2 per hr

The northern flank offers some classic Buckinghamshire villages. **Farnham Royal** and **Farnham Common** are strung between Beaconsfield and Slough. Huge houses set in several acres cost £800,000. Horse-riding is the popular pastime for wives left at home while their husbands are in the City. Both these little villages are right on top of Burnham Beeches.

For less expensive housing you have to look at somewhere like **Cippenham**, west of Slough, where Lovell Homes has built a new community of about 5,000 homes, with more in the pipeline. It has a Tesco and other stores and everything from one-bedroom starter homes for £80,000 to executive homes for £190,000.

The station is used by those who work on the Slough Trading Estate as well as commuters to London. It has only a small car park.

Taplow

This is where you start to find wonderful riverside villages with modest-sized yachts moored to the banks and anglers hunched beneath their green umbrellas. **Taplow** has lots of old cottages and a modern church with a distinctive copper spire. You can see Cliveden House, formerly the home of Lady Astor, in the distance on the cliffs above the river. Enormous houses with gardens running down to the Thames go for £800,000 to £1.5m, though in the village itself there are two-up-two-down Victorian cottages for around £145,000. There are also lots of flats. A one-bedroom converted flat in a large Edwardian house will fetch £75,000. People who live here might prefer to go to Maidenhead or Slough to pick up the faster train service to London and park the car more easily.

Journey: 28 min
Season: £1872
Peak: 2 per hr
Off-peak: 1 per hr

In Taplow there are enormous houses with gardens running down to the Thames that go for over £1m

Maidenhead

Journey: 32 min
Season: £1980
Peak: 4 per hr
Off-peak: 4 per hr

Maidenhead is an old Thameside town with an ancient heart, small shops and a High Street that is now fully pedestrianised. Big new facilities are on the way (multiplex cinema, health club, restaurants). Just outside the centre you will find grids of reasonably pleasant turn-of-the-century terrace houses. The ones with two bedrooms sell for up to £150,000. The modern developments are on the south-western outskirts, where three-bedroom semis cost £175,000 or more. The most sought-after areas, such as Maidenhead Bridge and Boulter's Lock, are close to the river. Here the houses are large, detached late Victorian, with big gardens and wealthy owners who can afford to pay £400,000 for four bedrooms. A short walk along the Thames is Brunel's Sounding Arch, a remarkably long brick viaduct built in 1838.

Bray, scarcely two miles out of Maidenhead, is a tiny picturesque village on the lip of the Thames and one of the costliest places to live even in

this expensive area. It combines closeness to London with a good train service, and has narrow irregular streets with timber-framed and Georgian houses. The Roux brothers have their famous Waterside Inn restaurant here and another Michelin star winner called The Fat Duck has joined it. There is a clutch of resident television stars so the mere act of buying a stamp in the local post office can bring you up against Michael Parkinson or Rolf Harris.

Restyled
Edwardian house,
near Maidenhead

The Fisheries offers huge mansions in a woodland setting with a river frontage – and prices running into millions. One of the things to watch for is the very occasional river flood.

Just outside the village is Bray Studios, where the Hammer House of Horror films were made and short television dramas are still made. Bray has a post office and small dress shop, plus a hockey club and tennis court. Tourist coaches tend to drive straight through because there is no tea-room. There are a few modern estates but they are hidden away. It is a conservation area and serious contender in the annual Britain in Bloom competition. If you want to build anything new, or change the exterior of your house, you can expect heavy opposition.

Heading south you come to **Holyport**, an attractive village set around a large green. This has a pond with two pubs on it, and annual village and steam fairs. Cricket on the green has been stopped because too many windows got broken, but the rounders matches still continue. Holyport has some huge Tudor and Georgian houses, and small former estate cottages. A house with half an acre might cost £400,000. The village is too spread out to have a strong sense of community, but there is an active preservation society. There are some council houses and new private estates, a handful of shops, a primary school and a special school for mentally handicapped children.

To the west is **Littlewick Green**, where the houses are built around the cricket pitch and the pub is called The Cricketers. The Courage Shire Horse Centre is a big draw for those with pony pashes. This and neighbouring villages attract a lot of commuters – people running private businesses and staff from Heathrow. Another pretty village, still within the two- to three-mile belt around Maidenhead, is **Pinkneys Green**. It has some huge old houses that sell for over £500,000, and a National Trust house, Maidenhead Thicket. The first Girl Guide troop was formed here by Olave Baden-Powell in 1910. Another village worth considering is **White Waltham**. It is very rural, has a thriving primary school, a small airfield, a thriving cricket club and detached estate houses that sell at £275,000. Then there is **Hurley**, on the Thames, with a lock, a 12th-century pub, a working boatyard and cottages costing around £250,000.

Branch line to **Marlow** via **Furze Platt, Cookham** and **Bourne End**

The service connecting these stations to Maidenhead is nicknamed the Marlow Donkey. It is very short and slow. The line follows the river and lifts its head out of the valleys to give good views. The area is close enough to London for people to commute by car, either on the M40 or on the M4. **Furze Platt** station was built in 1937 to serve north Maidenhead, which had been taken over by light industrial development. A spread of new housing has followed in its wake over the last 20 years. At **Cookham** you are in prize countryside now grazed by commuters and television celebrities, swags of it owned by the National Trust. The snob address is Cookham Dean, up on the common, where house prices start at £200,000 and go on to £3m for a large riverside house. Cookham Village is old and lovely, but the butcher and baker have long been replaced by chic little restaurants. Stanley Spencer lived here, and the Spencer Gallery shows some of his works. The Cookham Rise area was expanded in the Fifties, close to the brick and flint station building. A three-bedroom semi here costs around £175,000; or you might find a small cottage at around £150,000. The riverside towpath provides walks and rides for ponies but if

No through trains from Marlow. There is 1 through train per hr from Bourne End, peak only; otherwise change at Maidenhead.

Journey: 59 min*	
Season: £2220	
Peak: 2 per hr	
Off-peak: 1 per hr	

*From Marlow, changing at Maidenhead.

Schools in Berkshire

Ascot has five girls' private schools – Heathfield, St Mary's Roman Catholic school, Hurst Lodge, Marist Convent, and St George's. For boys the dominant school is Eton, at Windsor, which can count 19 former prime ministers among its old boys. There is also Pangbourne boarding and day school for girls and boys, which has a strong naval tradition, and Wellington at Crowthorne for boys (girls in the sixth) with a strong army tradition. A good state school is Newland Girls at Maidenhead.

Reading has Reading School, an unusual grant-maintained state day school for boys (some boarders) with a working week that extends into Saturday morning. For girls there are two independent schools – Queen Anne's boarding and day and The Abbey – as well as Kindrick Girls Grammar. For boys there is the public school, Bradfield College, and the Roman Catholic boys boarding school, The Oratory. Co-educational private schools include Leighton Park and Reading Blue Coat School (mostly boys).

Little Heath at Tilehurst is a good co-educational comprehensive. Further out towards Thatcham girls can attend Down House (boarding and day) where first-year pupils spend a term at a château in the Dordogne.

you want to swim or do the gym then the nearest leisure centre is at Maidenhead.

The river village of **Bourne End** is just as expensive, and much of the social life revolves around sailing. The Upper Thames Sailing Club is here, and at Spade Oak Reach there is a marina with timber chalet holiday homes. These are almost impossible to get hold of and will cost around £275,000, including moorings. A more substantial, secluded riverside home, typical of the area, with six bedrooms, a boathouse and half an acre running down to the river, would sell for over £750,000. A large proportion of the population commute to London, but they tend to drive to Beaconsfield (see page 137) and get the train to Marylebone rather than suffer the Marlow Donkey.

Marlow is also prime commuter country. Its ancient High Street stretches down to the river and has a proper fishmonger, chocolatier and Wednesday market. Burford County Combined School is a high-performer in the league tables. A two-bedroom Victorian cottage would fetch over £150,000; a three-bedroom terrace £150,000 to £200,000; a three-bedroom Edwardian house around £500,000. Large houses on the river rarely come up for sale and cost at least £1m. The west side of town is considered better than the east. At Marlow Bottom, two miles from the centre, is a huge modern estate with houses selling at £135,000. Since it is on the Berkshire, Buckinghamshire and Oxfordshire borders, parents can choose the local education policy that suits them. At **Bisham** nearby is the famous Compleat Angler restaurant and the Marlow Rowing Club, together with some very pretty Tudor cottages, but it is rather spoilt by the heavy through-traffic into Marlow. The parish council has bought an orchard for people to play in and have picnics. Bisham Abbey is a national sports training centre.

Continuation of main line
Twyford

Twyford is a typical small town surrounded by countryside. It has all the
essential shops and is referred to locally as "the village". There are rows of
Victorian terraces close to the station. Two-bedroom houses here sell for
£140,000, three bedrooms go for around £180,000. The huge, tightly-
packed new estate has starter homes at £82,000, up to four-bedroom
detached houses at £250,000. The older, more established and expensive
part of the town is Ruscombe, with house prices ranging from £350,000
to £800,000.

Journey: 40 min
Season: £2320
Peak: 3 per hr
Off peak: 3 per hr

    Waltham St Lawrence is two miles away, trapped in a rural world of
its own. The price of this in the form of a detached house with land is over
£500,000; a two-bedroom cottage is £210,000. Charming black-and-white
cottages mix with modern houses. The village owns its own pub, The Bell,
and has a general store with a post office. There is a good primary school
within walking distance, plus Brownies, playgroups and a football team
with its own pitch. The cricket team plays at **Shurlock Row**, which is
rather smaller. It has a much-respected butcher and a good pub called The
Royal Oak. It is also pretty, with a pond at the end of the main street.
Prices are slightly lower than in Waltham St Lawrence.

    For cheaper properties you have to look at the dense modern housing
at **Woodley**, built on the aerodrome used by Douglas Bader. Here a three-
bedroom detached house might cost over £130,000. At **Charvil**, a popular
commuter dormitory, a modern three-bedroom terrace could be had for
£120,000.

Branch line to **Henley** via
Wargrave and **Shiplake**

Wargrave lies on a charming stretch of the Thames, and its narrow streets,
trees and Georgian timber-framed houses on the river make it a rather
prestigious place to live. The Sultan of Oman and Paul Daniels have mansions nearby. You could get something with three bedrooms on a modern
estate for between £240,000 and £500,000, but good secluded houses start
at £400,000 and go up over the million mark. **Shiplake** is similarly expensive and exclusive. It has a number of new developments on which four-
to five-bedroom detached houses cost £290,000 to £1m.

Journey: 56 min*
Season: £2376
Peak: 2 per hr
Off-peak: 1 per hr
*From Henley,
changing at
Twyford. There
is only one
through train to
Paddington in the
peak period (jour-
ney 48 minutes).

    The rowing regatta, held during the first week in July, has put **Henley**
on the map. The first inter-university boat race was held there in 1829, and
by 1839 it had become a recognised annual event, the story of which is told

Riverside residence, Henley

in the new River and Rowing Museum. Hordes of people come to drink Pimms in the pink-and-white marquees and give the town an annual seizure. Though it remains pretty and rural, straddling the river by way of a lovely stone bridge, it has been affected by the influx of money. Small shops are closing and big supermarkets moving in. The battle to keep open the old cinema (complete with organ rising up out of the floor) has been lost and it has now become a three-screen complex. Two-bedroom Victorian cottages sell for around £160,000; larger terrace houses with no parking sell for around £300,000. Anything large with a river frontage would have a starting price of over £1m. Commuters often opt for flats with river views – two bedrooms might cost £250,000.

The hordes of people who now come to drink Pimms in the pink-and-white marquees give Henley an annual seizure

Hambledon, four miles away, is also worth looking at, if only to admire the cluster of houses around the huge chestnut tree with the village pump beneath. Film location hunters love it. The village has a church, general store and post office, cobbled pavements and a pretty little stream running through. Properties rarely come on the market here. A small cottage with no rear garden or parking might be picked up for £250,000.

Continuation of main line

Reading

Journey: 24 min
Season: £2600 (also valid to Waterloo)
Peak: 9 per hr
Off-peak: 6 per hr

Reading is a significant shopping and business centre, and a university town. Its prosperity used to be based on beer (Courage), bulbs (Suttons) and biscuits (Huntley & Palmer), but now it has a much higher profile as the gateway to the silicon valley. Seven out of 10 American IT firms have bases here, including Microsoft and Oracle. The train service to London is superb – one about every seven minutes – as it is one of the busiest rail interchanges in the country (see also **Waterloo to Reading**, page 205). Reading is also the terminus of the Kennet and Avon canal, which was reopened in 1990 and offers some marvellous walks to the west. Different areas of the city offer different things. **Caversham Heights**, on the Thames, has a mix of detached houses, flat conversions and modern flats, and is very residential. The most expensive address is The Warren, up on a hill with river views. A three-bedroom flat in an Edwardian conversion with a mooring and garden sloping down to the river would sell for around £250,000. A large five-bedroom Edwardian house in three-quarters of an acre would sell for £450,000 to £600,000. Prices in this area have risen hugely. **Lower Caversham** offers mainly Victorian terrace housing with some modern infilling. A three-bedroom terrace would cost £105,000; a modern flat on the river £148,000.

Caversham Park village is made up of town houses built a couple of decades ago. Prices tend to hover under £110,000, which makes it attractive to young families and first-time buyers. **Emmer Green** is very Thirties, with a lot of open land and golf courses. A three-bedroom semi here would cost around £200,000.

West and east Reading are cosmopolitan, and prices are slightly lower. A one-bedroom flat would cost £75,000; a three-bedroom Victorian house over £95,000. To the south is **Lower Earley** (see page 204) and to the west **Tilehurst** (see below), both with their own railway stations. A three-bedroom semi costs around £120,000 to £150,000. **Whiteknights Road**, where the university is, has large Edwardian houses that sell at around the £350,000 to £400,000.

The popular villages nearby include **Pangbourne**, **Goring** and **Streatley** (see page 156). **Sonning Common**, just inside Oxfordshire, is very sleepy and countrified. It has a few small shops but lacks a central focus. A two-bedroom detached bungalow might be bought for just over £130,000. Most of the villages to the south of Reading are not particularly outstanding in any way. **Burghfield** faces a huge population boom as extensive new building is planned.

Tilehurst

Tilehurst is a western suburb of Reading. A three-bedroom semi costs around £85,000.

Journey: 52 min	
Season: £2600	
Peak: 2 per hr	
Off-peak: 2 per hr	

Pangbourne

Pangbourne, just five miles off the M4, is a riverside commuter haven where the Thames meets the Pang. This is where Kenneth Grahame, author of *Wind In The Willows*, lived and where the buffoons in Jerome K. Jerome's *Three Men in a Boat* stopped off. Canoeists and boating tourists

Journey: 57 min	
Season: £2600	
Peak: 2 per hr	
Off-peak: 2 per hr	

now cavort in the shallows. Its discreet Georgian charm, with its square, weir and meadow, has developed a certain hustle as the population has swollen to 2,500. Local people say it is so busy that you can't cross the road in the rush hour, yet during the rest of the day it is so quiet you can lie down in it. There are old-fashioned shops – a butcher, baker – and it is known as an "eating village" because there are so many restaurants and take-aways. Pangbourne, the co-educational public school, stands on Pangbourne Hill. Prices are high. A modern semi in Kennedy Drive would cost £120,000; a Victorian terrace £165,000; a period detached house £300,000. Flats with river views will fetch £110,000. Much larger houses go for anything between £500,000 and £1m.

Goring & Streatley

Journey: 62 min
Season: £2600
Peak: 2 per hr
Off-peak: 2 per hr

Goring and **Streatley** sandwich the Thames between them. Both are expensive and pretty, with enough shops to make life manageable. A Victorian house with three bedrooms will cost £200,000 upwards. Streatley doesn't have the frill of modern housing on its outskirts that Goring has, and it has the Swan Inn on the towpath, which is now a conference centre.

Cholsey

Journey: 67 min
Season: £2600
Peak: 2 per hr
Off-peak: 2 per hr

Cholsey is sprawly, so the prices here are lower. Its main feature, a pretty village green edged with listed cottages, has to face down the parade of modern shops on the other side. The shops and post office are useful, though, and the parish magazine carries six pages of clubs and activities to join. It has a busy horticultural society, the Cholsey Silver band, and the Cholsey and Wallingford Steam Railway which is run by volunteers. The primary school is a very strong on music and has a nature reserve next door. Agatha Christie is buried in Cholsey. A three-bedroom house on a modern development would cost £110,000.

Didcot Parkway

Journey: 39 min
Season: £3108
Peak: 3 per hr
Off-peak: 1-3 per hr

Didcot itself lacks any romance, though its trains might be the envy of the west – the evening peak service pelts along at 95mph and completes the journey in 34 minutes. It has about 20,000 residents and is scheduled to expand even further. The shopping centre is adequate (as yet there is no theatre or cinema), but ambitious plans to completely overhaul the centre are in hand, as are plans to slip 3,500 new houses in around the edges. The most attractive part is **Northbourne**, which is old Didcot and still very beautiful. **East Hagbourne**, just outside, is distinctly special, displaying all the architectural eclecticism of the area – timber frame, thatch, zig-zag brickwork – clustered around the old village cross by the church. **West Hagbourne** is similar but quieter, with a village pond. Both are popular with staff at the Atomic Research Station at Harwell who can afford £250,000 to £300,000 for a three-bedroom 15th-century cottage.

16th-century thatched cottage, Blewbury

Perhaps the village with the most charm and vigour is **Blewbury**, set against the Downs. Blewburton Hill to the east is crowned with an extraordinary prehistoric camp. The village has pretty old inns, a football club, a cricket green, local wine-makers, church choir and a dramatic society. Once you get off the B4017 the prices are high. An early 16th-century cottage with four bedrooms and inglenook fireplace might fetch around £300,000, though you could pick up a four-bedroom modern house on a small new development for £160,000. **East Hendred**, to the west, is a typical Downland village peppered with thatch and timber. It is close to the ancient Ridgeway, which enables you to walk at a giddy height for miles in either direction. "It's very horsey and a bit arty crafty. Lots of Volvos with stickers saying Canine Defence League," is how one local resident describes it. **Harwell**, by comparison,

East Hendred is very horsey and a bit arty crafty. Lots of Volvos with stickers saying Canine Defence League

is plainer with plenty of workmanlike Victorian houses. An old three-bedroom farmer's cottage here can be had for £150,000 while four-bedroom modern houses cost £200,000.

The combination of riverside with proximity to London makes some of these villages obvious film-star territory. **Shillingford**, on a bridge over the Thames, and **Warborough** both reek of money. **Wallingford** has a pretty shopping centre with a notable bookshop and lots of Georgian houses. On the river front they cost from £500,000 into the millions, back in the streets a Victorian three-bedroom terrace will cost £200,000. The town is the fictional Cawston in the television drama *Midsomer Murders*.

Swindon

Swindon itself is architecturally brutal though wonderfully convenient for commuting, since the InterCity trains take a last breath here before sprinting on to the West Country. Big businesses like Motorola, Honda and the

Journey: 52 min	
Season: £4832	
Peak: 5 per hr	
Off-peak: 3 per hr	

Beyond Swindon you reach the great sweeps of the chalk uplands, with their pervasive atmosphere of antiquity

Nationwide have their headquarters here. Professionals, bank managers and the wealthier shopkeepers huddle together in the **Old Town**, in Victorian and Edwardian houses on the south side of Bath Road. A three-bedroom terrace at the cheaper end of the market here would cost £79,000. Four bedrooms in a more expensive road would fetch £170,000. **The Lawns**, near the lake and nature walks of Coate Water Park, is also sought after where five-bedroom detached houses with gardens cost £145,000. Or there is **Broome Manor**, with its golf course and a mix of modern Georgian, Regency and ranch-style houses selling at £280,000 and evoking the atmosphere of Dallas.

On the whole, people tend to flee Swindon for the chalk villages of the Marlborough Downs or the Vale of the White Horse. The east is more popular, with villages such as **Liddington**, **Wanborough**, **Bishopstone** (which still has its watercress beds) and **Aldbourne**. These are cohesive, and tend to have primary schools and huge churches and pubs that are still free houses. A four-bedroom house could be bought for between £240,000 and £275,000 depending on position. Ex-council properties sell at around £150,000. Although they are only just off the M4, they have some prime hacking country right on the doorstep and are seriously horsey.

A walk across the Berkshire Downs connects us to the past as surely as any history book. The white horse is at **Uffington** – against the Ridgeway near Dragon Hill, where St George is supposed to have killed the dragon. It is worth remembering that the further you go from Swindon, and the nearer you get to **Hungerford** or **Faringdon**, the more attractive the villages are, and the higher the prices – possibly £30,000 more for similar properties.

Country house, Swindon area

The National Trust owns much of the land to the north of Swindon, including the villages of **Coleshill** and **Buscot**. Here the infant Thames is hardly more than a stream running beneath the willows. **Lechlade** is idyllically pretty with a good collection of Georgian houses, but it fills with boating people in the summer and, being 10 miles from Swindon, is a bit of a slog to reach at the end of a hard day. The stone for St Paul's cathedral was loaded here. **Fairford** is worth considering. It is a thriv-

House style in the West

The great prize in the west is the Cotswolds, where the houses around the upper Thames, the Cherwell, the Evenlode, the Windrush and the Colne are built quite literally out of the landscape. They lie in the great belt of yellowy grey oolite which, when cut and dressed, makes each village street look as natural as an outcrop of stone.

Even the most humble cottages have a kind of a churchy grandeur given to them by the stone, and a decorativeness associated with wealth, including mullioned windows, arched doorways and drip-stones. The real money was made from the sheep dotted across the hillsides and the wool industry of the 14th and 15th centuries. The roofs, usually made with layers of stone slates and gabled windows to let the light into the top rooms, give that distinctive rhythm which brings tourists by the coachload to admire the scene.

Below Oxford you enter brick country, but there is also some clunch, taken from the Berkshire Downs, and around Aylesbury there is a chalk and clay mixture called "wichert". Many of the houses have lost the thatch they once had – a steep pitched roof is often a clue to the fact that a house was once thatched. Flora Thompson's *Lark Rise To Candleford* is perhaps the best description there is of cottage life in this area at the end of the last century.

Beyond Swindon you reach the great sweeps of the chalk uplands with their pervasive atmosphere of antiquity – burial mounds or barrows, and stone circles and white horses cut into the sheep-cropped hillsides. Eventually you come to the toffee-coloured stone of Bath, carved into the gracious 18th-century crescents and squares which gives the city its distinction and make it such an attractive place in which to live.

ing community, has a few shops, active local societies, and a church with 500-year old stained glass windows. A small Cotswold house with two bedrooms might sell for £160,000. The old gravel pits at **Whelford** are popular with watersports enthusiasts.

Villagers driving in from the west of Swindon have to cope with a traffic problem on their way into the city centre. **Wootton Bassett** is a large market town with a good range of local shops, including a delicatessen. Hackpen Hill nearby has a white horse on its flank. The weekly market used to be so disorganised that an early photograph shows a large cow emerging from a solicitor's office. You can get studio apartments for £35,000, and ordinary little three-bedroom houses for £90,000. The **Somerfords** (**Little** and **Great**, divided by the River Avon) both have a shop and post office, and are popular because they border the Cotswolds and are closer to the prettiness of **Malmesbury** and its beautiful 12th-century abbey ruins than to the dead weight of Swindon. They have lots of local societies, from under-fives to the Somerford Stages amateur dramatics group. Great Somerford also has a primary school. An interest in horses is a useful social passport. The Vale of the White Horse Hunt provides good hunting; there is polo at Cirencester Park, and endless bridleways and footpaths criss-crossing the Cotswolds. The price of a new detached house with four bedrooms, two bathrooms and a double garage hovers around £200,000. **Brinkworth** has lots of good points including its pub, The Three Crowns, and the gardening club called The Bramble Patches. It is notable for its extraordinary length – stretching to about five miles. A period house with four bedrooms here will cost over £220,000. Slightly to the east is **Lydiard Millicent**, typically north Wiltshire, with a pub, post office and green-belt buffer zone to insulate it from Swindon. A four-bedroom new detached house might cost £180,000. **Purton Stoke**, which has a pub and a village street that tapers into open countryside, is much nicer than its overblown neighbour **Purton**. A four-bedroom period house at Purton Stoke might have a price tag of £220,000. A three-bedroom reconstituted stone cottage would cost £140,000.

To the south there are a very few villages scattered in the sweeping chalk hills between Swindon and **Marlborough**, which actually lies closer to Pewsey station (see page 186).

Line to **Kemble**

Journey: 75 min
Season: £5112
Peak: 1 per hr (2 per hr changing at Swindon)
Off-peak: 1 per hr*
*Change at Swindon on most trains.

Kemble is a very pretty Cotswold village, often commended in best-kept-village competitions in Gloucestershire. Planning controls are tight, so that even the council houses are built in local stone. The village has a school and a general store-cum-post office, though most people do their major shopping in Cirencester. The abiding local interest is reflected in the biannual flower and vegetable shows. Three-bedroom former estate-workers' cottages sell for around £115,000; Victorian railway cottages for more; four-bedroom modern houses for £175,000 and above. Larger farmhouses can cost £400,000. "Location and rarity is everything," says one local agent.

Schools in Gloucestershire

The 11-plus still operates here so there are good grammar schools for those who excel but also good comprehensives and private schools. Villages between Cheltenham, Cirencester and Stroud are surrounded by choice. Cheltenham has the heavily oversubscribed Pate's Grammar for boys and girls, three impressive comprehensives, and strong private schools including Cheltenham Ladies' College, Cheltenham College for boys and girls, and Dean Close for both sexes. Stroud has two grammar schools – Stroud High for girls and Marling for boys. Wycliffe independent school for both sexes is at Stonehouse nearby, and Westonbirt for girls is to the south at Tetbury.

Cirencester has Rendcomb College independent school for boys and girls and two good comprehensives. Other strong comprehensives are in Chipping Camden and Fairford.

To the east is a belt of very desirable small villages and hamlets. **Poole Keynes**, the nearest, was little more than a farming hamlet with a medieval priory until the Sixties imposed a modern housing development on it. **Somerford Keynes** also has a lot of modern development but is socially very active. It has a thriving WI, plus bridge clubs, mothers and toddlers, and other groups. There is no shop, but the pub sells coffee and sugar, and bread is delivered three times a week. **Ashton Keynes** has a primary school, a petrol station, two shops and some lovely period houses close to the river. As you approach from South Cerney you will see some beautiful 17th-century cottages on the other side of the bridge. A large farmhouse in the countryside nearby would cost £300,000 to £400,000, while smaller houses are on a par with the rest of the area. **South Cerney** is close to the Cotswold Water Park – a collection of flooded gravel pits with water-skiing, sailing and fishing. A converted barn with four bedrooms in this area would cost around £300,000. The village is marred slightly by the large quarry with its constant lorry traffic. At least six miles from Kemble but well worth the journey is **Down Ampney**, the most charming of the Ampneys (the others being **Ampney St Peter**, **Ampney Crucis** and **Ampney St Mary**), famous as the birthplace of Ralph Vaughan Williams and much admired for its beautiful gabled manor house, Down Ampney Hall. Little here sells for less than £130,000. The larger, secluded country houses sell for £300,000 to £500,000.

Line to **Bristol Parkway**

The villages near here are perfect for commuters because the station is easy to reach and parking is plentiful. It also lies at the centre of a motorway network that can speed you north, south, east or west and link you with the major commercial centres of Wales as well as with Birmingham, Swindon and London. It is possible for a couple to live here and for one partner to work in Exeter and the other in London. It offers countryside, yet Bristol is on the doorstep. The station is on a spur that goes direct from Swindon, so you can be whisked to London in very little over an hour.

Journey:	80 min
Season:	£6508
Peak:	2 per hr
Off-peak:	1 per hr

Only six minutes from the station are the pricey villages of **Almondsbury** and **Awkley**. They are out of earshot of all the motorways, and an old stone house with four bedrooms might typically cost £250,000. Though they are out of the way, they are now seen as useful locations because of the second Severn Crossing, linked to Junction 17 of the M5. **Hambrook** is also a village with instant appeal. It has a greedy-corner bakery, a couple of pubs, a hotel and Hambrook Common at its centre. Four-bedroom houses easily creep up into the £250,000 range.

Also within six minutes of the station is **Stoke Gifford** – almost an ex-village (with a serious rush-hour problem) now that it has attracted big companies like Hewlett Packard, Sun Life and the Ministry of Defence. The village-proper is packed with old cottages, with those in Mead Road tending to be more expensive than the rest. A one-bedroom cottage will sell at around £55,000. A four-bedroom modern detached house will fetch £120,000. There is also a pair of Bovis housing estates, one being newer and much more popular than the other. The most sought-after roads are Touchstone and Fabian. Prices range from £47,000 for a one-bedroom house or two-bedroom flat, up to £100,000 for three bedrooms.

One partner can work in Exeter and the other in London

It is impossible to ignore the lake of housing at **Bradley Stoke** on its doorstep, billed as the largest development in Western Europe. Builders took over a decade to build around 11,000 houses with primary schools, sports centres, pubs and supermarkets. Unfortunately it developed the nickname Sadly Broke during the recession in the early Nineties, but things have picked up and estate agents are now calling it Bradley Hope. The housing is pick-and-mix, with one-bedroom flats being sold for £35,000, three-bedroom houses at £70,000 to £100,000, and four bedrooms at £110,000 to £175,000.

Much care was taken at Bradley Stoke to avoid the monotony of earlier new development grafted on to **Chipping Sodbury**. The old core remains a lovely old Cotswold town with a typically wide main street flanked with houses in Georgian brick and Cotswold stone. A 17th-century three-bedroom cottage would cost around £140,000. The nearby villages of **Winterbourne**, **Frampton Cotterell** and **Coalpit Heath** blend one into the other, offering a mixture of old and new with a few working farms in the outlying areas. At the bottom of the market you could buy a three-bedroom ex-council house for £100,000. At the top end you could pay £350,000 for a five- to six-bedroom Georgian mansion. **Iron Acton** is also very pretty, with a village green where girls dance round the Maypole in the spring, and two pubs.

If you are looking for a house around here it is worth remembering that in the area between Bristol and Wotton-under-Edge prices are affected by people who commute into Bristol. As you proceed beyond **Thornbury**, prices start to drop. On a bad day from this part, the journey to Bristol Parkway station could take 15 minutes, which many might consider too much.

Continuation of main line

Chippenham

Journey: 62 min (69 min peak)
Season: £5344
Peak: 2 per hr
Off-peak: 2 per hr
Chippenham has become the best-served station on this line for frequency (2 per hr) and speed (100 mph off-peak, 90 mph peak).

Chippenham is a town that has been busy rediscovering its old heritage – paving the old market square with York stone, bringing back market day, re-erecting the Butter Cross and cherishing its Roman remains. It has all the basic shops anyone would need and a £12m new classical-style shopping centre is being built in Bath stone on the banks of the River Avon. It is a place for small family businesses, with a new business park on the western outskirts. In 1962 the set-piece village of **Castle Combe**, five miles away, was declared the prettiest village in England. The arched bridge over the Bye brook, and little stone cottages with their steeply pitched roofs, were then transformed to serve as a seaport for the film of *Dr Dolittle*. It is a bit of a goldfish bowl for tourists, but at least the visitors are expected to leave their cars behind at the top of the village. Residents become very attached and properties rarely come on the market. A thatched cottage recently sold for £360,000. The pubs, Manor House hotel, school and post office make it a cosy community.

Far quieter and just as pretty is **Biddestone**, slightly closer to Chippenham, which has the classic village centre with stone houses, duck pond, pubs and a recreation ground for football and cricket. An older three-bedroom cottage semi will cost £180,000 to £200,000. To the north-east is **East Tytherton**, which is very small, has a village shop and attractive stone houses, and is close enough to the M4 to be favoured by those who prefer the car to the train. **Bremhill** is charming, too. A former resident, the vicar and poet Canon Bowles, kept the bells around the necks of his sheep tuned to thirds and fifths, and was a favourite visitor at Bowood House a few miles to the south. Bremhill has a post office-cum-general store, and a pub. A cottagey three-bedroom semi would sell at £150,000 to £200,000.

People much prefer **Corsham** which has a Cotswold stone heart and a delicatessen which proudly sells local produce. A new Wool and Stone Heritage Centre is planned. A handsome four-bedroom stone house and double garage sells for around £280,000 to £300,000 here. A restored Grade II listed house with five bedrooms would cost over £300,000. Further towards Bath on the A4 is **Box**. At one time it housed the workers building the Great Western Railway for Brunel; now it harbours the occasional rock star and is considered ideal by those who want to be within easy reach of **Bath** but also close to Chippenham railway station. Peter Gabriel's Real World Studios are here. The village has a general store which sells home-made quiches and pies, a chemist and a hairdresser, and two primary schools. There are lots of local activities and the village fête, known as the Box Revels, usually lasts for a week. House prices are reasonable at the moment, with three-bedroom stone cottages selling at about £150,000 – though larger houses will top the £250,000 mark.

At one time Box housed the workers building the Great Western Railway; now it harbours the occasional rock star

Local interests manage to be both horsey and cultural, and also sporting. Here you are in rugby country – thanks to the proliferation of boys' public schools and the huge success of Bath Rugby Club.

Marshfield, west of Chippenham on the A420, has a shop, butcher, doctor, pet and garden supplies. A three-bedroom terrace house, in what was once the last staging post to Bath, would cost around £210,000. The long grey-stone main street is dominated by the church tower and has some remarkable little almshouses dating from 1625.

Very few local sons and daughters can afford to buy homes in the villages they grew up in. First-time buyers are eased out into small towns such as **Calne** – an old woollen town with the site of an old Victorian bacon factory put down to grass in the centre. Flats can be bought for less than £40,000 for one bedroom. Another possibility is **Compton Basset**. It has been made a conservation area because of its delightful chalk-stone cottages and 12th- and 13th-century church. A stock of surplus Ministry of Defence houses which are eagerly snapped up by younger buyers is kept at arm's length and known as Lower Compton.

Other villages worth looking at include **Cherhill** (pronounced Cheryl), towards Marlborough, which stands beside a huge Iron Age camp and white horse, and has its own primary school. A 250-year-old whitewashed house with four bedrooms here would cost around £250,000 to £300,000. Then there is **Heddington** – a small village with infant and primary schools and an international meditation centre called The Pagoda. It is very upmarket: a three-bedroom family house with large garden would sell for around £130,000. Another very sought-after cluster of properties is at **Charlcutt**, north of Calne. The houses all have breathtaking views of the countryside for 20 miles in all directions. Something with five bedrooms and a double garage will cost over £265,000. Although **Sandy Lane** straddles the A342, south-west of Calne, it is very beautiful and has some lovely thatched houses. A two-bedroom cottage here might go for £185,000. Its population is mainly retired, and the residents tend to grow high beech hedges to guard their privacy. It is short of local activity but contains a great deal of wealth. One London commuter from here prefers to travel by helicopter rather than by train. Unfortunately the village is used as a short cut by motorists heading off the M4 for Southampton.

South of Chippenham the showcase village is **Lacock**, but the jumble of timbered houses in the gorgeous twisted streets around the Abbey are all in the hands of the National Trust. The fringe offers the occasional dream house. There is a new development where a five-bedroom semi can be bought for £300,000 to £350,000.

Part-time commuters might choose to live in some of the wonderful villages further south in the Avon valley, which are also served by the Melksham branch line to Bath (see ahead).

Schools in Bristol, Bath and Somerset

Good independent schools for girls in the Bristol area include Badminton for boarding and day, Clifton High, Red Maids' School day and boarding, Redland High and Colston's Girls'. Boys' independent schools include Bristol Cathedral School (girls in the sixth), and Queen Elizabeth's Hospital day and boarding school.

Co-educational independent schools include Clifton College boarding and day, Bristol Grammar day school and Colston's Collegiate. Good comprehensives includes The Castle Marlwood, The Ridings, and Wellsway.

Bath also has its share of educational successes, including Ralph Allen comprehensive, and three co-educational independents – King Edward's, Kingswood and Prior Park College. There is also the Royal High independent day and boarding school for girls.

Branch line to **Trowbridge,** via **Freshford, Avoncliff** and **Bradford-on-Avon,**

Freshford is favoured by retiring Bathonians. It is a strong little community, with its own shop and local railway station. Nipper trains drop you quickly into Bath, so there is no problem with parking the car

Bradford-on-Avon is so expensive that it vies with **Bath**. Indeed, it is built of the same limestone as Bath, on hills falling so steeply towards the Avon that the winding paths between the houses give one the feeling of being in a Greek village. Across the arched stone bridge, and open to the public, is one of the biggest tithe barns in the country. Bradford attracts many tourists who come in summer to wander the river and old shopping streets, and to buy from the craft shops. Any development is viewed suspiciously but nevertheless a huge old mill in the middle is being turned into rural lofts with more shops and cafés. It has a good swimming pool, rowing and sailing clubs, and an annual festival. There are also marvellous walks along the Kennet and Avon Canal.

The attraction of owning a house overlooking the tesselated rooftops of weavers' cottages, miniature 18th-century homes and narrow gardens bulging with hollyhocks, is difficult to quantify. There is a definite ex-military and ex-naval presence here. Larger houses sell for hundreds of thousands of pounds, but it is occasionally possible to find a period three-bedroom terrace house on four floors, with a tiny garden, at around £175,000. On the outer roads, three-bedroom ex-council houses in reconstructed stone will sell for around £80,000. Towards the higher end of the market on the edge of town you could get a four-bedroom Victorian stone semi, with outbuildings in over half an acre, for around £300,000.

Broughton Gifford, to the east, is much quieter, set in deep countryside with a village green faced by Gifford Hall, a 1688 village house. To the south, **Steeple Ashton**, like Bradford-on-Avon, was built on the profits of the wool industry. It has its own pub and post office, church with no steeple and a swag of new housing. A five-bedroom executive house with a paddock would cost around £375,000. Just next to it is **Keevil**, a collection of rather exclusive cottages with a stone manor house. It has a sub-post-office-cum-general-store and a primary school, and more than its share of resident doctors. A three-bedroom thatched cottage would sell for around £220,000.

Journey:120min (peak) and 90 min (off-peak) *

Season: £5404

Trains are infrequent

*There are no through trains to Paddington, change at Bath Spa or Westbury. There are through trains to Waterloo, but only off-peak.

Continuation of main line
Bath Spa

Journey: 74 min (82 min peak)
Season: £5484
Peak: 2 per hr
Off-peak: 2 per hr

People have been known to move to **Bath** and move out again within a couple of years – not everyone finds it easy to break into the social circles that centre on its elegant 18th-century squares and crescents. Its attractions are manifold: beautiful parks, specialist shops, some of them rather exclusive, and restaurants where the prices compete with Mayfair. The beauty of commuting from Bath, though, apart from its obvious physical splendour, is that you can live within walking distance of the station. Indeed you *have* to, otherwise the combined traffic and parking problems will sour your temper before the day has even begun.

The social hubs include the much-acclaimed international festival in June; the Theatre Royal, which is the starting point for many West End plays, the Royal Photographic Society, Bath Rugby Club, and of course the Pump Rooms, where balls are held regularly. The new Nicholas Grimshaw-designed £16m spa will add another life-enhancing experience. Various hotels, clubs and excellent restaurants rise and fall in the firmament as the right places to be seen at. Old Bathonians are extremely tight-knit. Public schools include King Edward's School, Kingswood School for boys and girls, the Royal High for girls, and Prior Park College, which is a Catholic school for both sexes.

The sought-after areas are the two hills to the north and south of the river. **Sion Hill** to the north is a sudden slope looking south over the city. This is where all the major crescents were built, including the Royal, for prominent figures in elegant 18th-century society. Very few of these are left intact: most have been split into flats. A first-floor, two-bedroom flat in Royal Crescent, would go on the market at around £250,000. Between the roads full of architectural gems you find a mixed bag of houses, though nowhere are prices cheap. A four-bedroom Victorian bay-fronted semi in a quiet road might sell for £325,000.

To the south of the river is **Bathwick Hill**, with Widcombe and Lyncombe Hills, where a sister spa to the famous central spa was found in the late 18th century. The architecture is equally fine, but the views from the houses are rather more rural than those from Sion Hill. Both attract businessmen, professionals and culture vultures, but people attach fiercely to their particular hill and would never swap.

It is possible to live outside the city in one of the villages, but driving into Bath is a problem

Living in the centre of Bath only became fashionable again in the early Eighties. For decades previously the Georgian architecture was not cherished, and the buildings had blackened and become gloomy. In the late Seventies, for instance, you could buy a complete Georgian town house in The Circus for £7,000. Now it would fetch close to £1m. There is a tendency for the houses to have tiny gardens because they were designed in the belief that people would take their recreation in the parks. If you own a house in a square, you will often have the right to buy a key to the central garden.

Elsewhere, a modest little house close to the canal with a little garden, two reception rooms and two bedrooms might be found for £150,000 to £175,000. Ex-council houses sell at £85,000 to £100,000.

It is possible to live outside the city in one of the villages,

Georgian town house, Bath

but driving into Bath is a problem. Parking adds an expensive premium to the season ticket, and traffic wardens are vigilant. To the south is the old Somerset coalmining area, still with the occasional slag heap on the horizon. **Peasedown St John**, an early mining town, has been rediscovered and is now a popular commuter haven.

Norton St Philip, however, has conservation status. It was built in local stone from the profits of the wool industry, and has some small modern culs-de-sac stitched unobtrusively into the whole. It has a shop but is best known for its pub, The George, which is one of the best preserved medieval inns in the country. Pepys paid a visit with his wife in 1668, dined on 10 shillings and noted a plaque in the church to twin ladies who had only one stomach between them. **Hinton Charterhouse** is similarly unspoilt but less self-sufficient, with the 13th-century ruins of Hinton Priory close by. The countryside is full of similar villages that you chance upon as you dip in and out of the valleys. But the farming crisis has affected them. In **Wellow** the local farmer no longer herds his cattle through the village at dawn and dusk. He has turned to arable and the barns have become houses. A small cottage will cost £150,000 to £175,000. It no longer has a post office, but the postmaster from Hinton Charterhouse comes to the village hall once a week to hand out the pensions. There are a lot of retired people, but also young families who enjoy the use of the primary school. Many people own horses, and there is a Trekking Centre that caters mostly for weekenders.

To the west are the villages served by the Bradford-on-Avon branch line (see page 165). To the north is another magical stretch of countryside where time seems to have turned everything to stone. **Charlcombe**, **Swainswick** and **Woolley** lie in a U-shaped valley in a landscape which is almost Welsh, and which at its northern end becomes positively austere. It is expensive. In Woolley even a two-bedroom cottage would sell for £150,000; a four-bedroom house for £300,000. To the east of the A46 is another stretch of villages which have that haphazard, ancient quality, including **St Catherine** and **Northend**. **Batheaston** is a favourite with commuters and the retired. Yet it manages to be a working village with a butcher, greengrocer, newsagent, florist and grocery shop, and a large council estate. It has 142 listed buildings altogether, which the Batheaston Society does its best to preserve. It has also been rescued from heavy traffic by a bypass. For breathtaking views across the watermeadows to the city you could look at **Bathford**, which has a busy village school and playgroup. Further north towards the M4, in villages like **Upper Wraxhall** and **North Wraxhall**, prices drop considerably but you become a little separated from the spirit, social life and interests of Bath.

Bristol Temple Meads

Journey: 92 min
Season: £6508 (also valid at Bristol Parkway)
Peak: 3 per hr
Off-peak: 2 per hr

Commuting from **Bristol** is never easy. Parking is difficult, and the station is hard to get at, being surrounded by rows of houses that have escaped from *Coronation Street*. There are huge traffic problems. The M32 regularly clogs into four-mile tailbacks, and there is no integrated public transport system yet to relieve the pressure in a city where a large number of major companies – Lloyds, British Aerospace and NatWest, for example – have their headquarters.

Culturally, however, it is rich, with the Bristol Old Vic, the theatre school and various pubs providing fringe theatre. The Hippodrome attracts the ballet and opera companies. Colston Hall is the rock venue, and the Watershed arts and media centre in the docks shows the arty films. Another big local interest is expressed through Bristol Rugby Club. The well-known public schools include Bristol Cathedral School, Bristol Grammar School, Clifton College, Colston's School and Queen Elizabeth's Hospital.

Clifton and Clifton Village are Bristol's Olympian heights, where the mix of Georgian, Regency and Victorian is very special

Clifton and **Clifton Village** are Bristol's Olympian heights, where the mix of Georgian, Regency and Victorian is very special and very expensive. Some of the houses are so large, with eight or nine bedrooms, that they have been divided into flats for upwardly mobile couples who will pay over £185,000 for something stylish with two bedrooms, marble fireplaces, balcony, ceiling mouldings and a drawing room with shutters. Most of these huge old places have coach houses at the back to serve as garages. In Cliftonville, many of the 10-bedroom Victorian mansions overlooking The Downs have been converted into offices. It has good independent schools – Clifton High for girls and Clifton for both sexes. A four-storey

Victorian house here would cost around £650,000 to £750,000. A four-bedroom Victorian terrace in Cliftonwood would cost £180,000 to £250,000.

Waterfront apartments, Bristol

More affordable but no less sought-after is the **Redland** area, offering a mix of Georgian, Victorian and Thirties in a distinctly bohemian atmosphere. The closer to the city centre you get, the more you feel the presence of students from Bristol University. A one-bedroom first floor flat in a Regency terrace in Redland, close to Clifton Downs, would be priced at around £90,000. A mid-terrace three-bedroom Edwardian house, or a charming four-bedroom town house, could be had for £220,000. The problems of getting to Temple Meads station are so acute, however, that people might prefer to drive out from here to Bristol Parkway (see page 161).

Another area worth considering, if you haven't got a family, is the Bristol **Docklands**. Huge new purpose-built Legoland-like developments are interspersed between old warehouse conversions. The idea is that if you live in Baltic Wharf or Merchant's Wharf you can get a river-taxi to Temple Meads station. One-bedroom flats cost around £95,000 with a view. Three-bedroom town-houses with a view are £235,000, without the view £180,000.

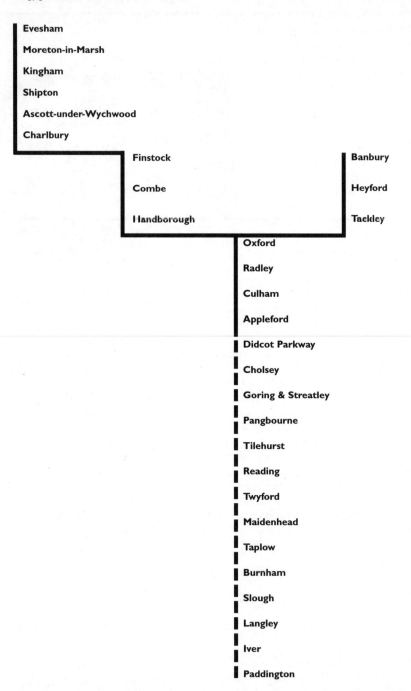

Evesham

Moreton-in-Marsh

Kingham

Shipton

Ascott-under-Wychwood

Charlbury

Finstock

Combe

Handborough

Banbury

Heyford

Tackley

Oxford

Radley

Culham

Appleford

Didcot Parkway

Cholsey

Goring & Streatley

Pangbourne

Tilehurst

Reading

Twyford

Maidenhead

Taplow

Burnham

Slough

Langley

Iver

Paddington

Paddington
→ **Oxford and Evesham**

For stations between Paddington and Didcot Parkway, see **Paddington to Bristol** line (page 147).

Appleford, Culham and Radley

Appleford is little more than a halt with a string of bunga- lows threaded to the railway line beside a good pub. **Long Wittenham** is a village in two halves, old and new, and is convenient for those who want to use The European School at **Culham**, which was established for the children of people working at the research station there. **Radley** has more trains serving it than the other two halts, but it is a bit betwixt and between to be really sought after. Its main feature is Radley College, the boys' public school.

Journey: 62 min, 81 min peak (from Radley)

Season: £3108 (all three stations)

Frequency: peak-hour trains from London in the evening, but none in the morning. Change at Didcot Parkway or Reading.

Oxford

Oxford can seem insufferably cliquey to some, but if you belong in some way to the publishing, university, hospital or industrial scenes then it is not too much of a problem. It was so nearly strangled by traffic that a new system has been introduced making it virtually impossible to drive into the centre. Park-and-ride is the way to do it. Travelling on the Oxford train can be a bit like attending a literary tea-party. As well as the city's obvious beauty, its schools are one of its greatest attractions to outsiders. Public schools abound – Magdalen College School, St Edward's, Radley College just outside, and the Oxford High and Headington School for girls. Prices in Oxford have simply blossomed in recent years.

Journey: 57 min
Season: £3108
Peak: 3 per hr
Off-peak: 2 per hr

The nicer bread-and-butter houses for those making a start in Oxford lie in **Osney** or **Jericho**, both within walking distance of the station. Osney is almost moated by a combination of the Thames and the canal. Two-bedroom Victorian

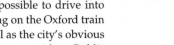

Private schools tend to grab the limelight, though there are some notable comprehensives

Schools in Oxfordshire

Private schools tend to grab the limelight, though there are some notable comprehensives. The latter include Lord William's at Thame and John Mason at Abingdon.

Oxford is the real educational powerhouse with a clutch of independent schools. Girls schools include the Oxford High (day), which tries to keep fees low, Headington for day-girls and boarders and Wychwood for girls, day and boarding. Boys have Magdalen College School and St Edward's, both for day-pupils and boarders.

Abingdon is the other bright spot. Here you find Radley, high in the public school firmament, for which you need to put your son's name down at birth, and Abingdon independent boys' day and boarding school, both keen on rowing. For girls there is the independent school of St Helen & St Katharine and Our Lady's Convent. Other girls independent schools around Oxfordshire include Tudor Hall at Banbury and St Mary's at Wantage. A good comprehensive can be found in Didcot Girls' at Didcot.

houses here sell for £170,000; three-bedroom houses for £200,000. Prices in Jericho are slightly higher, though the houses are small. Another area to consider is **Grand Pont**, where a Victorian house with three bedrooms would fetch £250,000.

For many, the only area to live is North Oxford, which is peppered with academics and successful professionals. It mushroomed in the 19th century after it was suddenly decided that dons should be allowed to marry. Huge Victorian houses on wide, tree-lined roads provided them with new homes, which now sell at around £850,000 to £1.2m There are just not enough of them to meet demand. Houses get smaller and slightly cheaper towards **Summertown**, where Cherwell comprehensive is a much-respected school, as is St Philip and St James' first school. **Wolvercote** village, a little further out, is particularly lovely, with The Trout Inn backing on to Port Meadow. Cheaper little brick-and-tile houses sell at around £150,000. There is a new development on which three-bedroom terrace houses sell at £190,000.

For many the *only* area to live is North Oxford, which is peppered with academics and successful professionals

Headington is popular with staff working at the hospital there, but it is the wrong side of Oxford for the station. Coaches heading for London (Victoria), stop there and many commuters use these instead. **Old Headington** and **Old Marston** are both charming old villages with crooked lanes and stone cottages that have been absorbed by the suburbs. Inhabitants tend to be rather rarefied. Pretty cottages in either might sell for £300,000 to £400,000. Oxford's equivalent of a stockbroker belt – large detached houses with the occasional tennis court or pony paddock – lies outside at **Hinksey**, **Cumnor** and **Boars Hill**. A Thirties house with five bedrooms, three bathrooms, lofts, outbuildings, swimming pool and over two acres of formal gardens in a woodland setting could be bought for around £750,000 to £1m on Boars Hill.

Line from **Oxford** to **Banbury**

Oxford is so strangled by traffic that new through trains from **Tackley** (68 minutes to Paddington, season ticket £3,108) and **Heyford** (72 minutes to Paddington, season ticket £3,108) now make this side of Oxford very appealing. **Steeple Aston**, a grey stone-walled village above the Cherwell, is definitely worth looking at. It has a village shop and post office, a choral society, Scouts and the Steeple Aston Players, who put on productions of plays written by local people. Commuters generally try to join in. The area is seriously horsey. **Hopcroft's Halt** nearby is where the French highwayman Claude Duval clattered about on his horse. The American Air Force Base at **Upper Heyford** used to cause noise nuisance but now that it has closed the great worry is that 1,000 new houses will be built there instead.

Then there are the **Tews** (**Great**, **Little** and **Duns**). Great Tew is particularly prized because it was a celebrated time-warp village (due to a neglectful previous owner it almost missed out on the 20th century). The combination of stone and thatch, punctuated by greens and clumps of ornamental trees, and the grey telephone kiosk (red would have spoiled it) seduced BBC location hunters when they were searching for somewhere to film the new production of *David Copperfield*. Even the overhead cables have been buried to keep the time-forgot atmosphere. Residents aren't antiques, however, and plenty of newcomers have arrived. A tiny two-bedroom cottage will cost £130,000 to £150,000.

For **Banbury** and **Leamington Spa**, see **Marylebone to Leamington Spa**, pages 144 and 145 for main entry. Through trains now take you to Paddington via Oxford on this line in 90 minutes (season ticket £3,132) during peak hours, but trains are scarce at other times.

The Steeple Aston Players put on productions of plays written by local people

From Banbury
Journey: 90 min
Season: £3132 (also valid to Marylebone)
Peak: 1 per hr (but only 1 every 2 hrs in the evening)
Off-peak: irregular (1 per hr at times, but with some 3-hr gaps)

Line from **Oxford** to **Evesham**

This line takes you to what many people think is the most beautiful side of Oxford to live, where villages of golden stone rise up from the fields. The skip-hop service to **Charlbury**, **Kingham** and **Moreton-in-Marsh** (better served than **Handborough**, **Combe**, **Finstock**, **Ascott-under-Wychwood** and **Skipton**, which are sandwiched in between them) has become more frequent in recent years. There are now many more through trains that run from Evesham to Paddington and stop at these three stations. Otherwise you have to get the local train and change at Oxford.

Charlbury

Journey: 72 min (61 min peak)

Season: £3896

Peak: 2 per hr

Off-peak: 1 per hr

This area is a tapestry of extraordinarily lovely villages. You have to watch for those which are under the Oxford influence and hence more expensive than those further afield. **Charlbury** is very elegant and has a few business units in the stables of Cornbury Park, Lord Rotherwick's estate. Modern three-bedroom boxes can be bought for £95,000, or four-bedroom period cottages for £250,000 to £300,000. It is just too far from Oxford to be really expensive, or to appeal to the young, who say they can find nothing to do in Charlbury.

Woodstock, which in Elizabethan times was the glove-making capital of the area, is slightly more expensive. Its old stone houses lie closer to Oxford and it is only two miles from **Combe** station. In summer it swarms with visitors who browse through it on their way to Blenheim Palace, eat at the Bear Hotel and walk along the banks of the River Glyme. **Bladon**, just apart from it, is more remarkable still. Its collection of ancient cottages is crowned by the elegant 15th-century chimneys of the old malthouse, and it is scarcely a mile from **Handborough** station. Sir Winston Churchill is buried here.

Cotswold house, near Moreton-in-Marsh

One of the best-liked small towns west of Oxford is **Witney**, which is rather less rarefied than some of the villages that surround it. Its fortunes were built on the blanket industry, which employed the waters of the Windrush and the wool from local sheep. It is a refreshing mix of old and new property, with greens at either end, raised pavements studded with limes, and modern shopfronts elbowing in between their Georgian neighbours. The central market place and the old covered butter cross give it a strong heart. Though it is only three miles from **Finstock** station, a lot of commuters from here choose to drive. The town is just off the A40, which now links easily to the M40. There are long rows of old blanket workers' cottages that sell for around £130,000 each. A huge new housing estate has mushroomed on the western flank, on which houses sell for between £70,000 and £250,000. More are to come to the north-east.

Kingham

The winding lanes, banked by streams and meadows overlooking the woodlands of the Evenlode valley, can make you feel quite isolated here. **Kingham** and all the villages around it are cut in fudge-coloured stone, with the occasional outcrop of council houses at the edge. People tolerate the longer commute to London from here because it is just out of reach of the Oxford influence and therefore cheaper. A handsome four-bedroom stone house could be bought for around £300,000; three bedrooms for £235,000; a smaller terrace for around £120,000.

Journey: 81 min
(71 min peak)
Season: £4148
Peak: 2 per hr
Off-peak: 1 per hr

The **Wychwoods** (**Milton-Under**, **Shipton-Under** and **Ascott-Under**) are closer to Oxford and slightly more expensive. Ascott-Under-Wychwood has its own station, served by regional trains running from Evesham to Oxford. Many people moving to the area will aim for the catchment of the popular Burford comprehensive school. A stone house with beamed ceilings, stone mullioned windows with leaded lights, Tudor fireplaces and five to six bedrooms might sell for around £400,000.

It qualified for extra coal rations because it was the coldest place in the region

Bourton-on-the-Water, though a model Cotswold village with its own model village, pushes commuter tolerance a little since it is about 10 miles from Kingham station. But with it come the **Slaughters** (**Lower** and **Upper**), the Lower set upon a stream that wriggles through little stone bridges and the Upper being right on the banks of the Windrush. Locals tend to be farmers, retired couples or craftsmen who don't mind being miles from anywhere. The nearest local shopping centre is **Chipping Norton**, an old market town where the huge old Bliss tweed mill was restored and sold as flats (priced at between £200,000 for two bedrooms and £250,000 for three). It has a reputation for being wet and windy. Locals say it qualified for extra coal rations in the war because it was the coldest place in the region.

Moreton-in-Marsh

Journey: 89 min (79 min peak)
Season: £4460
Peak: 2 per hr
Off-peak: 1 per hr

The perfection of towns such as **Moreton-in-Marsh** and **Stow-on-the-Wold** has meant torture by tourism. They seethe in summer and subside in winter. "The only people who live there are old dears in unmodernised houses who freeze every winter, or those involved in the tourist industry, or the very rich, who can spend the hundreds of thousands necessary to

Terrace cottages, Broadway

The area has proved popular with Londoners who swapped their Victorian terraces for the country, bringing higher prices with them

buy one of the lovely big country houses," says one local resident. That said, the area proved very popular with Londoners during the Nineties who swopped their Victorian terraces for the country, bringing higher prices with them. A little mid-17th-century cottage with three bedrooms would hit the market with an asking price of around £200,000. Large country houses can run into millions.

In Stow-on-the-Wold antique dealers have a dominating presence but there are two butchers, a bakery, two small supermarkets and a Tesco has arrived. A two-bedroom cottage could cost £120,000 to £140,000, a three-bedroom terrace on a new development £170,000.

Broadway and **Chipping Campden** are both beautiful towns, built mainly of stone. Chipping Campden attracts elderly people retiring from Birmingham, and it brims with local activities. The Chipping Campden Society looks after the historic buildings, and there are drama, hockey and football clubs. It has two primary schools and a comprehensive which brings in children from surrounding villages by the coachload. The 14th-century Woolstaplers Hall used to contain an interesting little local museum and tiny cinema but has recently closed.

Evesham

Though not a great many people would choose to commute daily from **Evesham**, many might consider part-time commuting. Its tree-lined walks, lawns along the Avon and some wonderful old buildings give it obvious charm. It also has two golf clubs. Property prices are lower here than up in the Cotswolds. A three-bedroom Victorian terrace might sell for £85,000; a three-bedroom modern detached house on an estate for £100,000. Two-bedroom cottages can be found in the surrounding villages for £115,000 to £120,000, with older four-bedroom detached houses costing over £150,000.

Journey: 104 min
(96 min peak)
Season: £4956
Peak: 1 per hr
Off-peak: 1 per hr

The Pershore side is particularly pretty, with picturesque black-and-white villages such as **Charlton**, **Cropthorne** and **Fladbury** (where the canoe club is run by a British national coach; it sends members to the Olympics). Fladbury tends to attract Birmingham rather than London commuters. The three new housing developments draw a constant flow of new people. It has an award-winning butcher, a florist, and a church primary school for five- to eight-year-olds. The middle school is in the neighbouring village of Pinvin, and the secondary is in Evesham. Further north of Evesham is another black-and-white village, **Norton**. It was once ruined by traffic on the A435, but has now been rescued with a bypass. The **Lenches** (**Church** and **Atch**) are also popular on this northern flank.

For truly grand landscape, however, you should look to the west, in the villages beneath Bredon Hill. The **Combertons** (**Little** and **Great**) are especially lovely. **Great Comberton** has a heady mix of half-timbered farmhouses and thatched cottages, while Little Comberton has a village dovecote with walls over 3ft thick and more than 500 nesting holes. Another red-brick dovecote in the village is even bigger, with 1,425.

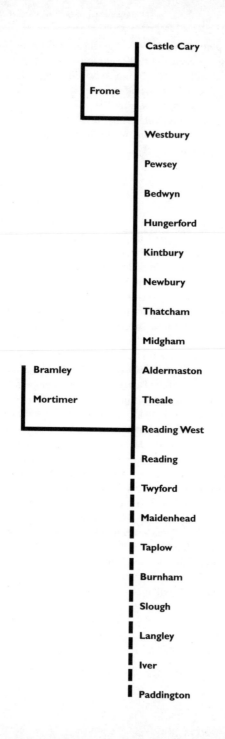

Castle Cary

Frome

Westbury

Pewsey

Bedwyn

Hungerford

Kintbury

Newbury

Thatcham

Midgham

Bramley
Mortimer
Aldermaston

Theale

Reading West

Reading

Twyford

Maidenhead

Taplow

Burnham

Slough

Langley

Iver

Paddington

Paddington ➡ Castle Cary

For stations between Paddington and Reading, see **Paddington to Bristol** line (page 147).

Reading West

Reading offers fast and frequent trains, a thriving commercial scene and reasonable house prices. Though it can't be described as particularly attractive, it lies within striking distance of beautiful countryside. For Reading main entry, see page 154.

Journey: 37 min
Season: £2600
Peak: 1 per hr
(plus 4 per hr, change at Reading)
Off-peak: 3 per hr (change at Reading)

Branch line to **Mortimer** and **Bramley**

Mortimer is the smaller and more rural of the two villages, but 100 new houses are planned and the parish council is hoping to screen them from view. A new minibus service to the station is a boon for commuters. Prices are quite high: £170,000 or more for a two-bedroom period cottage, £200,000 to £450,000 for a family house and large garden. **Bramley** is a linear dormitory village which grew up around the railway in the mid-1890s and has had to swallow a lot of new houses in the last few years. It has a green, a pond and a church. A two-bedroom flat on a new development will cost around £85,000, a larger three-bedroom semi £135,000.

No through trains.
Journey: 50 min
(from Bramley)
Season: £2620
Trains to Reading:
2 per hr

It is possible to go via Basingstoke to Waterloo (season £2568).

Reading offers fast trains and lies within striking distance of beautiful countryside

Continuation of main line
Theale

Journey: 54 min
Season: £2600
Peak: 1 per hr (plus
3 per hr, change at
Reading)
Off-peak: 1 per hr

Since getting into **Reading** is a nightmare, many people prefer to use **Theale** station instead. It marks the beginning of the Berkshire farming belt beyond Reading, yet is more accessible and gets the fast trains. The council has recently spent a large amount of money on restoring the town's Victorian image, reinstating cobbles and period lamp posts. Most of the main street, which has a butcher, baker, greengrocer and a few offices, is included within a conservation area.

Theale has accumulated large modern housing estates and an industrial area to the south, but environmentalists are thick on the ground and are fending off the considerable pressure for more development. A large business park accommodates major companies moving out of London, including Smiths Crisps and Panasonic. Another is planned, together with a new hotel. A new two-bedroom house is likely to cost around £115,000; three bedrooms £130,000. A turn-of-the-century, three-bedroom semi backing on to fields might fetch £150,000. Four-bedroom houses are in short supply.

Aldermaston

Journey: 49 min
Season: £2600
Peak: 2 per hr
Off-peak: 1 per hr
(change at
Reading)

Aldermaston is a very pretty village on the Kennet and Avon Canal, with a main street of red brick and timber houses sandwiched between Elizabethan cottages. To outsiders, however, it is best remembered as the starting point for the Ban the Bomb marches, chosen by protesters because of its proximity to the Atomic Weapons Research Establishment. Despite the traffic that thunders through it on the A340 to Basingstoke, the village has been well preserved. Until recently it was an estate village, and every third year on 13 December a candle auction is still held to determine the rent charged for a small piece of land called Church Acre – the end of the bidding is signalled by the extinction of a candle flame. The big house, Aldermaston Court, standing at one end of the main street, has been converted into offices. There is a parish hall, village green, store and post office. Bowls and cricket are played.

To outsiders, Aldermaston is best remembered as the starting point of the Ban the Bomb marches

The station itself is useful for shuttle services into Reading, whence fast trains to Paddington are plentiful. The proximity of the Atomic Weapons Research Establishment drags property prices down by 5% to 10%. Newcomers to the village graze the new Persimmon estate for purchases. A four-bedroom detached house can cost £190,000 to £270,000.

Midgham

Midgham station is actually in **Woolhampton**, but was renamed Midgham station in 1873 because of the likelihood of confusion with Wolverhampton. Most people drive to Thatcham anyway because there is only a handful of parking spaces at Midgham station. It is a linear village, "big in land but not in people," is how one resident puts it. There is, however, a good food-lover's pub called The Coach & Horses. You could buy a small period house for £220,000 to £230,000.

Woolhampton main street has half-timbered houses down one side and modern equivalents down the other, put up when the road was widened in 1931. The A4 and the railway thunder through making it too noisy to hear people speak. There are several shops, a post office, four pubs, an old forge and a fine watermill. A three-bedroom period house will cost around £170,000.

Journey: 53 min
Season: £2600
Peak: 2 per hr
Off-peak: 1 per hr
(change at Reading)

Thatcham

The old village of **Thatcham**, with the green at its centre, has swollen with new developments in the last couple of decades and more is yet to come. It has become a town, good for secondary shopping but Reading or Newbury (only two miles away) offer much more. The most sought-after new development is Dunston Park, within easy reach of the station and an established stamping grounds for professional couples and young families. Four-bedroom houses cost around £200,000. South Thatcham is less popular and sometimes less savoury (being close to the sewage works), so prices are lower. "Such a shame about the poo farm," says one agent. But lower prices mean good value and the average price for a four-bedroom house here is around £140,000.

Journey: 63 min
Season: £2600
Peak: 2 per hr
(plus 2 per hr, change at Reading)
Off-peak: 1 per hr

If you are not careful at Thatcham you can be stuck in your car at the crossing waiting for your own train to whoosh by

Thatcham station is served by the few through trains to London in the early morning. The snag is that you have to negotiate the level-crossing before you can park the car. "If you are not careful, you can be stuck in your car at the crossing waiting for your own train to whoosh by," says one exasperated commuter.

Cold Ash, a little over a mile north, is particularly popular, straggling fetchingly down a hill into the Kennet valley. It has about 2,300 residents, a community hall, a shop, a post office and some modern infilling. Property here sells quickly. You could expect to pay £290,000 for a four-bedroom bungalow; between £450,000 and £500,000 for a large five- to six-bedroom detached house in a couple of acres. The village of **Bucklebury** nearby, in an Area of Outstanding Natural Beauty, has some pretty cottages and a large common criss-crossed with footpaths. The Blade Bone pub has a copper-plated mammoth's shoulder bone on display, hence the name. Bradfield, the boys' public school, is close by. A small period cottage will cost £300,000, but anything larger with land attached will run up towards £1m. There is a curious little 17th-century painting of a fly and sundial in the local church, with the body and legs on one side of the glass and the wings on the other. *Tempus fugit* (time flies).

Newbury

From Newbury
Journey: 41 min
Season: £2648
Peak: 2 per hr (plus
2 per hr by chang-
ing at Reading)
Off-peak: 1-2 per
hr

**From Newbury
Racecourse**
Journey: 62 min
Season: £2648
Peak: 2 per hr*
Off-peak: 1 per hr
changing at
Reading
*A very restricted
return service
operates from
London.

Newbury is a prosperous former market town with a good train service to London, and attracts commuters like flies to a honeypot. It has a mass of pretty downland villages (*Watership Down* country) within reach and is positioned on the edge of the so-called Silicon Valley. The centre is mostly 17th- and 18th-century with a good range of shops, including an old-fashioned pork butcher and pie-maker. The Kennet & Avon canal provides scenic richness. Many people feel, however, that new buildings have erased all sense of the brick-and-tile traditional country town. Vodaphone has a massive presence (spread between 48 office buildings) and is planning to build a "business village" just outside to move into. "Fifty years ago I can remember cattle and sheep being driven in, and the circus arriving by train and walking from it through the town. It's hard to imagine any of that now," says one elderly resident.

A great mix of people are attracted to Newbury. Computer companies have brought in the upwardly-mobiles; the racecourse (which has its own weatherboarded train station) attracts the punters; the much-contested bypass has lured the protesters.

There is a shortage of two-bedroom houses for first-time buyers. Close to the centre you could find a two- or three-bedroom restored Victorian house for around £125,000. A standard executive house in Speen Lane could be bought for £230,000. In Garden Close or Tydehams, large houses built earlier this century in large private grounds will sell for £350,000 upwards.

Strings of racehorses in the narrow lanes can frustrate commuters driving to the station

The young tend to say that there isn't a lot to do in Newbury. Though there is a recreation centre and a swimming pool, the cinema has closed. Two new golf courses and a hotel have been built at **Donnington** just outside. The controversial bypass cuts a swathe straight across Enborne Chase, a beautiful belt of land south of the town. Villagers from as far to the north-west as **Lambourn** and as far south as **Hurstbourne Tarrant** will come in to use Newbury station. The National Hunt racehorse training centre is at Lambourn, so there are well over 1,000 horses in Lambourn and **Upper Lambourn** together, both busy working villages. Stable-hands work from about

Chalet-style house, Newbury

seven in the morning until midday, when they rush to the village to shop before starting work again at about four o'clock. Lambourn itself has a few general stores, a farm shop, butcher, delicatessen, post office and saddler. Upper Lambourn has very little other than a pub. A three-bedroom semi will cost £130,000. You need a car if you live here because buses to Newbury and Swindon are few. Strings of 20 to 30 horses, exercising in the narrow lanes across the rolling chalk hills, can frustrate commuters driving to the station to catch the early morning trains.

Eastbury, on the River Lambourn two miles closer to Newbury, is also a lovely village with a good pub, The Plough. Houses are built on the riverbanks, cleverly planted with shrubs and bulbs. It is a popular place to retire to. An old three-bedroom thatched house on the river would sell for around £250,000; a Sixties bungalow £220,000. In the neighbouring village of **East Garston**, you find another enchanting village full of thatched houses, with three stables, a shop-cum-post-office and house prices similar to Eastbury.

Further east are two more good chalk villages, **West** and **East Ilsley**, just off the A34. East Ilsley, slightly cheaper of the two, has a central square with a pond, and has resisted new developments apart from some sheltered housing for the elderly. Village life has changed dramatically over the years. This used to be the site of a twice-yearly sheep fair (the greatest sheep market in England after Smithfield, they say) and there were 13 pubs. Today only three pubs remain, and the place is largely inhabited by commuters. It has a shop-cum-post office, and all the walks that the nearby Downs can offer, including the Ridgeway, along which Neolithic and Bronze Age man once commuted. West Ilsley is the pretty cousin, with a church at its heart, a village green, cricket pitch and pavilion, a racing stables owned until recently by the Queen, and a good collection of cottages. It has a post office and a pub. Its social life tends to be dominated by the horse-racing fraternity. A four-bedroom period house set in half an acre would sell for around £300,000.

Stanford Dingley, set in the valley of the River Pang a good six miles to the north-east, is thought to be one of Berkshire's most beautiful villages. It has a classic mellow red-brick Georgian rectory, a 13th-century church screened by chestnuts, and two old inns called The Bull and The Boot. At The Bull a game called "Ring The Bull" is played, in which a ring

> **Prices are so high that an affordable housing scheme has been set up for villagers**

dangling from the ceiling has to be swung on to a horn. "We're an active village," says the parish clerk. "We have barn dancing and play boules on the little green opposite The Bull. We hold summer fêtes, usually in someone's garden. The River Pang runs through some of the gardens and at the fêtes we hold a tug of war over it, so that the losers fall in." Houses rarely come on the market because people tend to stay put. A typical early Victorian brick house with three or four bedrooms might be bought for under £400,000.

Yattendon, just north of the M4, has a picture-book village square surrounded by black-and-white 17th-century homes, backed up by Cromwellian red-brick houses. The partly-moated manor house, the church, rectory and malt house all look immaculately cared for. Robert Graves's ashes are in the churchyard. Yattendon has a general store and post office, butcher, hairdresser, smithy, The Royal Oak Hotel and a restaurant. Socially it remains fairly feudal. There are tennis courts and a cricket pitch. The village fête is the main annual event. Property prices here are so high that an affordable housing scheme has been set up to provide 12 houses at lower cost for native villagers. A modern four-bedroom detached house might cost £400,000. A house with six bedrooms in two acres will fetch £750,000 or more.

Much closer to Newbury, two miles north, is the village of **Bagnor**. It is scattered charmingly around a tributary of the Lambourn and remains fairly unspoilt, with a green, a pub called The Blackbird and a little theatre and restaurant, The Watermill, which attracts good productions. **Leckhampstead** also has a star quality setting, high above the Wantage to Newbury road, and wears its thatched cottages proudly around the small green.

Heading south you come to **Highclere** on the main Andover road, where houses range from £250,000 for four bedrooms to £280,000 for three bedrooms in a period cottage and half an acre. **Ecchinswell** is a handsome neighbour where a period four-bedroom cottage will cost around £300,000.

Kintbury

Journey: 76 min
Season: £2764
Peak: 2 per hr
Off-peak: 1 per hr

Kintbury is an unremarkable and yet endearingly compact and likeable village. It sits on the Kennet and Avon canal deep in agricultural Berkshire, where its position attracts an element of tourism. There is a full range of house types and prices, from new developments for first-time buyers to executive detached houses. Locals fear that too many commuters who don't join in village activities are moving in and sending prices "through the roof". Anything with three bedrooms will now cost £250,000 and even a starter home starts at £110,000.

Two miles away is **Inkpen**, a village strung out so thinly that you can't locate its centre (six hamlets have merged imperceptibly over the centuries). It is worth looking at, however, because of its position in the shadow of the Berkshire Downs. Steep winding lanes carry you hundreds of feet up to magical windy walks, and panoramic views from the gibbet on Walbury Hill.

Hungerford

Being just off the M4, **Hungerford** is a favourite starting-place for house-hunters in the area. It is on the twee side of pretty, with a pleasant wide High Street stretching down to the Kennet and Avon Canal and the River Kennet. The tea and trinket shops of tourism are combined with upmarket interior design shops and day-to-day needs. It is the local antiques capital, and has an antiques arcade which is open on Sundays. Cattle graze the huge 180-acre common – given by John of Gaunt in the 14th century – which gives way to chalk downs and wooded hills beyond.

Journey: 81 min	
Season: £2832	
Peak: 2 per hr	
Off-peak: 1 per hr	

The community is close and tightly knit. As the mayor says: "We have a cracking cricket team, a football team, choir, theatre club, band, good nursery school and so on. People get involved here. All the time something is happening, making it all tick." Ancient rituals are still observed. On the first Tuesday after Easter the Tutti men tour the town extracting kisses from all the women in return for oranges. There is also an arts festival and in December there is a pre-Christmas Victorian Extravaganza.

Black-and-white period house, Hungerford area

On the High Street you can buy older two-bedroom terrace houses for around £110,000. A larger four-storey Georgian house would fetch around £500,000. Standard four-bedroom houses on modern developments can be had for £200,000. But pressure on housing is a sensitive issue here. Plans to build 500 new houses were abandoned after every single person present voted against the plan at a public meeting.

The train service is good enough until about eight o'clock in the morning. After that the number of London trains dwindles to about one every hour or hour-and-a-half. Within easy reach of Hungerford is the village of **Chilton**

Tutti men tour the town extracting kisses from all the women in return for oranges

Foliat, a set-piece combination of brick, slate and thatch, with one shop and a pub. A three-bedroom thatched cottage on the main street would fetch £250,000. **Little Bedwyn**, on the Kennet and Avon canal, is lovely, too. It has an outstanding 18th-century farmhouse in chequered brick-work, with a rare octagonal game larder. The farmyard, with timber and brick barns, is right in the village centre. A four-bedroom Victorian detached house will cost £295,000.

Bedwyn

Journey: 88 min
Season: £2916
Peak: 2 per hr
Off peak: 1 per hr

Beyond this point the number of trains is much reduced. Beside the Kennet and Avon canal towpath is the Crofton Pumping Station, which houses the two oldest steam engines in the world that are still in working order. They are used to raise the water level in the canal. A large four-bedroom Victorian house with a good garden in **Great Bedwyn** will cost around £295,000.

Pewsey

Journey: 56 min
Season: £3760
Peak: 1 per hr
Off-peak: 1 approx
every 4 hrs

Daily commuters become rather thin on the ground here. The trains that serve it are mostly InterCity services from the west. There are special commuter trains each morning and evening. Otherwise it is always possible to get a train to Newbury and change.

Pewsey is a pretty agricultural town between Salisbury Plain and the Marlborough Downs. Some of the shops are still roofed in thatch, and a statue of Alfred the Great stands in the centre, overlooking the young River Avon and its resident ducks. It has a few supermarkets, estate agents, banks, bakery and so on, and its own comprehensive school, playing fields and swimming pool. The old hospital has been converted and the grounds filled with new houses. One of Wiltshire's six white horses was cut into the chalk hillside in 1785 and provides a potent local landmark.

A three-bedroom thatched cottage here could be bought for £175,000 to £200,000; a four-bedroom detached Victorian house for £300,000. Just outside the town is a Charles Church development where little two-bedroom houses are priced at £100,000; four-bedroom detached at £200,000.

The pretty villages nearby include **Manningford Bruce**, two miles away, where thatched cottages cluster around the church. A small house here could be bought for around £145,000. The whole of this area is classified as an Area of Outstanding Natural Beauty. A few miles to the north-west you come to **Stanton St Bernard**. The Pewsey Valley Riding Centre is here, and there are lots of weekend cottages and larger country houses. A four-bedroom detached Victorian house will cost around £300,000; a two-bedroom mid-terrace would be closer to £115,000.

Urchfont, though a little far from the station (nearly 10 miles west), is also extremely popular. It contains all the ingredients of the ideal village – thatched cottages, a couple of good pubs, 16th- and 17th-century houses around the greens, one of which is next to the church and has a duck pond. There is also a William and Mary manor house. A three-bedroom cottage on the green will cost £250,000; a five-bedroom house £350,000.

One of the advantages of living to the west is that you are within reach of **Devizes**, which is so attractive that it is a treat to go shopping there. The market square is surrounded by houses which are older than their Georgian facades. The town has good small butchers and bakers, a large Safeway on the outskirts and a new shopping centre planned. A small period terrace house will cost around £65,000; a three-bedroom period property £120,000. The Kennet and Avon Canal has a flight of locks, 29 over a two-mile stretch, rising 237ft to the town.

Marlborough is dominated by the boys' public school (it now takes some girls) and the tea-rooms where they buy their sticky buns

Less than three miles to the north-east of Pewsey is **Wootton Rivers**, where you pay a premium for prettiness. A three-bedroom thatched cottage here costs around £200,000 to £220,000 There is only one street, running up from the bridge over the Kennet and Avon Canal. Along the towpath you will find the lock and lock-house, both of which have recently been restored. The character of the place is so rural that even the churchyard seems merely an interruption in the farming landscape. The church itself is distinguished by a wooden belfry containing an unusual clock with a broomstick for a pendulum. Just to the north, for those in search of sylvan solitude, are the 2,300 acres of Savernake Forest.

East Grafton, a few miles further east towards Hungerford, offers slightly larger houses than some of the other villages. A thatched house with five bedrooms, stables and a few acres would cost over £500,000. The A338 runs through it, but it keeps away from the village proper, where there is a large green and a Victorian church edged with thatched cottages.

To the north is **Marlborough**, the old halt for 18th-century stage coaches on the run from London to Bath. Today the town is dominated by the boys' public school (it now takes girls) and the tea rooms where they buy their sticky buns. Marlborough is an extremely popular place in which to live – it is close enough to the M4 at Swindon, it has a good range of small specialist shops and is surrounded by spectacular countryside.

Thatch is noticeably absent. Terrible fires in the 17th century resulted in it being banned. The town has a Georgian feel, though there are plenty of half-timbered houses hidden down the small back lanes off the broad open High Street. A four-bedroom detached Georgian house might be had for £250,000 to £500,000. Two-bedroom Victorian terrace cottages sell at around £100,000 to £125,000. Apart from the leisure centre, there is very little for the young in Marlborough. The church is strong. There is a Church of England Society, a choral society, civic society and railway society that has restored the old railway track to Swindon as a cycle path. The Scouts and Cubs have taken it upon themselves to clean the chalk outlines of the white horses in the area.

Westbury

Journey: 70 min
Season: £5484
Peak: 1 per hr
Off-peak: 1 every 2 hrs

The train service is frankly thought to be better from Bath than it is from here. **Westbury** was once a charming small town (it still has a wonderful Victorian swimming pool), with Georgian houses grouped around the market place and church, but it has been swamped by new housing. Blue Circle cement has replaced the old glove-making industry as the dominant local employer. There are a few shops to meet basic needs: butcher, greengrocers, bank and supermarket with post office. Two-bedroom starter homes can be bought for £55,000, and three-bedroom semis for £72,000, though they tend to be small. High above Westbury stands the oldest white horse in Wiltshire, believed to have commemorated King Alfred's victory over the Danes in the ninth century.

Bratton, a couple of miles to the east, offers sleepy lanes where a small stream runs past some of the old cottages tucked into the hedgerows. The village has a post office, a store and a school. A 200-year-old three-bedroom cottage here would sell for around £135,000 to £175,000; a modern four-bedroom house for £165,000 to £200,000. **Edington** is similar, though more remote. This area is rather far from any large town so prices tend to be lower and commuting is rigorous. The number of daily commuters probably totals no more than a dozen.

Frome

Journey: 110 min peak; 120 min off-peak
Season: £5404
Peak: 1 per hr
Off-peak: 1 every 2hrs, poor connections
No through trains. London passengers must change at Westbury.

Frome is neither quite in the best countryside close to Bath nor in the most beautiful part of Wiltshire. It has a distinct character, however, with lots of stone buildings set on the steep eastern hillsides of the Mendips. The old market place is still there, though the cattle market moved out a few years ago. Its shopping centre is unimaginative, but the Black Swan art gallery is much admired and Sainsbury has made its presence felt on the edge of town. The narrow, twisted streets are worth walking through just to admire. The most famous of them is Cheap Street, which is cobbled and has a watercourse running down the centre.

An old terrace cottage with three bedrooms will cost £80,000 in the conservation area just off the centre. Modern estate homes on the outskirts range from two-bedroom flats at £35,000 to four-bedroom detached houses at £110,000 to £140,000. Trains are not frequent from Frome – the station is on the loop served by trains from Weymouth.

To the west and south-west are several villages that teeter on the edges of the old stone quarries. When you look, bear in mind that there are plans to expand the quarries at Whatley and Leigh upon Mendip. Three miles north is **Lullington**, a very pretty

Late Victorian house, near Frome

little hamlet with a green and a church but no shops, where an old stone house with three bedrooms might be had for £130,000.

Castle Cary

This is long-haul commuting, but people do it. Parking at the station is easy, and you can pick up the trains pelting back and forth to the Devon seaside. **Castle Cary** sits on the last few ripples of the Mendips before the relentless flatlands of the Somerset Levels. The town owes much of its

Journey: 89 min
Season: £5900
Peak: 1 per hr
Off-peak: 1 approx every 4 hrs

prosperity to agriculture and the horse-hair weaving trade. There is still a weaver in the town, though the hair is now imported from China. The remains of the old motte-and-bailey castle that gave the town its name are still here, and a small market is held on Thursday.

The mellow, golden local stone is what makes people fall in love with the place. There are a few traditional shops, a thatched hotel called The George and a notable rectory just outside at **Ansford**, which was once the home of the Reverend James Woodforde, author of *Diary of A Country Parson*. A three-bedroom period cottage would cost around £125,000. Larger hous-es lie on the edge of the town where something with three to four bed-rooms, a paddock and views across the fields would cost £220,000. A peri-od farmhouse would cost over £300,000. There are some modern estates on the outskirts, where a retirement bungalow costs around £110,000 and a modern, detached four-bedroom house £130,000.

Commuters necessarily have to live very close in to the station because of the length of the journey. A clutch of villages within the five-mile belt include the stone villages of **North** and **South Cadbury**, and **Yarlington**, which is a good agricultural working village with a mix of modern and old houses, priced very similarly to those in Castle Cary. To the north-west is **Ditcheat**, also a good working village. This is dairy country – rich, green and undulating – where much of the milk goes to butter and cheese-mak-ing factories.

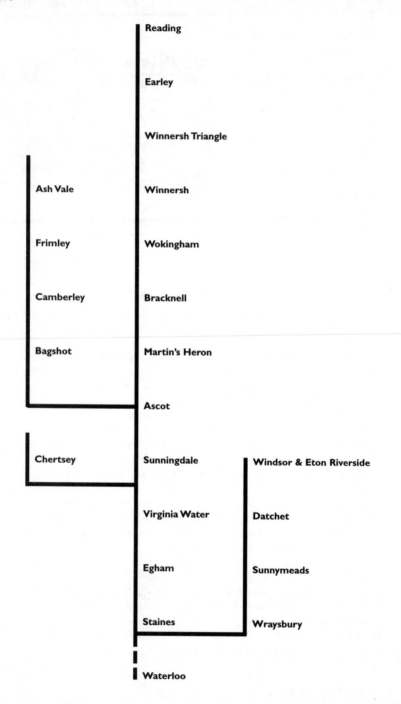

Reading

Earley

Winnersh Triangle

Ash Vale   Winnersh

Frimley   Wokingham

Camberley   Bracknell

Bagshot   Martin's Heron

                  Ascot

Chertsey   Sunningdale   Windsor & Eton Riverside

                  Virginia Water   Datchet

                  Egham   Sunnymeads

                  Staines   Wraysbury

Waterloo

Waterloo ➡ Reading

Staines

Staines has been an important communications point ever since the Romans established a river crossing here on their route from London to the west. Not all subsequent bridges have been successful – three of them had collapsed by the end of the 18th century. The present one, opened by William IV in 1832, survives despite the heavy traffic from the A30 and M25. A surprisingly small station car park, accommodating only 50 or so cars, means that the surrounding roads are clogged by all-day parkers. Commuters often prefer to travel from other stations if they can. There is a wide range of housing. Large developments offer flats and houses from £65,000 for a studio, £105,000 for a two-bedroom flat, £135,000 to £160,000 for a three-bedroom semi and £230,000 for a four-bedroom detached. Staines is one of Surrey's three main shopping centres. It keeps up to date and is augmented by new arts entertainment venues including a 10-screen Warner Brothers multiplex, health club and restaurants. The street market is on Wednesday and Saturday. The riverside is full of potential and the small roads leading off Laleham Road to the water are sought after. There is a sailing and a rowing club and plans for a new riverside park with a town pier, restaurants and pleasure boats.

Journey: 31 min	
Season: £1624	
Peak: 8 per hr	
Off-peak: 6 per hr	

Three bridges at Staines had collapsed by the end of the 18th century

Laleham, on the way to Shepperton, is the most favoured village, spread along a sizeable stretch of riverside. It has its own cricket club and a few basics, including a small grocery, antiques shop and three pubs, and what one local called a "cliquey atmosphere but a nice clique. Everyone gets on well". In the village centre which is predominantly Victorian a large four-bedroom detached house could be bought for £200,000.

A cliquey atmosphere but a nice clique. Everyone gets on well

Spur to **Windsor & Eton Riverside** via **Wraysbury, Sunnymeads** and **Datchet**

Wraysbury

Journey: 42 min
Season: £1708
Peak: 2 per hr
Off-peak: 1 per hr

Wraysbury spreads itself rather wantonly and has several distinguishing characteristics. It has two stations – Sunnymeads, only a mile away (see below), still counts as Wraysbury – and three miles of water frontage. It is surrounded by gravel pits which have been landscaped into 60 acres of lakes, providing sanctuaries for wildlife and a magnet for birdwatchers and sailing clubs. Until recently 80% of the houses were detached and individually built, though as a relatively new village it was rather looked down upon in its early days. Most roads are privately maintained by the residents, many of whom work at Heathrow which sends planes straight overhead. The M4 skirts the village without spoiling it, and counts as a convenience rather than a drawback. Wraysbury at one time was a weekend retreat for Londoners and there were many riverside shanties. These have given way to houses in the £350,000 to £650,000 bracket. There is a sprinkling of pre-Georgian cottages, a few Edwardian and Victorian terraces and some substantial small mansions. Modern three- and four-bedroom houses on a Barratt's development will cost £250,000 to £350,000. Wraysbury Hall, in a plum position on the river, was on the market recently at £2m. Surrounding green belt should provide protection against future development. There is a handful of local shops, including a pharmacy which makes its own aromatherapy remedies, a post office and a village green. One of the major features of life in Wraysbury is the number and quality of the local societies. These offer every option from cricket and fishing to history, drama, country & western and jazz – all well attended and well organised. Opposite the village is the island where Magna Carta was signed.

Opposite the village is the island where Magna Carter was signed

Sunnymeads

Journey: 44 min
Season: £1756
Peak: 2 per hr
Off-peak: 1 per hr

Sunnymeads, Wraysbury's second station, is on the boundary between Wraysbury and **Horton**, which is a rural village with a green, one shop and two pubs, both listed. It has proud historical connections with John Milton, who wrote some of his poems here, and with the Bowes-Lyon family. The local forge built the equestrian statue of George III, known as the Copper Horse, which stands on Snow Hill in Windsor Great Park. The snag is that the village lies directly in the path of most flights approaching Heathrow airport. "They fly over the listed buildings. As they bank, you see sprays of fuel coming out. Trees suddenly die but we keep on planting," said one local. The mix of properties ranges from a handful of listed houses to ex-council semis. Bell's Lane is a leafy haven where a three-bedroom semi would sell at around £150,000.

Datchet

Only a mile from Windsor, **Datchet** has avoided being overshadowed and retains a village personality. Physically it is compact and shaped like a letter H with two cross-bars. The left of the H is on the river (one of the ports of call in Jerome K. Jerome's *Three Men in a Boat*); the right is on the village green and the two cross-bars are High Street and Queens Road. The railway runs up the middle, regularly halting traffic at the level crossing (including government ministers complete with police outriders on their way to see the Queen at Windsor).

Journey: 45 min	
Season: £1780	
Peak: 2 per hr	
Off-peak: 2 per hr	

Until recently, most of the houses here were in the upper price bracket. In the last 15 years, however, new estates aimed at first-time buyers have appeared. Studios and one-bedroom terraces cost between £50,000 and £80,000. Elsewhere three-bedroom semis are from £150,000 to £200,000; detached houses with 150ft gardens and 45ft frontages over £250,000. Southlea Road is desirable and has some large 18th-century houses at £500,000 or more. Datchet has always attracted London commuters and there is a large station car park. The other strong connection is with Heathrow: both ground-staff and aircrew favour the village for its pleasant atmosphere and easy access to the airport. Datchet's charms have also attracted a share of past and present celebrities, including Sir William Herschel, the astronomer, Sir Robert Watson-Watt, the inventor of radar, and now a clutch of ageing showbiz personalities. There is a post office, a Montessori, local primary and secondary schools. Other social hubs include a local golf club with a long waiting list, a water-ski club, cricket (sometimes the village musters a showbiz eleven), sailing and a boatyard on the river which does daily hire.

Windsor & Eton Riverside

Windsor & Eton Riverside is **Windsor's** second station, a slightly slower route to London than the shuttle from Windsor & Eton Central to Slough (which picks up the InterCity service from London to Paddington). Commuters from both stations benefit from Windsor's attractive mix of quaint old streets below the castle and smart new shops – everything from

Journey: 49 min	
Season: £1800*	
Peak: 2 per hr	
Off-peak: 2 per hr	
*£1928 if also valid at Windsor & Eton Central.	

Dutch-style
family house,
near Egham

old family businesses to chain and department stores. It also has the 4,800 acres of Windsor Great Park close by. Apart from a few Georgian houses on Castle Hill, the centre of the town is composed mainly of Victorian terraces. A small cottage in need of improvement will cost £130,000 to £150,000; a three-bedroom house within walking distance of the town centre £200,000 and half as much again if very charming. The west and south of Windsor evolved in the Thirties and Fifties – semis now cost from £140,000 to £150,000. Development is restricted by Crown lands and green belt. However, a large new estate is to be built a mile outside on old Haileybury School grounds.

The most fashionable locations are St Leonard's Hill, King's Road, Queen's Acre, Adelaide Square and Bolton Avenue. Laing Homes is selling new four- to five-bedroom houses at King's Keep on Bolton Avenue for £475,000 and more smaller houses are being built. Nothing here is tailor-made for first-time buyers, who gravitate to Bracknell or Slough. The Guild Hall in the High Street includes a marvellous bit of architectural deception by Christopher Wren. When the town councillors saw his plans in 1687, they apparently demanded more columns to support the upper floor (and their own combined weight). Wren obliged, up to a point. The new columns all ended slightly short of the ceiling.

Eton is full of antique shops, restaurants, and schoolboys in wing collars and tailcoats

Old Windsor, south-east of the town, was described in the Domesday Book as the third largest town in Berkshire. It had a wooden Saxon palace which deteriorated after William built his castle, when it was reduced to a village. Today it is a small town with parades of shops, a post office, a bank and a convenient bus service into Windsor for major shopping. Large detached houses, some with river frontages, are a main feature of the market. The Friary is the road to aim for – Victorian houses in good sized grounds at £350,000 to £450,000. The main road is fringed with Twenties-built houses from £150,000, one or two large enough to satisfy those who want a private estate close to London. These are rare sightings in estate agents' windows, with price tags over £750,000. Elton John occupies one. Two large housing estates provide less expensive homes, priced slightly lower than their equivalents in Windsor where communications are better. Those who choose Old Windsor do so for its more rural atmosphere and its lively community with plenty of sporting and social opportunities.

Eton is full of antique shops, restaurants and schoolboys in wing collars and tailcoats. Inevitably, there is something of an us-and-them atmosphere. A three-bedroom Victorian house on the High Street could cost £300,000; a modern town house with three or four bedrooms down by the river £350,000. On one of the side roads off the High Street you might find a two-up-two-down Victorian house with small garden at £190,000.

Continuation of main line

Egham

Although **Egham** technically is a small town it retains an unhurried atmosphere from its village past. While Staines across the river is still bustling after dark, Egham shuts at 5.30pm and puts its feet up. There is a 17th-century coaching inn but most of the building is Victorian, some of it rather neglected. There are some new estates suitable for first-time buyers, however, where one-bedroom flats cost from £80,000. Two-bedroom Victorian semis in the town centre start at £140,000. The town has a good mix of local shopping, including a butcher and a baker whose families have been serving the community for more than 100 years. There are plenty of sports and social clubs, and an active conservation society.

Journey: 36 min
Season: £1708
Peak: 3 per hr
Off-peak: 4 per hr

To the west, **Englefield Green** is a prestigious address thought by some as rather twee. It comes with a green, traditional pub and little high street of shops including a baker. A two-bedroom terrace cottage will cost £140,000. To the south is **Thorpe**, a village bisected by the M25. Despite this apparent handicap, houses here are 15% or so more expensive than their equivalents in Egham. The smallest two-bedroom Victorian semi will cost around £160,000, and there is a preponderance of large houses in spacious plots. A four-bedroom detached house built in the Thirties or Fifties will fetch between £250,000 and £300,000; a four-bedroom 16th-century former pub and bakery sold recently for £380,000. There is a theme park just outside the village but the traffic to it does not pass through the village itself.

Virginia Water

Journey: 40 min
Season: £1800
Peak: 2 per hr*
Off-peak: 2 per hr*
* Additional trains
available by chang-
ing at Weybridge.

Virginia Water, brushed by the M25, has seen two enormous new developments in the last few years. Virginia Park and St Anne's Park are super-luxurious gated estates, each with a communal pool, gym, Jacuzzi, tennis courts and other Dallas touches. Their very presence has pushed prices up. A two-bedroom flat here will cost £300,000 (compared to £120,000 in the village). A five-bedroom detached house with a double garage will cost £750,000. The grand estate lifestyle all began with the Wentworth Estate, built here by a speculative developer called Tarrant in the Twenties, around the famous golf course. Celebrities flourish in its prosperous atmosphere – Russ Abbott, Bruce Forsyth, Nanette Newman and Brian Forbes have settled in very nicely. A five-bedroom family house on the Wentworth Estate will command upwards of £1m and much more. Similar houses in half an acre in Lower Wentworth, which does not overlook the golf course, will fetch £750,000. The atmosphere is quiet and rural – the first breath of real countryside outside London – but there is little sign of rural hardship. There are two parades of specialist shops, several excellent preparatory schools and parking at the station is cheap. Less expensive houses are few in number. For a two-bedroom Sixties semi you would pay around £200,000 – which represents a small premium over the next most prestigious area, Sunningdale. The stretch of water which gives the area its name is a great ornamental lake created in the 18th century by the Duke of Cumberland. He also built the nearby Fort Belvedere, later the home of Edward VIII, where the abdication was signed.

 ## Line to **Chertsey**

Chertsey

Journey: 63 min (44
in peak via
Weybridge)
Season: £1800
Peak: 1 per hr*
Off-peak: 2 per hr*
* Additional trains
available by chang-
ing at Weybridge
or Virginia Water.

Chertsey is reaping the commercial benefit of lying just inside the M25, an arbitrary boundary chosen by many London companies relocating their head offices. Eight new developments have gone up in the last few years to cope with the expansion. Very little remains of the famous Benedictine Abbey founded in 666. Henry VIII ordered the stones to be used in the rebuilding of his palace at Oatlands Park. But the handsome, seven-arched 18th-century bridge is still a landmark, and the town is in the throes of a 14-phase improvement scheme. There is a good selection of period properties which, foot for foot, offer better value than up-market Weybridge. Beside the park and woods of St Ann's Hill there are large detached houses with price tags which rise above £1m. Abbey Road is an equally prestigious address. Grove Road, by the football club offers more affordable Victorian houses which cost £140,000 for three bedrooms. First-time buyers will find a wealth of one-bedroom modern flats at £85,000. Good schools include Sir William Perkins' girls' grammar, and there is a very highly regarded hospital, St Peter's.

Lyne and **Longcross** are the most sought-after villages in the area (it costs 15% to 25% more to buy into them). There are some Victorian semis and modern bungalows at £180,000 to £300,000. They lack properties of real character but the agricultural smells and lack of a bus service are still enough to make country-lovers feel at home.

Continuation of main line
Sunningdale

The development of the Southern Railway at the turn of the century made **Sunningdale** accessible to London businessmen who wanted to build country mansions with golf and racing on their doorsteps. Several of these minor palaces still survive intact, but many were demolished in the Thirties and Sixties to make way for new development. Others have been converted into flats. It is a village of two parts – the old village around the church, and the busier shopping area near the station. Part of it lay within Surrey until 1991, when the whole was switched into Berkshire. The most sought-after houses are in Titlarks Hill (where Gary Lineker has taken up residence), leading to the golf course, and in Ridgemount and Priory Roads. Large houses in half to one acre sell for between £450,000 and £1m. Kenneth Branagh has completely rebuilt a house here. Sunningdale is not exclusively a playground for the rich, however-er. In the old village there are three-bedroom Victorian semis for between £160,000 and £200,000. Think twice before buying a house too close to the A30. When the M25 or M3 become clogged the traffic pours on to the other through roads and jams those, too.

| Journey: 46 min |
| Season: £2012 |
| Peak: 3 per hr |
| Off-peak: 4 per hr |

Sunningdale offers country mansions with golf and horse-racing right on their doorsteps

There is a good choice of state and private schools. Sport is plentiful, but rather exclusive. There are two top polo clubs, and golf at Wentworth and Sunningdale, which has the oldest golf club for women in the country.

Sunninghill to the west is a large parish covering several communities, none of which has retained its original atmosphere. The area known as **Cheapside** is small and sweet with The Thatched Tavern which is memorable for its good food. Sunninghill has a busy High Street with 50 or so shops, but its identity problem is not helped by the fact that Ascot station (see ahead) is actually in Sunninghill, and most people actually prefer it to Sunninghill station. All east-west trains stop at Ascot, and the car park in the past couple of years has been extended. Plentiful turn-of the century houses sell to London commuters or to those with jobs or businesses in Camberley or Heathrow. You would pay between £160,000 and £200,000 for a two- or three-bedroom semi. The church is very busy as is the dramatics society.

A couple of miles south of Sunninghill is **Windlesham**. It's a village with a stout heart that has fended off new development recently and obtained lottery money to refurbish the amateur Windlesham Club and Theatre. Semis can be bought for £130,000 to £200,000. Yet it flirts with the rich and famous, too.

The Al Maktoum family own three palatial houses and another 40 odd houses in the village; the Duchess of York famously let Ruby Wax into her rented house here (and showed her the fridge and T-shirt shelves) but she has since moved on. A five- or six-bedroom Thirties house standing in one or two acres in Westwood Road will fetch up to £2m.

Ascot

Journey: 51 min
Season: £2132
Peak: 4 per hr
Off-peak: 4 per hr

Because of its high racing and fashion profile, strangers expect **Ascot** to be a glamorous place to live. They are often surprised by its lack of real character. Its main attraction is the racecourse, which was laid out in 1711 for Queen Anne. The shopping centre consists of a row of small exclusive retailers. The level of wealth, however, can almost be measured by the height of the hedges – and they are lofty here. Racehorse owners (those who own a part-share of a horse rather than whole stables) pay a premium for four- to five-bedroom detached houses in Coronation Road and Kier Park. A seven to eight-bedroom house on five acres would cost £2m; a period house with five bedrooms, an annexe, needing a little work, could be snaffled for £750,000. You effectively buy into is a rich man's playground, close to Windsor and Heathrow Airport with golf at Hawthorn Hill and Wentworth, racing at Ascot and Windsor, polo at Smiths Lawn and the Royal Berkshire Polo Club, boating and sailing on the Thames. For the very rich there are some sizeable mansions. Not more than a mile away is Ascot Place and its several hundred acres, which last changed hands for £20m, one of the highest prices ever paid for a house in England. There are slightly smaller fry, though. In South Ascot there are Victorian railway workers' cottages as well as larger Victorian semis which sell at £400,000 to £500,000 for four bedrooms.

The level of wealth can almost be measured by the height of the hedges

North Ascot is quite different in character from the Ascot that surrounds the racecourse. Concentrated building began here in the 1880s and has been spreading north and west of the racecourse ever since. A Victorian semi in North Ascot will cost £175,000 to £225,000; a rare detached family house over £250,000. Three-bedroom semis on the 25-year-old infill developments start at around £150,000. Royal Ascot golf club is in the centre of the racecourse. There are also opportunities for squash, tennis and cricket in the area.

Parts of Ascot are in the parish of **Winkfield**, the largest in the county. It covers nearly 10,000 acres and contains several communities which are described as settlements rather than villages with traditional focal points. Winkfield itself is semi-rural, with some listed buildings and small terraces with modern infill, and has been earmarked for more new housing. There is a real worry that it will lose its identity and become "just a place from which to get to other places". It has several parks and recreation areas but no village green, though it still has an annual festival. A small parade of shops serves everyday needs. A small terrace house sells for around £200,000. A wing in a Georgian-style 1860s house in ample grounds is priced at around £500,000.

Most of the small communities in this area have their own local societies and, as this is partly Metropolitan Green Belt, the strongest voices belong to the residents' associations and conservation societies fighting against new development. Golf and polo are the favourite outdoor activities and there are numerous riding establishments. To avoid frightening the horses in the Cranbourne area you need to drive almost permanently in bottom gear.

Line to **Ash Vale** via **Bagshot, Camberley** and **Frimley**

Bagshot

Journey: 64 min
(56 min peak)
Season: £2192*
Peak: 2 per hr
Off-peak: 2 per hr
(change at Ascot
or Ash Vale)
*£2260 if also valid
via Ash Vale.

Once a wild heathland frequented by highwaymen (it was the perfect distance from London, reached by coach as dusk settled), **Bagshot** developed in the mid-19th century and is carefully maintaining its Victorian atmosphere. Lamp-posts are period-style, and new developments and refurbishments have to be in keeping. The area thrives because of the many London companies which have relocated in nearby Fleet. There is day-to-day shopping, good schools and plenty of opportunities for leisure. Connaught Park, a nine-year-old development on the outskirts, is often known as Terminal 5 because of the high concentration of airport personnel who live there – or alternatively as Little Australia, since several of the houses have been sold to Australian golfers. One-bedroom

To avoid frightening the horses in the Cranbourne area you need to drive almost permanently in bottom gear

houses here sell for around £75,000; four-bedroom detached houses for £225,000. College Ride is highly prized for its gardens backing on to Windsor Forest and a tract of land just made available by the Crown for public use (although it is reported to be "pretty overgrown and strictly for hearty walkers").

Victorian and Edwardian houses in a good position start at around £140,000 for two bedrooms. Commuters would be more likely to drive to Farnborough station (see page 210) and pick up the fast trains to Waterloo from Salisbury and Southampton than to use this smaller line.

Camberley

Journey: 55 min
Season: £2260
Peak: 2 per hr
Off-peak: 2 per hr
(change at Ascot or
Ash Vale)

Before the mid-19th century when the Royal Military Academy was established at Sandhurst, **Camberley** simply did not exist. Large houses with between six and 12 bedrooms were built for officers, with more modest developments and shops following between 1880 and 1910. At first there were two areas, Cambridge Town and York Town, named after the two dukes who had been heads of the academy. But when the mail kept going to the university town instead of the military one, the whole area was united under the single name, Camberley. Most of the largest old houses have gone, demolished to make way for new culs-de-sac. Those that remain will set you back by £500,000 to £700,000 for six bedrooms. A neo-Georgian detached house will cost £275,000 to £400,000. There are also some Victorian terraces which you can buy into for £150,000 to £200,000. One disadvantage of living in Camberley is traffic noise from the A30 and M3. Attractions include good high street shopping plus the Meadows shopping centre on the outskirts, the Arts Link Centre (with an independent cinema) and good local comprehensive schools.

For something more rural and very desirable, you need to look west of Sandhurst to **Eversley**, where £280,000 will buy a thatched cottage with three bedrooms, or £725,000 will buy a six-bedroom house with nine acres.

Frimley

Journey: 51 min (65
min peak)
Season: £2260
Peak: 2 per hr
Off-peak: 2 per hr
(change at Ascot or
Ash Vale)

Frimley is too modern to call itself a village. It is a one-high-street sort of a place, with all the basics and some good schools within walking distance. Most of the housing is contained on three large estates. Paddock Hill, for example, was built over a decade ago and offers one-bedroom maisonettes at £78,000, three-bedroom semis at £130,000 and Tudor-style four- and five-bedroom houses at £275,000. A lively young population entertains itself at Bagshot's nightclub or at Basingstoke's bowling alley, ice rink and cinema, 20 minutes' drive along the M3. Five minutes from the centre is Frimley Green, which has a very old heart. The roads off the green have a mix of houses built in the Thirties, Seventies and Eighties. Houses with a country feel on the Guildford Road cost £300,000 to £400,000 but you can pay much more for a period piece. Commuter parking is limited but most people either walk to the station or drive instead to Farnborough, whence the direct line to Waterloo takes only half an hour.

Ash Vale

Ash Vale is the place to hunt for more affordable houses in this otherwise prosperous belt around London. It is ideal first-time buyer country. For the main entry, see Alton section of the **Waterloo to Salisbury** line, page 208.

Continuation of main line
Martin's Heron and Bracknell

Nothing in **Bracknell** today suggests that in the early 19th century it might have been described as "a small thoroughfare hamlet adorned with many genteel residences and delightful villas". In 1948 it was incorporated as Berkshire's only New Town, planned for a London overspill of 25,000. It now has more than 52,000 inhabitants, all of whom must have chosen it for convenience rather than charm. The increase in commuter traffic was sufficient to require the building of a second station, Martins Heron, eight years ago. Property prices are relatively modest given that the journey to London takes less than an hour. One-bedroom flats can be found for £75,000 to £85,000; three-bedroom ex-council houses from £95,000; modern semis on private developments between £125,000 and £145,000, and four-

From Martin's Heron
Journey: 55 min
Season: £2156
Peak: 3 per hr
Off-peak: 4 per hr

From Bracknell
Journey: 58 min
Season: £2192
Peak: 3 per hr
Off-peak: 4 per hr

Modern two-up-two-down, near Bracknell

Nine Mile Ride was cut through the forest to enable ladies to follow the chase

bedroom detached houses at £175,000. Unkind critics attach the "concrete jungle" tag, but there is plenty of high-tech industry to keep a large proportion of the young population busy locally, with good sports facilities, every kind of club, and a "coral reef" water complex with a pirate ship, water slides and even an erupting volcano.

Three miles west of Bracknell is **Binfield**, which has outgrown its status as a village to become a suburb of Bracknell. Historically it is notable chiefly for its connection with Alexander Pope, who lived here as a boy in the early 1700s. It is loosely knit with greens, has a few shops, including an art shop, curry house, Chinese takeaway, some small business, the John Nike Sports Complex (for dry skiing, ice-skating and tobogganing), as well as the redoubtable Binfield Badger Group.

Modern estate housing includes Temple Park, overlooking the golf course, and Foxley Field where prices start at £115,000 for a two-bedroom detached, £165,000 for a three-bedroom detached, £310,000 for a five-bedroom detached. A community spirit still survives and young mothers, as well as the established older residents, are involved in the two community centres, drama club, Scout, Brownie and Guide groups, and line dancing. The local primary school has a good reputation, with secondary age children moving on to Bracknell.

Wokingham

Journey: 64 min
Season: £2264
Peak: 3 per hr
Off-peak: 4 per hr

Despite centuries of doffing its cap to nearby royals in Windsor Forest, **Wokingham** was not granted a coat of arms until coronation year, 1953. A relic of the royal hunt still survives in Nine Mile Ride, which was cut through the forest to enable ladies to follow the chase from their carriages. The town's millennium effort means that from now on every public and private space should be covered in a haze of bluebells every spring.

The old market town has expanded rapidly during the last two decades, swelling its population from 9,000 to around 30,000. Strategically it is extremely well-placed, being served by the A329 London to Reading road and by the M4 which links it to Heathrow airport, the West of England and South Wales. Bus services provide links to Reading and Bracknell. The town centre is surrounded by modern residential streets, many of which are still lined with old oaks and other forest trees. On the west side stands the Woosehill development, containing more than 2,000 houses plus shops, schools and community and health centres. Most of it went up in the Seventies and Eighties. The mixed estate offers flats and one-, two-, three- and four-bedroom houses at prices ranging from £85,000 to £275,000. One of the latest new additions, Keephatch Park, has five-bedroom detached houses at £415,000 and four-bedroom houses at £270,000.

A few handsome older buildings survive in the town centre. The best of them is perhaps Lucas Hospital in Luckley Road, which was built in 1665 to provide a home for 16 elderly men. The hospital is arranged around three sides of a quadrangle, with a chapel filling the right wing. Visitors are admitted by appointment. Elsewhere there are some attractive 16th- and 17th-century houses, particularly in Rose Street and Shute End. An 18th-century three-bedroom house in Rose Street with no garden could cost £240,000.

Wokingham is a good area for golf fanatics, who have five courses to choose from

The most expensive parts of town are in Murdoch, Sturges and Denton Roads, all just to the south-east of the centre, where large Edwardian houses, with four or five bedrooms and large gardens sell at £450,000 to £495,000. Priest Avenue and Rances Lane are also desirable, where three-bedroom houses in large gardens cost £260,000. Cheaper properties built in the Sixties are found around the Mulberry Business Park and along the Finchampstead and Luckley Roads. A three-bedroom semi here will cost around £140,000.

In the north the large Emmbrook development was begun in the Thirties, with additions in the Sixties, Seventies and Eighties. Modest estate-type housing predominates, with prices starting at £160,000 for a three-bedroom semi and rising to £200,000 for a four-bedroom detached chalet-style house.

Wokingham is a good area for golf fanatics, who have five courses to choose from. It also has public playing fields, a sports centre, indoor and outdoor swimming pools, a small theatre and a cinema. Shops include Tesco, Waitrose and W.H. Smith, but there is no major department store. Wokingham people tend to work and shop in Reading or Bracknell. Every November the town seizes up for the winter carnival, and each February it turns out for the half-marathon which attract around 1,500 entrants.

Winnersh and Winnersh Triangle

Winnersh has been built on old Windsor Great Forest land, starting in the Twenties and gathering pace in the last three decades. There is a supermarket, a large health club and DIY store for Sunday Black & Decker fiends. The new 12-screen cinema has upset older villagers who have described it as "a war-horse with neon signs". The Winnersh Triangle sounds dangerously exotic, but it's not

From Winnersh	From Winnersh Triangle
Journey: 68 min	
Season: £2320	Journey: 70 min
Peak: 3 per hr	Season: £2352
Off-peak: 2 per hr	Peak: 3 per hr
	Off-peak: 2 per hr

a place where boats disappear without trace – rather it's a large business centre. Traffic-hum from the A329M and M4 is a constant reminder of the quality of the road communications.

The most famous former resident of Winnersh was John Walter II, son of the founder of *The Times*. He built a Georgian mansion called Bearwood, which his son replaced with the present mansion, now a boys' private school. Walter also built the "model" estate of Sindlesham with its church, pub, school, dower house, cottages and farm. The rhododendron drive which he planted to the next village of Barkham still largely survives, though it has been hacked about a bit by new development. The model estate itself is now part of Winnersh and rather swamped, but Sindlesham manages to charm. Along the Reading Road are some good-value late Sixties and Seventies houses. The village is generally cheaper than Wokingham. A three-bedroom terrace house would cost £135,000. There are also some half-timbered houses

To the north lies **Hurst**, a "proper" village with a duck pond and green, much the nicest on this side of Reading. It has a shop and a butcher, a primary school and a strong cricket club. The most desirable four-bedroom cottages here sell for around £450,000, but there are cheaper properties, too.

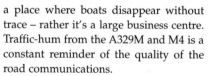

> The rhododendron drive still survives, though it has been hacked about a bit by new development

Earley

Journey: 73 min
Season: £2372
Peak: 3 per hr
Off-peak: 2 per hr

Despite the name – **Earley** derives from the Anglo-Saxon words for eagle and wood – there is nothing at all rural on the horizon here. There are three parts to Earley: Maiden Erleigh, Lower Earley and Earley proper. By some calculations Lower Earley is the third biggest housing estate in Europe, clamped to the southern underbelly of Reading, right beside the M4. Prices range upwards from £78,000 for one-bedroom to £300,000 for five bedrooms, but many residents describe living here as awful. The provision of facilities has not kept pace with new houses. Old Earley has the oldest and most expensive properties – older in this context meaning turn-of-the-century. Prices range from £100,000 for a two- or three-bedroom Victorian terrace to £160,000 for a three-bedroom semi and £500,000 for a large five-bedroom house. Maiden Erleigh Park is a belt of ancient woodland with a lake, kept as a commu-

> The third biggest housing estate in Europe, clamped to the southern underbelly of Reading

nity nature reserve. The area is nicer than the less appealing parts of Reading, but still rather a suburban sprawl. You might find the occasional 17th-century thatched cottage, for which you would probably have to pay something in the region of £280,000. The centre of Reading is about 15 minutes away by car, and the "village" – a misnomer if ever there was one – is enlivened by a large hall of residence for students of Reading University.

Reading

Reading offers fast and frequent trains, a thriving commercial scene and reasonable house prices. Though it can't be described as particuarly attractive, it lies within striking distance of beautiful countryside. For main entry, see **Paddington to Bristol** line, page 154.

Journey: 78 min*	*To Waterloo. For
Season: £2600 (also	faster services see
valid to	Paddington to
Paddington)	Bristol line,
Peak: 3 per hr	page 154.
Off-peak: 4 per hr	

Brockenhurst

Beaulieu Road

Ashurst New Forest

Totton

Redbridge

Dunbridge

Romsey

Salisbury

Grateley

Millbrook

Southampton Central

Andover

Bitterne

Woolston

Sholing

Netley

Hamble

St Denys

Swaythling

Southampton Airport Parkway

Whitchurch

Eastleigh

Shawford

Winchester

Micheldever

Overton

Hedge End

Botley

Fareham

Basingstoke

Hook

Alton

Bentley

Farnham

Aldershot

Ash Vale

Winchfield

Fleet

Farnborough

Brookwood

Woking

West Byfleet

Waterloo

Waterloo
➡️ Salisbury and Southampton

West Byfleet

West Byfleet is a large village that has expanded over the years to become inseparable from Woking. Property prices are high because of its closeness to London. A modern three- to four-bedroom town house will be unlikely to cost less than £325,000. An older similar sized house would be at least £350,000.

Journey: 37 min
Season: £1784
Peak: 5 per hr
Off-peak: 4 per hr

Woking

Woking is a busy but unremarkable commercial town, popular with commuters (75% travel to and from the town each day). The rail service is very frequent, even if available seats may be few, and it is conveniently placed for access to the A3, M3 and even the M25. The north side of the town is mostly given over to council houses and the south tends to be more sought after. A neo-Georgian three-bedroom house on a small development would start at around £150,000; a new four-bedroom detached house would cost £250,000. Hook Heath is where the wealthy gather, in mini-mansions on large plots which sell for over £500,000. For lower prices but a vast range of choice, you could look at Goldsworth Park, where 8,000 homes have been built over the last two decades. You could buy a two-bedroom terrace house for £95,000 to £120,000; a large four-bedroom detached for over £200,000.

Journey: 23 min
Season: £2020
Peak: 11 per hr
Off-peak: 10 per hr

Horsell, on the outskirts and separated by the canal, tends to be slightly more expensive than Woking proper. H.G. Wells lived in Woking for a time, and in *The War of the Worlds* he described the Martians landing on Horsell Common. A Thirties detached house with three bedrooms would cost around £200,000 to £250,000.

For a vintage Home Counties village there is **Chobham**, two miles to the north-west, no weakling in the Best Kept Village stakes. Lorries have been banned from the High Street, which is very much a conservation area – full of antique shops, with a pretty hump-backed bridge over the Bourne brook. Chobham Common is a precious green lung in this part of Surrey, providing wooded bridleways for pony-lovers. People from outside the village run the football, tennis and cricket, but the Brownies, Guides and

WI are domestic affairs and the Venture Scout troop is second to none. The village is very sought after, so a small period cottage will cost at least £165,000. For a larger period house, perhaps with a paddock, you must expect to pay £750,000.

Brookwood

Journey: 33 min
Season: £2120
Peak: 4 per hr
Off-peak: 3 per hr

Brookwood has the edge on Woking because people prefer the idea of living in a village, no matter how built-up it has become. The strangest fact about the station is that is was built originally to serve the enormous cemetery (created to take 1854 London typhoid victims), not for the convenience of commuters. Small culs-de-sacs of fairly new houses abound. A three-bedroom Thirties detached house would cost around £180,000.

 Fork to **Alton**

Ash Vale

Journey: 37 min
Season: £2260
Peak: 3 per hr
Off-peak: 2 per hr

Ash Vale is usually considered a rather unfashionable address, though it has the attraction of affordable prices for first-time buyers. It consists mainly of Victorian terraces arranged in grids around the railway station. A two-bedroom house would start at around £110,000.

Aldershot

Journey: 42 min
Season: £2260
Peak: 3 per hr
Off-peak: 2 per hr

Aldershot is an army town with a pretty rough feel to it. There are 10,000 soldiers and their families, compared to 31,000 civilians. The good thing is that it has terrific sports facilities, including games pitches and an Olympic-sized swimming pool. Victorian terraces went up in Aldershot like mushrooms in a cow pasture. You could buy a two-bedroom terrace now for around £85,000. In the nearby dormitory of Fleet (see page 210), the same house would cost £10,000 more. Aldershot's terraces are surrounded by lots of army married quarters, built in the Thirties and Sixties. Prices rise a little on the Farnham side of town, where a three-bedroom detached house will cost around £150,000.

Farnham

Journey: 48 min
Season: £2344
Peak: 3 per hr
Off-peak: 2 per hr

Farnham is something of a refuge from Aldershot, having a lovely Georgian heart with the castle at its centre. People living anywhere between the two towns will always say they live in Farnham. The south side is more upmarket than the north. It has more of a country feel, even though it is very well-connected to London by train and the A3. A three-bedroom detached Thirties house in a quiet road will cost £250,000; a more spacious five-bedroom house £350,000 to £450,000. There are some modern apartments on the south side, where a three-bedroom unit will cost around £150,000.

Bentley

Bentley is an older village of attractive cottages and houses which has become more sought after since the new bypass put the A31 further east. There are one or two discreet modern estates, and a small Charles Church development of large four-bedroom houses with double garages selling at around £230,000. Smaller three-bedroom period terrace cottages may be bought for around £180,000. Jane Austen's brother was once curate of Bentley; Robert Baden-Powell lived in Pax Hill house; and a director of the White Star Shipping line, owners of the *Titanic*, lived at the big house, Jenkyn Place. It is has a school and shop and strong sense of community. The station is some distance from the village near Alice Holt forest.

Journey: 56 min
Season: £2364
Peak: 2 per hr
Off-peak: 1 per hr

Alton

Alton is a handsome little market town whose square still fills with stalls every Tuesday. The station building is painted in the old Southern Railway livery of green and cream. The community of 6,000 is essentially a rural one, though there are quite a number of commuters who have been attracted by the lovely countryside that surrounds it. At the lower end of the market you might find a mid-terrace Grade II listed house with two bedrooms, beams and an inglenook fireplace dating from 1800, all for around

Journey: 63 min
Season: £2452
Peak: 2 per hr
Off-peak: 1 per hr

Old manor house,
Alton area

£120,000. Newer three-storey town houses with three bedrooms start at £130,000. A new development on the fringe of the town has five-bedroom houses from £225,000.

Period five-bedroom thatched houses in the lanes will cost from around £450,000 up to £600,000. One of the most sought-after villages is **Chawton**, a mile away, though the stone-and-thatch cottages only rarely come up for sale. Chawton's main claim to fame is that Jane Austen lived in a small cottage with her parents and wrote most of her novels here. Her nephew, Edward Knight, lived in the manor house. The cottage is now open to the public.

Continuation of main line

Farnborough

Journey: 31 min
Season: £2280
Peak: 3 per hr
Off-peak: 2-3 per hr

It is socially advantageous to have some connection with flying if you live in **Farnborough**. This is where the Royal Aircraft Establishment is, and where the Farnborough Air show is held. The heart of the town has been fairly unceremoniously ripped out. What remains is a shopping arcade and some small Victorian terraces, suitably priced for first-time buyers at around £55,000 each. Further out, the housing is of Sixties vintage: three-bedroom semis at £75,000 to £80,000; four-bedroom detached houses at between £110,000 and £175,000.

Fleet

Journey: 49 min
Season: £2304
Peak: 3 per hr
Off-peak: 2 per hr

The army is to **Fleet** what the air force is to Farnborough. There is a huge camp here. The train service to London is good, and it is popular with commuters. Another great attraction nearby is Fleet Pond, 133 acres of freshwater lake, woodland, heath and reedbed which are fiercely protected by the Fleet Pond Society. Fleet itself divides neatly into quarters, each one conveniently date-stamped. If you have a taste for the Twenties, you'll find a good selection of Arts and Crafts houses with three-bedroom semis in the £150,000 range. If you prefer the architecture of the Fifties and Sixties, closely-packed in leafy roads, then you'll find a range of choice at between £150,000 and £170,000. The other two quarters are modern, built

Fleet divides into quarters, each one conveniently date-stamped

in the last two decades, with many of the three- or four-bedroom houses aimed squarely at that archetypal creature of the Eighties, the yuppy. You could pay over £200,000 for four bedrooms; £350,000 to £400,000 for a house with five bedrooms and three or four reception rooms. Creatures of the Nineties are here, too –

1,000 new houses have been built in recent years and groundbreaking for another 1,700 is already in progress.

Winchfield

Around the station there is scarcely a village to speak of. Little more than a mile away, however, is **Hartley Wintney**, practically two centuries removed from Fleet. It has old coaching inns with archways leading into cobbled yards, five village ponds and five village greens with ancient oaks, and the second oldest cricket ground in England. The centre is full of antique shops and has an art gallery which specialises in English water-colours. "Very Hampshire," says one local. There is a butcher (with a fish-monger and game counter), a bakery and a coffee shop. Social highlights include productions by the local dramatic society, and there are all the usual clubs and societies – WI, Scouts, Brownies and so on. As usual, high prices follow the 17th- and 18th-century architecture. Council houses are tucked out of sight. A classic four-bedroom cottage overlooking the cricket ground might cost £300,000. A modern four-bedroom house would be in the range of £200,000, while a two-up, two-down Victorian cottage on the common might be had for £135,000 to £150,000.

Journey: 54 min
Season: £2336
Peak: 3 per hr
Off-peak: 2 per hr

Hook

Hook is modern-day Commuterland as opposed to Metroland, with a major Tesco and hundreds of new houses arranged in estates. The London-bound trains are frequent, and it is very close to Junction 5 of the M3. Four-bedroom detached houses start at around £170,000, rising to £260,000 for one from the up-market builders Charles Church. There is a big helicopter base a couple of miles away at RAF Odiham. Thomas Burberry, of raincoat fame, had a house here called Crossways, the site of which is deluged with modern developments.

Journey: 58 min
Season: £2380
Peak: 3 per hr
Off-peak: 2 per hr

Basingstoke

The station car park is capacious and there is a good selection of fast trains. Some actually start from here; others come through from Bournemouth and Weymouth. Thirty years ago **Basingstoke** was a com-paratively sleepy market town with a few local engineering firms and a population of 25,000. Now it is a London overspill town with a population of 90,000 and more than 400 companies, including the Automobile Association, IBM, Sony Broadcast and Sun Life of Canada. The shopping centre, refurbished and pedestrianised, has all the usual chain stores.

Journey: 41 min
Season: £2568
Peak: 5 per hr
Off-peak: 4 per hr

Watercress beds are a particular feature of the local countryside

Basingstoke Leisure Park has a 10-screen cinema, 26-lane 10-pin bowling rink, swimming pool, championship-size ice-rink and golf driving range. The old town is the place for wine bars, pubs and restaurants. It is also the place for two-up-two-down Victorian terraces, priced from £110,000, and four-bedroom Thirties houses at £275,000. In the quiet of Cliddesdon Road, large, detached five-bedroom Victorian and Edwardian houses sell for over £400,000. Further out, you come to the council estates and more sedate private bungalows. The modern estates are on the outskirts. North Chineham is one of the most popular because it has matured over a decade and has a shopping centre with a Tesco superstore. There are also plans for a new station here. Three-bedroom semis can be bought for £120,000; five-bedroom detached houses for £200,000. Hatch Warren is very similar.

Watercress beds are a particular feature of the local countryside. Old Basing, Mapledurwell, St Mary Bourne and Whitchurch all have them. One of the best-known villages, only four miles to the south-west, is **Dummer** – a small linear village that found itself besieged by the world's press at the time of Prince Andrew's wedding, being the home of his then parents-in-law. Perhaps because of its exposure it is rather a tight-knit community. A two-bedroom period cottage will cost at least £180,000 to £200,000. A larger Georgian pile with land will cost at least £700,000.

Actually Mapledurwell is more Land Rovers, Upton Grey more Range Rovers

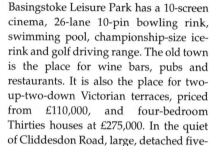

Very close to Basingstoke's eastern flank is **Old Basing**, where old brick cottages are prettily arranged around the church, the River Lodden, and what remains of Basing House. The house was a glamorous Tudor mansion which became the focus of a two-year siege by the Roundheads during the Civil War and was eventually destroyed. Some of the stone was salvaged and used to build houses in the village. There is a strong village spirit and, says one local, "the place is alive with horses". A two-up-two-down period cottage would cost £120,000 to £140,000. Two villages nearby, **Mapledurwell** and **Upton Grey**, are the stuff of an adman's dream, with Range Rovers carelessly parked outside idyllic thatched cottages. "Actually Mapledurwell is more Land Rovers, Upton Grey more Range Rovers," says one insider. Upton Grey has a duck pond, willow trees, some 17th-century cottages, and the fight is on to save the village shop. Prices vary from over £325,000 for a thatched cottage to around £600,000 for a new four-bedroom house.

Fork to **Salisbury** ⬅

Overton

Overton used to be rather pretty and had a defined role as a venue for sheep fairs and silk mills. Now it is where the paper for our banknotes is made. It still retains a certain appeal, though it has become extremely corpulent with new housing estates pushing at its seams. There are some thatched cottages, shops, pubs and restaurants, and a gun shop. A 17th-century, four-bedroom house in the centre will cost around £350,000 to £400,000. Family houses on the new developments cost up to £180,000; large individual houses around £400,000. Winchester Street is considered the poshest bit.

Journey: 54 min
Season: £2584
Peak: 2 per hr
Off-peak: 1 every 2 hrs

Whitchurch

Whitchurch is another old silk-mill village on the River Test. The mill on Frog Island is now restored and sells extremely expensive silk-lengths. But Whitchurch, too, has grown fleshy with huge council estates and private developments designed for those who made money in the Eighties. At Lynch Hill Park, for instance, are huge mock-Tudor and mock-Georgian houses selling in the £300,000 to £350,000 bracket. At the lower end of the market are two-bedroom terrace houses at around £100,000. To the west of the village newly-built four-bedroom houses fetch around £275,000. On the village doorstep is the wonderful rolling chalk downland that envelopes the River Test, the landscape used by Richard Adams in *Watership Down*. An 18th-century brick-and-flint farmhouse in this area would start at £500,000.

Journey: 59 min
Season: £2648
Peak: 2 per hr
Off-peak: 1 every 2 hrs

Andover

Andover had the stuffing knocked out of it in the Sixties and is now a town of shopping malls and modern housing. However, it is well-placed for the M3/A303 magic carpet to the West Country and it sits plum in the middle of some of Hampshire's prettiest countryside. Not even Andover's best friend would call it a cultural oasis, but there is the Cricklade Theatre, and there are drama and music societies. One of the most prominent new shopping centres is the Chantry, which takes up much of the old upper High Street. The tapering market place has survived the onslaught and there is a general street market on Thursday and Saturday.

Journey: 62 min
Season: £2796
Peak: 2 per hr
Off-peak: 1 per hr

In the few Victorian streets that remain, you might buy a three-bedroom terrace for around £90,000. Some of the most popular properties are

The chalk hills around Andover hold some of
the loveliest villages in the country

the Twenties and Thirties semis which sell at around £120,000 to £140,000 for three bedrooms. The west of the town is where the newest housing is to be found. At Weyhill, for example, you could buy a four-bedroom detached family house for about £190,000.

The chalk hills around Andover hold some of the loveliest villages in the country. All those along the Bourne Valley, from Hurstbourne Tarrant down to Longparish, have a definite social cachet.

Hurstbourne Tarrant sits in the valley bottom with Hurstbourne Hill casting a steep green shadow in the background. Stage-coaches used to change horses here before tackling its merciless incline. William Cobbett visited on his *Rural Rides* – his initials are on a brick in the garden wall of Rookery Farm, where a former owner used to put out plates of food for hungry travellers. Jane Austen's parson brother also lived here and she visited frequently. To move here now you have to pay through the nose, though, fortunately, new low-cost housing is allowing some local people to stay. A two-bedroom period cottage could cost £130,000; a four-bedroom period house £325,000.

St Mary Bourne is further east along the sparkling chalk River Bourne – often called the Swift by locals, especially when it is in full spate. The village is a wonderful muddle of brick-and-flint, oak beams, wattle-and-daub and thatch. It has 15 listed buildings and a lovely Norman church with a black marble font. There is a very traditional village primary school, three pubs, and all the usual village societies. Some of the local families have lived here for centuries, as an 1842 tithe map has proved.

"Our main worry," said the parish clerk, "is that new people moving in want to throw a glass dome over the place and don't want it to change, even though the demands of the village are changing." A two-bedroom thatched cottage will cost from £135,000; a modern four-bedroom house £250,000 and up.

Longparish, at the lower end of this exclusive corridor, is indeed a very long parish, threading along three-and-a-half miles of winding lane and the meandering River Test. Some of the field walls and the thatched cottages are built of clunch (chalk stone), with some modern estates sandwiched in between. The big flints in the fields are known as "Hampshire diamonds"; the other white specks are sheep. Property prices are similar to those in St Mary Bourne.

Ludgershall, to the north-west, offers housing even cheaper than Andover's – if you can bear the development going on all around you. "There are hundreds of houses going up. It's out of control," said one villager. A three-bedroom terrace house built in the Twenties will cost around £80,000; a two-bedroom terrace around £65,000. Further west are **North**

Tidworth and **South Tidworth**, both of which offer outstanding value for money but have rather transient populations. The army, which has a strong presence in the area, has been shedding staff, with the result that you might pick up a two-bedroom flat for £45,000, or a three-bedroom house for £65,000.

Shipton Bellinger is very ordinary and again dominated by the army. Three-bedroom semis fetch around £75,000 to £85,000. Closer to Andover itself is the rather more cosy community of **Penton Mewsey**, where you might buy a four-bedroom period house for £275,000 – around £50,000 less than it would fetch in the Bourne Valley.

To the south-west is **Monxton**, with the Pill Hill brook gambolling through it under a small bridge. It is a very compact village with some timber-frame and thatched cottages, a small green, a pub but no shops. It is popular with retired people, but there are also some young families with children at the local playschool. Village barbecues are a regular social event. A small thatched terrace cottage would be likely to cost over £140,000; a four-bedroom modern house over £225,000. **Abbotts Ann**, close by, is also pretty. Its status has risen to rival the villages of the Test or Bourne valleys, though it is feeling rather bruised by the number of recent incomers. You could buy a thatched cottage with three or four bedrooms for £275,000; a four-bedroom detached modern house for about the same.

There are hundreds of houses going up in Ludgershall. It's out of control

Stockbridge, further south, has enormous cachet. It lies in breathtakingly lovely countryside and is a great angling centre for some of the best and most expensive fishing in England, along the River Test. The Grosvenor Hotel, with its huge overhanging porch, might as well be an exclusive club for fishermen. The wide main street, edged with Tudor and Georgian houses, a superb butcher and other good shops, belies the village's size for there are very few back streets.

Stockbridge Down, a mile away, is dotted with ancient earthworks, and up in the hills are the Iron Age forts of Woolbury Camp and Danebury Ring. A two-bedroom period terrace house with a small garden in Stockbridge will cost £155,000; a more substantial Georgian terrace £190,000 to £200,000. Half a dozen new six-bedroom detached houses carry a value of £295,000 or more. An oddity close to Stockbridge is **Leckford** – an estate village of tied thatched cottages owned since 1928 by John Lewis. All the properties are occupied by retired former employees of the John Lewis Partnership, and all the gables and woodwork are painted John Lewis green.

Grateley

Journey: 75 min
Season: £2932
Peak: 2 per hr
Off-peak: 1 every 2 hrs

Grateley proper is an old-fashioned farming village. Many of the period properties have been in the same families for years and few come on to the market. The range of property is wide, however. You could pay just under £115,000 for a two-bedroom Victorian slate-roofed terrace house; up to around £300,000 for a four-bedroom period house if you are lucky. The Andover side of the village is best. There is a newer area of development around the station, where there are starter homes and council houses. To the south, **Over**, **Middle** and **Nether Wallop** are attractive villages with some nice period properties, but surrounded by a sea of post-war council estates. A four-bedroom white-washed thatched cottage at Nether Wallop sold recently for £200,000.

Salisbury

Journey: 79 min
Season: £3176
Peak: 2 per hr
Off-peak: 1 per hr

The city of **Salisbury** is full of visual treats, architectural nooks and crannies, gabled houses, half-timbering and Chilmark stone. Unlike Winchester, which grew out of medieval clutter, it was built on a grid pattern and so has a greater sense of space and order. At the heart of it is the confluence of the rivers Avon and Nadder, spanned by medieval bridges. Another remnant of medieval life is the open-air market on Tuesday and Saturday. Shops in the city centre tend to be small and specialised, with Waitrose and Tesco kept out of sight on the edge of town. The Salisbury Playhouse is the main theatrical venue, with the Salberg providing productions on the fringe. The Arts Centre has celebrity lectures.

On Salisbury Plain, the magic of a country walk might be exploded by a training exercise

The top of the property pyramid in Salisbury is the Cathedral Close, once home to the novelist Henry Fielding and now to Edward Heath, right beside the river. It is regarded as one of the most beautiful closes in England, dating from the late 18th century when graves were pushed to one side and some remarkable houses built for the city's more important residents. One of them, Mompesson House, is now in the hands of the National Trust. The close is perfectly quiet, shut away behind locked gates at night and as expensive as Chelsea or Westminster. A 10-year lease here will cost £200,000; a freehold could well top £1m. There are some other good streets near the cathedral, overlooking Queen Elizabeth Gardens. In this area you might pick up a four-bedroom turn-of-the-century terrace house with a 60ft garden for around £250,000 upwards. A short distance away is Fisherton Island, a small group of detached houses built in the Sixties

Schools in Wiltshire

Salisbury gets all the accolades. The Goldophin is an independent day and boarding school for girls, and there are two grant maintained grammar schools – Bishop Wordsworth's for boys and South Wilts Girls' – both of which get excellent results. Other strong independent schools include St Mary's at Calne for girls, Dauntsey's in Devizes for girls and boys and Marlborough in Marlborough for girls and boys. Good comprehensives include those in Wootton Basset, Corsham and Sheldon school in Chippenham.

which also command high prices – around £265,000 for four bedrooms. It is also possible to buy into one of the oldest streets in Salisbury, Guilder Street, where an old brick-and-timber cottage with two bedrooms might cost £90,000. Popular schools include the Cathedral School, The Godolphin, Bishop Wordsworth's Grammar and South Wilts.

At the lower end of the market are hundreds of turn-of-the century terraces fronting directly on to pavements. Beware the terrible parking problem. You might get a two-bedroom terrace house for just over £75,000. In the gentrified streets – identifiable by the hanging baskets – you could pay £85,000, and in St Anne's Street over £80,000.

On the city outskirts, areas like Shady Bower offer retirement flats at around £85,000 and modern three-bedroom houses at £165,000. For a more villagey feel, look to the leafy lanes of Milford, where four-bedroom detached houses fetch around £175,000.

Outside Salisbury, the Wiltshire chalk downlands and the five valleys of the Avon, Wylye, Nadder, Ebble/Chalke and Bourne provide the setting for some very attractive, unspoilt villages. Those to the south tend to be more popular. Those to the north are on the edge of Salisbury Plain, where there is a massive military presence and the magic of a country walk might be exploded by a training exercise.

Penetrating quite deeply into the south you come to **Fordingbridge**. This is rather far for regular London commuters, but people's fondness for it is such that it acts as a magnet for the villages between it and Salisbury. Its best asset is the River Avon, crossed by a seven-arched medieval bridge and overlooked by a statue of Augustus John, who once lived here. It has shops good enough to meet day-to-day needs, as well as a bookshop, antiques shop and china shop. It is ideally placed for people who like to hack across the New Forest and for anglers with rods on the Avon. Inevitably, it is also popular with retired people. There is a real mix of housing, from the often flimsily built but very sought-after houses of the New Forest, for which you could pay £165,000 for two bedrooms, to huge Twenties set-pieces in 20 acres of ground at £875,000. Pony paddocks are very expensive here. On one of the several modern developments you would pay £130,000 for a three-bedroom detached house; £160,000 for four bedrooms.

Nearby is **Breamore**, pronounced "Bremmer", a typical Wiltshire brick village. "It's a horsey, hunting, shooting village. Brilliant," said one happy local. Breamore House, the home of the Hulse family, is an Elizabethan manor overlooking the Avon valley, open to the public. There is a good choice of period houses, with three-bedroom brick-and-tile cottages at around £200,000 and larger, thatched brick cottages at around £275,000 or more. Villages slightly to the west within this group – **Rockbourne** and **Martin**, for example – are also very rural and pretty, with properties selling at similar prices. Rockbourne and Damerham operate one of the first federated primary schools in the country, sharing teachers and facilities. Its reputation is good.

Thatched cottage, Chalke Valley

Midway between Salisbury and Fordingbridge, is **Downton**, a village that once depended on lace-making, flour-milling and paper-making. It

has an authentically ancient atmosphere, especially in the lovely main street, The Borough, where you would pay over £150,000 for a 16th- or 17th-century house. It is a large village, with a population of around 2,500, so it has better amenities than most, including shops, a medical centre, a couple of banks and a library. Villagers usher in the spring with the annual May Cuckoo fair.

Closer in, lying beside Salisbury's watermeadows, is **Britford**, a sleepy collection of brick cottages and farmhouses on the River Avon. It has a school and a common, but there are no shops and it has to share its vicar with other villages. Residents have a reputation for being rather reclusive and rarefied – particularly those who occupy the large houses on the lower road along the river bank. "People who live there really think they're something," carped one neighbour. A good period house with four bedrooms would cost well over £300,000. Nearby are **Odstock** and its neighbours **Nunton** and **Bodenham**, where the social life is rather more robust. People who have moved away find themselves drawn back for the annual fête, to join in the river raft races and dance the night away. Odstock has a school, a pub popular with doctors from the nearby hospital, and the designer Georgina von Etzdorf's silk screen printing works. Prices are similar to Britford's.

The Chalke Valley to the south-west is also a good hunting ground. **Bowerchalke**, though very much a one-road village, occupies a beautiful position in an Area of Oustanding Natural Beauty surrounded by the

Downs, just before the countryside tips over into Dorset. It has a mix of brick-and flint, cob and green sandstone, and with some modern houses, too. Everyone knows everyone else. There is no pub, but it has battled to keep its general store open, and there is also a playgroup. Incomers are not always a bad thing, as one villager recalls: "Everyone used to inter-marry. The IQ of the village was saved by the arrival of the bicycle." There is a trout farm and a small stream running through, and endless walks. Houses here and in the neighbouring village of **Broad Chalke** are usually easy to sell. A 19th-century two-bedroom cottage will fetch £150,000; a modern four-bedroom house in vernacular style £275,000. Broad Chalke is right on the Ebble where it meets the Chalke, and it regards itself as the capital of the Chalke valley. It lies between two chalk ridges, Here Path and Ox Drove Road, which both provide challenging walks. There is an ancient pub, and shops which include a butcher who makes his own fag-gots. The village school is still going strong, and there is a doctor's surgery. One of the most successful of its many clubs and societies is the Wilton and District Youth Band. Owners of swimming pools in the village allow their neighbours to use them. South Street is particularly pretty because of its thatched cottages.

The town of **Wilton**, three miles west of Salisbury, is spoilt by its position on the A30 and A36, though it has a good market square peppered with antique shops, and some nice old houses. A two-bedroom cot-tage could be picked up for around £100,000. This is where the Royal Wilton Carpets are made. Much of the town is owned by the Pembroke estate. The near-

Villages retain their sense of remoteness and yet have easy access to the city

by Wilton House, built by the Earl of Pembroke, is open to the public.

The next spoke in the wheel of valleys around Salisbury is the Wylye Valley to the north-east. The villages here both retain their sense of rural remoteness and yet have easy access to the city along the A36. **Codford St Mary** and **Codford St Peter** are rather strung out along the road and have plenty of modern houses. They have one of the only village theatres in the country. A four-bedroom house would cost around £150,000; a three-bed-room Thirties semi around £110,000.

To the north of Salisbury, the Woodford Valley is given particular charm by the River Avon. There is a dearth of smaller cottages so this is not first-timer country. A four-bedroom period family house, possibly with a paddock, is likely to fetch over £400,000. There are people here whose fam-ilies have lived in the area for centuries; many of the newer arrivals have military connections. **Lower Woodford**, **Middle Woodford** and **Upper Woodford** are all very strung out, so there is no very strong sense of com-munity. There is no shop or post office, though there is a pub, a church and a football team (the cricket team has died out) at Middle Woodford. Heal

House, where Charles II sheltered after the Battle of Worcester in 1651, opens its gardens to the public. Lower Woodford has a pub, beside some old thatched chalk cottages. **Great Durnford** also lies in this exclusive belt and is similarly expensive.

Further north, a couple of miles from Stonehenge, is **Amesbury**. This is in the neighbourhood of three army camps – Larkhill, Tidworth and Bulford – and the army personnel help keep the first-time-buyer market ticking over. A mass of new developments has sprung up in the last two decades alongside the older brick-and-flint cottages, and more growth is likely. On the new estates you would pay around £70,000 for a two-bedroom house, £90,000 for a three-bedroom semi, £120,000 for a four-bedroom house. Older three-bedroom cottages fetch around £95,000. There are a handful of select roads such as Countess, and London, where large detached houses built in the early part of the 20th century sell for close to £190,000.

Just to the east of Salisbury is **Laverstock**, separated by the River Bourne. Large riverside houses appeal to the local bank-manager class, and there are one primary and three secondary schools which have good reputations. A modern detached house with four bedrooms will cost around £170,000.

Fork from **Basingstoke** to **Southampton**

Micheldever

Journey: 78 min (53 min peak)

Season: £2688

Peak: 3 per hr*

Off-peak: 1 per hr

*Some by changing at Basingstoke.

The countryside really takes over here. **Micheldever** has a good collection of old thatched cottages arranged haphazardly by the Dever brook and around a triangle of grass with a seat and a tree on it, known as the Crease. Duke Street is perhaps the prettiest for terrace cottages: two bedrooms will cost around £140,000. There is an old-fashioned village school, a store and a pub. The station is a couple of miles from the old village, but has had a whole new community spring up around it.

There are Fifties and Sixties estates and bungalows, where a family-sized house might cost £250,000. The area has been earmarked for new town development. The main road at one end of Micheldever does tend to impinge on the rural dream, but most people hear the A33 and M3 only as a low growl on quiet nights.

Winchester

Its beautifully simple Norman cathedral, boys' public school and streets lifted straight from Jane Austen give **Winchester** a compelling appeal. Winchester society is a force to be reckoned with. Much of it revolves around a tightly-knit farming set, for whom the sporting weekend is essential. There are several fashionable hunts and shooting estates, and the Houghton Club on the River Test provides some of the best trout fishing in the country. The shopping centre is much as you would expect, rather upmarket, with pricey toy shops – the kind that sell hand-made rocking horses – and Jaeger and Laura Ashley, plus an antiques market in King's Walk. There are lots of pubs and restaurants. Art exhibitions are held at the Guildhall Gallery, the Winchester Gallery and the Heritage Centre;

Journey: 55 min
Season: £2936
Peak: 3 per hr
Off-peak: 4 per hr

House style in Surrey and Hampshire

A wonderful mixture of styles is packed between the metropolitan hard edges of south-west London and the retirement haven of the south coast. Through the sandy heaths of Surrey, the collectors' items are the houses designed by Edwin Lutyens in gardens by Gertrude Jekyll. Lutyens's architecture combines formality with naturalness, texture with geometry.

Then comes Hampshire, where stockbroker belt meets Georgian good manners and beautiful villages laze in the folds of the chalk valleys around Winchester and Andover.

You have to marvel at what can be done with a stone as soft as chalk. Around Petersfield there are farm walls made of clunch (chalk stone). When it is combined with flint and arranged in a chequerboard pattern or horizontal stripes, it turns humble cottages into architectural curios.

When the chalk gives way to the poor soil of the New Forest, you find a range of brick and timber, brick and flint, thatched and even cob houses. Particularly pretty are the one-and-a-half storey thatched houses or "bun" cottages, with steep roofs that look as if they have risen like loaves of bread.

The New Forest itself often disappoints. The original houses were small and low, and now would be considered scarcely habitable. Those that still stand have often been changed and extended beyond all recognition. The exceptions lie in the wealthier villages such as Beaulieu and Bucklers Hard in the south, where shipbuilders' oak went into the houses.

Bungalow-itis is ever-present along the coast, but makes a strangely natural partnership with the old defence fortifications around Southampton.

concerts at the Guildhall and in the cathedral. Chesil Theatre and John Stripe Theatre are busy with amateur theatrical productions, while the Theatre Royal (reopening in 2000 after refurbishment) attracts national and international stars and shows newly-released films.

Little Minster and Great Minster, right by the cathedral and close to Winchester College, are two of the best addresses in the country outside London. Tourists are the main drawback. Flocking through to see where William the Conqueror claimed his crown, and where King Canute and Jane Austen are buried, they can't help pausing to look at the beautiful 18th-century houses, too. Small terrace houses in Cannon and Colebrook Streets are also extremely sought after, though life here can be inconvenienced not only by the seriously difficult parking problem, but also by

Little Minster and Great Minster, right by the cathedral and close to Winchester College, are two of the best addresses ourside London

film units seeking period backdrops. A tiny flat-fronted terrace house could cost between £160,000 and £180,000; a larger imposing Georgian house £450,000. At the cheaper end of the market, two-bedroom Victorian terrace houses fetch between £130,000 and £160,000, rising to £220,000 to £280,000 for three- to four-bedroom semis. The area down by the watermeadows in **St Cross** is popular with young professional families. Here you can buy two-bedroom Victorian terrace houses, or two-bedroom flats in converted houses at around £160,000 to £190,000. Two more areas that are within walking distance of the city centre and are coming up are **Hyde**, where you would have to pay £165,000 for a three-bedroom Victorian terrace, and **Fulflood**, which is slightly cheaper.

Some people prefer the comparative peace of some of the avenues away from the city centre – Chilbolton and Bereweeke Avenues, for example, where houses range from Victorian to Sixties and a four-bedroom detached could be bought for £300,000 to £450,000. Just outside Winchester is a large modern development called Badger Farm. One-bedroom flats here cost £55,000; two-bedroom terraces £70,000; four-bedroom houses rise to £180,000.

The neighbouring villages compete to be the most beautiful and socially spirited. The particularly desirable area to the north-east contains **Itchen Abbas**, a village described by Charles Kingsley in *The Water Babies*. The Pilgrims' Way runs through it, as does the River Itchen. There is no

Old Alresford attracts day-trippers because of the Watercress Line

shop, but the village does have a primary school, the usual local societies and a football pitch. A four-bedroom period house here would cost £450,000. For cricket you must follow the river down to **Easton**, another pretty village with a mix of thatch and half-timber, Victorian and modern, with the snarl of the M3 in the distance. **Avington** is also in this select group. Most of its old brick-and-flint cottages are protected within a conservation area. Its flagship is Avington Park, a fine Carolean mansion set in ancient parkland with a lake, which is open to the public. You could expect to pay £150,000 to £170,000 for a two-bedroom thatched cottage in any of these villages.

Old Alresford attracts day-trippers because of the Watercress Line, an eccentric railway which offers a half-hour return journey through Hampshire farmland, chalk cuttings and hills. Antique and curio shops have sprung up as a result. Nevertheless, small two- and three-bedroom Georgian terrace houses around the centre can be bought for £250,000. To the south is **New Alresford**, which is *so* new that some of the houses haven't yet been sold. A four-bedroom detached family house costs between £200,000 and £240,000.

To the north-west is **Crawley**, where there are some picturesque thatched cottages by the village duck pond. It has the kind of star quality that earns it regular appearances on scenic calendars. As an old estate village it was planned as a whole, and some of the architecture is flamboyant. You could pay £400,000 for a detached bungalow or £325,000 for a semi-detached period cottage with three bedrooms. A larger detached house with grounds could reach £1m to £2m. Prices have risen rapidly.

Sparsholt is rural and convivial, and provides the opportunity of walks from the back door into the thousand acres of hills and woodland in Farley Mount Park. The village is particularly proud of its church-controlled primary school, though the influx of new home-owners tend not to use it. Villagers feel that the new five-bedroom executive houses, selling at £600,000 each, jar in the landscape. There is a village shop and a new hall, funded partly through the efforts of the local community, where country dancing is a regular event. Property prices are similar in most of the villages throughout this area.

Due south of Winchester the M3 has snaked its way across Twyford Down to join the M27, leaving the old M3 a bizarre sight in a conservation area with the old motorway bridge surrounded by grass.

Shawford

Shawford is bisected by the M3, so one of the major factors governing prices here is whether properties have been affected by it or not – hundreds of home-owners are filing for compensation. You would pay just over £130,000 for a two-bedroom Victorian or Edwardian terrace away from the main road, 10% less if it's in the traffic zone. Towards **Compton** there are some huge individual houses, built on large plots, that sell for £500,000 to £800,000, though some of these, too, are affected by the motorway.

Journey: 93 min
(70 min peak)
Season: £2944
Peak: 3 per hr*
Off-peak: 1 per hr
*Some by changing at Winchester.

Eastleigh

Eastleigh is quite a come-down after Winchester. It was built around the railway and still has a large railway works, though it is now attracting new companies (such as Pirelli) and has a new shopping centre. It also has the headquarters of the Royal Yachting Association. In the early days the social divisions between railway employees were underlined by their choice of address. Drivers and inspectors lived in the north; everyone else in the south. Today the north is still the better side of town, and properties here sell for slightly more. Its basic stock in trade is a mass of late Victorian

Journey: 71 min
Season: £3044
Peak: 3 per hr
Off-peak: 2 per hr

Modern
development,
Chandler's Ford

terrace houses, fronting the pavement and selling at between £70,000 and £80,000.

Bishopstoke and **Fair Oak** were once older villages but they now behave more like comparatively prosperous suburbs of Eastleigh. Bishopstoke has new estates where you might buy a three-bedroom house for less than £90,000, or a four-bedroom detached house with two en-suite bathrooms and double garage for £160,000. Fair Oak is slightly more up-market, with its old village square still intact.

The stockbroker belt is at **Chandlers Ford**, parts of which consider themselves to be more Winchester than Eastleigh. Much of it is modern. The Hiltingbury area, developed in the Sixties, has three-bedroom semis at between £100,000 and £120,000; three-bedroom detached houses at £135,000; chalet-style houses at £150,000. The Oakmount area, which followed in the late Sixties and early Seventies, has two-bedroom maisonettes now costing around £75,000 and three-bedroom terraces at £85,000. In the Eighties came Valley Park. You could buy a five-bedroom house for £270,000 here, though you might think they were rather tightly packed. The expensive side of Chandlers Ford is Hocombe, built in the Thirties when little heed was paid to land values. Substantial four-bedroom houses with spacious sitting and dining rooms spread themselves over large gardens and change hands at £400,000 to £450,000. This is where the IBM executives from Hursley tend to congregate. Also on the northern side are two good comprehensive schools, Toynbee and Thornden, which themselves are an attraction to the area. Layers of new housing continue to be added, especially now that the M3 slicing past it offers easier access to the rest of the country.

Fork to **Fareham** via **Hedge End** and **Botley**

Journey: 117 min*
(from Fareham)
Season: £3044 (also valid via Southampton or Fratton and also to Victoria via Hove)
Peak: 2 per hr

Off-peak: 1 per hr from Waterloo, 1 per hr from Victoria; 4 per hr from Waterloo changing at Winchester or Fratton

*93 min peak, also 96 min off-peak by changing at Winchester.

It is also worth considering **Hedge End**, **Botley** and **Fareham**, strung below Eastleigh, because they now have direct train services into London, supplemented by services which involve changing at Winchester. Hedge End can be reached with a journey 106 minutes (season ticket £3,044). while Botley can be reached in 110 minutes (season ticket £3,044). Botley has some good 16th- and 17th-century houses and sits at the head of the tidal reach of the River Hamble. The National Trust has bagged a few acres along the river to preserve them for the future. Fareham takes 117 minutes (season ticket £3,044). Beyond that Gosport looms like an ugly giant.

Continuation of main line
Southampton Airport Parkway

This station is really here for the convenience of Southampton Airport. The train service as a result is fast and frequent, but the station car park is rather expensive. Many of the houses are close to the railway line. A three-bedroom Victorian terrace would cost between £65,000 and £75,000.

Journey: 64 min
Season: £3296
Peak: 2 per hr
Off-peak: 3 per hr

Swaythling

Swaythling is an area of Victorian terraces with prices lower than Eastleigh's. A two-bedroom house might cost £60,000. Many workers from the nearby Ford factory have their homes here, and it can seem as if nearly all the 30,000 students from Southampton University have their digs here, too.

Journey: 76 min
Season: £3296
Peak: 2 per hr*
Off-peak: 1 per hr*
*Change at
Southampton
Airport Parkway.

St Denys

This is one of the older parts of Southampton and a happy hunting ground for first-time buyers. Turn-of-the-century terraces and semis sell for between £60,000 and £70,000.

Journey: 79 min
Season: £3296
Peak: 2 per hr*
Off-peak: 1 per hr*
*Change at
Southampton
Airport Parkway.

Branch line to **Hamble** via **Bitterne, Woolston, Sholing** and **Netley**

Bitterne, Woolston and **Sholing** float on the skyline like a sea of chimney-pots. This is probably the cheapest part of Southampton, composed mainly of turn-of-the-century terraces but with some Thirties housing stitched in, too. It lies on the east side of the Itchen River, crossed by a tollbridge which can seem a bit of a bother. A three-bedroom terrace would cost around £70,000; a three-bedroom Thirties semi about £80,000, possibly with good views thrown in. Houses backing on to the river cost rather more.

Netley is given a certain status by its pebbly shoreline on Southampton Water. It leads to the Royal Victoria Country Park – a mar-

No through trains.
Journey: 94 min
(from Hamble)
Season: £3296
Frequency: 1 per
hr to St Denys/
Southampton
Central

vellous place for picnics, and a vantage point for watching the ferries and tankers chugging across to the Fawley oil refinery on the other side of Southampton Water. Netley also has the remains of the Royal Victoria Hospital, where Florence Nightingale nursed casualties from the Crimea. Large four-bedroom family houses, built in the early Eighties, might cost around £180,000. More modestly, a small two-bedroom terrace house would fetch around £55,000. Part of the old military hospital has been converted into flats, selling at around £160,000 for two or three bedrooms.

Hamble (together with the village of Warsash on the other side of the Hamble River) was used as the setting for the television series *Howard's Way*. It is one of the most concentrated yachting centres in the country, positively bristling with marinas and boats for hire. It is very smart, though in spite of all the visible wealth it still retains the atmosphere of a village. There is a green and a church, and a huge common that leads down to the water. It was a working fishing village until 1914. Some pioneering aviation work was also carried out here, and in World War II the Americans used it as a base to prepare for the D-Day landings. Property prices can break the £600,000 barrier, but you could find an ordinary three-bedroom semi for around £110,000.

Continuation of main line
Southampton Central

Journey: 72 min
Season: £3296
Peak: 2 per hr
Off-peak: 4 per hr

Southampton is a busy modern city that has managed to attract some sizeable companies to relocate – Price Waterhouse and Skandia Life, Meridian Television and the Department of Transport's Marine Directorate. Its increasingly aggressive commercial face, excellent shopping centres and proximity to the sea and the New Forest are all major assets. It can also offer five museums, numerous cinemas, nightclubs and discos, an art gallery, the Mayflower Theatre, the Gantry arts centre and Southampton University, which has its own gallery, theatre and concert hall. The Dell will be losing Southampton Football Club to new premises in 2001; there is first-class cricket at the Hampshire county ground and races at Goodwood, a 30-mile run east on the M27. Participation sports include golf, plenty of tennis, athletics, and swimming in a new £10m swimming complex at The Quay. There is also a choice of health and fitness clubs. Southampton Airport provides flying lessons for those with strong stomachs and the money to match. But the principal leisure activity is still sailing. There are clubs, moorings and dinghy schools all around the coast.

Ocean Village is the place for weekending sailors – a mixture of docklands architecture, frivolous shopping, bars and restaurants, the Port Grimaud of southern England, where a lot of the early property buyers turned out to be interested in investment only. A two-bedroom apartment with a berth for the boat costs £165,000 or more; a town house might cost £200,000, rising towards £240,000 if it has a berth.

Old Southampton is also thought to be rather special. The old town stretches from Bargate in the north to Town Quay in the south – a good vantage point from which to watch the QE2 or Canberra sail into port. The medieval town wall is

A surprising number of people cannot resist living along the coast to the west

another reminder of the city's long maritime history. (It was not until the 18th century that it became a fashionable resort.) One of the most popular old/new developments is a listed warehouse which has been converted into luxury apartments overlooking the old pier. You can expect to pay around £190,000 for four bedrooms. There is a restaurant on the ground floor. Inner Avenue is one of the best places to look for older town houses. A two- or three-bedroom house within walking distance of the city centre would cost between £80,000 and £90,000. For cheaper housing you could look at **Shirley**, where a two-bedroom turn-of-the-century terrace would fetch just over £67,000.

Further out from the town centre is **Bassett**. This has become rather chic because of its proximity to Southampton Common, the university and two good schools, King Edward VI independent school for boys (girls admitted to the sixth form), and Atherley independent school for girls. A three-bedroom Thirties semi here might cost £100,000; a three-bedroom detached house around £150,000. There are some larger, rather distinctive, four-bedroom houses which sell for over £180,000.

North of Southampton is **Chilworth**, which is considered irredeemably smart. Wealthy businessmen are attracted to the individually built large houses with anything from half an acre to two acres of ground. Smaller three- or four-bedroom houses start at around £230,000, with prices rising inexorably towards the £800,000 mark as you enter the minimansion market.

Millbrook

A surprising number of people cannot resist living along the coast to the west, or in remote parts of the New Forest, even though it means taking this sweeper service into Southampton. At **Millbrook** you are still in the Southampton suburbs, where late 19th-century terrace houses can be picked up for around £75,000.

Journey: 82 min
Season: £3296
Peak: 1 per hr*
Off-peak: 1 every 2 hrs*
*Change at Southampton Central.

Redbridge

Journey: 86 min
Season: £3296
Peak: 1 per hr*
Off-peak: 1 every 2 hrs*
*Change at Southampton Central.

By **Redbridge** you are hitting the modern estates, where a one-bedroom flat might cost around £40,000 and a two- to three-bedroom semi around £80,000.

Branch line to **Romsey** and **Dunbridge**

No through trains. Change at Southampton Central.
Journey: 110 min (from Dunbridge)
Season: £3308
Frequency: 1 every hr from Romsey; 1 every 2 hrs from Dunbridge

Romsey scores high marks for quality of life. It is a classic English market town with a strong agricultural base. A general market is still held once a week just off the market square (overlooked by a statue of Lord Palmerston). The silent simplicity of the Abbey, which is essentially Norman, gives the centre of the town a tremendous architectural and spiritual uplift. It has a lavish leisure centre and small specialist shops, with Southampton near enough for major purchases. It also has its own newspaper and a local theatre, The Plaza, bought by the amateur dramatics society and used by the Romsey Art Group. In the centre of town a restored two-bedroom Victorian terrace house would cost around £125,000. The small farms and older country houses dotted along the Test Valley start at over £300,000 and run into millions. Broadlands, once the home of Lord Mountbatten and now occupied by his grandson Lord Romsey, is nearby.

Michelmersh, where David Frost has a house, is a rather sought-after village which spreads itself out through the lanes like the fingers of a hand. Part of it is a designated conservation area. Its exclusivity is guaranteed by some of the country's best, and most expensive, trout fishing on the Test nearby. It also contains a brickworks that still produces handmade bricks. You could buy a four-bedroom house for around £280,000, but prices vary enormously depending on position and age.

The post office in Mottisfont is known for its superior cream teas

Mottisfont is another of the area's wonderful surprises, owned mostly by the National Trust. You will need at least £325,000 to be in the running for one of the handful of houses left in the open market. The post office is known for its superior cream teas, and is a stop-off point for ramblers on a trail that runs from Totton, close to Southampton, along the chalk downs to Inkpen Beacon. Mottisfont Abbey, with its gardens of old-fashioned roses beside the River Test, also belongs to the National Trust.

Continuation of main line

Totton

Totton likewise is part of the Southampton sprawl, being joined to the city by a causeway across the River Test. It offers a wide variety of new estates, with four-bedroom, double-garage detached houses priced at over £160,000. The Woodlands side of Totton, which faces on to the New Forest, is distinctly more up-market. Here you could pay £250,000 for a three-bedroom house with a paddock; £180,000 for a modern bungalow with two double bedrooms.

Journey: 81 min
Season: £3332
Peak: 2 per hr
Off-peak: 1 per hr

Ashurst New Forest

Ashurst New Forest station was the closest to **Lyndhurst** that the powerful local landowners would allow the railway to come. Lyndhurst, known as the capital of the New Forest, is exquisitely pretty but seizes up with tourist traffic in the summer. People come to visit the church, with its stained glass by William Morris and Burne-Jones; to admire Swan Green with its cordon of thatched cottages, and to visit the new audio visual centre. The Forestry Commission has its local headquarters here in the Queen's House, a former royal hunting lodge. Lyndhurst has proper shops, including a marvellous butcher, and a fruit and veg shop.

Journey: 92 min
Season: £3332
Peak: 1 per hr
(plus 1 per hr by changing at Southampton Central)
Off-peak: 1 every 2 hrs, change at Southampton Central

Property prices in the New Forest are high, despite the fact that the scarcity of building materials means that the quality of the older houses is often rather poor. Prices in Lyndhurst start at around £100,000 for a two-bedroom terrace and rise effortlessly to £400,000 in sought-after Pines Hill Avenue. A new

This was the closest the local landowners would allow the railway to come to Lyndhurst

development in the centre provides cheaper property, with three-bedroom detached houses at around £150,000 and four-bedroom versions around £200,000. An owl and otter park set in 2,000 acres of woodland, is nearby.

Beaulieu Road

At **Beaulieu Road** you come to a rather isolated part of this ancient bog-and-bracken landscape, where there is little more than a handful of cottages and a hotel. This is where the New Forest ponies are sometimes rounded up

Journey: 96 min	*Change at Southampton Central.
Season: £3400	
Peak: 2 per hr*	
Off-peak: 1 every 2 hrs*	

and sold. **Beaulieu**, four miles to the east, is the most exclusive village in the area, where people compete for invitations to Lord Montagu's drinks parties. A three-bedroom thatched cottage costs around £250,000 to £300,000; a six-bedroom house with a couple of acres on the Beaulieu River, fit for the occasional stray pop star, sells for several million.

New Forest
Thirties-style
house

Brockenhurst

Journey: 87 min
Season: £3528
Peak: 2 per hr
Off-peak: 2 per hr

Brockenhurst is blessed because it receives the fast trains from Weymouth. They stop here, at Southampton Central, Southampton Airport Parkway and Winchester, then go non-stop to Waterloo. This is a pretty, vibrant village with some gracious old houses set in half-an-acre or so, for which you might pay £375,000 and more, and some new estates within walking distance of the centre where you could pay £225,000 for four bedrooms. Brockenhurst teems with tourists in the summer. The nearby Beaulieu Motor Museum is a great attraction. The village of **Pilley Bailey**, known locally as Pilley, is a little less expensive. It is very small, with a pub, a church and a shop. A two-up-two-down cottage here would fetch around £130,000. The whole of this area is very close to the sea, and in particular to **Lymington** – an extremely expensive but rather quaint yachtsman's playground. A former shipbuilder's cottage with a downstairs bathroom and three bedrooms will cost £160,000 here. A fast shuttle train links it to Brockenhurst.

Commuters are now prepared to move even further down the line to Bournemouth

As rail services have improved,

Schools in Hampshire

People move to Winchester just for the schools. Winchester College independent boys' boarding school (with some day boys) has a formidable academic reputation. Girls have St Swithun's independent boarding and day school, which still teaches lacrosse. Among the co-educational comprehensives are Perin's and Westgate. The latter takes both boarders and day pupils, and provides an evening meal for children of working parents.

At Petersfield there is the progressive school, Bedales, an independent co-educational day and boarding school, as well as Churcher's College, a co-educational independent day school. At Hook there are two independents – Lord Wandsworth for boys' (girls in the sixth) boarding and day, and North Foreland boarding and day school for girls. At Farnborough there is Salesian College, an independent Roman Catholic school for boys, and Farnborough Hill Roman Catholic girls' day school. Good comprehensives are at New Milton, Ringwood and Yateley.

Southampton also has some popular schools. King Edward VI is a selective entry co-educational independent; St Anne's a grant-maintained comprehensive for girls, with priority given to practising Catholics.

Portsmouth's best include the Grammar, a co-educational independent day school to which the brightest children will travel from miles away; and Portsmouth High independent day school for girls.

commuters are now prepared to move even further down the line to **Bournemouth**, attracted by its pine-cloaked valleys, sandy beaches and breezy clifftops. It is also a commercial success story, attracting big insurance companies to relocate and establishing its name as a major conference centre. The journey to London can be done in 105 minutes, an annual season ticket costs £3,904, and there are two trains per hour. Incomers are attracted to the purpose-built leasehold flats in blocks with sea views along the Eastcliff, each of which has its own price hierarchy. A middle-market block will yield up a one-bedroom flat from £60,000; two-bedrooms for £115,000 to £120,000; three-bedrooms £130,000 to £140,000. You will be extremely lucky to find a freehold house facing full frontal to the sea; should such a rarity come on the market, you could expect to pay £250,000 to £300,000 for three bedrooms, a roof terrace and cliff top access.

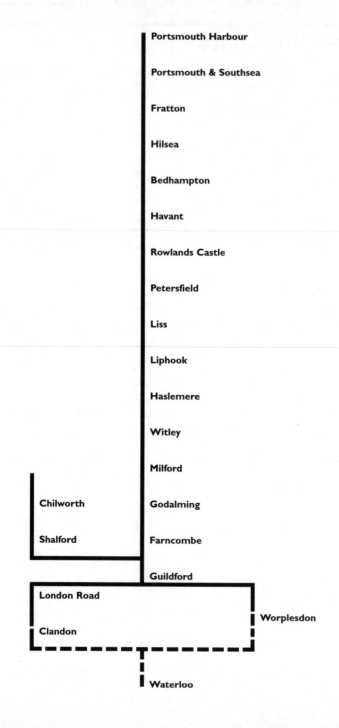

Portsmouth Harbour

Portsmouth & Southsea

Fratton

Hilsea

Bedhampton

Havant

Rowlands Castle

Petersfield

Liss

Liphook

Haslemere

Witley

Milford

Chilworth   Godalming

Shalford   Farncombe

Guildford

London Road

Clandon   Worplesdon

Waterloo

Waterloo ➡ Portsmouth

Worplesdon

Worplesdon, sandwiched between Woking and Guildford, is a main-road village with the A322 cutting straight through it. The station is at least a mile from the centre but is close to some rather nice private roads running off Goose Rye Road. Large Twenties and Thirties detached houses here sell for £380,000 upwards. A four- or five-bedroom gabled and dormered house with a detached granny-annexe will fetch around £550,000.

Sutton Green, a mile south-east of the station, is semi-rural. Sutton Place, one of the finest Tudor houses in the country, is owned by an American foundation which uses it to exhibit works of art. A two-up-two-down turn-of-the-century cottage will cost around £160,000; a four-bedroom detached house of the same period will be over £400,000.

Journey: 46 min
(34 min by chang-
ing at Woking)
Season: £2040
Peak: 3 per hr
Off-peak: 2 per hr

Guildford

Even though it is so close to London, **Guildford** offers rich pickings for shoppers and culture vultures alike. The steep, cobbled, pedestrianised High Street has a wide variety of boutiques and specialist shops, and the Friary shopping mall has all the major chain stores. The Roof Garden Food Court on the top floor is the place to snatch a snack. Architectural highlights include the 1683 Guildhall with its famous projecting clock, and one of the country's few modern cathedrals, designed by Sir Edward Maufe with a very plain interior. The Yvonne Arnaud Theatre has a very good reputation and attracts London-bound shows on their way to the West End, and the nine-screen cinema keeps film buffs happy. The Guildford Harmonic Orchestra is also widely respected. Sports enthusiasts head for the Spectrum leisure centre which has an athletics track, ice-rink and 10-pin bowling.

It is possible to live right in the centre of the town. A one-bedroom flat over the High Street shops will cost around £70,000; a purpose-built, three-bed, two-bathroom flat just off the High Street around £175,000. There are some streets of old houses around Guildford Museum, near the remains of the 12th-century castle at the bottom of the High Street. Most

Journey: 32 min
Season: £2200*
Peak: 5 per hr
Off-peak: 4 per hr
*Also valid via
London Road
(Guildford), see
page 249

Small modern
estate house,
Guildford area

have been converted to business use, but the occasional three-bedroom terrace comes up for around £185,000.

On the north side of town, in the **Woodbridge Hill** area, are the typical bay-fronted, net-curtained, respectable mind-you-own-business streets of provincial England. The houses are solid, with good-sized rooms, but even though it is convenient for the hospital, the cathedral and the university, nobody rushes to live here. A three-bedroom Thirties detached house will cost around £160,000; a three-bedroom semi £135,000. Cornhill Insurance has its headquarters here.

Much more popular is **Fairlands**, where housing of the Sixties and Seventies has bedded down and matured nicely, and where a good community spirit has evolved around the school, the doctor's surgery and so on. It even has its own free local news magazine, and residents are trying to upgrade the name of the place to Fairlands Village. It is a good place to look for a bungalow – three bedrooms for £150,000 to £180,000. A three-bedroom semi-detached house will cost slightly less.

On the north-eastern fringe is **Burpham**, no longer a village but a sea of modern houses, designed with enough breathing space to make them palatable. There are four developments: Weybrook Park, Weyley Farm, Merrow Park and Bowers Farm. A tiny studio costs just under £60,000; a three-bedroom semi £135,000; a large four- or five-bedroom house between £275,000 and £335,000. There are also some large early 20th-century houses with five bedrooms and four reception rooms that sell in the range of £300,000 to £375,000. Nearby **Merrow** is now also a suburb of Guildford. It has a golf course and leafy private roads where houses built in the Thirties now have the occasional bungalow wedged between them. Both bungalows and houses, with four to five bedrooms, tend to sell in the £350,000 range.

The south of the town is particularly well-heeled and attracts successful local professionals. In White Lane are some large houses, built in the Twenties and later, with big gardens and views across to the North Downs. The likely price for one of these would be over £650,000. Further to the south-west is Loseley Park, an Elizabethan country house which is open to the public and whose farm produces the well-known dairy products that bear the Loseley name.

A very popular village to the south-east is **Cranleigh** (see entry for Ockley on the line to Horsham, page 280). Closer to Guildford's southern flank is **Bramley** – well-liked and rather expensive. Its

Its exclusivity is well expressed by the presence of a busy Ferrari dealer

exclusivity is well expressed by the presence of a posh car dealer and well-subscribed golf club. Another attraction is the girls' private school, St Catherine's, which is the sister school to Cranleigh School for boys. A modest three-bedroom semi here will cost £170,000. A four-bedroom detached with a large garden and driveway could go well over £400,000.

To the west of Guildford is **Wood Street**, a large linear village surrounded by farmland, with an ample village green, church and post office. The council housing is discreetly tucked away and there is quite a lot of property built between the Thirties and the Sixties. For £150,000 you might pick up a three-bedroom Edwardian semi, or a more modern three-bedroom detached house with a large garden backing on to fields.

North Downs line east to Shalford and Chilworth

Shalford

Shalford is a one-street village of period houses and cottages with a green. Two-bedroom Victorian terrace houses start at £120,000 to £140,000. Five- or six-bedroom houses can cost £350,000 or more. Shalford Mill, an 18th-century tile-hung watermill on the River Tillingbourne, is now in the hands of the National Trust.

Journey: 47 min
Season: £2380
Peak: 2 per hr*
Off-peak: 1 per hr*
* change at
Guildford

Chilworth

Chilworth spreads itself rather uneasily along the A248, a bland mix of houses and bungalows built in the Thirties and Fifties. Cars tend to park along both sides of the road as few of the houses have garages. Chilworth has its own primary and middle school, and an old gunpowder factory on the banks of the Tillingbourne which is open to the public. A three-bedroom Thirties semi would cost £175,000 at the better end of the village; £135,000 at the other.

Journey: 51 min
Season: £2380
Peak: 2 per hr*
Off-peak: 1 every
1.5 hours*
* change at
Guildford

Continuation of main line

Farncombe

Journey: 39 min
Season: £2208
Peak: 3 per hr
Off-peak: 2 per hr

Farncombe is the poor man's Godalming (see below), of which it is really now a suburb. It does have its own recognisable centre, however, graced by the presence opposite the playing field of 10 early 17th-century red-brick almshouses, still administered by the Worshipful Company of Carpenters. A four-bedroom Victorian terrace house in Farncombe will sell for around £180,000; a Twenties detached three-bedroom house for £150,000; a modern two-bedroom terrace for £120,000 or slightly less.

Godalming

Journey: 40 min
Season: £2216
Peak: 4 per hr
Off-peak: 2 per hr

Forever prosperous, **Godalming** thrived first on the wool trade, then as a coaching stop on the London to Portsmouth road. Since the 1870s it has been the home of Charterhouse, the private school for boys and girls. The High Street contains a wonderful collection of 16th-, 17th- and 18th-century buildings, and in the centre is The Pepperpot, a distinctive colonnaded building with a clock tower. Godalming was further distinguished by being the first town to replace gas street lighting with electric. Its shopping is typically small-town, with one or two specialist shops and a Sainsbury on the edge.

There are good walks along the River Wey from Godalming Wharf to the Thames at Weybridge, complete with locks and weirs. For autumn colour the place to walk is the National Trust's Winkworth Arboretum.

> The church is set apart on a mound next to a thousand-year-old yew tree

The two most fashionable areas of Godalming are **Busbridge** and **Charterhouse**. Busbridge has quiet leafy streets lined with properties spanning every period from Victorian to the Thirties, and a famous water tower converted into an eccentric house. A three-bedroom detached house here will set you back £450,000, though you could pay up to £650,000 for a large house with half a dozen bedrooms and a capacious garden. Charterhouse is similar, though the houses tend to be larger. The tail-end of Mark Way is a private road where some of the older houses were built in such enormous acreages that strips of garden were sold off for building plots in the Fifties. A four- or five-bedroom house set in a third of an acre will cost at least £550,000. At the lower end of the market are some two-bedroom terraces on small modern developments that sell for around £125,000.

The nearby village of **Dunsfold** is lovely if you can afford it. The houses, some of them dating from the 15th and 16th centuries, are gathered around an open common, with a pub, small shop, nursery school, and church picturesquely set apart on a mound next to a 1,000-year-old yew tree. Even a tiny two-bedroom period farmworker's cottage here will fetch £180,000 to £200,000. Larger houses start at £500,000.

Milford

Milford has been rather carved up by main roads (including the A3), but there are compensations in the pretty rambling-and-riding countryside that surrounds it. The village sprawls around the shops and church and provides a broad range of properties. You might pay just under £100,000 for a two- or three-bedroom ex-council house; £130,000 for a modern three-bedroom semi; £160,000 for a Thirties semi; £400,000 and over for a four- to five-bedroom Victorian or Edwardian family home.

Journey: 48 min
Season: £2228
Peak: 3 per hr
Off-peak: 1 per hr

Elstead, three miles to the west, is more rural, with some bracken-covered Surrey commons within walking distance. Sir Edwin Lutyens spent the early part of his career working in the area, which contains a large number of his houses. Elstead itself has one good example – Fulbrook, built in 1896. The village also has a pretty watermill, the only survivor from six, a 12th-century bridge, plus a green and a couple of pubs, but the

Schools in Surrey

Guildford has a highly-valued independent boys' day school, The Royal Grammar, which creams off the top 10% of the ability range in the area if it can. There is a choice of three independent schools for girls – Guildford High day school, St Catherine's day and boarding, and Tormead day school. The two co-educational comprehensives of note are Guildford County and George Abbot.

Other good independent schools are scattered throughout the county. They include Charterhouse for boys (girls in the sixth) and Prior's Field for girls at Godalming, and Cranleigh School for boys (girls in the sixth) at Cranleigh, Caterham for both sexes and Woldingham for girls at Caterham, Dunottar for girls and Reigate Grammar for both sexes at Reigate, The Royal School for girls at Haslemere, the Notre Dame for boys and girls at Lingfield, St John's for boys (some girls) in Leatherhead, Notre Dame Senior for girls and the Yehudi Menuhin for the musical at Cobham.

Good comprehensives can be found at Dorking, Redhill, Leatherhead and Oxted.

fight is on to slow the traffic with 20mph speed limits and plenty of sleeping policemen. A one-bedroom flat in a converted Edwardian house will cost just over £80,000; a Victorian two-up two-down terrace just over £120,000; a two-bedroom Thirties semi £140,000. A large detached house, built in the early part of this century and backing on to the commons, will cost £500,000 upwards.

Witley

Journey: 45 min	
Season: £2248	
Peak: 3 per hr	
Off-peak: 1 per hr	

Witley is spread out over several miles, with housing estates from the various 20th-century building booms linking arms around the half-timbered and tile cottages of the old village centre. You would pay anything from £130,000 for a two-bedroom terrace to well over £400,000 for an early 20th-century detached house with five bedrooms. Witley Common, 500 acres of National Trust land, is a great local asset.

The station is a mile to the south at **Wormley**. This is a quiet residential area where a detached house built in the Twenties, shielded from the road by a bank of trees and a long driveway, is likely to cost around £350,000. On a hilltop eminence is King Edward's private school for boys and girls.

‘

Chiddingfold green hosts a massive bonfire night party with 400 torchbearers

’

Hambledon, a mile to the east, is a more conventional village. It lies in a hollow surrounded by hills and woods, with good views of the Hog's Back. The village has a pretty green with a cricket pavilion and pond. Just off the green, one of the oldest houses, Oakhurst Cottage, is kept by the National Trust as a 17th-century museum. The village school is now a nursery, the shop closed but has since been revived by the community and is staffed by volunteers, and the old workhouse is being converted to housing. Houses rarely come on the market, and the tiniest of cottages would be likely to fetch £200,000. A 17th-century Grade II listed house with three bedrooms set in half an acre would start at £400,000; grander houses would fetch over £650,000.

Chiddingfold, two miles south of Witley station, is also tailored to the traditional image of a perfect English village. The green in the centre hosts a massive and spectacular bonfire night party with 400 torchbearers. It is overlooked by the oldest pub in Surrey, the Crown Inn, and by an 11th-century church. Other events on the green include an annual fun day. Shops include a newsagent, chemist, greengrocer, a post office, hairdresser, and there is a fishmonger who calls on Wednesdays. Outside the general store is an ancient thorn tree, supposedly a 1,000 years old, which is now held together with hoops. In the reign of Elizabeth I there were around a dozen glassworks in

‘

The lichens are an attraction to botany students from all over the country

’

the village, the profitability of which can be seen in the lovely half-timbered houses of the period. The church is notable both for its Chiddingfold glass windows and for the huge collection of lichens in the churchyard – an attraction to botany students from all over the country. The large 16th-

and 17th-century houses on the green would break the £1m barrier if they ever came on to the market. There are a couple of small modern developments where you might buy a four-bedroom modern detached house for £240,000.

Haslemere

Repossessions have hardly been heard of in **Haslemere**. This is rich commuter territory, surrounded by National Trust land and with a pretty High Street stiff with half-timbered 16th-century buildings. The shops are intimate and intriguing. One of the town's best-known features is the Dolmetsch Workshops, founded by a Swiss, Arnold Dolmetsch, who helped to revive an interest in early musical instruments including the recorder. Replicas are still made, and the public can visit the workshops by appointment. There is a festival of early music every July. Another attraction is the Haslemere Educational Museum, which contains displays of British birds, geology, zoology, local history and so on – the mummy with one toe exposed is a big hit with schoolchildren.

Journey: 46 min
Season: £2412
Peak: 5 per hr
Off-peak: 4 per hr

There are very few houses in the centre. In Lower Street you might find an artisan's Victorian two-bedroom cottage for £120,000. In Petworth Road you might get a large detached Victorian house with walled gardens for £600,000. Ubiquitous Thirties semis spread outwards from the centre, selling for £160,000 and upwards depending on the street.

The mummy with one toe exposed is a big hit with schoolchildren

A lovely address to aspire to is Tennyson Lane, named for the poet who lived here. The huge Victorian and Edwardian mansions have large grounds with views of Blackdown Hill (National Trust), and are within 15 minutes' walk of the centre. The larger ones sell for vast sums, though some of the smaller interlopers, slipped on to remnants of garden, might be had for £500,000. Scotlands Lane is similar, though the houses are later (Twenties and Thirties) and the road itself is not so quiet.

On the Wey Hill side of town you find the Victorian terraces, with banks and building societies, small supermarkets and chip shops complimenting the large Tesco. A two-bedroom terrace house here will sell for just over £120,000. There is some new development, too. On the Deepdene estate you might buy a two-bedroom terrace for £85,000, a three-bedroom semi for just over £155,000 or a four-bedroom detached house with a garage from £220,000.

North of Haslemere is the 900ft Gibbet Hill which, if you are up to the climb, gives lofty views over the Weald and the South Downs. To the west is the open heathland of Frensham Common with Frensham Great and Little Ponds. Both have sandy (and rather dirty) beaches. They were created in the 13th century to supply fish to, among others, the Bishop of Winchester.

Between these two beauty-spots lies **Hindhead**, which was once rather fashionable – Sir Arthur Conan Doyle, George Bernard Shaw and Lloyd George lived here. But it has had its nose put out of joint by the A3, which comes to a standstill here quite regularly, while vital bypass plans remain on hold. There are still some huge houses that sit snugly behind their shields of greenery, but there's little point considering them unless you have upwards of £500,000 to spend, though you could buy into a modern development for £350,000. Hindhead Common, 1,100 acres of heath and woodland, is a major local attraction.

Though it has a proper little shopping centre, **Grayshott** is still at heart a village where those who can afford it retire for peace and quiet. "It's a lovely little village, Everyone pulls together. It sounds corny, I know. We have local village clear-up days," said one happy local. A two-bedroom Victorian house will cost £90,000 to £100,000; a large Thirties-built house with several acres and a pony paddock around £475,000. **Grayswood**, on the lip of Haslemere, is less exclusive but still in the top drawer. Twenties and Thirties detached houses come onto the market priced at around £250,000 for three bedrooms; and two-bedroom Victorian semis for £165,000.

The Surrey/Hampshire boundary looms large in people's minds because there is intense rivalry between the two counties

Seven miles south, beyond the Blackdown Hill, is **Midhurst** – a market town on the River Rother whose attractions include the Cowdray Park polo ground. It is in many respects a rather plain town, but at least the shops have not been completely homogenised and there are some very attractive houses. Next to the church, for example, is a Queen Anne terrace with likely price-tags close to £350,000. The parklands of some of the largest houses in the town – Heatherwood, Elmleigh, Guillards Oak and Heathfield Park – have been developed as small housing estates. The average price for a four-bedroom detached house (of which there is a great number) is £250,000. Heathfield Park also has some pseudo-Georgian three-bedroom terraces, priced at around £135,000. Another good area is Close Walks Wood. A dozen or so houses have encroached into the woodland and would fetch around £375,000 for four bedrooms. Elsewhere in the town you could find an ordinary three-bedroom turn-of-the-century terrace for around £90,000.

Liphook

The Surrey/Hampshire boundary looms large in people's minds because there is intense rivalry between the two counties. **Liphook** just falls into Hampshire. It is cheaper than Haslemere because it is further south, and it doesn't have the same character. A bypass has recently relieved it of the A3. The Square, where six roads converge, is a conservation area dominated by the 17th-century Royal Anchor Hotel. Otherwise there is quite a lot of post-war development. Loseley Park, built roughly a decade ago, is a network of terraces and small developments of detached houses. A three-bedroom semi will cost £125,000; a four-bedroom detached £200,000. Victorian three-bedroom semis in Liphook fetch between £140,000 and £200,000.

Journey: 54 min
Season: £2440
Peak: 3 per hr
Off-peak: 2 per hr

Liss

Liss is sliced in two by the railway and River Rother. It is very mixed and not greatly sought after, though it does provide a good range of houses. One-bedroom modern flats start at £55,000. Two-bedroom Victorian terraces cost £95,000; three-bedroom modern detached houses £145,000. There are some large Victorian properties at Liss Forest – an extension of the village where a four-bedroom house will cost £200,000 or more. On the outskirts, four- or five-bedroom period houses set in a few acres start at £450,000.

Journey: 60 min
Season: £2520
Peak: 3 per hr
Off-peak: 2 per hr

Four miles north-west is **Selborne** – an idyllically pretty village slightly handicapped by a main street too narrow for the volume of traffic. The Wakes, former home of the naturalist Gilbert White, is an attraction to tourists, as are the beech hanger and meadows (now owned by the National Trust) which he described in his classic book *The Natural History of Selborne*. The Wakes also contains a permanent exhibition dedicated to Captain Oates, companion to Captain Scott on his ill-fated exhibition to the Antarctic. The High Street is lined with picturesque brick-and-limestone cottages, some thatched, some early Victorian, though it turns into something of race track during rush hours. A small, late 19th-century stone cottage here will sell for around £150,000. A larger four-bedroom cottage on the hillside, with large grounds and lovely views, could fetch £400,000. There is a small amount of modern housing. The price for four bedrooms and a double garage is around £250,000.

The High Street is lined with picturesque brick-and-limestone cottages, some thatched

Petersfield

Journey: 58 min
Season: £2612
Peak: 4 per hr
Off-peak: 2 per hr

The countryside to the west of **Petersfield** is a designated Area of Outstanding Natural Beauty which is often referred to as Little Switzerland or the Hampshire Alps. A line of hangers, or hanging beech-woods, follows a meandering escarpment from Binstead, just to the west of Alton, down to Petersfield where it connects with the South Downs and rises to a 900ft peak at Butser Hill. Butser is within the Queen Elizabeth Country Park, four miles south of the town, which is the place for picnics, pony rides and even grass skiing.

With this remarkable landscape to hand, and with Winchester and Chichester only half an hour by car, it is not surprising that Petersfield is a very desirable, and hence expensive, place to live. (Beyond Butser Hill to

Fifties detatched
house, Petersfield

the south, property prices drop rapidly as you move outside commuting range.) Petersfield owed its initial prosperity to wool, leather and its use-fulness as a coaching stop on the road to Portsmouth. Its charm comes from the grouping of ancient buildings around The Square, a former market place. Running off it is Sheep Street, lined with 16th- and 17th-century houses. A small two-bedroom house here would cost around £110,000. The

Spain is a kind of unexplained opening in the original street plan, now containing some good Georgian houses. Petersfield was once a predominantly agricultural town, but is now popular with retired couples as well with commuters to London and Portsmouth.

Just a short walk from the High Street is a pond and 69 acres of heath. Here are boats for hire, a cricket pitch and golf course, as well as lonelier spots where you come across Bronze Age burial mounds. The Heath every October is the scene of the Taro Fair, once a horse fair but now featuring roundabouts and stalls. The best addresses in town are on The Heath. Imposing Victorian or Edwardian detached houses, with possibly eight bedrooms, several reception rooms and a billiards room, sell for between £400,000 and £600,000. Typical residents are successful local solicitors and retired naval officers.

On the outskirts are some substantial houses built in the Twenties. Four bedrooms will cost from £320,000. A few major new developments have appeared during the past two decades. Herne Farm is still under construction and offers everything from one-bedroom flats at £60,000 to five-bedroom detached houses at £325,000. The Village, built in the centre of the town, is of "olde worlde" design and colourfully painted. A three-bedroom house here costs £160,000; four bedrooms £200,000 or more. Stoneham Park, built in the Seventies, has two-bedroom houses at £80,000; four bedrooms at £150,000. The Gallifords is slightly cheaper.

A notable feature of village life are the social events at Bedales

Surrounding Petersfield are some beautiful villages. Two miles north is **Steep**, a trickle of houses across a hillside which they share with the co-educational private school Bedales. There are dramatic views of the beechwoods, to which you can walk by taking a route across the common, past the primary school and up into the hangers. A notable feature of village life are the social events at Bedales, which include plays in the new Olivier Theatre, concerts and talks. There is also an art gallery open to the public. You could buy a small period cottage in Steep for around £100,000; a three-bedroom Victorian semi for £200,000; a four- or five-bedroom detached Victorian house for up to £200,000. A one-off five-bedroom detached modern house with an acre of garden could start at £375,000. The Petersfield bypass is a sore point in the village because it comes rather close.

Sheet, one mile north-east of Petersfield, exudes an historic charm. An ancient horse chestnut stands on the village green close to the Queen's Head pub, with the church and a terrace of old cottages nearby. Two former mills set off some of the larger houses very nicely. The village sustains a large primary school which also serves the extensive Thirties housing estate. Prices have risen since the bypass drained traffic away from it. A two-bedroom period cottage will cost around £120,000; a three-bedroom

Thirties detached bungalow £200,000. A four-bedroom Georgian house might fetch around £350,000.

To the south-east of Petersfield is **South Harting**, recognisable from a distance by its octagonal copper church spire seen against the backdrop of Linch Down. The main street, running uphill to the church, has thatched and timber-frame cottages, hairdresser, post office and art shop. Villagers have secured the future of the village shop through a community share-ownership scheme. A three-bedroom half-timbered cottage in South Harting will cost just over £200,000; a three-storey Georgian house with four bedrooms around £325,000. The village hall is the meeting place for all the local clubs and societies, including WI, the Harting Society and a four-days-a-week playschool. There is football and cricket on the recreation ground. Uppark, the house restored by the National Trust after it was burnt down, is a mile away up the hill.

Rowlands Castle is a village for IBM executive types where you need a really new Volvo estate and a headscarf to pick up the children from school

To the west is **West Meon**, which suffers from traffic on the A32, and its sister village **East Meon**, both lying in the shadow of the Downs. West Meon has a primary school, a post-office-cum-store, plus all the usual clubs and societies. A 16th-century four-bedroom thatched cottage in need of modernisation might cost a little under £250,000; a Seventies-built three-bedroom semi around £120,000. East Meon is the prettier of the two, with the River Meon flowing beneath a sequence of little bridges. There are one or two 14th-century houses, plus some Tudor and Georgian, and a working forge. A four-bedroom Georgian house with two or three reception rooms would be likely to cost over £350,000. Leydene Park is a new development a few miles to the south with giddy views of the south coast, tennis courts and five-bedroom detached houses for over £400,000.

Rowlands Castle

Journey: 74 min
Season: £2752
Peak: 3 per hr
Off-peak: 1 per hr

Rowlands Castle has all the appearances of a traditional English village – a crescent of green at the centre, flanked by terrace cottages, Georgian and Victorian houses. A large country house, Deerleap, stands behind a flint wall opposite, and has in its grounds the remains of the castle which gave the village its name. The place is stiff with money and retired naval officers. "This is a village for IBM executive types, where you need a really new Volvo estate and a headscarf to pick up the children from school," is how one local observer put it. There is a long waiting-list of people eager to pay the not inconsiderable fee to join the golf club. The village has its own primary school, a few shops, football and cricket pitches, and a tennis club with courts open to the public. Huge detached houses built in the Twenties and Thirties with an acre of garden sell for around £350,000 in Links Lane, which is the smartest address. Bowes Hill is also smart, with four- and five-bedroom houses of the same period priced between £250,000 and £300,000. Nearby is Ditcham Park, the private school for boys and girls, which has a liberal tradition but is not as fashionable as Bedales. Rowlands Castle is strung between the ancient Forest of Bere and Stansted Park, the family seat of the Earl and Countess of Bessborough, which is open to the public.

Havant

Havant, too, is fairly sedate. It lies inland from Langstone Harbour, which is a popular sailing and watersports centre with good moorings and a sailing club. The town is also well placed to take advantage of the cultural riches offered by Chichester, 10 miles to the east. Another major attraction is the old shore path to Warblington and Emsworth, running past Hayling Island and a much-prized area of marsh and mudflats designated as a Site of Special Scientific Interest. The older part of Havant is now masked by modernity, notably by the Meridian shopping centre, with library and multi-storey car park en suite. A short walk away is The Parchment, so called because the new flats and mews houses here are built on the site of an old parchment-making works. A two-bedroom flat will cost £60,000; a four-bedroom house with two bathrooms £120,000. More up-market areas are Meadowlands and Wade Court, both within half a mile of the town centre. Individually designed detached houses with four and five bedrooms, built in the Twenties and Thirties with plush gardens, sell for between £250,000 and £350,000.

Journey:	72 min
Season:	£2880
Peak:	4 per hr
Off-peak:	3 per hr

6

A major attraction is the old shore path to Warblington and Emsworth running past Hayling Island

Two miles to the east is **Denvilles**, a comforting Thirties suburb where three-bedroom detached houses with large gardens sell for around £110,000 and humble three-bedroom semis can come as cheap as £90,000. A four-bedroom detached house on a Seventies estate would fetch £120,000 to £140,000. There is also a huge Fifties council estate, Leigh Park, built to house Portsmouth overspill.

Bedhampton

Journey: 82 min
Season: £2880
Peak: 2 per hr
Off-peak: 1 per hr

Bedhampton is, with Denvilles (see previous page), one of the prime residential areas of Havant. It was developed in the Fifties as a series of bungalow estates where something with three bedrooms will now cost £110,000 to £120,000. There are three-bedroom semis for around £90,000 and detached houses for £125,000.

Housing developments cling on to Havant for several miles around, and to the north they don't let go until you get beyond Clanfield. Within this built-up area are former villages such as **Cowplain**, where there are 20- and 30-year-old estates and bungalows. A three-bedroom detached house on a Sixties development might cost £120,000; a bungalow of the same size maybe £125,000. **Denmead** village proper is very sought-after, though it stands in a sea of anywhere-modernity. It has shops, pubs and a village green. A turn-of-the-century cottage with three bedrooms and a bit of land could fetch £200,000. There are also plenty of small new developments, popular with young families because of the local school. Prices are similar to those in Waterlooville.

Waterlooville is a very modern quiet suburb, around 80% of which was built during the last decade. Off Tempest Avenue, which runs from one end to the other, is a run of culs-de-sacs with mixed housing in each. A studio apartment will cost £30,000, a three-bedroom semi £85,000 and a four-bedroom detached house £120,000 to £130,000. **Purbrook** has an air of retirement about it. The streets are quiet, the population is older, and there are some turn-of-the-century houses between the bungalows. A two-bedroom bungalow will cost £100,000.

The navy dominates Portsmouth. Along with IBM it is the biggest employer, though it can sometimes create a them-and-us feeling in the city – particularly when hordes of Americans land and head straight for the nightlife in Southsea

Hilsea

Journey: 100 min
(85 min by changing at Havant)
Season: £3044
Peak: 3 per hr
Off-peak: 1 per hr

Hilsea is really north Portsmouth (see ahead). Streets of houses built in the Thirties fan out around the station. A three-bedroom semi will cost between £90,000 and £100,000.

Fratton

Fratton is the home of Portsmouth Football Club, known to friend and foe alike as Pompey. For the rest it is very Coronation Street, like much of Portsmouth. Flat-fronted two- to three-bedroom terrace houses sell for around £55,000.

Journey: 81 min	
Season: £3044	
Peak: 3 per hr	
Off-peak: 3 per hr	

Portsmouth & Southsea and Portsmouth Harbour

The navy dominates **Portsmouth** Along with IBM it is the biggest local employer, though it can sometimes create a them-and-us feeling in the city – particularly when hordes of Americans land and head straight for the nightlife in Southsea. The dockyard has been home to the Royal Navy for 500 years, and the fleet is still serviced here. It is not only a good place for spotting modern warships, there is also an impressive collection of historic ships, including *HMS Victory* and the *Mary Rose*, which attracts tourists all year round. On top of the naval traffic are the constant comings and goings of the Cherbourg, Le Havre, Caen, St Malo and Santander ferries into Albert Johnson dock.

From Portsmouth & Southsea
Journey: 85 min
Season: £3044
Peak: 3 per hr
Off-peak: 3 per hr

From Portsmouth Harbour
Journey: 89 min
Season: £3044
Peak: 3 per hr
Off-peak: 2 per hr

In the Mountbatten Centre, the city has one of the best leisure centres in southern England, which also doubles as a conference and trade show venue. Portsmouth Grammar School is the local private school that takes both boys and girls.

Fogeys might prefer to browse among the bay-fronted Victoriana of North End

Portsmouth Harbour station is close to Gosport, **Old Portsmouth** and the ferry terminal for the Isle of Wight. An 18th-century four- or five-bedroom house in Old Portsmouth would cost around £250,000. Quaint little cottages of the same period, built along cobbled streets, cost between £150,000 and £200,000. North of Portsmouth Harbour is **Port Solent**, a product of the high-earning, fast-living Thatcher years. The marina is the centrepiece, with the surrounding houses, shops, restaurants and sailing school offering "the ultimate maritime lifestyle". A two-bedroom flat will cost around £130,000; a three-bedroom town house with a berth £180,000.

Throughout the city, first-time buyers compete for two-bedroom Victorian and Edwardian houses, priced at around £55,000. A third bedroom puts the price up to around £60,000. Those who are looking for their second or third purchase on the housing ladder, and who are attracted to

Edwardian family
home, Portsmouth

modern property, could look in **Anchorage Park**. This is a huge development in the north of the city, built in the last decade, where a studio costs £30,000; four-bedroom detached houses £120,000. Fogeys might prefer to browse among the bay-fronted Victoriana of **North End**, an area undergoing gradual gentrification. A three-bedroom terrace here would cost around £75,000.

Southsea has more the feel of a seaside resort, with two piers, a shingle beach, permanent funfair, ballroom and the King's Theatre. It is packed with shops, restaurants and pubs. The Pyramids leisure centre is a wonderland of fun pools, water chutes and so on. Running back from the seafront are plenty of Victorian and Edwardian houses. You would pay around £80,000 for three bedrooms; up to £150,000 for a three-and-a-half bedroom corner house.

Waterloo to London Road (Guildford) via Clandon

Clandon

Journey: 45 min
Season: £1932
Peak: 3 per hr
Off-peak: 2 per hr

West Clandon and **East Clandon** both command very high prices. The station is at West Clandon, a linear village, part of which is protected as a conservation area, part devoted to council housing. Until 1900, East Clandon was an estate village attached to Hatchlands Park, a National

Trust house with splendid Robert Adam interiors and gardens by Repton and Gertrude Jekyll. A terrace period cottage in either village could cost between £150,000 and £225,000.

London Road (Guildford)

Guildford lies at the core of sought-after Surrey, an area which appeals to international buyers and in which house prices have more than bounced back since the slump. London Road is Guildford's second station. For Guildford main entry, see page 233.

Journey: 50 min
Season: £2060
Peak: 3 per hr
Off-peak: 2 per hr

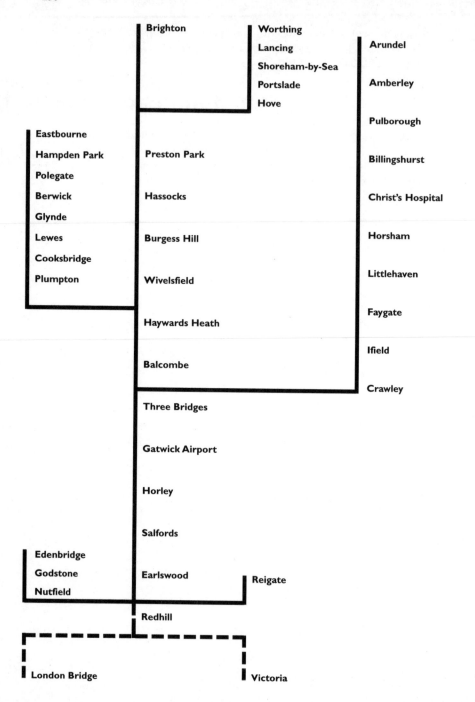

Brighton

Worthing

Lancing

Shoreham-by-Sea

Portslade

Hove

Arundel

Amberley

Pulborough

Eastbourne

Hampden Park

Polegate

Berwick

Glynde

Lewes

Cooksbridge

Plumpton

Preston Park

Hassocks

Burgess Hill

Wivelsfield

Haywards Heath

Billingshurst

Christ's Hospital

Horsham

Littlehaven

Faygate

Balcombe

Ifield

Crawley

Three Bridges

Gatwick Airport

Horley

Salfords

Edenbridge

Godstone

Nutfield

Earlswood

Reigate

Redhill

London Bridge

Victoria

Victoria/London Bridge
➡ Arundel and Brighton ⬎

and on to Eastbourne, Lewes & Worthing

Many services on the line from Brighton to London Bridge proceed to Blackfriars
City Thameslink, Farringdon and Kings Cross Thameslink. Season ticket prices cover
this at no extra cost (but do not cover the Underground).

Redhill

Redhill has now outstripped its older neighbour **Reigate** (see page 253), though it only began to sprout in about 1841 when the railway arrived. It is now heavily commercialised. There is a huge new shopping centre called The Belfry anchored around a large Marks & Spencer, as well as a theatre, The Harlequin, and a sports centre, The Donyngs, with saunas, Jacuzzis, swimming pool and gym.

Redhill is slightly cheaper than Reigate. There is an abundance of good old Thirties semis and detached houses with bay windows and steep cottage-style rooftops. Buy-to-let investors have been snapping up flats and pushing up prices. One-bedroom flats now cost £65,000, two-bedroom flats £100,000. You can get little two-bedroom cottages for around £110,000, three-bedroom terrace houses for £125,000 and three-bedroom semi-detached houses for £140,000 to £180,000. Something more sumptuous, with a third of an acre and a heated swimming pool in the garden, could be bought for £450,000.

To Victoria	
Journey: 28 min	
Season: £1840	
Peak: 2 per hr	
Off-peak: 3 per hr	

To London Bridge	
Journey: 26 min	
Season: £1840	
Peak: 2 per hr	
Off-peak: 3 per hr	

North Downs line east ⬅
to Edenbridge

Nutfield

Nutfield is little more than a ribbon town which has grown up along the A25, with the pedigree of a 13th-century church on the High Street. You can buy two-bedroom maisonettes in converted Victorian houses for £140,000 to £75,000. A substantial house with five or six bedrooms in this area could cost £450,000. **South Nutfield** (where Nutfield station is situated) has a school, two grocers, a post office and the local watering hole is the Station Hotel. A turn-of-the-century terrace house here might cost £140,000; but again there are some very exclusive properties, particularly in The Avenue, which sell for over £500,000.

To London Bridge	
Journey: 32 min	
Season: £1840	
Peak: 1 per hr plus 1 per hr changing at Redhill	
Off-peak: 1 per hr	

Godstone

To London Bridge
Journey: 37 min
Season: £1912
Peak: 1 per hr (plus 1 per hr changing at Redhill)
Off-peak: 1 per hr

Godstone is right on the A25 with a one-way traffic system that turns the centre into an alternative bottleneck when the M25 is blocked. It is no longer the rural backwater where William Cobbett spied double violets as large as small pinks. But it still has the neat gardens he admired, the green, the pond and the White Hart Inn where he stayed. A three-bedroom Georgian terrace house on the High Street was offered recently for £150,000. A Grade II listed house with four to five bedrooms, formerly the tea rooms, would be priced at £220,000.

Edenbridge

To London Bridge
Journey: 43 min
Season: £1912 (also valid at Edenbridge Town), or £2180 via Tonbridge
Peak: 1 per hr (plus 2 per hr changing at Redhill or Tonbridge)
Off-peak: 1 per hr

Edenbridge has two stations, the other being Edenbridge Town on the Hurst Green to Uckfield line (see page 287). The stations are a mile apart, and the two railway lines hold the worst bit of town in a pincer-grip between them. The area is a depository for factories and former council estates. The best parts of town are in the north and south. First-time starter flats cost around £60,000; attractive new one-bedroom terrace houses around £75,000. Four-bedroom houses on a well-kept estate like The Ridgeway, built in 1959, cost about £230,000, including a 200ft garden.

Although Edenbridge is not one of the gems of Kent, it does have its attractions. It is an hour from London and the same from the coast. Gatwick is only half-an-hour away, but not so close that aircraft noise is a worry. The town has a seemingly endless High Street, a string of beautiful half-timbered houses by the River Eden with Duncan Goodhew's restaurant in a restored mill. The south-eastern portion of the town, towards Hever, is more pleasing, especially where it turns into the hamlet of **Marsh Green**, which has a cricket pitch on the green. The south-west end of town, towards **Haxted**, is also inviting. Haxted has a large watermill which is currently closed, but the stables next door have been turned into a restaurant which serves Dover sole and roast pheasant by candlelight or on the terrace by the millpond in summer. On the northern flank of Edenbridge is a mini-industrial estate and a very large, sprawling London overspill council estate called Spittals Cross, where the houses have thin slit windows and flat roofs. Wits say that Edenbridge is a tale of two towns, offering a spectrum of urban blight to rural delight within one-and-a-half miles. There are all the usual sports: cricket, football, tennis, badminton, rugby, hockey, bowls and golf.

The villages surrounding Edenbridge are much more scenic than the town itself. They have a number of fine timber-framed houses from the 16th century, built on the proceeds of the iron industry which collapsed in about 1700. The magnificent old half-timbered houses of **Chiddingstone**, often used for film locations, are in the hands of the National Trust and are let to tenants.

North Downs line west to Reigate

Reigate is Redhill's older brother, tucked under the North Downs, with rows of quiet residential streets and a shopping centre with a significant Safeway. Sunday afternoon walks are taken on Reigate Heath, 130 acres of open space on the edge of the town, where there is a restored windmill that is used as a church. Education is shared with Redhill. There is a Roman Catholic/Church of England co-ed comprehensive called St Bede's that prepares students for A-levels and Oxbridge entrance. East Surrey College offers degrees in art, design, science and computing.

To Victoria
Journey: 46 min
Season: £1840
Peak: 4 per hr*
Off-peak: 1 per hr*
*Change at Redhill, except for 2 through trains to London Bridge

Reigate has a greater quantity of properties at the top end of the market than Redhill. The most exclusive areas are High Trees Road and just off Reigate Hill. A large family home on Pilgrims Way with two-thirds of an acre, garaging for three cars and four double bedrooms would cost £500,000 to £650,000. A little detached Victorian house with three double bedrooms, close to the High Street, could be bought for rather less, at £250,000.

Continuation of main line
Earlswood

It is hard to find a dividing line between **Earlswood** and Redhill. Many of the people who live here work at the nearby East Surrey Hospital. There are also plenty of commuters, travelling to both Croydon and London. Earlswood is not as sought after as Redhill, but it does have a beautiful common and two lakes for boating and fishing. A purpose-built two-bedroom flat would cost £85,000; a three-bedroom turn-of-the-century semi £120,000.

To London Bridge
Journey: 35 min
Season: £1840
Peak: 2 per hr plus 2 per hr to Victoria
Off-peak: 1 per hr

Salfords

Salfords is nice in parts but has the disadvantage of straddling the A23. It has a village shop-cum-post-office, and a brace of newsagents, but people tend to aim for Redhill, Horley or Hookwood for their major shops. There is a primary school, but older children have to go by bus to Horley or Redhill for secondary schools. Long-suffering parents spend a lot of time chauffeuring their children about because there is not much for them to do in the village itself (the Scout group is at neighbouring Sidlow). The nearby aerodrome is a thorn in the side. Night-flight training programmes for light aircraft and helicopters are a regular irritation. A three-bedroom semi

To London Bridge
Journey: 39 min
Season: £1936
Peak: 2 per hr plus 2 per hr to Victoria
Off-peak: 1 per hr

with a long garden here might cost £135,000 and a bungalow with two double bedrooms would cost slightly more because of its rarity value. Larger properties in leafier roads lie to the east.

Horley

To Victoria
Journey: 42 min
Season: £2120
Peak: 4 per hr
Off-peak: 1 per hr

To London Bridge
Journey: 42 min
Season: £2120
Peak: 2 per hr
Off-peak: 1 per hr

Compared to the two commercial bullies, Reigate and Crawley, that lie on either side of it, **Horley** is a mute backwater. "A lot of people think it is *too* quiet," says one resident. It does, however, have a swimming pool at the Horley Anderson Centre, plus cricket, hockey, bowling and football clubs. Gatwick Airport is a big local employer. The two main thoroughfares are the A23 and a modest high street. The local comprehensive, Oakwood School, is well-liked. In the sea of Thirties semis you could pay between £130,000 and £140,000 for three bedrooms. There are also some Victorian terraces where three-bedroom houses start at around £120,000. The modern Langshott estate, with over 700 houses on it, won awards for landscaping and design when it was built. A five-bedroom detached house here would cost over £300,000. The area is earmarked for another armful of new housing soon.

The village of **Charlwood** struggles admirably to hang onto its rural image, in spite of the fact that Gatwick Airport is only a few miles away and is constantly wanting to expand towards it. A formidably active parish council keeps a watchful eye on all planning applications and development proposals. Villagers lovingly nurse the large number of listed buildings, which include a Grade I listed Norman church. The village has a newsagent which also sells fruit and groceries, a post office, a soft furnishing shop, a pine shop and a builders' merchants. There is a school for the under-sevens. People living here have the choice of commuting either from Horley or from Gatwick, where the service is fast and frequent. A brick-built two-bedroom cottage might be bought for £120,000; a third bedroom puts the price up to around £140,000.

Smallfield, to the north-east, has been greatly affected by the development of Gatwick. Aircraft noise is a problem, and the very presence of an airport has allowed more industrial development than there would otherwise have been. It has a burgeoning population, with a good mix of young and old, yet it is straggly and has no real centre. Local shops include a greengrocer and butcher, local events take place in the new Centenary Village Hall. There is an annual flower show, a carnival each July, and dinner-dances in the church and school hall. Prices are similar to those in Horley. A two-bedroom Victorian semi-detached cottage sells for £120,000 and a detached three-bedroom house for £150,000. Modern four-bedroom detached houses cost around £200,000.

Gatwick Airport

Gatwick Express trains whistle into London from here at a frequency of one every 15 minutes, making it a popular choice for commuters in a hurry. People living in the villages to the west might prefer it to stations on the nearer but much slower **Victoria/Waterloo to Horsham** line (page 277).

To London Bridge	To Victoria
Journey: 28 min	Journey: 30 min
Season: £2188 (Thameslink); £2608 (all operators, all routes)	Season: £2120 (Connex); £2460 (Gatwick Express); £2608 (all operators, all routes)
Peak: 3 per hr	Peak: 6 per hr
Off-peak: 4 per hr	Off-peak: 8 per hr

Grade II listed house, Charlwood

Three Bridges

Some of the better parts of Crawley such as **Pound Hill** and **Copthorne** are close to this station. One-bedroom flats cost about £70,000; three-bedroom detached houses about £120,000 (see Crawley). **Three Bridges**, so-called because of the bridges that cross Gatwick Brock nearby, was a village in its own right before Crawley was first thought of. It contains some Victorian terraces that sprang up around the railway station, but the bulk of it was built in the early Fifties when more than 2,000 houses were put up for 4,800 newcomers. Prices are slightly higher than those in Crawley (see page 256)

To Victoria
Journey: 42 min
Season: £2280 (£2620 if Gatwick Express included)
Peak: 3 per hr
Off-peak: 3 per hr

To London Bridge
Journey: 34 min
Season: £2232 (£2280 if also valid to Victoria)
Peak: 3 per hr
Off-peak: 2 per hr

Main line from Three Bridges to **Arundel**

Crawley

To Victoria
Journey: 46 min
Season: £2280
(£2620 if Gatwick
Express included)
Peak: 2 per hr
Off-peak: 2 per hr

To London Bridge
Journey: 53 min
Season: £2240
(£2280 if also valid
to Victoria)
Peak: 2 per hr
Off-peak: 1 per hr

Crawley is not much loved by anyone and can't avoid the nickname Creepie Crawley. A few years ago the young here felt they had nothing. "There isn't even a Miss Selfridge," whined one. Now there is a Miss Selfridge, and two nightclubs as well. But the great plus here for the young is that unemployment has hardly touched it. Jobs at Gatwick Airport are plentiful, and the factory estates and business parks that have grown up around it include every kind of industry from light manufacturing to pharmaceuticals and foodstuffs.

It was developed as a New Town after the war – the only one in the south of England – for people moving out of London. The design was originally anchored around nine neighbourhoods (now there are 13 with one at planning stage), each with a population of 6,000. Each would have its own shopping parade, primary school, church, pub, community hall and playing fields. The first new-towners moved in during 1949, when Gatwick Airport was no more than a war-time runway on boggy ground on the town's outskirts, a far cry from the noisy, air-polluting monster that it has become.

People moving to the area would probably choose to live in one of the neighbouring villages, or closer to Three Bridges station, and go into Crawley only to take advantage of County Mall, the biggest covered shopping centre in the south-east, and the new Crawley Leisure Park which has

House style in Sussex

The tile-hung cottages of Sussex, with their hipped roofs, rich timbering and modest proportions, give the most sought-after villages their texture and colour. Set against the drama of the North and South Downs, often tucked into folds or valleys, their russets and terracottas glow in the landscape.

The tiles themselves are hooked over battens, often fastened only every third or fourth course with nothing more than oak pegs. Baking in the kiln caused them to become slightly distorted, so that they form a pleasingly uneven line with small variations in colour. Line them up, row upon row, and you get a kind of decorative architectural needlework. Vary the shapes by introducing diamonds and fish-tails, and the humblest of cottages looks as prettily feathered as an exotic bird.

Architectural deceit is something to watch for in this part of the country. For here it was that

mathematical tiles were invented – tiles to look like bricks – in the 18th century. The theory is that this was done as a means of avoiding Brick Taxes, but it may have had more to do with vanity. Brick was the fashionable building material of the time. The deceit continues as mathematical tiles often fool modern housebuyers who believe them to be brick. The key to their detection is the absence of lintels and arches over windows and doors.

East and West Sussex are also counties which have provided great wealth and pleasure. This is where William the Conqueror built some of the first Norman castles and established the feudal system. Later royals used the seaside towns as their favoured watering holes, hence all the Regency froth and finery of Brighton. The town was transformed with squares and crescents by the Prince of Wales in the early 1800s.

a fitness club, bowling, restaurants and a Virgin Megaplex Cinema. Other attractions include Tilgate Park, which has a rare and domestic animal collection, and the 18-hole municipal golf course.

For £110,000 it is possible to get one of the original three-bedroom semis put up at the beginning of the new town. Studio flats cost around £45,000 and one-bedroom flats £55,000. The original neighbourhoods are still identifiable. West Green, for instance, was one of the first, and it still has rows of brick terraces and some older labourers' cottages. The less popular and less successful neighbourhoods are Broadfield, which has a lot of council housing, Bewbush, which was hastily built to accommodate second generation Crawley families, and Langley Green.

Ifield

Ifield is on the outskirts of Crawley, but at least there is a conservation area which contains the old village green, St Margaret's Church and the Plough Inn. The old Ifield Watermill sits beside a millpond and has been partially restored as a museum. A larding of new houses was added in 1956. Today the population stands at 8,500. You can get three-bedroom semis for £105,000 and two-bedroom cottages from £110,000.

To Victoria	To London Bridge
Journey: 59 min	Journey: 56 min
Season: £2280	Season: £2240
(£2620 to include	(£2280 if also valid
Gatwick Express)	to Victoria)
Peak: 2 per hr	Peak: 2 per hr
Off-peak: 1 per hr	Off-peak: 1 per hr

Faygate

This little station is only served in the rush hour. Property is a little more expensive in **Faygate** than in Crawley because people like the intimacy of scale offered by the village, but in truth the semi-rural atmosphere is negated by the dual carriageway screeching past. Something with four bedrooms will cost over £180,000.

To Victoria
Journey: 63 min
Season: £2320
(£2620 to include
Gatwick Express)
Peak: 1 per hr
(plus 2 per hr
changing at Three
Bridges or
Gatwick)
Off-peak: 1 every 4
hrs

Littlehaven

Littlehaven was once a separate village, but is now essentially a part of Horsham with modern estates providing the putty between the two. The older houses are in Rusper Road, but much of the property for sale is modern, with three-bedroom semis sensibly priced at around £140,000. Wise advice from one seasoned commuter: "The station platform is only four carriages long so you have to make sure you're in the right bit of the train or you can't get off."

To Victoria	To London Bridge
Journey: 64 min	Journey: 62 min
Season: £2440	Season: £2400
(£2620 to include	(£2440 if also valid
Gatwick Express)	to Victoria)
Peak: 2 per hr	Peak: 2 per hr
Off-peak: 1 per hr	Off-peak: 1 per hr

Horsham

To Victoria
Journey: 55 min
Season: £2440
(£2620 if Gatwick
Express included)
Peak: 3 per hr
Off-peak: 3 per hr

To London Bridge
Journey: 65 min
Season: £2400
(£2440 if also valid
to Victoria)
Peak: 2 per hr
Off-peak: 1 per hr

Horsham is a busy little Sussex town which manages to combine its old character as a smugglers' haunt and late 18th-century garrison town with plenty of interesting little shops and local businesses. It has a population of 40,000 which is expanding fast. It is in a marvellous position with a good train service to London, but with house prices lower than they are across the border in Surrey. Chichester and Guildford are close enough for theatres though Horsham has its own small theatre, and the sea is 20 miles away over the South Downs. You can go to the races at Goodwood, show jumping at Hickstead, hunt with the Crawley and Horsham Pack, and there are golf clubs at Pulborough, Mannings Heath, Pease Pottage, West Chiltington and Ockley. It also has Christ's Hospital public school for boys and girls, where there is a separate railway station (see ahead).

Some of the houses in the town are collector's items. Walk down Pump Alley and into the Causeway, for example, and you find a street that is much as it was 300 years ago. These houses with bulging walls and uneven roofs very rarely come on the market, and could fetch around £375,000. For something more ordinary – a detached Thirties house with three bedrooms, within walking distance of the town – you could pay £250,000. A small modern two-bedroom house would cost around £95,000. There are council estates to the east and west of the town.

Local villages also maintain strong links with the past. **Slinfold**, to the west, has a good collection of Georgian houses hemmed in by tall hedges and walls, strung out along a very pretty winding lane. It still has a village shop and school. A classic Sussex tile-hung house with four bedrooms, two bathrooms and large gardens backing on to fields would cost around £360,000. Closer to Horsham, separated from it by the A24, is **Broadbridge Heath**, which has a sports centre, Tesco, and a house called Field Place, the birthplace of Shelley, occasionally opened to the public.

Further south is **Itchingfield**, which has an intriguing priest's house attached to the church; and **Southwater**, which is little more than a dormitory to Horsham and free-fire zone for new housing. Moving east you come to **Nuthurst**, a delightful village with 16th-century houses and a timber-framed inn.

Lower Beeding is small, elongated and has a small post-office-cum-shop. An old gardener's cottage with three bedrooms and outbuildings in three quarters of an acre might fetch just under £300,000. The big house, Leonardslee, has rhododendron gardens that are occasionally open to the public. The countryside lapses back into heathland here in St Leonard's Forest – 12,000 acres of old royal hunting ground, once thought to have harboured dragons and to which (within living memory) pigs were driven up from Brighton to snuffle for acorns. To the south is **Cowfold**, which has lost some of its character through being a junction for the A272 and the

A281 but it is still well-liked. Flats here start at £65,000, but a country house in the area with six bedrooms, three bathrooms and three acres would cost £550,000.

North of the forest is **Rusper**, an enchanting village with an ancient church (origins in the 13th century), a high street full of black-and-white timber buildings and two pubs, The Plough and The Star, which are centuries old. On this side of Horsham you have to beware the noise of aircraft from Gatwick.

You need to remember that stations south of Horsham have a much less frequent service to London

Christ's Hospital

Christ's Hospital, hardly distinct from Horsham, is dominated by the public school, fondly known as C.H. by local people, which disgorges pupils in their distinctive blue and bright yellow uniform. Around it has grown a low-level brick settlement, largely 20th-century, which looks to neighbouring Southwater for small-time shopping. It is a much sought after area, with a disproportionately large railway station. Straightforward two-bedroom modern houses sell for between £120,000 and £140,000, three-bedroom semis from £165,000 to £185,000 and four-bedroom red-brick turn-of-the-century cottages at £200,000 to £220,000.

To Victoria
Journey: 59 min
Season: £2460
(£2620 if Gatwick Express included)
Peak: 2 per hr
(plus 1 per hr to London Bridge)
Off-peak: 1 per hr

Billingshurst

Billingshurst feels more like a small town than a large village, with some fine 15th-century houses beached on a shore of modern developments. It is very much divided by the A29, which follows the route of the old Roman road, Stane Street. Commuters love it because it is more intimate than Horsham or Crawley yet has the fast rail links. "Our looks and intelligence distinguish us from other villages," says one resident. A two-bedroom turn-of-the-century cottage will cost £140,000.

To Victoria
Journey: 66 min
Season: £2480
(£2620 if Gatwick Express included)
Peak: 2 per hr
(plus 1 per hr to London Bridge)
Off-peak: 1 per hr

Wisborough Green, two miles away, is literally a film-set village, regularly used by film directors as a backdrop. It has a cricket green that borders the A272, a village shop-cum-post-office and two inns. A Grade II listed period tile-hung cottage with four bedrooms, two bathrooms, gardens and 10 acres of paddock would cost around £450,000. You need to remember that stations south of Horsham are much less well served by trains to London.

Pulborough

To Victoria
Journey: 73 min
Season: £2600
(£2620 if Gatwick
Express included)
Peak: 2 per hr (plus
1 per hr to London
Bridge)
Off-peak: 1 per hr

This is where the Arun valley becomes spellbindingly beautiful, and houses backing onto it are extremely sought after. "The wetlands, the bird sanctuary, the downland walks, make it an absolutely glorious place to live, full of sunny corners," says one happy local resident. This rather belies the fact that **Pulborough** is under a lot of development pressure, and local conservationists are battle-scarred. Local societies eddy and bubble – there are Cubs, Brownies, rugby, cricket and plenty of vigorous football. The green fingered work hard on the allotments and join the horticultural society. The village has two butchers, a supermarket, and a grand new village hall. In the jumble of brick, flint and thatch you could pick up a little three-bedroom detached house for £150,000.

Many of the villages on the felted slopes of the South Downs are very lovely. **West Burton** and **Sutton**, for instance, are very small and rural, no more than a handful of cottages and a pub. A three-bedroom cottage will cost over £300,000; a four-bedroom house over £400,000.

Nutborne, just to the north-east, is another little hamlet with a pub, a local vineyard, and you might find a two-bedroom cottage for £200,000. Northeast of West Burton and Sutton you come to what local people tend rather dismissively to call the Surrey part of Sussex – meaning that it is more suburban in character than the wilder countryside to the east. A three- to four-bedroom bungalow in comparatively manicured **West Chiltington** will cost £275,000 to £375,000. It is close to the shops at **Storrington**, a village that long ago burst its boundaries with new houses but which offers a reasonable range of shops and two ponds with ducks and swans. The River Stor also bursts its boundaries regularly so ask about flood risk if you are buying a house here. Dying here poses problems because the graveyard is full (so in recent years people have been under pressure to be cremated), but thankfully a field has now been consecrated to take the overspill.

Period town house, Petworth

The star in the west is **Petworth**, the town that stands at the gates of Petworth House, with hundreds of acres of National Trust land and a house begun by the Duke of Somerset at the end of the 17th century. The old timber-frame houses in the tangle of narrow streets around the square attract lots of tourists in the summer. The large local car park is full by breakfast-time, much to the annoyance of the local shoppers. Petworth is also an antiques centre, with more than 30 antique shops. There aren't a lot of other shops, though there is a gunsmith for the sporting fraternity. Villagers feel oppressed by the traffic coming through on the A285 and the A272; a by-pass has been talked of since 1935 and has now developed into grand ideas for a tunnel through which cars could mole in order to avoid the town. A brick-and-tile house with four bedrooms, a garage and garden, would cost around £220,000. Commuters have the choice of using the faster line into Waterloo from Haslemere, which is 10 miles away.

A bypass has been talked of since 1935 and there are now grand ideas for a tunnel

Fittleworth, closer to Pulborough, is a more mixed kind of village where neighbours find it difficult to get to know each other. It has its own shop, church and inn, and is close to marvellous riding country in Bedham Woods and on the Downs. A four-bedroom Sussex tile-hung house set in one acre would cost something over £350,000.

Amberley

Amberley is another of the many villages in this area that have hung onto their character. It is protected from heavy traffic on a side road off the B2139. Old flint-and-thatch cottages with old-fashioned cottage gardens cluster around Amberley Castle, once the residence of the Bishops of Chichester and dismantled by Parliamentarians during the Civil War. A footpath to one side leads to Amberley Wild Brooks, protected water meadows visited by migrating birds. The village has a shop-cum-post-office. A four-bedroom cottage could be bought for £350,000. House prices remain on the steep side in several other popular villages further from the station such as **Houghton** and **Bury.**

To Victoria	
Journey: 79 min	
Season: £2620	
Peak: 1 per hr	
Off-peak: 1 per hr	

Arundel

Arundel is a busy old town on the River Arun, dominated by its castle which is often described as Windsor in miniature. The High Street, winding steeply between the river and the castle, has plenty of antiques shops but none of the standard chain stores. There is a butcher and two bakers, general stores, a fine-wine-cum-deli, antique shops, and a walking-stick shop. Chichester is only 10 miles away with its attractions for yachtsmen and theatre-goers (though Arundel has its own Priory Playhouse for smaller-scale productions); Goodwood racecourse is a mere three miles up on the Downs, and there are plenty of golf courses. The sea is three miles

To Victoria	
Journey: 84 min	
Season: £2620	
Peak: 2 per hr	
(plus 1 per hr to London Bridge)	
Off-peak: 1 per hr	

away, and there is a good beach at Climping. The River Arun has to be watched. It is tidal, and one of the fastest flowing rivers in the country after the Severn. The Arundel Wildfowl Trust, founded by Sir Peter Scott, runs special events for children during the school holidays.

You could buy a two-bedroom cottage now for £90,000. For a building in traditional brick-and-flint, you will have to pay a premium of around £10,000. For three-bedroom houses the price jumps to over £150,000 – though you might be lucky and find a three-bedroom terrace for around £140,000. People either opt for old Arundel, which climbs steeply up the hill, layer upon layer towards the castle, or they look at the larger Fifties houses on the Chichester side. These have large gardens and garages, are within walking distance of the town and are rather more suburban. A four-bedroom house in this neighbourhood will cost between £200,000 and £350,000.

The villages of **Burpham** and **Wepham** lie to the east, on the way up to the top of Harrow Hill where the views are wonderful. Both are popular, and a thatched two-bedroom semi with small garden would cost £190,000. **Slindon**, to the west, is the kind of village people wait years for a chance to move into. Not only because of its beauty but because the involvement of the National Trust means that very few houses are still freehold. A period house with three to four bedrooms could cost close to £500,000. The village has its cheaper end where two-bedroom bungalows sell for around £145,000.

Main line from **Three Bridges** to **Brighton**

Balcombe

To London Bridge
Journey: 39 min
Season: £2280
(£2320 if also valid to Victoria and £2620 if Gatwick Express included)
Peak: 1 per hr (plus 1 per hr changing at Three Bridges or Gatwick)
Off-peak: 1 per hr

Its position on a railway line set deep in an Area of Outstanding Natural Beauty has gilded the house-price lily in **Balcombe**. Commuters now have quite a strong presence there, most of them high earners. They usually begin by sending their children to the local nursery and primary schools, but switch them into the private system later. The village has an old quarter and a modern quarter, and its great good luck is that the new estates have been planned well enough to avoid any feeling of claustrophobia. Just off the village centre in the old quarter, Victorian semis with three bedrooms, three reception rooms and a garden sell briskly in the £185,000 range.

The village is described by the parish clerk as "happy, friendly and caring". Strangers are soon spotted by vigilant members of the Neighbourhood Watch. Among the myriad clubs and activities is a Care Group which arranges to take people to hospital, collect prescriptions and so on; and a Christmas Tree Society to aid the needy. There are societies to cover the needs of every age group from mixed Cubs to pensioners, plus tennis, cricket, football and badminton clubs. The actor Paul Schofield lives here.

It is close to Ardingly (the last syllable rhymes with eye) Reservoir where people sail, windsurf and fish at weekends. Mostly it is used by students from Ardingly College, the independent school for boys and girls which sits on the bank. The hill-ridge village of **Ardingly** is best known for the National Trust's Wakehurst Gardens. These are leased by the Royal Botanical Gardens at Kew and for the South of England Showground. The three-day agricultural show every June makes it the agricultural capital of Sussex. The grounds are also used for antique shows and Pony Club displays. Ardingly's village hall is heavily booked with ballet classes, mothers and toddlers groups, playgroups and horticultural society meetings. A Thirties semi with three bedrooms in a quiet cul-de-sac within walking distance of all these activities sells at around £165,000.

Haywards Heath

This is prime commuter country, close to the M23 and the M25, fed by fast trains to London yet close enough for trips to the sea. Successful local businessmen and airline pilots from Gatwick also help to put up prices. The town feels hugely superior to Burgess Hill, which is three miles away and probably has slightly better shops, though **Haywards Heath** has both a Marks & Spencer and a Sainsbury. Property prices are high. A simple one-bedroom flat will cost around £60,000, rising to between £65,000 and £72,000 for a two-bedroom flat and £78,000 to £90,000 for a two-bedroom house. A detached four-bedroom house with two bathrooms is likely to cost around £200,000. Better parts of town are in the conservation areas at Lucastes and Lewes Road. Also popular is Muster Green, where the large Victorian and Edwardian houses have ample gardens around an open space that has much of the character of a village green.

You can throw money at houses in the Haywards Heath area. Villages such as **Wineham** are very popular. Here, a grand Twenties mock-Tudor house with nine bedrooms, 88 acres and a lodge, recently appeared on the market with a price tag of around £1.75m. **Lindfield** has all the ingredients of the perfect village – a high street with tile-hung Sussex houses, a pond with ducks and swans, a large open common and a historic parish church. It is in two halves. One half remains Elizabethan. The other half consists of ex-council housing. Stockbrokers' houses are slipped into the lanes round about. A five-bedroom Georgian house on the Lewes Road would fetch around £450,000. A modernised and extended farmhouse with four bedrooms, fabulous views and three acres just to the north will cost around £550,000.

To Victoria
Journey: 45 min
Season: £2560
(£2620 to include Gatwick Express)
Peak: 5 per hr
Off-peak: 3 per hr

To London Bridge
Journey: 41 min
Season: £2520
(£2560 if also valid to Victoria)
Peak: 3 per hr
Off-peak: 4 per hr

Further north still, **Horsted Keynes** is another village that mutated during the Fifties. You drive through the centre thinking how lovely the village green is, then turn a corner and confront a mass of cheap housing. The pretty bit is still very popular and commands higher prices than Haywards Heath. A two-bedroom bungalow with views over the countryside would cost around £150,000. About a mile away is the privately-run Bluebell Railway, a great delight for steam-train enthusiasts. **Paxhill Park** is popular for its golf course but lacks a real village spirit.

Unusual tile-hung cottage, Wivelsfield

To the west is **Scayne's Hill**. It has been sliced in two by the A272 but has some dignified Victorian houses, with prices starting at £85,000 for two bedrooms in the quieter parts. **Fletching** is tiny but has a lovely collection of 16th-century houses and a couple of pubs (see page 291).

Less than two miles to the west of Haywards Heath is the tall spire of **Cuckfield** parish church, which German bombers used as a landmark during the Second World War. Beyond it you negotiate a tortuous bend, then climb the beautiful 15th-century high street, lined with medieval cottages. At the brow of the hill the spell is broken and medieval England dissolves into Victorian and modern. A well-presented Eighties five-bedroom family house and garden sells at around £450,000.

Since the village was once a staging post it is well-endowed with pubs – five altogether, for a population of 2,000. Cuckfield is extremely active and shows its independence in eccentric ways. A fight with the district council over the ownership of the green resulted in the village declaring independence and producing its own passports, currency and stamps. It still holds mock elections for a mayor every year, and residents pay one penny to vote. The Independent State of Cuckfield is the eccentrically named local pressure group which does much charity fund-raising and has fought off plans for a rubbish tip. Cuckfield has its own museum, library and local beauty spot, New England Wood.

To the west are the more remote hamlets of **Bolney** and **Warninglid**. Both had strong connections with the medieval iron industry, and are now very quiet and beautiful, and kept scrupulously tidy by elderly inhabitants. A four-bedroom chalet bungalow in Bolney with three quarters of an acre would cost around £275,000.

Wivelsfield

Wivelsfield station is actually two-and-a-half-miles away on the edge of Burgess Hill. The village is split, with the older part gathered around the church and school, and the newer part on the east of the B2112 at Wivelsfield Green. Property prices are similar to those in Burgess Hill (see below). People tend to pass through it on their way to Haywards Heath or Lewes. The influx of London and Brighton commuters since the war has doubled the population to around 1,200, but the old village families are still involved in agriculture and Young Farmers' events are well attended. It has a post-office-cum-village store which stretches to delicatessen food and French bread, and a garage. The primary school is popular though the Victorian buildings are worn and torn. Older children move on to Haywards Heath comprehensive and a tertiary college at Chailey. There are lovely old tiled cottages in some of the older roads, such as Church Lane. A modernised, tile-hung terrace house with three bedrooms and a 150ft garden backing onto open countryside sells at around £130,000.

To Victoria
Journey: 54 min
Season: £2580
(£2620 to include Gatwick Express)
Peak: 3 per hr
Off-peak: 2 per hr

To London Bridge
Journey: 44 min
Season: £2540
(£2580 if also valid to Victoria)
Peak: 2 per hr
Off-peak: 1 per hr

Burgess Hill

Burgess Hill was an intimate little place until a few decades ago. In 1951 its population was just 8,000. Since then it has been overwhelmed by new estates built to soak up London overspill. The population has shot up to 27,000 and is still climbing as big companies including British Oxygen and American Express move in. A new relief road and link to the A23 has unlocked pockets of building land for thousands more new houses but a grass buffer to the west of town called the Green Crescent provides a protective belt of sorts. The old Sixties shopping centre, The Martletts, has been redeveloped in a new Nineties mould. There is a Waitrose and Tesco, but otherwise the shopping is unimaginative. Cultural treats can be had at the cinema and the Burgess Hill Theatre (venue for local dramatic and choral societies), and muscle tone can be developed at the Triangle Leisure Centre. The comprehensive school is oversubscribed; the fee-paying alternative for girls is Burgess Hill School.

To Victoria
Journey: 61 min
Season: £2580
(£2620 to include Gatwick Express)
Peak: 3 per hr
Off-peak: 1 per hr

To London Bridge
Journey: 46 min
Season: £2540
(£2580 if also valid to Victoria)
Peak: 2 per hr
Off-peak: 2 per hr

The town is downmarket of Haywards Heath and probably offers the lowest property prices to be found in this expensive mid-Sussex belt, though still higher than south Sussex. Two-bedroom houses start at around £75,000; three-bedroom houses at £85,000; four-bedroom detached houses at £150,000. Silverdale Road, Keymer Road and Folders Lane are where you find the most expensive older houses, with company directors and airline pilots settling at around £300,000 to £600,000. A few very old farmhouses still survive on the former commons.

Hassocks

To Victoria
Journey: 64 min
Season: £2600
(£2620 to include
Gatwick Express)
Peak: 3 per hr
Off-peak: 1 per hr

To London Bridge
Journey: 50 min
Season: £2560
(£2600 if also valid
to Victoria)
Peak: 2 per hr
Off-peak: 1 per hr

Hassocks likes to think of itself as a village, but it is actually town-size with a population of 9,000 containing quite a high proportion of retired people. It snuggles up to **Hurstpierpoint** and **Keymer**, though the people of Hurstpierpoint regard themselves as quite separate. The small shopping parade meets basic needs, but for serious food shopping people go to Waitrose or Tesco at Burgess Hill.

Hassocks is not architecturally distinguished. It grew up around the railway in the 19th century, with new developments appearing in the Thirties and Fifties. But it does sit under the wing of the South Downs, so there are magnificent views of the Jack and Jill windmills on the crest where you can also take lonely windblown walks.

You would pay around £160,000 for a three-bedroom modern detached house, but older properties go for much more. For example a four-bedroom Victorian or Edwardian semi would set you back by £250,000 to £300,000. Hassocks has primary and secondary schools which are thought to be good. There is a Beacon Club for the mid-teens, but not much for older teenagers to do. The old Sussex game of stoolball is still played here, kept alive by the Stoolball Association. It is a form of rounders, invented by milkmaids who wanted a recreational use for their three-legged milking stools. There is an amenity association which looks after conservation, plus drama and horticultural societies.

Ditchling, just to the east, is one of the most rarefied spots in this part of Sussex, luxuriating in a dramatic valley beneath the spine of the South downs, though it is hammered by traffic heading straight through for Brighton. During the last century it has attracted a succession of artists and calligraphers, originally attracted by a Roman Catholic artistic community (including Eric Gill) which settled up on the Downs. A gracious, four-bedroom Thirties house in an acre of garden would cost around £350,000. On the outskirts, where a council estate seems to have approached almost by stealth, a three-bedroom semi might be picked up for around £120,000, as houses at the cheaper end of the market tend to stick because people moving to Ditchling want something rather more special. Over the years it has attracted many famous inhabitants, including the actress Dame Ellen Terry and currently Dame Vera Lynn. It has a few basic shops, teashops, an art gallery, a good primary school and a Museum of Local Life. It is particularly proud of its choral society. Nearby is Ditchling Common, offering nearly 200 acres of walks; and Ditchling Beacon, over 800 ft high, where a fire was lit to warn of the approach of the Spanish Armada.

The illustrator Raymond Briggs lives in the nearby hamlet of **Westmeston**, which is also a beautiful quiet retreat at the foot of the Downs. Residents recently raised money to have the unsightly overhead wires buried underground; the village pulse can be taken in the new

Parish Room where events are held. There is no shop or post office but it does have a public telephone box. The nearest primary school is in Ditchling and there are secondary schools in Lewes, Chailey and Hassocks.

Preston Park

Preston Park is a part of Brighton that particularly attracts commuters because of its railway station. Small Victorian and Edwardian houses with two bedrooms sell for between £120,000 and £125,000. It is much leafier than the Victorian streets of North Laines and Westhill, which are both close to the station in Brighton proper.

To Victoria
Journey: 73 min
Season: £2640
Peak: 2 per hr
Off-peak: 1 per hr

To London Bridge
Journey: 57 min
Season: £2640
Peak: 2 per hr
Off-peak: 1 per hr

Brighton

Brighton is busy trying to metamorphose into London-on-Sea, developing an increasingly sophisticated and cosmopolitan air, playing up its strengths as a conference centre and weekend retreat. It is short on domestic gardens and garages, but the frivolity of the Royal Pavilion, the beautifully landscaped parks and the backdrop of the Sussex Downs make it an enviable place to live. The Brighton Festival (May) is England's biggest arts festival. There is a plethora of restaurants and the Theatre Royal attracts many plays on their pre-London tours. There has always been a theatrical crowd in Brighton – Lord Olivier once lived here – attracted by the Regency terrace houses of Montpelier with their canopied bow fronts and panelled drawing rooms. Brighton has always been *the* place to have a flat, and the various building booms of the last few decades have provided plenty of them, both in purpose-built blocks and in large houses that have been converted. There is also now a boating crowd, drawn by the marina.

To Victoria
Journey: 71 min
Season: £2640
Peak: 3 per hr
Off-peak: 1 per hr

To London Bridge
Journey: 55 min
Season: £2640
Peak: 2 per hr
Off-peak: 4 per hr

Commuters tend to live within walking distance of the railway station, which is very central and within half a mile of the seafront. The shops, seafront and residential areas are so closely knit that many people don't have cars at all. There are various interlocking conservation areas which househunters might aim for. **North Laines**, **Westhill** and **Clifton** are close to the station, all now rather gentrified with little boutiques and antique shops. In the Clifton Conservation Area, a substantial Victorian corner house sells for around £320,000.

Millionaires' Row is at **Roedean**, just beside the girl's private school and opposite the marina. Large houses with six bedrooms sell here for anything up to £600,000. If you are thinking about buying anything facing the sea, however, do consider the havoc wrought by salt-laden winds on your exterior paintwork and the extra decorating bills you'll have to face as a result.

Schools in East and West Sussex

The ample arms of the North and South Downs give Sussex's schools the most beautiful settings, with huge acreages and lofty views down to the sea. At Crawley in West Sussex, occupying a 19th-century mansion with a monastery and abbey attached, is Worth School, an independent boarding school for boys. Not far away is Burgess Hill independent day and boarding school for girls.

Haywards Heath offers a choice of popular private and state schools. These include Ardingly, the co-educational boarding and day school, and Warden Park, the co-educational comprehensive. At Horsham, choices include the comprehensives Millais, Tanbridge House, as well as nearby Christ's Hospital independent co-educational boarding school (where the fees are means-related) and Farlington independent girls boarding and day school. East Grinstead has the Sackville and Imberhorne co-educational comprehensives.

Brighton has attracted a rash of independent schools. These include the girls' day school Brighton & Hove High, and the independent co-educational day and boarding school Brighton College. Roedean boarding school for girls is nearby, as is Lancing, the boys' boarding and day school (girls in the sixth), which has a commanding position set in 550 acres on the top of the Downs.

Eastbourne has the Moira House independent boarding and day school for girls and Eastbourne independent boarding and day school for boys (with girls in the sixth), set in wonderful cloisters around a cricket square.

Another school which is spoken highly of in the East Sussex area is St Leonards-Mayfield, near Crowborough, an independent Roman Catholic school for girls.

 # Fork from **Plumpton** to **Eastbourne**
Plumpton

Journey: 57 min
Season: £2580
(£2620 to include Gatwick Express)
Peak: 1 per hr (plus 1 per hr to London Bridge)
Off-peak: nil

The railway line divides **Plumpton** into two parts, Plumpton proper and **Plumpton Green**. The latter consists of modern estates close to the railway station, with the National Hunt racecourse to the south. A good five-bedroom modern family house with a double garage will cost £275,000. The old village is anchored to Plumpton Place, a 16th-century moated manor. It has a general store-cum-post office, a couple of garages and a primary school, and is the home of the East Sussex Agricultural College. There is wonderful riding over the Downs if you have your own horse. The wildflowers on the Downs are prized by honey farmers. **East Chiltington** is very close by and untouched by repeated housing booms. Here you could pay £300,000 or more for a family house with four double bedrooms, double garage and half an acre.

Cooksbridge

The desirability of **Cooksbridge** is reduced because it sits on the main road to Lewes and on the railway line, both of which can be noisy. A two-bedroom flat could be bought for £67,000; a three-bedroom end-of-terrace house for £80,000. Ex-railway workers' cottages with three bedrooms sell for around £95,000.

Journey: 61 min
Season: £2580
(£2620 to include Gatwick Express)
Peak: 1 per hr
(plus 1 per hr to London Bridge)
Off-peak: nil

Lewes

Large parts of **Lewes** are still medieval – particularly along the main street, which follows the route of an ancient causeway. The passages winding away from it are an irresistible invitation for shoppers to explore. Bookshops, antique shops and 15th-century timbered cottages lean against colour-washed houses. The Bloomsbury Group connection (Vanessa Bell and Duncan Grant used to live here, and Virginia Woolf lived at Rodmell two miles away) has left an arty-crafty atmosphere. It is the county town of East Sussex and is always alive with exhibitions and craft shows. It has its own coterie of resident artists, several of whom work in studios at the Star Brewery.

Journey: 62 min
Season: £2580
(£2620 to include Gatwick Express)
Peak: 1 per hr
(plus 1 per hr to London Bridge)
Off-peak: 2 per hr

Property is more expensive than in the surrounding areas. A two-bedroom terrace house costs just under £130,000. It would be likely to have a mean garden or a small courtyard since the town is tight for space, and this means that parking is difficult, too. The tiny cobbled streets just off the High Street have a particular cachet, and houses here don't often come on the market. There is a high proportion of council housing – the highest per capita in East Sussex – as well as some bland modern private estates which generate little interest among incomers.

Shopping is adequate. Lewes has Boots, Safeway, Tesco, Iceland and Next, and Eastbourne and Brighton are not far away. The local private school is The Old Grammar School. The great social occasion of the year is the huge Bonfire Night party which commemorates the burning, not of Guy Fawkes but of a batch of Protestant martyrs.

There are some extraordinarily lovely downland villages around Lewes. **Kingston**, in the south, has a street of distinguished old houses and a modern estate where four-bedroom houses sell for around £175,000. The village is something of an enclave for Sussex university professors. Then there is **Rodmell**, which seduced the Bloomsbury Group with its mix of flint-and-thatch and tile-hung cottages. A two-bedroom cottage will cost almost £180,000; a four-bedroom house backing on to fields is likely to reach £375,000. Neither of these villages has shops. Any house with views of the Downs sells for 15% to 20% more.

To the north is **Barcombe**, which has prices to match its beauty. A modest four-bedroom detached house with a garden and double garage would cost £275,000; a more lavish four-bedroom house with a large garden might fetch £350,000 to £400,000. It is really a village of three parts. There is Barcombe Cross, which has tile-hung houses and shops, plus a pub and a 16th-century Forge House. Then there is Barcombe Mills, on the River Ouse, where people go for picnics. And there is Old Barcombe, by St Mary's Church, abandoned by the population during the plague. **Ringmer** is more of a dormitory to Lewes, where houses sell briskly on the prettiness factor. Three-bedroom semis fetch about £120,000; four-bedroom detached houses around £180,000. The centrepiece is the village green, fringed with old cottages overlooked by the parish church, where cricket is played in the summer.

Glynde

Journey: 87 min (67 min peak)
Season: £2640
Peak: 1 per hr to London Bridge
Off-peak: 1 per hr changing at Lewes

Glynde consists of little more than the big house, Glynde Place, an 18th-century church and a grassy bank that becomes a cloud of daffodils in spring. Mount Caburn , one of the highest points along the South Downs, looms above. The Glyndbourne Opera House, which draws the dinner jackets with their picnic hampers between May and August, is on the parish boundary with Ringmer. Much of the local property is in private ownership and leased to villagers.

Berwick

Journey: 93 min (75 min peak)
Season: £2640
Peak: 1 per hr (plus 2 per hr changing at Haywards Heath)
Off-peak: 1 per hr changing at Lewes

Berwick is best known for having a church decorated with murals by Duncan Grant and Vanessa Bell – so vivid that they caused an outcry when they were painted in the Forties. Unfortunately it draws coach parties in the summer, as does Drusilla's Zoo theme park. Houses close to the station were built during the Thirties, many of them offering good views of the Downs and Arlington reservoir. A three-bedroom semi sells for around £150,000 to £160,000; a four-bedroom detached house for over £200,000.

Polegate

Journey: 78 min
Season: £2700
Peak: 1 per hr (plus 1 per hr to London Bridge)
Off-peak: 2 per hr

Polegate is really the outer rim of Eastbourne. It is a village that billowed during the Thirties and again during the Eighties. The single High Street has everything from a greengrocer to a hairdresser. Victorian two-up-two-down workers' cottages sell at about £60,000; Thirties and Fifties semis at £85,000 to £95,000. You could pay £120,000 for three bedrooms and clipped lawns in a tidy road. Polegate sprawls in its egalitarian way towards Hampden Park, and there is no distinct division between the two.

Hampden Park

There are expensive and cheap sides to **Hampden Park**, which glories in all the variations on the theme of suburban mock-Tudor that you could imagine. In a good area three-bedroom terrace houses sell for £65,000; detached houses for around £200,000. There is nothing in the Victorian department. This is where Eastbourne has its industrial estate, and all the hangar-sized stores such as B&Q and a 24-hour Tesco have been built here, too.

Journey: 94 min
Season: £2700
Peak: 1 per hr
(plus 1 per hr to London Bridge)
Off-peak: 1 per hr

Eastbourne

Eastbourne is still very much a holiday resort and retirement town. Attractions such as Fort Fun and the Treasure Island theme parks resound in summer to the shrieks of holidaying children, who then make for the beautiful Victorian pier to gorge themselves on ice-cream. Adults can indulge with a trip to the Winter Gardens, Devonshire Park or the Royal Hippodrome Theatres. There are also nightclubs and cinemas. Healthier pursuits include stupendous cliff walks over Beachy Head and those vast switchbacks of chalk, the Seven Sisters.

Journey: 85 min
Season: £2700
Peak: 1 per hr
(plus 1 per hr to London Bridge)
Off-peak: 2 per hr

To live within walking distance of the station you have a choice of Edwardian and Victorian houses, or some Thirties detached. Prices vary enormously depending on size. You could pay £180,000 for three bedrooms; up to £280,000 for a mock-Tudor with five bedrooms. The cheaper flats start at over £30,000. One of the most prestigious addresses is The Meads, a conservation area that attracts professionals and couples who have retired early. A modest semi here might cost £150,000.

You can expect to pay a premium price if you want to live near any of the three golf courses – The Royal, The Downs or The Willingdon.

Thirties Tudor-style house, Eastbourne

Spur from **Preston Park** to **Worthing**

There are some other stations along this route but the London trains don't stop at them. For Preston Park, see page 267.

Hove

Journey: 62 min
Season: £2640
Peak: 2 per hr (plus 1 per hr to London Bridge)
Off-peak: 2 per hr

Hove is much more sedate and "respectable" than its neighbour Brighton, though the two are now officially joined at the hip by the Brighton and Hove Council established in 1999. Its image has been that of a haven for the elderly, and indeed it does have plenty of sheltered housing and low-level flats. However, as part of its campaign to attract a younger set, Hove has built up a sporting image with two sports complexes offering everything from martial arts to synchronised swimming. The King Alfred Leisure Centre is being redeveloped to include a multiplex cinema, casino and restaurants.

Georgian terrace house, Hove/ Brighton area

Hove suffered in the Thirties when many of its most important houses were demolished and replaced with 10-storey blocks of flats. Nevertheless, there are still some classic, sweeping Regency curves to be found in the Brunswick area; some good Sussex cottages near the King Alfred Centre; and some fine Victorian and Victorian Gothic houses in The Avenues, Willett Estate and Cliftonville.

Property tends to be cheaper on the outskirts, where the modern estates are. Two-bedroom flats start at around £65,000. There are plenty of Thirties developments, too, built with the ubiquitous shopping parade, where a semi might cost £100,000 and a two-bedroom bungalow £95,000. The most expensive roads are Tongdean Avenue, Tongdean Road and Dykeroad Avenue. Seafront flats with film-star interiors are also hugely expensive, fetching upwards of £250,000.

While Sussex County Cricket Club still calls Hove home, Brighton and Hove Albion FC has been moved into temporary quarters at the Withdean Stadium in Brighton while the powers that be contemplate its future. There are two golf clubs, the West Hove and the Brighton

Just as Hove has had a complex about Brighton, so Portslade has one about Hove

and Hove. And there is also, of course, the beach. In the last decade this sedate old lady of a town has developed a certain sparkle by acquiring a galaxy of restaurants along Church Road which are good enough to lure foodies from Brighton and the surrounding area.

Portslade

Just as Hove has had something of a complex about Brighton, so **Portslade** has one about Hove. It might not look particularly impressive as you drive through, but if you turn off the main road you will find some 16th-century flint cottages and a church dating back to 1100. Portslade's recent history is not very distinguished. Two decades ago it was known locally as "Nappy Valley" because it offered a mass of housing cheap enough for young couples to buy and breed in. Housing is still relatively inexpensive. Two-bedroom terrace houses sell for around £85,000, three-bedroom terraces for £100,000 and three-bedroom semis for £120,000 to £140,000. Repossessions have melted away recently.

Villagers have succeeded in protecting from development an old field in the centre, so there is a green of sorts for people to walk on. More recently money has been spent on restoring Portslade's main streets. They have re-paved, installed Victorian-style street lamps and renovated the Victorian red-brick water tower which used to supply an isolation hospital. American Express has sponsored the installation of a camera obscura, which gives a wonderful panoramic view of the South Downs.

Journey: 68 min
Season: £2640
Peak: 2 per hr
(plus 1 per hr to London Bridge)
Off-peak: 1 per hr

Shoreham-by-Sea

Shoreham is a Victorian seaport which still imports two million tonnes of cargo each year. The High Street, which has the River Adur running along the bottom of it, has basic shops for day-to-day needs, and the Holmbush Centre has brought Marks & Spencer and Tesco. Shoreham is relatively free from hotels and B-and-Bs and does not feel like a seaside resort. It does have a sandy beach at low tide, however, and a popular pit-stop for wildfowl in the Widewater, a lagoon behind a man-made shingle bank.

Journey: 69 min
Season: £2680
Peak: 2 per hr
(plus 1 per hr to London Bridge)
Off-peak: 2 per hr

> A colony of wooden huts, made largely from disused railway carriages, were occupied by the London Music Hall fraternity

Shoreham Airport (whence the first commercial flight was made in this country) still runs charter flights and is the base for several flying schools. Across the river on the shingle spit is the site of what was once Bungalow Town – a colony of wooden huts, made largely from disused railway carriages, which were occupied by the London Music Hall fraternity. Some early films were made there, but most of it was destroyed in the Second World War to prevent its use as a beachhead.

Commuters gravitate towards North Shoreham and the town centre where modern three-bedroom terrace houses sell at around £85,000. A two-bedroom bungalow with a sun-room would fetch around £125,000; a third bedroom would put the price up to nearer £160,000. For a Marbella-style seaside hacienda, you would have to pay upwards of £300,000. There are two secondary schools, the most popular being Kings Manor Comprehensive on the border of Shoreham and Southwick; the boys' public school at Lancing is nearby.

Bay-fronted
bungalow,
Shoreham-by-Sea

Lancing

Journey: 76 min
Season: £2720
Peak: 2 per hr (plus 1 per hr to London Bridge)
Off-peak: 1 per hr

Old north and south Lancing have blended into one, and the once pretty High Street has been spoilt by tasteless development. Many people commute to Gatwick and Brighton from here but few to London. There is still a smattering of thatch-and-flint in the north and fishermen's cottages in the south. A two-bedroom flat will cost £60,000, but a period cottage or a new substantial detached house is likely to be nearer £160,000. The boys' public school, Lancing College, which takes girls in the sixth form, stands in 550 acres on a spur of the Downs overlooking the sea. There are several primary schools which feed the state secondary school, Boundstone Community College.

Worthing

Worthing has become increasingly popular with commuters over the last decade, absorbing housebuyers displaced by high prices from Surrey. To be within walking distance of the station and shops you would need to live in one of the Edwardian terraces north of the town centre. The price you pay for such convenience is that it is difficult to find a parking space. Spacious three-bedroom houses sell for between £90,000 and £110,000. B-and-Bs are concentrated in the centre, near the four large hotels, nightclubs, theatres and cinema. The shopping centre is surprisingly varied, with specialist shops. So don't imagine a town full of little old ladies in fluffy hats: the largest segment of the population is the 16-44 age group, and the adult education centre is very well subscribed. Big businesses, including Beechams Pharmaceutical, have settled here too. Worthing is proud of the fact that it is the home of bowls. One small warning: the seafront can get rather smelly when the seaweed is churned up from the Bognor Regis beds.

Journey: 75 min
Season: £2720
Peak: 2 per hr
(plus 1 per hr to
London Bridge)
Off-peak: 2 per hr

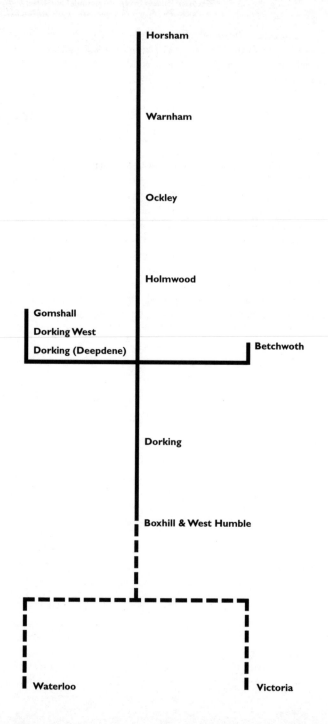

Horsham

Warnham

Ockley

Holmwood

Gomshall
Dorking West
Dorking (Deepdene)

Betchwoth

Dorking

Boxhill & West Humble

Waterloo

Victoria

Victoria/Waterloo ➡ Horsham

Boxhill & West Humble

Just beyond the M25, London suddenly lets go and gives way to one of the best known beauty-spots in the south-east. Box Hill itself rises to nearly 400ft above the River Mole and affords panoramic views of the surrounding chalk downland and glimpses of the South Downs. But this does not necessarily make it a good place to live. The approaches to it are given over to caravan sites, and estate agents tend to say that **Box Hill** is more a place to look at, and look from, than to live in.

West Humble is no more than a handful of houses at the foot of Box Hill. Norbury Park is close by. There are three working farms and Bocketts Farm, a rare breeds farm open to visitors.

To Victoria
Journey: 45 min
Season: £1800
Peak: 1 per hr
(plus 3 per hr to Waterloo)
Off-peak: 1 per hr

Dorking

Dorking is an ancient market town shot through with antique shops, some new buildings and a couple of delicatessens. It prides itself on its variety of restaurants, from Thai to French. Reigate Grammar and St John's at Leatherhead are the two popular local public schools. Guildford is close enough for smart shops and the theatre. Most trains terminate here during the daytime (you have to change if you want to travel further out of London), which makes it one of the most convenient stations on the line. The web of villages that surround it have much to offer.

Property prices in and around Dorking are fairly constant. A three-bedroom semi with work to be done on it sells for around £150,000. One in better condition will fetch around £170,000. One-bedroom flats sell for between £70,000 and £80,000.

Five miles west is **Shere**, a leafy village with a stream bubbling through. It's so pretty that British Gas used it to illustrate the rural idyll in an advertising campaign. The square is picturesquely framed with old houses; it has a 12th-century church, several shops, a post office, tea-rooms and a couple of antique shops. Social activities abound – a gardening club, youth and old folks' organisations – and for the moment it still retains its village school. The dramatic society is shared with **Peaselake**, which backs on to Hurtwood Common, one of the many Surrey commons

To Victoria
Journey: 46 min
Season: £1860
Peak: 2 per hr
Off-peak: 2 per hr

To Waterloo
Journey: 40 min
Season: £1860
Peak: 3 per hr
Off-peak: 2 per hr

The poor soil made it unsuitable for farming, so it became a refuge for smugglers and squatters

that are covered in golden broom and gorse, with shelter-belts of pine. The village has a green with a war memorial.

Another popular village is **Abinger Hammer**, which has a green, a working blacksmith and an insatiable passion for cricket. The full Australian team was invited to play here, and the villagers managed to make the return match, too. There is also an annual celebrity match. Men swap their white flannels for green tights when the annual medieval fair comes round to Abinger Common. Opposite the pub is a clock tower from which a little man emerges every hour to strike the bell with a hammer – hence the name of the village.

Nearby is **Holmbury St Mary**, which has a green and a post office run by volunteers but has lost its school. This was once considered to be one of the most remote places in Surrey. The poor soil made it unsuitable for farming, so it became a refuge for smugglers and squatters and only began to be recognised as a village in the 1850s. Then it became popular with weekenders who built the first large Victorian houses up on Holmbury Hill, whence there are magnificent views over the Weald. By far the most remote spot here now is **Coldharbour**. Designated an Area of Outstanding Natural Beauty, it clings to the side of the 960ft Leith Hill, from which, on a clear day, you can see the Channel. It is a mountain in the middle of Surrey. The narrow winding roads that lead up to Coldharbour are often cut off in winter. There is no school, though it has a pub, a church and good-neighbourly residents who take elderly villagers into Dorking.

Victorian houses on Holmbury Hill have magnificent views over the Weald

To the east is **Brockham**, with 18th-century houses overlooking the green, pubs, a primary school and 16th-century church. You can easily spend £350,000 to £600,000 on a large house here, but there are some superb smaller ones which start at around £200,000. The main event of the year is the bonfire on Guy Fawkes night, which draws thousands of people from miles around. **Leigh** (pronounced Lye) is also an extremely popular small village with a 16th-century priest's house on the green, and a weatherboarded pub. **Newdigate**, which is tucked right away from the main roads, has an excellent farm shop, a blacksmith and a new estate of executive homes.

North Downs line west to Gomshall

Dorking Deepdene is a good-quality residential area, close to the station yet set in beautiful woodland. It takes its name from the Deepdene Estate, which was owned by the Howard family. Large detached houses sell for around £400,000; three-bedroom semis for around £200,000. **Dorking West** is partly residential, partly commercial, with new business parks springing up. A small terrace house would cost around £130,000; a semi £165,000. **Gomshall** is an expensive village marred by traffic. A Victorian two-bedroom semi would cost just under £180,000.

No through trains
Journey: 60 min
(from Gomshall)*
Season: £2124
Peak: 2 per hr*
Off-peak: 1 per hr*
*To Dorking
Deepdene
(footpath links to
Dorking)

North Downs line east to Betchworth

Sitting on the banks of the River Mole, surrounded by the North Downs, **Betchworth** is something of a local beauty spot. It has some 17th-century houses inhabited by retired High Court judges and diplomats who can play golf at nearby Betchworth Park. A four-bedroom detached house is likely to cost £400,000; a two-up-two-down further out at Peeble Hill would start at £150,000.

No through trains
Journey: 60 min
(from Betchworth)
Season: £1860
Peak: 2 per hr*
Off-peak: 1 per hr*
*To Dorking
Deepdene
(footpath links to
Dorking)

Continuation of main line
Holmwood

Note that after Dorking the rail service is not as good and late night trains are infrequent. Some villages have been badly affected by the A24 cutting south. **Beare Green** straddles it, and now consists mainly of houses built during the Seventies and Eighties. These sell for less than those in Dorking, of which it is effectively a dormitory. The **Holmwoods** (**North** and **South**) are also staked out along the A24. North Holmwood retains its green and pond but has been submerged by new housing. The surrounding countryside is lovely, however, with 600 acres of common offering pony treks and long walks. Just to the north is a memorial to Alfred

To Victoria
Journey: 55 min
Season: £2140
Peak: 2 per hr
Off-peak: 1 per hr

Gwynne Vanderbilt, a member of the American millionaire family, who sacrificed himself by handing his lifejacket to a woman passenger when the *Lusitania* sank.

Ockley

To Victoria

Journey: 58 min	
Season: £2140	
Peak: 2 per hr	
Off-peak: 1 per hr	

Ockley's prettiness is being spoilt by traffic on the A29, but it has some strong points, including a cricket pitch (visible from the main road), a conventional green with old houses around it, and its own school. This whole area lies close enough to Guildford for commuters to take advantage of the fast trains into Waterloo (see page 233) as well as the local theatre and shops. Other commuters choose to jump a station by driving to **Clandon** (page 248), where it is easier to park.

Cranleigh, strung between Ockley and Guildford, would meet many people's idea of the perfect small town. This is where the first cottage hospital was established. The main street has a story-book intimacy and, despite a population of 12,000, the town still thinks of itself as a village. It has a cricket green and a cinema, food shops, gift shops, shoe shops, delicatessens and a gun shop (the green Wellington fraternity has a strong presence here). A three-bedroom period cottage might cost between £200,000 and £300,000; a larger old house with three acres and a tennis court could fetch over £500,000. Modern houses sell for less – four bedrooms for around £275,000. The area is wealthy, popular with executives in insurance, banking and oil, those who own successful local companies,

Modern family house, Horsham area

TV personalities and ageing rock stars. Cranleigh School is the local boys' public school; the sister school, St Catherine's, is at Bramley near Guildford (see page 235).

Warnham

A sign warning that deer may cross the road is the first thing you see as you approach **Warnham** and its deer park. The old farming community has now been largely replaced by commuters to Guildford, London and Horsham, who are attracted by the green, pubs and old houses. A small semi in need of modernisation might sell for £100,000 in Bell Road. Larger detached houses start at around £225,000.

To Victoria
Journey: 64 min
Season: £2360
Peak: 2 per hr
Off-peak: 1 per hr

Horsham

Horsham is a bustling Sussex town with the South Downs in its sights and some attractive villages around it. The faster route into London is via Gatwick Airport. For main entry see **Victoria/London Bridge to Arundel/ Brighton** line, page 258.

To Victoria	To London Bridge
Journey: 55 min	Journey: 65 min
Season: £2440	Season: £2400
(£2620 if Gatwick	(£2440 if also valid
Express included)	to Victoria)
Peak: 3 per hr	Peak: 2 per hr
Off-peak: 3 per hr	Off-peak: 1 per hr

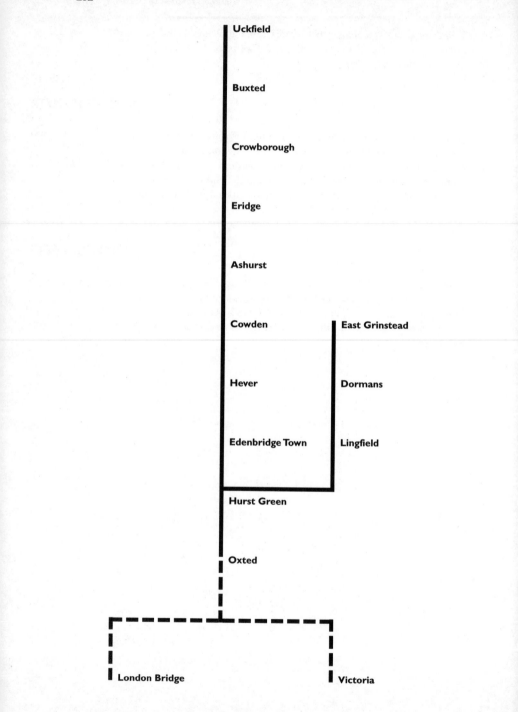

Victoria
➡ Uckfield

Oxted

Oxted is everything that most people would want a small town to be. It is safe for children and pleasant to live in, but not so pretty that it suffers invasion by tourists. It has a population of around 14,000, and all its vital organs are centralised within walking distance of each another – station, cinema, shops and Tandridge Leisure Pool which has a gym. The cinema is old-fashioned and privately owned – the lady who sells the tickets also holds the ice-cream tray. It gets all the new releases, yet the atmosphere is cosy enough for parents to allow their children to go unaccompanied. The town is also reasonably safe to walk around in after dark.

To Victoria
Journey: 36 min
Season: £1560
Peak: 2 per hr
(plus 3 per hr to London Bridge)
Off-peak: 2 per hr

16th-century
cottage, Oxted

Teenagers looking for a good night out head for East Grinstead or Croydon, where there are nightclubs. Older funsters go into London for theatres, or to country restaurants

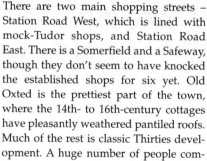

There are two main shopping streets – Station Road West, which is lined with mock-Tudor shops, and Station Road East. There is a Somerfield and a Safeway, though they don't seem to have knocked the established shops for six yet. Old Oxted is the prettiest part of the town, where the 14th- to 16th-century cottages have pleasantly weathered pantiled roofs. Much of the rest is classic Thirties development. A huge number of people commute to London or Croydon; otherwise people work in local shops or in the factories at Hurst Green. The wealthier residents live in the private wooded roads of Rockfield Road and Icehouse Wood, where large detached houses cost at least £500,000. Nearly all the gardens in the town are large by London standards, most extending to half an acre or more. Even the few modest two-bed Victorian terraces, selling at £125,000 to £150,000, have 100ft gardens.

Teenagers looking for a good night out head for East Grinstead or Croydon, where there are nightclubs. Older funsters go to London for theatres, or to country restaurants. There are golf courses nearby at Tonbridge and Limpsfield.

Limpsfield and **Limpsfield Chart** are five minutes away by road. Both villages are occupied almost exclusively by newcomers, and both are split by the A25. A car is essential for living here. Limpsfield is olde worlde and expensive, its main street eyecatchingly lined with old stone cottages.

A stretch of common land tumbles over the edge of the Weald. In spring the woods are carpeted with bluebells

There are a few shops, a pub, a very good bookshop and a highly-rated restaurant called The Old Lodge. Limpsfield Chart is also attractively set in National Trust landscape. The Chart is a stretch of common land which tumbles over the edge of the Weald, offering superb views as you head south and containing remnants of an old Roman road. In spring the woods are carpeted with bluebells. A grand four-bedroom house on the common overlooking the North Downs, with tennis court and two acres of garden, could sell for over £650,000.

The village of **Tandridge** is less expensive, with Sixties and modern housing added to the mix. Three-bedroom Victorian houses and artisans' cottages cost over £200,000. Tandridge has a pub and a primary school, and has the feel of a proper village even though it is only two miles from the M25. It does, however, have traffic problems. The north is the nicest part, with a lovely church and steeple standing on a little hill.

Hurst Green

Hurst Green is more mundane and sprawly than Oxted, and cheaper. But it is a popular choice for people moving out of London looking for varied house types at low prices. On the Sixties Home Park estate, for instance, you could buy a two-bedroom house from £100,000, or three bedrooms for £120,000. There is a Wates estate, where one-bedroom starter homes on Barnfield Way cost around £70,000, and a couple of council estates with some ex-council houses for sale. The town is very segmented, and some of the segments are much nicer than others. The Green itself is picturesque. It is surrounded by older houses which have the advantage of being only a short walk from a splendid shop called Hobbs Stores, purveyor of fresh French bread and much else besides. It would be possible to do your entire weekly shop here. A detached three-bedroom house nearby could fetch around £250,000. Other parts of Hurst Green harbour the odd factory or two. All the segments have infant and junior schools, churches, post office and shops. Between Hurst Green and Edenbridge lies Staffhurst Wood, famous for its bluebells.

To Victoria	
Journey: 38 min	
Season: £1600	
Peak: 2 per hr	
(plus 3 per hr to	
London Bridge)	
Off-peak: 2 per hr	

Fork from **Hurst Green** to East Grinstead

Lingfield

Lingfield and Dormansland (see page 286) are glued together by Lingfield racecourse. Lingfield is the larger and older of the two villages, with a population that now reaches nearly 5,000. There has been very little new development, so the marvellous collection of 15th-century, Tudor, Jacobean and Georgian properties has been kept intact, and many of the buildings are scheduled as ancient monuments. Modern interlopers include the occasional Thirties house and a small Eighties estate.

To Victoria	
Journey: 44 min	
Season: £1800	
Peak: 1 per hr	
(plus 2 per hr to	
London Bridge)	
Off-peak: 2 per hr	

The area is very popular with people who need to be close to Gatwick airport. Pilots, air hostesses and ground staff live here; so do many business travellers. There are excellent communications. The M25 is only eight minutes' drive away and the M23 is also close by. Lingfield has a typical range of village shops including two small supermarkets, a butcher and a baker. Next to the pond at the heart of the village is a strange stone structure roofed with iron bars. This is the so-called "cage", built in 1473 and thought to have been used as a

There is a splendid shop called Hobbs Stores, purveyor of fresh French bread

lock-up for poachers and drunkards. House prices cover an enormous range, from a two-bedroom flat at £80,000 to a five- or six-bedroom detached family house in a couple of acres for £500,000 to £750,000. There is no such thing as a "typical" Lingfield house to extrapolate average prices from, but a three-bedroom terrace might go for £120,000; a three-bedroom detached for £170,000. Houses at the top end of the market might come with their own equestrian facilities though the racecourse, one of the first in Britain to have an all-weather surface, has not attracted many trainers or jockeys to live in the area. The style is more pony-club and conspicuous wealth. The village has a primary school. Older children are bussed to Oxted.

Dormans

To Victoria
Journey: 47 min
Season: £1800
Peak: 1 per hr (plus 2 per hr to London Bridge)
Off-peak: 2 per hr

Dormansland is slightly smaller than Lingfield, with a population of just under 4,000 if you include Dormans Park. It has a post office, a hairdresser, a couple of pubs, a church and a primary school. Houses are largely Victorian with a smattering of modern and small council estates. **Dormans Park**, which is actually closer to the station than Dormansland itself, has a curious history. It grew up when rich Victorians used to come down from London for Lingfield races. A number of little summer houses were built around the Dormans Hotel (now disappeared), where many of them liked to stay. The summer houses grew grander, and Dormans Park became the sort of place where the playboys of the time liked to entertain their mistresses. Nearly all the houses are large, detached villas in sizeable plots surrounded by countryside. A six-bedroom affair with a paddock and outbuildings might sell for £750,000. The area is rather secluded and has no local facilities of its own.

East Grinstead

To Victoria
Journey: 52 min
Season: £1900
Peak: 1 per hr (plus 2 per hr to London Bridge)
Off-peak: 2 per hr

The town of **East Grinstead** itself retains the characteristics of the market town it once was, though it now has a relief road and other modern appendages. It consists of two parts: the old town, which includes much of the High Street; and London Road, which contains the new major shops. It is becoming more of an industrial and commercial town, with new offices springing up. East Grinstead draws in people from the surrounding villages for their regular shop, though large or specialist items have to be sought in Croydon or Crawley. The Kings Centre provides a swimming pool and sports complex for hearties, while The Atrium has a nightclub, two cinemas and 10-pin bowling for night owls. The Chequer Mead Art Centre has a little 320-seat theatre. One of East Grinstead's attractions to commuters is that its station is at the end of the line, so there is no danger of going to sleep and missing your stop. There are some pretty old buildings in the centre of the town, including 14 hall houses in the High Street. Particularly handsome is Sackville College, a Sussex sandstone almshouse with high chimneys, quadrangle and gardens, which is now converted for sheltered housing. Otherwise there is a wide range of housing, quite a lot of it on new estates which have sprung up in the last 20 years.

Cheap starter homes and flats cost between £65,000 and £85,000. A larger modern mock-Georgian four-bedroom house will fetch over £200,000.

Two manor houses outside the town are put to strangely contrasting uses. Saint Hill Manor, to the south, is the headquarters of the Church of Scientology. Gravetye Manor is one of the best small country house hotels and restaurants in Britain. For fishing, sailing and walking there is Weir Wood Reservoir. To the south is Ashdown Forest, where the countryside becomes very beautiful. Here you come up on to the High Weald, where you find some of the last remaining heathland in the south-east.

Fork from **Hurst Green** to **Uckfield**
Edenbridge Town

Edenbridge is not one of the gems of Kent but it is nicely positioned half-way between London and the coast – both are well within reach. For main entry, see **Victoria to Brighton** line, page 252.

To Victoria	
Journey: 49 min (40 min peak)	Peak: 1 per hr (plus 1 per hr to London Bridge and 2 changing at Oxted)
Season: £1912 (also valid at Edenbridge)	Off-peak: 1 per hr* *Change at Oxted.

Hever

Hever is one of the area's tourist attractions, popular with visitors en route to Hever Castle, where Henry VIII courted Anne Boleyn. The village is unspoilt and is an extraordinarily small place to command its own railway station. A house here in consequence will cost around £100,000 more than a similar property in Edenbridge. For a detached four-bedroom house you will have to pay in the region of £450,000. There is no cheap property in Hever, but the least expensive are the former labourers' cottages from the Astor estate. These have been sold and, as the locals put it, "tweed up" by their new owners. The village has a church, a few houses, a golf course and the Henry VIII pub. Beyond a massive stone gateway you enter the drive to Hever Castle and its strange mock-Tudor village, which is hired out for

To Victoria
Journey: 52 min
Season: £1920
Peak: 1 per hr (plus 1 per hr changing at Oxted)
Off-peak: 1 per hr* *Change at Oxted. No peak trains from Victoria

conferences. In high summer, plays and concerts are held in the castle's Italian gardens; in winter a Christmas Fair raises money for the local church and school.

Hever's Church of England primary school has such a good reputation that it reverses the usual demographic trend. Instead of children being bussed from village to town, children from Edenbridge are brought to Hever. Locals, however, have still had to fight to prevent it from being closed. Village life is lively though there are no shops and the nearest post office is three miles away in Edenbridge. Horticultural shows and WI markets are held in the village hall. Although Hever proper is small, the parish has 800 on the electoral roll and is quite far flung. As there is absolutely nothing for teenagers to do, it is probably just as well that the population consists of solicitors, commuters, retired people and minor landed gentry.

Cowden

Journey: 57 min
Season: £1940
Peak: 1 per hr (plus 1 per hr changing at Oxted)
Off-peak: 1 per hr*
*Change at Oxted. No peak trains from Vicoria.

Cowden is very pretty village cushioned amid the quiet leafy lanes that wind through the Weald. Its main street has a curious symmetry, with a housing estate at each end and a pub in the middle, and it contains the village's oldest houses, many of them 400 years old. Buses do exist here but you would be seriously inconvenienced without a car. There are no shops. It pays to get on with the neighbours because the same people are likely to belong to all the same societies and to turn up at all the same events – the horticultural society, British Legion and WI. There is no school, and teenagers have little to do except gatepost-hang. A modern four-bedroom house designed in the Kentish farmhouse style, with a small garden and double garage, might cost £400,000.

Ashurst

Journey: 61 min
Season: £1960
Peak: 1 per hr (plus 1 per hr changing at Oxted)
Off-peak: 1 per hr*
*Change at Oxted. No peak trains from Vicoria.

Ashurst is very rural and slightly reserved. You may have to spend six months waiting on the platform with the other six passengers at Ashurst station before they get round to acknowledging you. Though the village is very small a smart new village hall opening in summer 2,000 is the focus for grand plans for keep-fit groups, dancing classes and IT tutorials. Property in Ashurst is more expensive than nearby Eridge (see ahead), but houses in both villages rarely come up for sale and you'll have to move quickly if you want to buy. There is a bus service of sorts but, as ever in this area, car ownership is practically essential.

The larger villages of **Langton Green** (see page 297) and **Groombridge** are also close to Ashurst. Groombridge straddles the county boundary with the new, modern dormitory village forging into Sussex and lovely Old

Groombridge lingering in Kent. The old part, including the 16th-century terrace cottages, the Crown Inn which faces the triangular green, the 17th-century moated manor house, Groombridge Place, and its 200-acre estate, was marketed in 1992 with an asking price of £3.25m. The big house (used by the director Peter Greenaway for his film *The Draughtsman's Contract*) is now used mostly at weekends. The gardens are open to the public in the summer.

Eridge

Eridge is a very small village best known for its huge park, which is scored with footpaths. It has a church, but has lost its store and post office. Much of it was once part of the Abergavenny estate. Some of the old estate cottages still occasionally come on to the market.

Journey: 67 min
(53 min peak)
Season: £1980
Peak: 1 per hr
(plus 1 per hr to London Bridge and 2 changing at Oxted)
Off-peak: 1 per hr*
*Change at Oxted.

Crowborough

Crowborough is one of those strange areas that are sedate and suburban to the core, yet lack a proper focus or a shopping centre. It began as a series of big hilltop hotels built around a golf course. Later it became a popular retirement haven and then, in the early Fifties, came an explosion of housing estates which turned it into a commuter dormitory with a population of 20,000. The only cinema closed down a few years ago but there is a leisure centre with swimming pool, badminton and squash, and two supermarkets.

Journey: 75 min
(60 min peak)
Season: £2000
Peak: 1 per hr
(plus 1 per hr to London Bridge and 2 changing at Oxted)
Off-peak: 1 per hr*
*Change at Oxted.

The Warren is the smartest part of town, built to the north and looking down over Ashdown Forest. Homes in the Warren are mainly detached houses with four or five bedrooms, priced in the £300,000 to £500,000 bracket. Most of the larger houses once stood in extensive grounds but have since had smaller houses or flats built around them. This infilling has spoiled the previously rather gracious character of the area.

Groombridge Place was used for the film
The Draughtsman's Contract

On the newest estates a one-bedroom starter home costs £65,000, a three-bedroom house £125,000. Much of the building in and around the town centre is Victorian, and the least attractive streets are those near the station and the industrial estate. Further out are a number of former 16th- and 17th-century farmhouses. Sir Arthur Conan Doyle lived at Hurtis Hill, and when he died in 1930 he was buried in his back garden overlooking Crowborough Common and the golf course. His body was later exhumed and re-buried in Minstead Churchyard in the New Forest. The house has since been converted into an old people's home called Windlesham Manor, but the town still fills up with Sherlock Holmes fans for the annual Conan Doyle festival.

Rotherfield nearby has at its core a conservation area studded with listed buildings, antique shops and Victorian terraces. A small cottage costs around £135,000.

Buxted

Journey: 80 min
(65 min peak)
Season: £2100
Peak: 1 per hr (plus
1 per hr to London
Bridge and 2
changing at Oxted)
Off-peak: 1 per hr
*Change at Oxted.

Buxted is mostly modern but nevertheless quite attractive. It has a population of around 4,000, and real shops that sell clothes and food rather than antiques. Property prices are about the same as Uckfield's (see below).

Uckfield

Journey: 86 min (72
min peak)
Season: £2200
Peak: 1 per hr (plus
1 per hr to London
Bridge and 2
changing at Oxted)
Off-peak: 1 per hr*
*Change at Oxted.

Uckfield is a rapidly expanding "strip" town. The population currently stands at around 13,000 but new houses are going up all the time. Older properties are mainly Victorian – a three-bedroom semi of this period will cost around £130,000 to £145,000. Locals describe the rail service as abominable, and suggest that it would be quicker to travel by pram. For a smallish town there are a lot of facilities, including a leisure centre, cinema, library, bowling green and the nearby Piltdown golf club. It is also surrounded by lovely countryside, ideal for walking or cycling. To the north-west the country lanes wind into Ashdown Forest. Here there are also some rather grand houses – five bedrooms, paddock and enormous garden would cost over £500,000.

Because of the shortcomings of the local rail service, many London commuters prefer to drive the 12 miles to Haywards Heath (page 263) and use the faster service from there. Uckfield used to be a notorious bottleneck on the A22 to Eastbourne but is now bypassed. Fortunately all public car parks in the town are free – a mercy for people from the surrounding villages who have very

Locals suggest that it would be quicker to travel by pram

few shops of their own. The beautiful villages nearby are **Fletching**, **Nutley** and **Barcombe Cross**. Fletching is the most desirable. It has no new estates and is set in the Ashdown Forest, making it ideal for walks and pony rides. This is a village like villages used to be, with a close-knit community and a good village centre with beamed pubs. Many of the houses are picture-postcard trim. Three-bedroom houses, some with half an acre of land, sell for around £250,000 to £300,000.

Little Horstead, to the south, is popular with golfers because of its proximity to Horstead Place, a large country estate with hotel and golf complex.

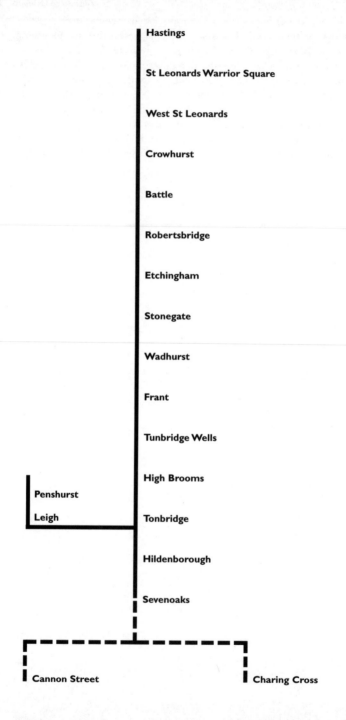

Hastings

St Leonards Warrior Square

West St Leonards

Crowhurst

Battle

Robertsbridge

Etchingham

Stonegate

Wadhurst

Frant

Tunbridge Wells

High Brooms

Penshurst

Leigh

Tonbridge

Hildenborough

Sevenoaks

Cannon Street

Charing Cross

Charing Cross and Cannon St
➡ Hastings

All trains are to Charing Cross except where specified.

Sevenoaks

Sevenoaks has been a commuter town ever since the railway arrived in 1862. Recently it has developed a reputation for wealth – a survey showed more cars per head of population than any other town in England. The concentration of private schools is another reliable money indicator. There is Sevenoaks School for boys and girls, Walthamstow Hall for girls, and a clutch of prep schools. The childrens' fathers are surveyors, accountants, solicitors and other successful professionals. The shops are good, and there is a Sainsbury and 24-hour Tesco, though many locals prefer shopping in Bromley or Tunbridge Wells. Outsiders meanwhile flock into Sevenoaks for the quaint little shops in Dorset Street, Bank Street and Well Court. Other attractions include the Stag Cinema and Stag Theatre, the swimming and sports centres, an abundance of golf courses, and The Vine, the pitch on which the first-ever nationally reported cricket match was played. Sevenoaks Cricket Week happens every July, and if the sound of ball on bat is not music enough to your ears, then there is the Sevenoaks Summer Festival of music, drama and art. Nearby are the wooded walks of the North Downs Way, the lakes and grassland of the Sevenoaks Wildfowl Reserve, and Knole – one of the largest private houses in Britain, set in a vast deer park, where the writer Vita Sackville-West spent her childhood.

Journey: 31 min
Season: £1740
Peak: 4 per hr
(plus 3 per hr to Cannon Street)
Off-peak: 4 per hr

A survey showed more cars per head of population in Sevenoaks than in any other town in England

Some of the most expensive addresses are on the Wildernesse Estate, where small mansions were developed on two-acre plots during the Thirties. Many of these now have smaller modern houses squeezed in beside them, often bought by what estate agents refer to as New Money. A five- to eight-bedroom house here will cost £600,000 to over £1m with a swimming pool and all the trimmings. The **Kippington** area is also popular, offering a mix of Victorian, Thirties and post-war housing priced in the £500,000 range. Throughout the town you can buy four-bedroom family houses of varying periods at prices between £350,000 and £500,000. One of the quaintest old streets is Six Bells Lane, where tiny one-bedroom 18th- and 19th-century cottages cost around £120,000. There is a snag here, however. If the cottages score points for charm, they lose them on parking difficulty. The large houses around the Vine cricket ground harbour a few flats, the cheapest of which sell at around £150,000. There are more flats in a purpose-built block also overlooking the Vine, where a really spacious apartment with views would cost over £250,000.

Hildenborough

Journey: 39 min
Season: £2080
Peak: 3 per hr (plus 2 per hr to Cannon Street)
Off-peak: 1 per hr

Hildenborough is something of a poor relation to its wealthy neighbours. It has the occasional shop and garage but no real centre, and the B245 makes it a place to drive through rather than to stop in. For affordable housing, however, it's worth a look. A two-bedroom house will cost around £100,000; three-bedroom £150,000 to £200,000.

Tonbridge

Journey: 39 min
Season: £2180
Peak: 5 per hr (plus 3 per hr to Cannon Street)
Off-peak: 4 per hr

Tonbridge has none of the glamour of Tunbridge Wells, to which it gave its name, though it does have the remains of a motte-and-bailey castle on the banks of the River Medway in the town centre. It is a busy one-street town with quite a few businesses and small industries. It also has the private Tonbridge School for boys and two grammar schools for girls. A studio flat in Tonbridge will cost £50,000; a two-bedroom terrace house £70,000; a three-bedroom detached £170,000.

North Downs line west to Leigh and Penshurst

From Leigh To London Bridge	From Penshurst To London Bridge
Journey: 53 min	Journey: 50 min
Season: £2180	Season: £2180
Peak: 3 per hr*	Peak: 3 per hr*
Off-peak: 1 per hr	Off-peak: 1 per hr
*Change at Tonbridge or Redhill. There is 1 through train to London Bridge.	*Change at Tonbridge or Redhill. There is 1 through train to London Bridge.

Leigh (pronounced *Lie*), is very much a dormitory village. It has a huge green canopied with conker trees, and traditional tile-hung and weatherboarded Kentish houses. There is a general store and post office, and a butcher. The primary school flourishes, and organised activities include mothers-and-toddlers and a cricket club. Leigh is popular with London solicitors and bankers, which explains the arrival of a new development of executive houses. A five-bedroom period property with four reception rooms, granny annexe, tennis court and swimming pool would cost £750,000 or more. **Penshurst** nearby is an attractive, straggly Kentish village with some nice old tile-hung cottages and its own primary school. The heavy influx of commuters here has resulted in a certain them-and-us feeling. Commuters are often referred to as "invisible parishioners", so slight is their involvement in village activities. At least membership of the village football and cricket teams is growing again. When Penshurst's general store closed, Lord de L'Isle of Penshurst Place opened up a post office and grocery store in the village garage for the convenience of the elderly. Unfortunately Penshurst Place and Hever Castle bring tourists as well as patronage – an irritant in the summer. Activities include amateur dramatics, bridge, dancing and stoolball (a cross between rounders and cricket, played with a round wooden bat). Property is now so expensive that it is beyond the means of local young people. A two-bedroom cottage might cost £125,000, a five-bedroom period stone house £500,000, a substantial Queen Anne house over £800,000. **Chiddingstone** is also a show-stopping village. The main street, with Chiddingstone Castle at one end, is owned by the National Trust (the castle made an excellent Toad Hall in the recent film of *The Wind in the Willows*). Prices are slightly less than those in Penshurst.

Continuation of main line
High Brooms

High Brooms, dominated by out-of-town retail stores, is the industrial face of Tunbridge Wells – a steep hill lined with streets of Victorian terraces, most of them built in brick from the old Tunbridge Wells brick company, whose workers lived in them. It is within reach of the more elegant part of town, but property prices are low enough to attract young commuters. A two-bedroom terrace will cost around £95,000; a three-bedroom semi around £120,000. On the eastern side are Sherwood Park and Home Farm, two areas where new housing estates burgeoned during the Eighties. A two-bedroom house here will cost £95,000; four bedrooms around £150,000.

Journey: 49 min
Season: £2300
Peak: 3 per hr
(plus 1 per hr to Cannon Street)
Off-peak: 2 per hr

Tunbridge Wells

Tunbridge Wells is to Kent what Bath is to Avon. The gracious crescents and elaborate terraces, designed by Decimus Burton to serve its image as a fashionable 18th-century watering hole, still give it an air of great prosperity. Beau Nash was master of ceremonies at the wells from 1735, and you can still take a foul-tasting sip from the dipper at the Pantiles. For a more complete re-creation of the past there is "A Day At The Wells", one of those sight, sound and smell museums that aim to leave as little as possible to the imagination. Modern Tunbridge Wells caters for recreational

Journey: 53 min
Season: £2340
Peak: 3 per hr
(plus 1 per hr to Cannon Street)
Off-peak: 2 per hr

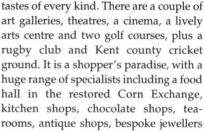

tastes of every kind. There are a couple of art galleries, theatres, a cinema, a lively arts centre and two golf courses, plus a rugby club and Kent county cricket ground. It is a shopper's paradise, with a huge range of specialists including a food hall in the restored Corn Exchange, kitchen shops, chocolate shops, tea-rooms, antique shops, bespoke jewellers and many more indigenous exotics.

Undoubtedly the best address in Tunbridge Wells is Nevill Park, a private road with lodge gates at each end, 10 minutes' walk from the station, where large and sumptuous houses dating from the 1800s to the present day overlook the town from a ridge. On one side is the green expanse of Tunbridge Wells Common; on the other is Hungershall Park where a grandly-proportioned house with five bedrooms, three reception rooms, and perhaps a Victorian conservatory at the back might cost between £700,000 and £1m.

You will need a similarly deep pocket if you want to consider one of the 21 exquisitely-designed houses by Decimus Burton in Calverly Park, some of which are sub-divided into smaller houses. A four-bedroom house might cost around £650,000; double it for a well-maintained whole house. In Calverly Park Crescent, where shops were originally designed into the ground floors beneath heavily-gardened balconies, you could find a home for around £350,000. The imposing private houses built along Mount Ephraim are also sought after, though 70% of them have been turned into flats. A three-bedroom flat with grand reception rooms will cost between £225,000 and £275,000. There are some smaller ones at around £175,000.

Ordinary family houses are to be found in Royal Chase and Culverden Down, behind Mount Ephraim and only a short walk from station and shops. Many of them were built during the various building booms of the 20th century. A four- to five-bedroom tile-hung Thirties house in three-quarters of an acre will cost over £500,000. Those of more modest means head east to the tightly-knit area of terraces and semis where

Stable block conversion, near Tunbridge Wells

a three-bedroom semi with no garage will cost between £150,000 and £200,000. The reputation of the local schools is another major factor in the town's popularity. They include Skinners, a boys' grammar school; Tunbridge Wells Boys' Grammar; Tunbridge Wells Girls' Grammar, and two comprehensives. All are close to St John's Sports and Indoor Tennis Centre and swimming pool.

For years the stationmaster at Frant ran a wellie-warming service for homebound commuters

Tunbridge Wells is surrounded by rich riding country well provided with bridleways and livery stables. The Eridge and South Downs Hunt and the Pony Club are both vigorously attended. **Langton Green**, two-and-a-half miles to the west, is a favourite with local businessmen. It has its own village shops, pubs, some old village houses and cottages, plenty of new housing and a popular mixed prep school called Holmwood House. A four-bedroom detached house here will cost between £250,000 and £350,000, a two-bedroom cottage £150,000. Immediately to the north of Tunbridge Wells is **Pembury**, which has a bypass and offers a large volume of middle-range modern housing. A three-bedroom detached house here would cost around £200,000, but you need to avoid the roads used as peak-time rat runs. See also Penshurst, Leigh and Chiddingstone on the **North Downs line** (page 294).

Frant

The most striking feature of this hilltop village is its green. Surrounded by superb timber-frame and Georgian houses (one of which reputedly sold for over £1m in 1999), it makes a perfect setting for village cricket. A modern four-bedroom house in **Frant** would fetch around £375,000. The village has its own shop, a bowling green and a well-attended primary school, though the rural idyll is marred slightly by lorries using the village as a cut-through. The station is actually at Bells Yew Green, where for years the stationmaster ran a wellie-warming service for homebound commuters. Post-journey comfort these days is more likely to be found at the Brecknock Arms, just around the corner.

Journey: 57 min
Season: £2360
Peak: 2 per hr
(plus 1 per hr to
Cannon Street)
Off-peak: 1 per hr

Lamberhurst is definitely a village worth looking at. It is hammered by the A21 but a bypass has long been talked of and the welcome quiet it would provide would push property prices up by 10%. Lamberhurst has some good oak-framed houses, antique shops, a village store-cum-post-office, and a vineyard. Two-bedroom cottages sell for around £140,000; three bedrooms up to £200,000. This is too much for some local people, so affordable housing is being built for those with proper village connections.

Wadhurst

Journey: 61 min
Season: £2420
Peak: 2 per hr (plus
1 per hr to Cannon
Street)
Off-peak: 2 per hr

Wadhurst is a narrow, busy and attractive village set in an Area of Outstanding Natural Beauty in the High Weald. It is big enough to have around 30 shops including a couple of banks, butchers, doctors, dentists, solicitors and so on. Lying on the borders of Sussex and Kent, it offers the choice of two different county education systems. Some people choose Wadhurst's own Uplands Community College, which combines the role of good comprehensive school with adult education and sports centre. Others shuttle their children across the border into Kent to take advantage of the old-fashioned grammar schools in Tunbridge Wells. Lots of teenagers ride and there is a local livery stable.

Lying on the borders of Sussex and Kent, Wadhurst offers the choice of two different county education systems

A two-bedroom village house, old or new, will cost around £110,000 – about the same as a one-bedroom flat in one of the small modern developments. Three-bedroom terrace houses built in vernacular style fetch around £125,000; five-bedroom executive houses with 2,400sq ft of space are around £300,000. A decent period house with four bedrooms and a garden will cost around £275,000; something more lavish with five bedrooms, tennis court and swimming pool will be around £500,000.

Stonegate

Journey: 67 min
Season: £2480
Peak: 2 per hr (plus
1 per hr to Cannon
Street)
Off-peak: 1 per hr

Stonegate itself is tiny and is becoming increasingly desirable. It is something of a drive-through village with a good primary school and several modern executive developments. Victorian three- to four-bedroom semis sell at around £180,000; four-bedroom Edwardian detached houses at £450,000.

Neighbouring **Ticehurst** is attractively set around a central square in a conservation area. Three horse chestnut trees guard the bus stop in the old village pump shelter. Shops include a village store, baker, butcher, haberdasher, dry-cleaner and greengrocer. There are also estate agents and a handful of pubs.

Ticehurst has its own primary school and a good choice of local societies. Prices are lower than in Wadhurst because it is thought to be more out-of-the-way. A small semi in a cul-de-sac will cost £85,000; a weatherboarded two-bedroom cottage £100,000; a three-bedroom bungalow

£145,000. The big house in the village has been split and converted – a four-bedroom slice of it will cost £160,000.

Etchingham

Etchingham is popular because it is reasonably good to look at and has the convenience of its own railway station. The village winds up the hill from the railway, offering a sprinkling of traditional weatherboarded properties among the 18th-century houses and a Fifties estate. There is also a modern development opposite the village hall. Etchingham has a general store, post office and a butcher that has been in the same family for generations. There is a much-loved primary school, and the Etchingham British Legion Club where people meet for billiards and darts. A small semi in the village might cost between £110,000 and £125,000; a three-bedroom detached house down one of the lanes would be around £200,000 to £225,000.

Journey: 72 min
Season: £2520
Peak: 2 per hr
(plus 1 per hr to
Cannon Street)
Off-peak: 1 per hr

Burwash is more attractive than Etchingham and is well known for its striking High Street of white weatherboarded and tile-hung houses, tea-rooms, brick footpaths and lime trees. Not so well-known is its warmth and friendliness. Prices are similar to those in Etchingham – held down by the fact that they are further from the station. On the edge of the village are some five- and six-bedroom modern houses, each one set in half an acre of garden, selling for £395,000. Half a mile away is Bateman's, where Rudyard Kipling lived and wrote *Puck of Pook's Hill* in 1906.

To the north-east, back over the border into Kent, is **Hawkhurst**, a village in two halves. Housebuyers would probably avoid the half that contains the junction of two main roads in favour of an area known as The Moor in the neighbouring valley. This has a large village green, playing fields and small shops and cottages. A two-bedroom terrace house will cost around £70,000; a three-bedroom semi

Half a mile away is Bateman's, where Rudyard Kipling lived and wrote *Puck of Pook's Hill*

£100,000; a four-bedroom detached modern house £180,000. A four-bedroom period house in one of the lanes will fetch over £250,000. Both Hawkhurst and its much smaller neighbour **Sandhurst** are within the catchment area of Cranbrook School, one of the most highly respected schools in Kent, run on traditional grammar school lines. Hawkhurst also has a clutch of private schools, including Marlborough House, and Bedgebury Lower School for girls.

Robertsbridge

Journey: 76 min
Season: £2560
Peak: 2 per hr (plus 1 per hr to Cannon Street)
Off-peak: 1 per hr

Considering the prettiness of the countryside that surrounds it, **Robertsbridge** is surprisingly unprosperous. There is no major town or city centre close enough to attract regular commuters, and those who come here tend to want escape. Hastings, it has to be said, does not offer much of a diversion. Robertsbridge's lovely village high street has now been relieved of through-traffic by a bypass. It has a sub-post office, part-time bank, butcher, chemist, greengrocer, general store and two hairdressers. The new village hall hosts regular meetings of the archaeological society, playgroups and dancing classes. There is also football, stoolball for women and, especially, cricket. The Gray-Nicholls factory makes bats out of locally grown willow (and also the round wooden bats for Sussex stoolball). A three-bedroom cottage will cost £85,000 to £95,000, a three-bedroom modern house £120,000 to £170,000, and a larger country house with extensive grounds £300,000 to £400,000. Its most famous former resident was the late thinker and journalist Malcolm Muggeridge. Current residents include the mild-mannered members of a commune who live in the beautifully-restored old TB sanatorium. They are very self-contained, make their own clothes and educate their own children. The women distinguish themselves by always wearing dark blue spotted headscarves.

Battle

Journey: 77 min
Season: £2620
Peak: 2 per hr (plus 1 per hr to Cannon Street)
Off-peak: 2 per hr

Battle is as self-contained, charming and spirited as any market town in England might have been before the 20th century came along to ruin it. Its most famous asset is the remains of Battle Abbey, on the site of King Harold's defeat by William the Conqueror in 1066. A spectacular bonfire is lit on the playing fields on Guy Fawkes Night, big enough to rival the one in Lewes. The town's High Street is full of shops and inns, some of them timber framed or weatherboarded, and there are some nice old tea-rooms for connoisseurs of the sticky bun. A first-time buyer could find a two-bedroom period cottage in need of renovation for just under £90,000. Three-bedroom semis come at between £80,000 and £90,000; four-bedroom detached houses at £165,000 to £175,000.

In the lanes around Battle are some rather grand houses in the £300,000 to £500,000 range. A converted oast with 30 acres and a barn for conversion would be likely to fetch in excess of £400,000. Of the neighbouring villages, **Sedlescombe** is particularly pretty with a traditional village green fringed with brick and tile-hung cottages. It has a post office, a tea-room, a pub, a hotel, a restaurant, a good primary school and societies on every night of the week. Villagers have recently acquired a site on which to build a new village hall. **Catsfield** and **Ninfield** are so popular that most of the house-moves involve people already living there. Social trends have been reversed here because a new shop *and* a new pub have opened. For utter rural tranquillity there is **Penhurst**, a picturesque hamlet set in deep Sussex countryside. Prices in all the villages are roughly similar to those in Battle itself.

Crowhurst

The station makes **Crowhurst** an extremely sought-after village. The electrification of the line was followed by an influx of buyers from outside the area (two-thirds of people looking for property at that time were from London). You can now expect to pay £100,000 to £120,000 for a three-bedroom semi; anything from £225,000 to £400,000 for an older detached house. As you come down the hill from Bexhill you see the remains of the old medieval manor house next to the Norman Church. There are some lovely tile-hung houses and the oldest yew tree in the county – it may have been here to welcome William the Conqueror. Crowhurst has often been voted "best kept village", though the judges have criticised it for the clods of mud left by the herds of cows that plod through for the morning and evening milking. The Plough Inn runs an annual pumpkin show, providing plantlets to people on a specific date so that all the competitors start level. The village has a post office-cum-grocer which stocks locally grown fruit and vegetables, locally made craft goods and takes in dry cleaning. Other plus points are the primary school, clubs, sports groups from tennis to cricket, a horticultural society, and a busy drama group. Tesco at Hollington sends a bus to the village each week, and there is a shopping and recreational complex at Glyne Gap, between Bexhill and Hastings.

Journey: 87 min
Season: £2632
Peak: 1 per hr
(plus 1 per hr to Cannon Street)
Off-peak: 1 per hr

Grade II listed terrace cottage, East Sussex

West St Leonards and St Leonards Warrior Square

West St Leonards
Journey: 92 min
Season: £2640
Peak: 2 per hr (plus 1 per hr to Cannon Street)
Off-peak: 1 per hr

St Leonards Warrior Square
Journey: 87 min
Season: £2640 (£2800 if also valid to Victoria via Eastbourne)
Peak: 2 per hr (plus 1 per hr to Cannon Street)
Off-peak: 2 per hr

Though the stations are only three minutes apart, many trains do stop at both. **St Leonards** was created by James Burton and his son Decimus as a bit of early speculative development. It was conceived by them as a dignified residential area, but time has taken its inevitable toll. A string of fish-and-chip shops and restaurants overlook the seafront. Conservationists are beginning to pamper the bits they can such as Victorian Southwater which has attracted lottery funding. People from South London and Tunbridge Wells tend to move here for the sea air and the comparatively low prices – though the serious retirement area is to the west, at Bexhill-on-Sea. Recovery from the Nineties' recession was slow. Studio flats start at only £8,000, with smarter one-bedroom units at up to £20,000. A sea view can affect prices in boom time, but in a time of glut it tends not to make much difference. Three-bedroom houses of any period tend to cost between £55,000 and £75,000. There are also some very large six-bedroom Victorian houses in more salubrious areas such as Upper Maze Hill and The Green.

Hastings

Journey: 90 min
Season: £2640 (£2800 if also valid to Victoria via Eastbourne)
Peak: 2 per hr (plus 1 per hr to Cannon Street)
Off-peak: 2 per hr

Hastings has never quite caught the limelight in the way that Brighton has. Much of it has a slightly down-at-heel look, though the population still swells with trippers and holidaymakers during the summer. There are good walks along East Cliff across the gorse-covered valleys to Fairlight. Hastings seafront is much like any other, with a fine pier built in 1872. The castle ruins now tell the 1066 story audio-visual style. The White Rock Theatre does a good line in variety shows, concerts and plays, and there is a cinema. The High Street shops and the new £50m Priory Meadows mall draw shoppers from the neighbouring villages. You can buy fresh fish from fishermen pulling their boats up on to the beach.

Much of Hastings has a slightly down-at-heel look, though the population still swells with trippers and holidaymakers during the summer

Much of the housing is Victorian. Commuters usually prefer to live within walking distance of the station, close enough to the William Parker comprehensive if they have families. A two-bedroom house in this area would cost around £55,000; four bedrooms £80,000. One-bedroom flats in a converted house come at around £25,000. A view, or even a squint of the sea, will add a small premium. A two-bedroom top floor flat with a sea view will cost around £30,000.

One of the smartest areas is **St Helen's**, close to Alexandra Park, where a three-storey, four-bedroom Victorian house will cost £80,000 to £90,000, and a three-bedroom semi with 100ft garden over £75,000. For modern properties people look to **Parkstone**. A two-bedroom bungalow here will sell for over £90,000; a four-bedroom detached around £110,000. Property prices in other parts of Hastings have fallen steeply. If you don't mind it being in need of repair, you might get a little Victorian house for £45,000. The most expensive area is probably the **Old Town**. Some people find it too claustrophobic, with tourists pressing their noses against the windows in summer, but others find the innate charm of the close ancient streets well worth the extra money. Here you might pay £50,000 for a two-bedroom flat; up to £150,000 for a four-bedroom Edwardian terrace.

If you don't mind it being in need of repair, you might get a small Victorian house for as little as £45,000

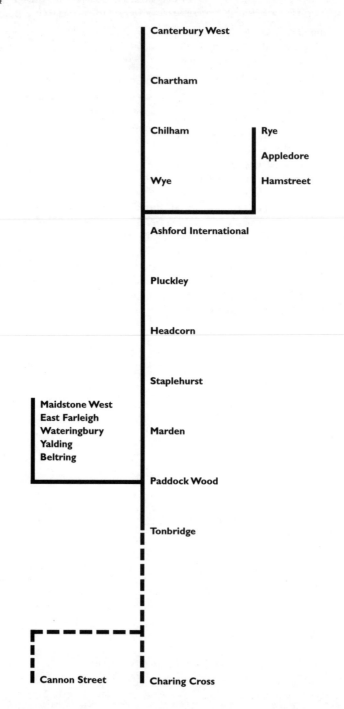

Canterbury West

Chartham

Chilham

Rye

Appledore

Wye

Hamstreet

Ashford International

Pluckley

Headcorn

Staplehurst

Maidstone West
East Farleigh
Wateringbury
Yalding
Beltring

Marden

Paddock Wood

Tonbridge

Cannon Street

Charing Cross

Charing Cross/Cannon St ➡ Canterbury
(via Tonbridge and Ashford)

All trains are to Charing Cross except where specified

Tonbridge

Tonbridge is the plain industrial cousin to Tunbridge Wells just down the road. It is also much more affordable. For main entry see **Charing Cross/Cannon Street to Hastings** line, page 294.

Paddock Wood

Londoners have always been attracted to **Paddock Wood**. Those with happy memories of hop-picking settled here after the war. More recently there has been a steady trickle of suburban refugees from Bromley and Orpington. Paddock Wood now is a town with little romance, large enough to support a department store, Tesco, a sports and leisure centre and some light industry. Its comprehensive school has a good reputation and doubles as an adult education centre. Property prices are lower than in the surrounding area, with second-hand three-bedroom semis at between £100,000 and £115,000. Four-bedroom detached houses cost £170,000 to £270,000. The Finches and Warrington are good areas to look. It would be misleading to describe all the property here as cheap, however. The convenience of the journey into London means that a large detached houses with land could fetch up to £950,000.

Journey: 47 min
Season: £2320
Peak: 3 per hr
(plus 2 per hr to Cannon Street)
Off-peak: 2 per hr

Branch line to **Maidstone West** via **Beltring, Yalding, Wateringbury** and **East Farleigh**

Close to **Beltring** station is the Hop Farm. It contains the largest group of Victorian oast houses in the world, and the complete brewing process is demonstrated to the public here. Apart from this, Beltring offers little more than a clump of houses. Nearby **Laddingford** is a true hamlet on the River Tiese, a trout stream. It has a pub

No through trains
Journey: 67 min
(from East Farleigh)
Season: £2360
Frequency: 1 per hr*
Change at Paddock Wood.

It is also possible to travel to Charing Cross via Strood in the opposite direction.

called The Chequers, and a clutch of four-bedroom Eighties houses with 200ft gardens backing onto open fields which sell at around £186,000.

Yalding is a lovely old village served by winding country lanes, with a few shops, a post office, a working forge, a beautiful 14th-century bridge and a Church of England primary school. Two-bedroom period terrace cottages start at around £90,000. A three-bedroom house with a handkerchief garden will cost £160,000; a newish five-bedroom three-bathroom house £310,000 (add £50,000 to £100,000 for a period version).

The innate prettiness of **Wateringbury** is marred by the busy A26 Tonbridge to Maidstone road which thumps through it. It has some shops, a post office and a Church of England primary school. Even small period cottages can cost £140,000. You would have to pay over £160,000 for a four-bedroom detached house; over £450,000 for a large period detached house with land. The village has some fine stone-built Georgian houses and creeping modern development.

East Farleigh is much quieter than Wateringbury (though it is increasingly used as a rat run to Maidstone) and just as attractive with a five-arch 14th-century bridge pinning the centre together. It has a county primary school, and a shop-cum-post-office run by villagers from a Portakabin in the pub car park. Again, small cottages are expensive – at least £135,000. A spacious three-bedroom bungalow might cost £235,000; a four-bedroom house might cost £300,000.

For **Maidstone**, see page 314.

Continuation of main line
Marden

Journey: 53 min
Season: £2360
Peak: 1 per hr (plus 2 per hr to Cannon Street)
Off-peak: 1 per hr

Marden is a substantial, pretty village with Kentish weatherboarded houses, genuinely useful shops, including a butcher, greengrocer, post office, library and an excellent primary school. Modern three-bedroom semis sell for around £90,000, with more mature semis at over £120,000. You might find a small three-bedroom period terrace cottage at less than £160,000, but a larger four-bedroom Georgian house will fetch £300,000 at least.

Just over four miles to the south is **Goudhurst**. It is set on a hilltop surrounded by orchards, cornfields and hop gardens and has lovely views across the Low Weald. This is a classic English village with half-timbered cottages and a duck-pond. It is a self-sufficient community with its own primary school, shops, the Hughenden restaurant and tea-shops for the summer visitors. A small terrace house can be bought for £100,000; a period house with land £350,000. At **Bedgebury**, just over two miles to the south, there is a huge privately owned forest called the Bedgebury Pinetum.

Goudhurst is a classic English village with half-timbered cottages and a duck pond

Staplehurst

Staplehurst has a little light industry and a large Mazda warehouse by the station. Sprawling along the A229 south of Maidstone, it is a plain village in comparison with some of the jewels of the Kentish landscape which lie to the south. The busy High Street has a pedestrianised section ideal for its population mix of elderly people and young families. It has its own primary school, a herb farm and farm museum. Three-bedroom semis on the Sixties estates sell for around £90,000; four-bedroom detached houses at least £150,000. Period properties carry the expected premium, with two- and three-bedroom cottages at over £125,000 and larger, more secluded detached houses with pony paddocks around £275,000.

Journey: 57 min
Season: £2420
Peak: 2 per hr
(plus 2 per hr to
Cannon Street)
Off-peak: 2 per hr

Cranbrook has a special appeal for Londoners worried about schooling. Cranbrook Grammar for boys and girls has a reputation sufficient to add a premium to property prices within its five-mile catchment area. Parents living outside it will even pay for their children to board, since the school straddles both private and state education systems. Cranbrook is a compact town of weatherboarded houses (all listed) with a well-preserved black-tarred smock mill at its centre. New houses are being slipped in all the time. The town used to be cut off in winter because of the deep mud on the roads, and this has given it a lingering feeling of insularity. Small two-bedroom houses, old or new, start at just under £75,000. Three-bedroom weatherboarded semis cost £110,000 to £150,000; three-bedroom modern detached houses £130,000; period farmhouses on the outskirts up to £600,000.

A mile up the cramped lanes from Cranbrook is **Sissinghurst** – a pretty one-street village of weatherboarded and half-timbered houses with a pub and primary school, close to Sissinghurst Castle (National Trust), where Vita Sackville-West and her husband Harold Nicolson created their wonderful gardens. **Benenden** is just over seven miles from Staplehurst (15 minutes by car) and is popular with commuters. It is a perfect Kentish village set around a green (cricket is played in summer) beside the William IV and The Bull pubs. There is a handsome range of brick and weatherboarded cottages and old hall houses, close to the parkland of Benenden, the girls' public school. Prices in both Sissinghurst and Benenden are similar to those in Cranbrook.

Headcorn

Headcorn is very popular with commuters, not least for its large station car-park. It is big enough to support a busy shopping centre which includes restaurants, though serious shopping means a trip into Maidstone or Ashford. Other assets include a primary school, village green, a flower farm and vineyard, an aerodrome and the Lashenden Air

Journey: 62 min
Season: £2460
Peak: 2 per hr
(plus 2 per hr to
Cannon Street)
Off-peak: 1 per hr

Warfare Museum. Well-heeled commuters pay over £350,000 for large houses with an acre or two on the outskirts. Medieval timber-frame cottages are silent reminders of the past. An old timbered farmhouse with 20 acres and an oast might cost £700,000. Within the village itself, a period four-bedroom house will fetch around £200,000. There are also some new developments (those built in the Sixties now look rather tatty) where a four-bedroom detached might be bought for £145,000. A three-bedroom semi right in the centre will cost £95,000.

Smarden, three miles to the east, is a beautiful well-kept village with listed cottages grouped around a 14th- to 15th-century church. It is too small to have a shop, but there is a post office and a butcher. The mobile library calls once a week and there is a primary school. The village teems with activities, including a history society and gardening club. It tends to be popular with families. Large, family-sized period houses with perhaps two acres will cost £400,000 to £450,000. A three-bedroom semi-detached period cottage will cost £150,000; a two-up-two-down terrace cottage £100,000.

Biddenden, three miles south of Headcorn, is favoured because of its closeness to Tenterden, a stylish Wealden town that has become something of a local antiques centre. This is also where you find Kent's oldest commercial vineyard and can buy the locally made ciders, wines and apple juices. An 18-hole international golf course, Chart Hills, designed by Nick Faldo is nearby. A three-bedroom terrace house looking onto farmland could cost £95,000; a five-bedroom detached house with an inglenook fireplace and rural views £335,000.

Pluckley

Journey: 68 min
Season: £2520
Peak: 1 per hr (plus 2 per hr to Cannon Street)
Off-peak: 1 per hr

The countryside around **Pluckley** will be familiar to anyone who watched the television serialisation of H.E. Bates's *Darling Buds Of May*. The influence of the Dering family – previous lords of the manor of Surrenden Dering – is very obvious here. Kentish ragstone was used for many of the older houses, most of which have distinctively-arched Dering windows. The village has managed to stay small, with a population of just over 1,000 served by two shops, four pubs, one church, and a Church of England primary school. Leisure opportunities include cricket, tennis, and Pluckley Pantomime Unlimited. Houses are expensive. The smallest detached cottage can fetch £150,000. A new interloper could be bought for £200,000 to £250,000. A period country house with three acres on the outskirts will cost £395,000.

Bethersden, a couple of miles south of the station, is another pretty conservation village of listed weatherboarded and tile-hung houses. It clusters around two shops, a post office and general store, a church, three pubs, garage and primary school. Bethersden is cosy and comfortable in character rather than smart like Smarden. A two-bedroom Victorian brick semi will cost just over £95,000. A three-bedroom semi in a quiet lane will fetch over £100,000; a three-bedroom Georgian semi with a half-acre garden £145,000.

Ashford International

Ashford still has a tiny medieval core but the 20th century has not been kind to it. Now, with the new international passenger terminal serving the Channel Tunnel, it stands on the brink of a further metamorphosis. For Ashford main entry see **Victoria to Ashford International** line, page 318.

Journey: 72 min
Season: £2560 (also valid to Victoria)
Peak: 2 per hr (plus 2 per hr to Cannon Street)
Off-peak: 3 per hr

Branch line to **Rye** via **Hamstreet** and **Appledore**

Hamstreet has had some of its tranquillity returned thanks to the arrival of a bypass. It has a green and a duck-pond by the village hall and is built on land reclaimed from Romney Marsh. It has a primary school, post office/general store, and antique shops and is attracting new houses. A rare two-bedroom Victorian brick house will cost just over £65,000; a modern three-bedroom semi £75,000. A flashy modern four- to five-bedroom house with three reception rooms in a third of an acre will fetch £175,000. Just to the north are the Hamstreet Woods, a linked series of five woods in a nature reserve famous for its nightingales.

Journey: 105 min (from Rye)
Season: £2800 (also valid to Charing Cross/Victoria via Hastings)
Frequency: 1 per hr*
*There are no through trains. All services change at Ashford International.

    Appledore is a delightful village and one of the best places to slip off the main road to enjoy the eerie flat landscape of Romney Marsh just to the east. It has lovely old black-and-white houses and a particularly attractive street, Court Lodge Road, which leads to the church and pub. Unfortunately Appledore has lost its primary school – due in part to the incomers' preference for private education. The result is that village children are now bussed three miles to Wittersham. The village has a bric-a-brac shop, a gift shop and two tea-shops. The Royal Military Canal – built in the 19th century as a second line of defence inland from the Martello towers – runs along the margin. Houses sell very quickly here, with buyers always waiting for an opportunity. A 100-year-old three-bedroom terrace will cost over £85,000; a modern four-bedroom detached house £165,000; an old farmhouse with land and stables over £350,000. The only things that sell slowly

Appledore is a delightful village and one of the best places to slip off the main road to enjoy the eerie flat landscape of Romney Marsh

Rye is regarded as one of the most picturesque towns on the south coast

in Appledore are the ex-council houses – you can pick up a three-bedroom semi for £85,000.

Rye is regarded as one of the most picturesque towns on the south coast. Two miles into the mouth of the River Rother, it was once a flourishing port huddled behind protective sea walls. Now its cobbled streets and Tudor, Stuart and Georgian houses attract hordes of summer tourists. It is an intimate place in which to live – most people seem to know what everyone else is doing. There are plenty of shops selling food, antiques and souvenirs, but going to the cinema means a trip into Hastings. Rye has all the usual clubs and societies, including the Rye Players, who perform a Christmas pantomime each year, and the Rye Medieval Association organises an annual Medieval Week. Well-known local residents include John Ryan, the creator of Captain Pugwash, and Spike Milligan lives nearby in Udimore. A two-bedroom Victorian terrace house in Rye will cost £60,000 to £75,000 or more. The picture-postcard streets include Church Square, Watchbell Street and Mermaid Street, steep and cobbled, where a romantic bow-windowed cottage would cost around £170,000.

Line from **Ashford** to **Canterbury**
Wye

Journey: 99 min
Season: £2580
Peak: 1 per hr (plus 1 train to Cannon Street)
Off-peak: 1 per hr to Victoria*
*Or change at Ashford International for Charing Cross.

Wye is possibly the most sought-after village in the Ashford area. Not only does it have the station, but it has a remarkable street called Bridge Street in which many of the medieval houses are reached by stone steps. Their purpose originally was to raise the buildings above the stream that once ran down the middle. The Great Stour does still run through the village and is overlooked by the Tickled Trout pub. Two-bedroom period cottages here are likely to start at £90,000, with Victorian semis starting at £140,000. Larger period houses cost £200,000 in town and £300,000 on the edge. A new but cottagey two-bedroom mews house could be bought for £100,000. The village has shops enough for anything you're likely to need. There are also two banks, a garage, a primary school and The Wife of Bath restaurant. Wye College, London University's agricultural college which is soon to merge with Imperial, introduces an unusually young, cosmopolitan element. The college has an annual rag week and celebrates Bonfire Night with a torchlight procession to the Crown – a chalk image cut into the Downs. There are good walks along the North Downs Way, which passes through the village, and in the Wye Nature Reserve. The latter contains a deep wooded hollow known as the Devil's Kneading Trough.

Chilham

The central square of 14th- and 15th-century black-and-white houses in Chilham is an irresistible draw for tourists, film crews and wealthy house-hunters. The church is known for its roughly chequered flint tower. The gardens at the privately owned Chilham Castle – a Jacobean mansion with a 12th-century keep – were laid out by the 17th-century botanist John Tradescant. The mulberry trees there are said to be 500 years old. Properties rarely come up for sale in Chilham but, if you were lucky, you might snatch a four-bedroom Georgian house just off the square with a postage stamp garden for £215,000. A family-size Tudor house will cost at least £280,000 to £300,000. On the outskirts a five-bedroom modern house might come up for resale at £335,000. It is a village with a strong community spirit. There is football, cricket and tennis, and in May the square is closed for a huge fair at which the villagers dress in period costume. Chilham also has the considerable advantage of being only five miles from Canterbury.

Journey: 105 min
Season: £2580
Peak: 1 per hr
(plus 1 train to
Cannon Street)
Off-peak: 1 per hr
to Victoria*
*Or change at
Ashford
International for
Charing Cross.

Old Wives Lees, a mile to the north, is a cheaper alternative, known to locals as Old Wives Knees. There is plenty of modern development here. A three-bedroom older house might cost £150,000.

Chartham

The River Stour, which divides before it enters the village, was for centuries the source of power for the local paper mills – one of which is still in production. Chartham is not as smart as Chilham. It has a mix of old houses – some of the nicest are by the little green and the 13th-century church – plus Victorian and modern estates built on the sites of old orchards and a mental hospital. A three-bedroom end-of-terrace in Chartham would cost around £95,000; a four-bedroom period house £175,000. It is quite a large village served by a handful of small shops and its own primary school.

Journey: 109 min
Season: £2580
Peak: 1 per hr
(plus 1 train to
Cannon Street)
Off-peak: 1 per hr
to Victoria*
*Or change at
Ashford
International for
Charing Cross.

Petham, three miles to the south-east, also has a mix of old thatched cottages, turn-of-the-century and new houses in a lovely setting. It has a church, a primary school and a garden centre. A three-bedroom bungalow might cost £190,000; a four-bedroom cottage in the heart of the village £195,000; a five-bedroom converted oast £255,000.

Canterbury West

Being both a cathedral city and a university city, **Canterbury** has a liveliness and style unlike other settlements in the eastern heel of Britain. It is far quicker to travel in from Canterbury East station. For main entry see **Charing Cross to Canterbury** line via Rochester, page 335.

Journey: 85 min
Season: £2580 (also
valid at
Canterbury East)
Peak: 1 per hr
(plus 1 train to
Cannon Street)
Off-peak: 2 per hr
to Victoria*
*Or change at
Ashford
International for
Charing Cross.

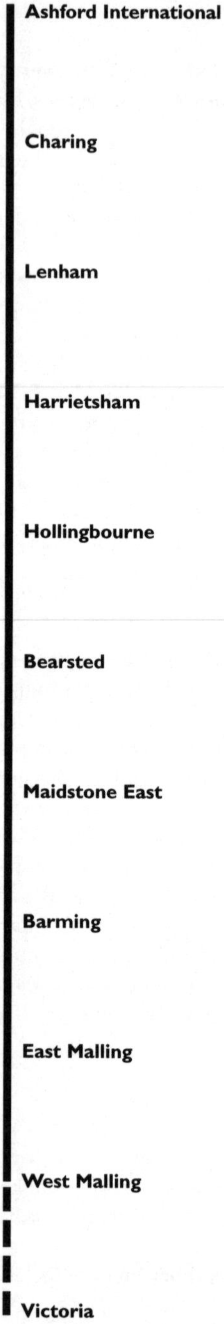

Ashford International

Charing

Lenham

Harrietsham

Hollingbourne

Bearsted

Maidstone East

Barming

East Malling

West Malling

Victoria

Victoria

Ashford International
(via Maidstone)

West Malling

Considering its closeness to London, **West Malling** is surprisingly unspoilt. The old High Street, in parts Tudor and Georgian, opens out into what was once the market square. There is a Tesco, a delicatessen, bakers, and a store which sells everything from plimsolls to vests. Cake decorating, knitting and sewing are practised in the local craft centre. The village has two primary schools and a 900-year-old abbey. As always, there are a number of local stalwarts who keep the social wheels turning, running the conservation society and fending off new development. The fields that cushion the village from Maidstone are guarded with particular vigilance. The local airfield, an old World War II fighter station, has been turned over to housing with a business park called Kings Hill. Four- and five-bedroom houses here start at £270,000. The M20 is close enough to be audible from the nearby woods. A four-bedroom period house in the main street at West Malling is unlikely to cost less than £180,000, though you might pick up a two-bedroom modern box for as little as £80,000.

Journey: 37 min
Season: £2208
Peak: 2 per hr
Off-peak: 3 per hr

East Malling

East Malling is much smaller than West Malling and its property prices are slightly lower. The old heart is picturesque with a church and village green but ex-council estates tend to dominate. The East Malling Research Station, which develops new fruit varieties, is based in Bradbourne House, a Queen Anne-style mansion. A three-bedroom Victorian terrace cottage might cost £130,000.

Journey: 54 min
Season: £2220
Peak: 2 per hr
Off-peak: 1 per hr

Barming

Barming lies on a beautiful stretch of the River Medway. It was crossed by a 1740 wooden bridge until the county council condemned it and had it removed. To outsiders it may seem like a suburb of Maidstone. To those who live here, however, it is very definitely a village. The old centre has been swallowed by new development, yet it is still extremely popular. A

Journey: 57 min
Season: £2280
Peak: 2 per hr
Off-peak: 1 per hr

two-bedroom 19th-century cottage will cost over £75,000; a three-bedroom modern semi around £110,000. The post office-cum-general store sells everything from wine to plants.

Maidstone East

Journey: 45 min
Season: £2360 (also valid at Maidstone West)
Peak: 2 per hr
Off-peak: 3 per hr

Detached period house, near Maidstone

Maidstone looms rather brutishly on the Kentish landscape – particularly if you approach it from the pretty southern villages. Nevertheless, it is a friendly and workmanlike hilly town where people manage to have the time to say good morning. Its focus is the River Medway, with the Archbishop's Palace (used as a place of rest on journeys to Canterbury) on the bank. A Saturday park-'n'-sail scheme allows boats to be brought upriver from Allington for Christmas shoppers. The remains of some 14th-century collegiate buildings are now occupied by the Kent Music School. The Maidstone Museum and Art Galley are in Chillington House, a 16th-century manor. The Corn Exchange is a cultural centre, too – home of the Hazlitt Theatre and a venue for concerts, dances and conferences.

Maidstone has always had a commercial and agricultural bias. In earlier centuries it supplied hops, linen, paper, ragstone and gin to London. Today it is particularly strong on shopping. The Chequers Centre has a host of major high street names, all gathered together under a single roof. The Royal Star Arcade has more upmarket specialist shops; Starnes Court is a Victorian-style arcade of designer-shops set around a courtyard. Beside the river on Lockmeadow there are weekly mar-

kets for furniture, bric-a-brac and agricultural produce. Mote Park, being the former parkland of an old country house, is a popular venue for boating, fishing and football. The Maidstone Leisure Centre has rock-climbing as well as leisure pools and health-and-fitness equipment. The town has the benefit of three Kentish grammar schools, two for boys and one for girls, plus a Mid-Kent College of Higher and Further Education.

Much of the housing in Maidstone is Victorian. There are terraces of small artisans' cottages where you might pay £65,000 for two bedrooms, or £75,000 for three. The houses get larger as you move further away from the centre. A four-bedroom terrace with three reception rooms and a walled garden could cost as little as £125,000.

The huge new Grove Green estate is densely built but popular. You could buy a two-bedroom terrace here for £82,000; a three-bedroom semi for around £125,000, or a four-bedroom detached for £160,000 to £250,000.

To the south-east is **Sutton Valence**, a pretty hilltop village with views over the Weald of Kent. It is marred by the busy A274 running through it but remains popular because of Sutton Valence School, a co-educational private school for older children. There is also a prep and a local primary. The village has lost most of its shops but still has a village store and

House style in Kent

Medieval England is clearly reflected in Kent's many hall houses. They were built with great arched, interlocking timbers, each one carefully notched and marked like a huge rustic modelling kit. Beneath the common roof the entire household would huddle around the central hearth (chimneys didn't appear until the late 16th or early 17th centuries).

Hall houses these days can be initially hard to recognise because they have been divided up into smaller rooms or had upper floors inserted into them, but the magisterial timbers soon give them away. You can see beautifully restored examples of early houses at the Weald and Downland Museum at Singleton in West Sussex.

Timber for these old buildings was felled from the great woods which stretched across the Weald (Anglo Saxon for wooded country). The intricate brick- and and tilework, made from the local terracotta clays, did not develop until the 17th and 18th centuries, when it was most lavishly applied to the houses of high clergy at Canterbury.

Alec Clifton-Taylor described the tile-hanging of Kent in his book The Pattern of English Building: "A good tile-hung wall is a creation of infinite subtlety, an agglomeration of shallow and slightly irregular convexities, seemingly held in place, under the right conditions of light, by a fine mesh of shadow."

Weatherboarding is the other familiar sight among these Kentish villages, looking strangely ephemeral for a building material. Cranbrook, built upon the wealth of the Flemish clothworkers who settled here, is like a toy-town made of wood. The clothworkers also left behind them a string of cloth halls and weavers' cottages.

newsagent. At the centre is an enclave of old houses – some black-and-white half-timbered and some weatherboarded. On the outskirts a good address might cost £400,000, a two-bedroom period cottage in need of renovation £135,000. In the churchyard is a memorial to John Willes, the man who introduced round-arm bowling to cricket.

Due south of Maidstone, and hardly separate from it, is one of those lovely English villages that everyone would like to call home. **Loose** owes its attraction to its position on the steep valley slope of the fast-flowing Loose stream. Old mills litter the wooded streambanks, which are overlooked by the church and pub called The Chequers. The 15th-century half-timbered Wool House is now administered by the National Trust and open to the public on written application. The village has a primary school, a post office-cum-shop and antiques shop. Half-timbered and weather-

The annual fair, with old-fashioned stalls and silly races, is a great occasion for pulling together

boarded cottages rise on terraces over the springs which feed the stream. On the outskirts you might find a two-bedroom beamed cottage for £120,000. A fine family-size Tudor house in the centre would fetch closer to £500,000; a listed oast with 10 bedrooms in need of renovation could be had for £765,000.

To the north is **Boxley**, set in an Area of Outstanding Natural Beauty with the North Downs Way and the Pilgrims Way running close by. The Channel Tunnel rail-link is unfortunately carving its way through Kent just 100 yards from the village but trains will be hidden by cut and cover. Alfred, Lord Tennyson, lived at Boxley Place. At the top of Detling Hill a couple of miles away is the Kent County Agricultural Showground.

Bearsted

Journey: 50 min
Season: £2360
Peak: 2 per hr
Off-peak: 2 per hr

Bearsted, insulated from Maidstone by a belt of green, is a very popular village, though in recent decades it has become rather bloated with new development. The older part, to the north of the A20, has a core of 17th-century houses around a large green on which is one of the earliest cricket pitches in the county. The poet Edward Thomas lived by the green, close to where the shops now stand – there is a bakery-cum-butcher locally famous for its pies, a newsagent and two pubs. Baroness Orczy also lived here which is why the Scout troup is called The Scarlet Pimpernels. A Grade II listed cottage with two bedrooms could cost £107,000. A family-sized Tudor house would reach £300,000 or even £400,000.

A disadvantage of Bearsted is that the old and the new sides of the village are rather split, each having its own village hall. An effort is being made by the old village not to make the new village feel left out. The annual fair, with old-fashioned stalls and silly races, is a great occasion for pulling together. The new estates to the south have their own supermarket and parade of shops. A four-bedroom detached house on the Meadow Hill development is priced at around £235,000.

The first pocket of rural life on Maidstone's eastern flank, but closer to Bearsted, is **Otham**. There is a 900-year-old church, a few ancient half-timbered houses, and a tradition of parish life which is maintained in spite of the massing of new houses around the margins. The WI hall also does duty as a village hall and nursery school. There are some pretty walks up the valley around the River Len, where you could keep in training for the egg-and-spoon race at the annual fête. In the Len valley is **Downswood**, an area of high-density modern housing estates set in farmland, with four shops, where you might buy a three-bedroom semi for £100,000 or a four-bedroom detached for £170,000.

Hollingbourne

Hollingbourne is one of the prettier villages in this part of Kent, though it lies in the path of the Channel Tunnel rail-link which will tunnel underground in order to minimise disturbance. The High Street for practically the whole of its length is lined with half-timbered houses. A small two-bedroom cottage away from the rail-link will cost £85,000; a three-bedroom Victorian house at least £200,000. The upper village clusters around the Elizabethan manor house, with the shops kept in their place at the lower end. There is also a primary school, a football team and an architecturally admired early council housing estate built just after World War II. Hollingbourne church contains the 300-year-old embroidered Culpeper cloth. The North Downs Way passes through the village and affords some breathtaking walks.

Journey: 64 min	
Season: £2384	
Peak: 2 per hr	
Off-peak: 1 per hr	

This is also the station for Leeds Castle. The castle was built in 1192 in the middle of a lake formed by the River Len, and given by Edward I to his wife Eleanor of Castile. It was given to the nation in 1974 and is now a venue for conferences, open air concerts, balloon events and so on. Prices in **Leeds** are similar to those in Hollingbourne. It merges into the neighbouring village of **Langley**, where there is a shooting ground and a golf course, and where you can spot deer in the woodland. A three-bedroom semi will cost £105,000.

Harrietsham

Harrietsham is split by the A20 and has been heavily developed. It has a village shop and an Indian restaurant and two pubs. A three-bedroom modern semi will cost around £120,000; a new three-bedroom detached chalet £165,000; a tile-hung five-bedroom house with a generous garden £350,000. Among the older properties you might stumble across a strange anachronism – a cottage with a flying freehold on a bedroom in the house next door.

Journey: 68 min	
Season: £2404	
Peak: 2 per hr	
Off-peak: 1 per hr	

Lenham

Lenham is a large working village with a population of around 3,500. It combines a pretty central market square, surrounded by Wealden hall houses and Georgian-fronted buildings, with a strong industrial base. Marley Tiles established itself here in the Twenties (its three factories are quite well hidden), and in the Seventies the Lenham Storage Company set up Freightflow, one of Britain's first international customs depots. This brings a lot of trans-continental lorries to (but not through) the village. The parish hall is on the square and is heavily used by organised groups rang-

Journey: 71 min	
Season: £2436	
Peak: 2 per hr	
Off-peak: 1 per hr	

ing from badminton to British Legion. The village is particularly strong on football – there are several junior teams – bowls and cricket. It has its own primary and secondary schools. Because of the changes in farming methods, ramblers often now find themselves prairie-walking rather than following the ancient footpaths, but the village's saving grace is that it lies just at the foot of the North Downs, which is a designated Area of Outstanding Natural Beauty.

Prices don't vary much in the villages between Maidstone and Ashford. Small cottages start at around £90,000, with prices rising to around £700,000 for the largest period properties. For a three-bedroom semi on a modern estate you would have to pay around £110,000.

Charing

Journey: 76 min
Season: £2496
Peak: 2 per hr
Off-peak: 1 per hr

At the heart of **Charing** is the old Archbishop's Palace, once used by Archbishops of Canterbury but now a private house. The green – a favourite place to sit in summer – overlooks the market place, where a modern library has replaced the old pig slaughterhouse. The main street with its Elizabethan and Georgian-faced houses is a whole town in miniature. It has two butchers, an interiors shop, two grocers, a watchmaker, an electrician and hardware store, and a doctor's surgery. Charing likes to be thought of not just as a pretty village, but as a hard-working one, too. A two-bedroom period cottage here would cost £95,000, a large, family-size period house around £320,000 and a four-bedroom modern detached house £200,000. There are also some flats in Elizabethan Court on the High Street priced at around £70,000 for two bedrooms. The village has a primary school and a host of clubs and societies. The WI holds a weekly market in part of the Archbishop's Palace.

A modern library has replaced the old pig slaughterhouse

Ashford International

Journey: 84 min
Season: £2560 (also valid to Charing Cross)
Peak: 2 per hr
Off-peak: 1 per hr
See also Charing Cross to Canterbury West, page 311.

People are not kind about **Ashford**. If Kent were ever to need an enema, they suggest, then Ashford is where you'd insert the tube. In the Seventies it was designated as a growth area. Thousands of new houses were built, the population swelled to nearly 100,000 and a lot more housing is planned. Ashford is zoned for growth. Beside the domestic station used by Connex trains there is now the International Passenger Station used by Eurostar, with combined traffic of around 8.5m passengers each year. Lydd Airport is just a few miles away; Sainsbury and Tesco and Cineworld multiplex cinema have set up shop alongside junctions 9 and 10 of the M20.

House prices in Ashford tend to be 10% lower than they are in Maidstone or Tonbridge, because of the distance from London. A three-bedroom semi with a garage will cost £75,000 to £90,000; a modern four-bedroom detached house £110,000 to £200,000. A two- to three-bedroom period cottage will be over £100,000. Ashford has two good grammar schools, Highworth School for Girls and Norton Knatchbull for boys, and three mixed high schools. Ashford Girls' School is private and takes both boarders and day-pupils.

Boughton Aluph's church is a mile away since the village was displaced by the Black Death

On the slopes of the North Downs are several tiny hamlets amounting to little more than clusters of houses. **Boughton Aluph** (pronounced Borton Aluf) is rather more substantial. It is centred around a village green on which cricket has been played since 1752. This is flanked on one side by neo-Georgian houses and on the other by the green-painted, corrugated iron village hall, known as the Iron Room. The village has one or two distinguished Elizabethan houses but there is no shop, and the church (a mile away since the village was displaced by the Black Death) is used only in summer. In winter it is too expensive to heat. The Stour Music Festival is an annual thrill for lovers of early music. The big house, Eastwell Manor, has become a hotel. A two-bedroom cottage in Boughton Aluph will cost £90,000 to £100,000; a family-size period house over £250,000.

Challock Lees, also to the north, is similarly priced. The Lees which gives the place its name is 16 acres of common land. It has a 12th-century church and a primary school but little else, for this is another village that moved at the time of the Black Death. **Challock** (pronounced Chollock) proper has a considerable number of new houses squeezed between the old, and there are a couple of modern closes. A large modern detached house will cost between £180,000 and £300,000. Challock is high up on the Downs, 630ft above sea level, and there are some spectacular footpaths and bridleways. The price you pay is that it can be very cold, windy and foggy in winter. The village has a post office-cum-general store and a farm shop.

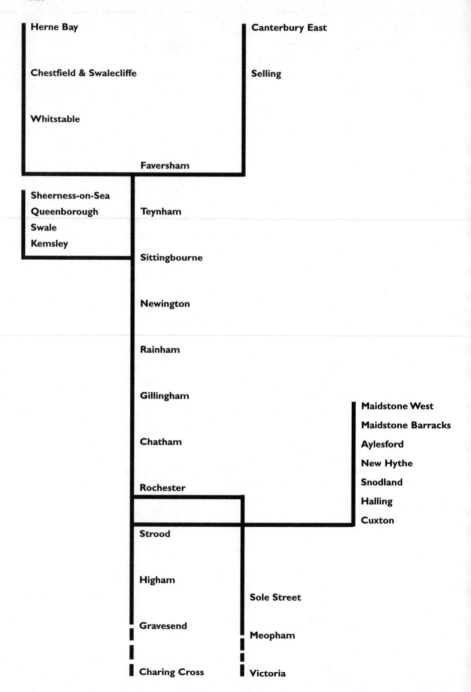

Herne Bay

Canterbury East

Chestfield & Swalecliffe

Selling

Whitstable

Faversham

Sheerness-on-Sea
Queenborough
Swale
Kemsley

Teynham

Sittingbourne

Newington

Rainham

Gillingham

Maidstone West

Maidstone Barracks

Aylesford

Chatham

New Hythe

Snodland

Rochester

Halling

Cuxton

Strood

Higham

Sole Street

Gravesend

Meopham

Charing Cross

Victoria

Charing Cross/Victoria
➡ Herne Bay and Canterbury
(via Rochester)

Line from Victoria to **Sole Street**

Meopham

The cricket green at **Meopham** really grabs all the attention, being over-looked by a marvellous wooden smock mill. The village is long and strag-gly with a seemingly endless main street dotted with 16th- and 17th-cen-tury houses mixed with new. You would pay £85,000 to £100,000 for a two-bedroom cottage; around £135,000 for a three-bedroom semi built in the Sixties or Seventies.

Journey: 44 min
Season: £2020
Peak: 3 per hr
Off-peak: 2 per hr

Sole Street

Sole Street is deceptively small and, because it really is very rural, it can be rather expensive. It has a general store, a pub, a little shop and a post office. The Tudor Yeoman's House is owned by the National Trust, though you have to make a written request to see it. Older, two-bedroom Victorian terrace houses sell for around £85,000; four-bedroom modern detached houses for £180,000 to £300,000. There are some large individual properties built with large gardens around 1920, for which you would probably have to pay upwards of £300,000.

Journey: 46 min
Season: £2020
Peak: 3 per hr
Off-peak: 2 per hr

Cobham is a very pretty north Kent village in an Area of Outstanding Natural Beauty on the crest of a hill. The big house, Cobham Hall, is now a girls' boarding school, but the grounds – landscaped by Repton – and the deer park are often open to the public in summer. The Street has a good range of 18th-century houses, some Victorian and some weather-boarded, plus the village hall and three pubs, including the Leather Bottle – a pub which Dickens used as a setting in *Pickwick Papers*. There is also a Victorian flint primary school and a general store that sells meat. It is a very expensive village in which a one-bedroom 18th-century cottage will cost upwards of £80,000 and a three-bedroom cottage £140,000-£150,000. A modern detached house will be at least £200,000.

Main line from Charing Cross

Gravesend

Journey: 51 min
Season: £1720
Peak: 4 per hr (plus
3 per hr to Cannon
Street)
Off-peak: 4 per hr

For centuries the local economy of **Gravesend**, London's trade and defensive gateway, has been bound to the River Thames. Many of the traditional riverside industries have closed down now, but the paper mills and cement works are still going. The riverside part of town is heavily atmospheric, with narrow streets and alleyways peppered with old churches, inns and historic fortifications. The best place to watch river traffic ploughing the Thames is from the Gordon Promenade gardens, where you can look across the water into Essex.

Efforts to work the London Docklands miracle by replacing old industrial sores with mix-and-match housing are well under way. The district council and Kent County Council together have allocated funds for a town rejuvenation scheme which they have called Towncentric, but its thrust is mainly commercial. The headquarters of the Port of London Authority and Customs and Excise have moved here, and by 2002 there should be a new international station with a fast track to London. There are swathes of Edwardian and Victorian houses, and some handsome Georgian houses (which have been sadly neglected). It is a good hunting ground for first-time buyers. A small two-bedroom Victorian house would cost around £80,000; a slightly larger, typically bay-fronted one around £100,000. Almost on the river an old brewery building has been converted into flats selling at around £60,000; and there are some new developments in which two-bedroom flats with river balconies sell from around £100,000. Large Georgian terrace houses with four or five bedrooms can be bought for around £160,000 to £190,000.

Property prices are higher to the south of the town, especially in the Thirties-built roads around the golf course. A large detached house will cost from upwards of £200,000 to around £425,000, for which you would also get a very large garden. Another more expensive part of Gravesend is the Windmill Hill conservation area, a mile from the town centre, where some of the houses have giddy river views. A two-bedroom Victorian house would cost at least £85,000. Some of the larger houses have been converted into flats. These don't often come on the market but would command a price of up to £65,000 for one bedroom. If you were looking for a house on a decent modern estate, then the answer could be Rivermount, built in the Eighties, where a four-bedroom detached house costs £185,000, a three-bedroom semi £95,000, and you might get a good view thrown in. The village of **Shorne**, two miles east, is pretty and old (though with its fair share of new), and very much sought after since this part of north Kent can seem rather bleak. It is also close to the A2. Snob value adds to the prices of the 15th- and 16th-century timber-framed cottages. You'd have to pay £120,000 for one-and-a-half bedrooms, £130,000 for a modest three-bedroom house in a terrace. There are a few three-bedroom detached Sixties houses, valued at around £265,000.

Higham

Higham station car park has now closed, leaving commuters to use the increasingly congested streets. There are a few older properties, but most of the houses were built in the Sixties and Seventies. A Victorian two-up-two-down will cost around £85,000; a modern three-bedroom semi around £100,000. There is a butcher, a hairdresser, greengrocer, pub and takeaway. Gad's Hill Place was Charles Dickens's home from 1856 until the end of his life, and is now an independent girls' school. He left *Edwin Drood* unfinished when he died in 1870.

Journey: 58 min
Season: £1920
Peak: 3 per hr
(plus 2 per hr to
Cannon Street)
Off-peak: 2 per hr

Strood

Strood is linked to Rochester by a bridge over the River Medway. Its small High Street has a broader choice of shops than Rochester's, and B&Q, Homebase and Safeway draw people from over the water. The houses in the centre are flat-fronted, late-Victorian terraces, which – at between £50,000 and £55,000 for two bedrooms – are attractive to first-time buyers. Close to the station is a surge of Fifties housing where a three-bedroom home would cost around £70,000. In the more sedate Thirties developments near the fringes of the town, a three-bedroom house would cost around £90,000.

Journey: 63 min
Season: £1960
Peak: 3 per hr
(plus 2 per hr to
Cannon Street)
Off-peak: 2 per hr

It is a popular area for boating. Further out along the Medway estuary, the marina at **Upnor** throngs with hundreds of small craft. Developers have begun to cater for the sailors' needs by providing small town houses and semis along the riverbank. Prices are similar to those in Strood. The main street is rather pretty, with old weatherboarded houses. Upnor Castle, now a museum, was built in the mid-16th century to defend Chatham dockyard. The Isle of Grain, which thrusts out like a hammerhead over the mouth of the estuary, is deeply unattractive, bristling with oil terminals and refineries. It is one of the fastest growing container ports in the country. British Gas has 900 acres of land earmarked for future industrial development.

Developers have begun to cater for the sailors' needs by providing small town houses and semis along the riverbank

Branch line to **Maidstone West** via **Cuxton, Halling, Snodland, New Hythe, Aylesford** and **Maidstone Barracks**

No through trains. It is possible to travel in the opposite direction and change at Maidstone Barracks (footpath to Maidstone West. Journey: 83 min (from Aylesford) Season: £2300 (£2360 if valid via Maidstone) Peak: 3 per hr* Off-peak: 2 per hr* *Change at Strood.

Cuxton is one of the Medway villages that boomed with the cement industry during the 19th century. It has an attractive mock-Tudor station with a hand-operated level crossing and an old-fashioned signal box. Some of the houses are Victorian terraces suitable for first-time buyers, selling for around £65,000 to £75,000 for two bedrooms.

On the boarders of Cuxton, **Halling** is dominated by the large riverside cement works. This part of north Kent is not very popular, but it does offer the prospect of affordable housing and property here is selling fairly fast. A detached family house on a new development can be bought for £175,000. **Snodland**, too, has been stigmatised by association with the cement industry. Blue Circle and the area around the cement works is plagued by dust and lorries. Snodland has a plain Victorian centre where terrace houses sell for between £65,000 and £75,000. On the new developments around the margins you would expect to pay up to £75,000 for a two-bedroom terrace, and around £90,000 for a three-bedroom semi.

New Hythe is very close to the old Aylesford paper mills, which have now been converted to light industrial use. Victorian and Thirties semis range from £90,000 to £100,000. **Aylesford** is marginally more appealing and is thought to offer good value for money. It has a 14th-century ragstone bridge and some very old houses overlooking the River Medway. These might sell in the region of £120,000 and upwards. There are also lots of old terrace properties with two or three bedrooms, selling in the £75,000 to £80,000 range. For **Maidstone** see main line to Ashford via Maidstone, page 314.

Converted oast house

Continuation of main line

Rochester

Most of this apparently seamless string of north Kent towns looks as if it might have detached itself from the north of England and slipped southwards during the night. **Rochester**, however, is something of an exception, having managed to sustain a policy of architectural conservation on the back of the Charles Dickens industry – just as in the past it was able to create fine buildings on the back of its maritime trade. The pedestrianised High Street has an intimate villagey atmosphere with tourist shops, gift shops, antique shops and small businesses packing the narrow streets around it. It is pleasant to stroll and enjoy some of the older Elizabethan buildings and excellent Georgian houses. The town is stiff with locations used by Dickens in his novels. The Royal Victoria Hotel is The Bull in *Pickwick Papers*; The Bull is The Blue Boar in *Great Expectations*; Miss Haversham's home was loosely based on Restoration House; *Edwin Drood* was set in Rochester. The Charles Dickens Centre at Eastgate House has the reconstructed Swiss chalet workshop in which the author worked while he lived at Gad's Hill. Every year the town dresses itself in 19th-century costume for the summer Dickens Festival and Christmas Dickensian festivities.

To Victoria	
Journey: 40 min	
Season: £2200	
Peak: 3 per hr	
Off-peak: 3 per hr	

To Charing Cross	
Journey: 66 min	
Season: £2200	
Peak: 2 per hr	
(plus 2 per hr to	
Cannon Street)	
Off-peak: 2 per hr	

One of the most prestigious areas is close to the castle. This was built during the reign of Henry I, and has a well-preserved square keep that overlooks the river. Nearby are the cathedral, largely

Rochester is stiff with locations used by Dickens in his novels

12th-century, and King's School Rochester, the co-educational public school. One of the best places for period properties is St Margaret's Street, where a four-bedroom early Georgian house with garage will fetch £250,000. In the streets just off it, and lying within the same conservation area, are large, five-bedroom Victorian houses which fetch around £275,000 to £300,000. For less expensive homes you need to travel five or 10 minutes outwards from the centre. Here you will find row upon row of Victorian terraces. They front straight on to the pavement and sell at around £55,000 for two bedrooms.

New building has been kept at bay, but there are a few small estates where you could buy a four-bedroom, box-shaped detached house for upwards of £150,000. To the south is a large area of Thirties housing with some bay-fronted terraces and semis, and a few bungalows. The average price for a three-bedroom semi in good condition is £115,000.

You have to suffer a little to commute from Rochester. The one-way system makes driving to the station difficult, and parking is not easy. For this reason many people prefer to travel from Chatham.

Chatham

To Victoria
Journey: 41 min
Season: £2200
Peak: 4 per hr
Off-peak: 4 per hr

To Charing Cross
Journey: 69 min
Season: £2200
Peak: 1 per hr (plus
3 per hr to Cannon
Street)
Off-peak: 2 per hr

Little flat-fronted Victorian terraces, ideal for first-time buyers at between £40,000 and £50,000, cram the steep hillsides around **Chatham** dockyards, once the industrial heart of the town. Its first ship was launched in 1586 to join the fleet against the Spanish Armada. Four centuries and 400 Royal Navy ships later, the docks were closed in 1984 and handed over to a trust. The 80-acre site, which contains 47 scheduled monuments, is the most complete Georgian and early Victorian dockyard in the world, and has recently been grandly renamed World Naval Base. Now it is almost as much of an attraction to house-hunters as it is to tourists. Part of it has been turned into a living museum where you can see rope- and sail-making. Other parts have been converted to residential use with a choice of both restored and new properties. The new developments include one- and two-bedroom flats ranging from £85,000 to £120,000, and town houses modelled on the Georgian officers' terraces, priced at £180,000 to £200,000. Restored properties include 12 houses in a terrace built on five floors between 1722 and 1732. These have relatively plain interiors and are priced at £475,000. Old naval stable blocks have been converted into three-bedroom mews houses selling at between £150,000 and £160,000. Outside

Schools in Kent

Kent still has some of its old grammar schools, though parents should remember that entry is highly selective. At Tonbridge there are two grammars for girls and Judd for boys – as well as Tonbridge independent boarding and day school for boys.

Tunbridge Wells is full of good schools, which include Tunbridge Wells Girls Grammar, Tunbridge Wells Grammar for boys, as well as Skinners for boys, plus Kent College Pembury independent girls boarding and day school.

Sevenoaks is rightly proud of Sevenoaks School, an independent co-educational day and boarding school beside Knole Park, and Walthamstow Hall independent day school for girls.

At Cranbrook, close to Staplehurst station, is the Cranbrook co-educational grant-maintained day and boarding grammar school. It is so popular that houses within a five-mile catchment area may carry a premium price. Nearby is the girls' public school Benenden.

Maidstone has its Girls' Grammar and Maidstone Grammar for boys (girls in the sixth). Nearby is Sutton Valence, an independent co-educational day and boarding school. Girls can also look to Ashford where there is Highworth Grammar for

Girls, Invicta Grammar, and Ashford independent day and boarding school. Boys in Ashford can go to Norton Knatchbull which does well in the school league tables.

Canterbury offers a wide choice. King's Canterbury, the independent co-educational day and boarding school, is set in the cathedral precinct and has a strong musical tradition. Its rival is Kent College, the independent co-educational day and boarding school with its own 90-acre farm. There are also two grammars – Simon Langton Boys' and Simon Langton Girls'.

Gravesend has Gravesend Boys' Grammar and Gravesend Girls' Grammar. Chatham has Chatham Girls' Grammar, which is grant-maintained and allows boys into the sixth form. Chatham Boys' Grammar also performs well in the school league tables, as does Ford Pitt Grammar. Other good grammar schools include those at Gillingham, Broadstairs, Sittingbourne and Faversham.

Rochester also has its own cathedral school, mostly for day pupils. King's is co-educational, independent and fiercely no-nonsense. Rochester Girls' Grammar was founded in the 1880s to produce girls "fit to adorn the homes of England".

the dockyard you can find three-bedroom ex-naval Georgian town houses selling for around £145,000.

For cheaper modern housing you could look at the Walderslade area, a huge estate with one-bedroom starter homes at £40,000, two-bedroom terraces at £60,000 and four-bedroom family houses at £140,000.

Gillingham

Gillingham is the largest of the Medway towns and commercial big brother to Chatham, with which it shares the now defunct naval dockyards and depot. The large shopping centre has a pedestrianised High Street with the usual chain stores. There are very good leisure facilities – an ice rink, leisure centre, leisure pool, indoor bowls and cricket, and Gillingham Football Club, currently playing in the second division of the Football League. The dockyard here is ringed by an old Georgian fortification system called the Brompton Lines, one-and-a-half-miles of moats and ramparts overlooked by the Napoleonic Fort Amherst.

Near the town centre many of the tightly-packed Victorian streets are still very run down but first-time buyers can pick up small terrace houses for around £50,000. One of the better areas is Darland, a Thirties estate where four-bedroom detached houses sell for upwards of £200,000.

To Victoria	
Journey: 45 min	
Season: £2260	
Peak: 4 per hr	
Off-peak: 4 per hr	
To Charing Cross	
Journey: 72 min	
Season: £2260	
Peak: 1 per hr	
(plus 3 per hr to	
Cannon Street)	
Off-peak: 2 per hr	

Rainham

Rainham is much more suburban in character than either Gillingham or Chatham, with the atmosphere of a dormitory town. It was once popular with hop-pickers coming down from London. The station is large and the London trains are fast. Housing is a mixed bag, from turn-of-the-century farmworkers' terraces at £55,000 to £60,000 to architect-designed Thirties houses in the Wigmore area, where four-bedroom detached houses now sell from £140,000 upwards. Hempstead is another attractive area with an old villagey heart and an outgrowth of new estates: you can pay from £65,000 for a starter home right up to £250,000 or £400,000 for a large detached house. The Riverside Country Park, which extends along the southern shore of the Medway Estuary between Gillingham and Rainham, offers escape from the relentless housing. The park was formed from reclaimed saltmarshes and is linked from west to east by the Saxon Shore Way – a coastal footpath which runs 140 miles between Gravesend and Rye.

To Victoria	
Journey: 49 min	
Season: £2280	
Peak: 3 per hr	
(plus 3 per hr to	
Cannon Street)	
Off-peak: 4 per hr	

The Saxon Shore Way runs 140 miles between Gravesend and Rye

Newington

To Victoria
Journey: 71 min
Season: £2340
Peak: 1 per hr (plus
2 per hr to Cannon
Street)
Off-peak: 2 per hr

The countryside does try to breathe here but it is soon submerged again by Sittingbourne. **Newington** is thought to be more rural, but in fact it's bisected by the busy A2 and is beginning to merge at one end with Sittingbourne and at the other end with Hartlip. You can't call it pretty, though the planned bypass may help. A two-up-two-down terrace will cost just over £60,000; a modern three-bedroom semi close to £90,000. Calloways Lane is particularly smart. A large five-bedroom detached house on up to an acre of ground here would sell for over £250,000.

Hartlip, a mile or so to the south-west, is far more sought after. It has more of a villagey feel and is close to the Medway Towns. This is one of the first conveniently placed, attractive villages that you reach on your way out of London through this part of Kent. The conservation area in the village centre encompasses a handful of listed buildings, 15th-century thatched cottages and a fine half-timbered pink-and-white house. The rest is brick and weatherboarding, plus some modern houses built in the Eighties. It is a good address. You will have to pay £375,000 or more for a four-bedroom period property with an acre of ground, £250,000 or more for a modern four-bedroom detached house. There is a primary school with about 85 pupils, a church, a Methodist chapel and a village hall. The local parish pump is The Rose and Crown – symbolic of Kent's reputation as the Garden of England and its allegiance to the Sovereign. The village is friendly to newcomers and used to commuters. The main worry is that Gillingham might burst at the seams and engulf it.

Sittingbourne

To Victoria
Journey: 56 min
Season: £2380
Peak: 3 per hr (plus
3 per hr to Cannon
Street)
Off-peak: 4 per hr

Like the Medway Towns, **Sittingbourne** is more affordable for first-time buyers. Much of the town centre looks more like Coronation Street than Kent, with terraces fronting straight on to the pavement. A two- or three-bedroom house here could be bought for between £45,000 and £60,000. Yet it is still only an hour by train from London. The favoured side of town is the south, where Thirties detached houses and semis – some of them with good long gardens – sell for between £125,000 and £250,000. There are new estates here, too, with three-bedroom semis at £75,000 to £85,000, and two- or three-bedroom terraces at just over £65,000.

The mile-long High Street still displays something of its history as a market town (there are Wednesday and Friday markets) and coaching stop. Pilgrims used to rest here on their way to Canterbury. The Red Lion, George and Bull inns are still there, and there is evidence of Georgian buildings behind the High Street's modern facades. Sittingbourne was also once a busy harbour town. The muddy Milton Creek that runs into town

from The Swale is lined with warehouses, factories and reedy inlets. The Dolphin Yard Sailing Barge Museum repairs and restores barges. The town's prosperity used to depend on the hugely expanding demand for bricks, paper and cement in the late 19th century. Of these traditional local industries only paper-making now remains, the rest have been replaced by modern light manufacturing. For recreation there is a huge, multi-million-pound leisure centre called The Swallows.

Restored timber-frame house, north Kent

House prices rise a little as you move out to the villages. To the west is **Stockbury**, where it would be difficult to find a property at less than £130,000, for which you might be lucky enough to get a two-bedroom bungalow. Most houses will cost around the £240,000 mark, though those nearer to the gypsy camp tend to fetch less. Closer to Sittingbourne is **Borden**. It is quite smart, and attracts executives. Some parts of it are very old indeed: a 13th-century church is set in the conservation area which contains some quaint, white-painted weatherboarded cottages. You would pay £95,000 for a small period cottage. Four-bedroom detached houses range from around £200,000 to £250,000. Much of the building is in brick, with some timber-frame and some modern infilling. At the heart of the village is the Playstool – an old Kentish name for a playing field on two levels. From the top level you have wonderful views across the countryside. The main street is called The Street and has a pub, and a general store with a post office. The village has a high proportion of elderly people as well as a thriving primary school.

Less than a mile away is **Tunstall**. Prices here are similar to those in Borden, though the village itself is very tiny, with a small primary school but no shops, and has become almost a suburb of Sittingbourne. Due south of here is **Milstead**. Opinions and signposts vary about the correct spelling (several maps and guides, though not the Ordnance Survey, omit the *a*) though there's no doubt about its status as the most sought-after village in the area. It has a truly Kentish feel to it, with leafy lanes on the slopes of the North Downs giving on to a church, a pub, a thatched cricket pavilion, a primary school and old thatched cottages which tend to be occupied by well-paid professionals. A three-bedroom detached cottage will come with a price tag of over £250,000. The village itself is a conservation area. The surrounding countryside is a designated Area of Outstanding Natural Beauty. At the centre is a tiny green with an old cedar tree growing on it, framed by a row of tile-hung cottages, the church and Milstead Manor. It is a busy place. The cricket attracts people from neighbouring villages, and the school just outside the village has a swimming pool. It is worried about becoming a dormitory village, though there are truly local families who have lived here for years. A car is essential for all those who don't want to have to use the post bus.

Branch line to **Sheerness-on-sea** via **Kemsley, Swale** & **Queenborough**

No through trains.
Change at
Sittingbourne.
Journey: 77 min
(from Sheerness)
Season: £2380
Peak: 3 per hr*
Off-peak: 2 per hr*

Kemsley was built to house workers from the nearby papermills and is rather formally laid out with a central square containing a modern social centre built in Queen Anne style. The area is not greatly sought after. Three-bedroom terrace houses cost only around £52,000. There is also a large new estate on the outskirts where prices are low: one-bedroom starter homes sell for just over £45,000, three-bedroom semis for £82,000 and four-bedroom detached houses for £120,000.

Swale station is in a bleak and remote spot where the only housing to speak of is the occasional farmhouse on the flattest of horizons. It was named after the channel that separates the Isle of Sheppey from the mainland, now spanned by the Kingsferry Bridge (the central section of which opens up for coasters). The Royal Society for the Protection of Birds' Elmley Marshes Nature Reserve begins here and stretches across the southern part of the island. At **Queenborough** once again you find the typically north Kentish combination of relentless turn-of-the-century housing in a harbour setting. The High Street ends in an esplanade where you can watch the boats using the new all-tide landing gear. Queenborough is popular as a safe haven for ships caught in storms but not so much as a place to live. Two-bedroom Victorian terrace houses sell for £38,000 to £45,000.

Sheerness-on-Sea is where Nelson's body was brought in *HMS Victory* after the Battle of Trafalgar in 1805

Sheerness-on-Sea, at the north-west tip of the Isle of Sheppey, is protected by a massive sea wall above the clean shingle beach, from which there are good views over the Thames estuary. The design of the old dockyards was supervised by Samuel Pepys in his capacity as Secretary to the Navy Board in 1665. This is where Nelson's body was brought in *HMS Victory* after the Battle of Trafalgar in 1805. Today Sheerness has a flourishing container port. Most of the town consists of Victorian terrace housing, built for dockyard workers and now selling at around £45,000 for two bedrooms. Ex-council semis sometimes fetch about £60,000. **Minster**, two miles to the east, is more popular. Semis and bungalows here tend to sell in the range of £80,000 to £90,000. Established between the wars by speculative developers who sold plots to Londoners who wanted seaside homes, Minster has had another development spurt during the last 30 years. The coast from Minster to Leysdown is a more or less continuous run of caravan sites and chalets.

Continuation of main line

Teynham

Teynham is a sprawling village unromantically sandwiched between the A2 and the railway. It was once 10 hamlets, hence its name. Though only a few trains stop here in peak hours, Teynham is very much a commuter village. Most of the houses were built during the Sixties and Seventies. A three-bedroom semi of that vintage will sell for around £80,000. A run of older, turn-of-the-century housing flanking the A2 provides two- or three-bedrooms for around £65,000. Outside the road-rail sandwich lie the hopfields which supply the Faversham breweries.

To Victoria
Journey: 80 min
Season: £2400
Peak: 1 per hr
(plus 2 per hr to Cannon Street)
Off-peak: 2 per hr

Faversham

Faversham is a hugely popular old market town. The historic Market Place lies within a mainly pedestrianised conservation shopping area, and still has markets on Tuesdays, Fridays and Saturdays. Tudor and Georgian houses exude period charm, and Faversham Creek brings the sights and smells of the river. It was this navigable tidal inlet that earned Faversham its status as one of the Cinque Ports. The warships built there won it the further title of King's Port. There are still some medieval warehouses left on its banks, though today it is the brewing industry that dominates.

To Victoria
Journey: 65 min
Season: £2440
Peak: 3 per hr
(plus 3 per hr to Cannon Street)
Off-peak: 4 per hr

Small plain terrace houses sell for between £55,000 and £60,000. For more expensive property, one of the most sought-after streets is Abbey Street, which contains some of the oldest half-timbered buildings in Kent. They very rarely come on the market, but their current value is probably in the £170,000 to £230,000 range. People looking for new houses should consider the Preston Park estate in the south-east. This offers a range of housing from two-bedroom terrace houses at around £85,000 to four-bedroom detached at around £180,000.

The villages around Faversham benefit from their proximity to such an attractive and popular town. Stretched along a valley bottom to the south-west is **Newnham**, which has a conservation area and a pub, and where everyone knows everyone. A one-bedroom weatherboarded cottage might fetch £75,000; a two-bedroom period house £125,000; a four-bedroom detached £250,000 to £265,000. Newnham's big house is an interesting Tudor pile with two chalk fireplaces and decorative plasterwork in the form of tumbling leaves. It is privately owned.

The harbour area in Whitstable now contains the largest oyster hatchery in Europe

Eastling, a mile from Newnham, has 14th- and 15th-century timbered hall houses and ancient weatherboarded houses scattered along country lanes. The cheapest two-bedroom weatherboarded house would be likely to cost around £110,000. The village has a pub and a church (with a yew tree reputedly over 900 years old), and a primary school with a toddlers' group, but there are no shops. Though the village has a number of vigorous societies, the character of the place has changed over the years as commuters have replaced agricultural workers. Two or three miles away is Belmont House, an 18th-century mansion set in fine parkland which is open to the public.

Boughton village, a couple of miles east, has a charming main street lined with period houses, laced with a few shops and two good pubs. It has a complete cross-section of residents, including quite a few commuters. A modern three-bedroom semi with a garage and garden would sell for £85,000. A larger six-bedroom early Victorian house would be expected to fetch around £225,000 to £260,000.

Fork from Faversham to **Herne Bay Whitstable**

To Victoria
Journey: 76 min
Season: £2500
Peak: 2 per hr (plus 2 per hr to Cannon Street)
Off-peak: 2 per hr

The sea can be a force to be reckoned with in **Whitstable**. New sea defences now keep it snug and dry, but in the terrible storm of 1953, waves breached the sea wall and the tide surged miles inland. The oyster industry was severely disrupted, though it has been built up again so successfully that the harbour area now contains the largest oyster hatchery in Europe. There is an annual summer oyster festival, and the beginning of the oyster season is marked by the blessing of the sea.

The housing market has been frisky recently, boosted by commuters and second-home hunters. The town centre is full of little Victorian terraces of two-up-two-downs. The shabbier ones sell at £55,000; restored ones at £70,000. There are also some well-established newer developments. In Bay View, for example, a neo-Georgian semi here would cost in the region of £90,000. On the seafront there are some 200-year-old smugglers' and fishermen's cottages with added cutesey value. Expect to pay £100,000 or more for a three-bedroom semi. Also overlooking the sea is a small development called Cushions View. A one-bedroom flat here costs £80,000; a larger town house probably £145,000. As a resort Whitstable is fairly restrained, though there are the usual seaside amusements and it is popular for yachting and watersports. The rows of weatherboarded fishermen's cottages and old boat sheds along the shingle beach (there is sand to the east and west) are the subject of a Turner sketch.

Tankerton, on the east side of Whitstable old town, is sedate, slightly more expensive and a popular retirement haven. Houses on the seafront sell for between £180,000 and £300,000, and overlook the Tankerton Slopes, a wide grassy verge that runs down to the beach. Extending from the beach is a long shingle spit known as The Street. This is where two tides meet, and at low water you can walk right out along it into the sea. **Seasalter**, to the west, is another retirement area with its own parade of shops and ration of bungalows. In Joy Lane you will find some of the most expensive houses in the area. This is where Somerset Maugham, whose uncle was vicar of Whitstable, learned to ride his bicycle. If you fancy one of the large detached houses he must have wobbled past, you'll need to spend anything from £250,000 up to £325,000.

Chestfield & Swalecliffe

There is a bit of snob value attached to **Chestfield**. It is a cut above the seaside tat, thinks of itself as a village and has a private golf club. The new dual carriageway on the A299 has affected it, though. There are some very large period houses that sell for over £400,000. Between these are new developments or individually-built modern houses on small plots that sell in the £150,000 to £180,000 range. On the Chestfield Park estate, Tudor-style family houses sell from just under £180,000 to £250,000. The village does also have some properties for first-time buyers. Expect to pay around £70,000 for two bedrooms. Chestfield now spills over into **Swalecliffe** which has lots of ex-council houses in the £50,000 range and some cheaper bungalows at £65,000 to £75,000.

To Victoria
Journey: 80 min
Season: £2508
Peak: 2 per hr
(plus 1 train to
Cannon Street)
Off-peak: 1 per hr

Herne Bay

The Victorian seaside resort has spread its tentacles over quite a large area now, and much of **Herne Bay** feels like a retirement town. Spacious Victorian terraces on three storeys line the seafront, selling at around £200,000 or more and there are a few restored two-bedroom terrace houses at £70,000. Numerous roads lead down to the sea, fitted with snug

To Victoria
Journey: 81 min
Season: £2560
Peak: 2 per hr
(plus 2 per hr to
Cannon Street)
Off-peak: 2 per hr

two-bedroom bungalows priced at around £80,000; two- to three-bedroom terrace houses at around £70,000; and modern detached houses which rise to £150,000 or £200,000 depending on the views. Herne Bay's long exposed foreshore can be sealed off when there are severe storms; otherwise it is extremely popular with day-trippers, and with sailing and fishing enthusiasts. The seafront has had a £3.5m makeover, though not the pier (the second longest after Southend), which was damaged by storms in 1953 and 1978. However, the Twenties' Art Deco bandstand is now gleaming with fresh paint.

Large family house, Herne Bay

One mile inland is the parent village of **Herne**, a collection of pretty white weatherboarded cottages on a hillside with a restored working 18th-century smock mill. A mid-terrace cottage here would cost just over £65,000.

Main line from **Faversham** to **Canterbury East**

Selling

To Victoria
Journey: 76 min
Season: £2440
Peak: 1 per hr plus 2 per hr changing at Faversham
Off-peak: 1 per hr

This is a nice position to be in. You are close to the pretty market town of Faversham, near enough to Canterbury for special shopping, and also handy for the sea. The countryside starts to roll south-east of Faversham, and at Perry Wood is a huge area of unspoilt accessible woodland. From the Pulpit, a wooden structure built on a mound at the highest point, you have panoramic views over Kent. There are some very fine half-timbered houses and oasts scattered in the deep lanes around here. A three-bedroom oast conversion might cost £260,000.

Canterbury East

Canterbury charmingly combines modernity and tourism with its medieval heritage. The centre was bombed out in World War II. Beneath the modern shopping precinct that replaced it are Roman mosaics which are open to the public. Much of the centre is pedestrianised, which makes it a pleasant place to shop, and it is also very beautiful. Despite the bombs, much of the old medieval city remains in the narrow streets of timber-framed houses around the cathedral, where Thomas Becket was murdered. The most sought-after area is within the city walls, close to the cathedral and King's co-educational public school. The latter occupies many of the buildings that were formerly part of the monastery attached to the cathedral. Old Grade II listed houses here are snapped up very quickly. Anything with a garage sells at a premium; parking in Canterbury is a nightmare. At the cheaper end of the market, a tiny turn-of-the-century terrace cottage within the city walls would be likely to fetch between £70,000 and £90,000.

To Victoria
Journey: 82 min
Season: £2580 (also valid at Canterbury West)
Peak: 1 per hr plus 2 per hr changing at Faversham
Off-peak: 2 per hr
See also Canterbury West, page 311.

The city margin is ringed with roomy Victorian detached and semi-detached houses. In Ethelbert Road, to the south, the houses have as many as 10 bedrooms and sell for around £400,000. Unsurprisingly, very few of them remain intact as single homes. Many have been converted into flats – priced at around £60,000 for one bedroom. There are also plenty of modern developments from the Fifties, Sixties and Eighties. A 10-year-old

6

Wickhambreaux once formed part of the Kentish estates of Joan Plantagenet, the Fair Maid of Kent

9

detached house with four bedrooms in the south of the town would cost around £180,000. Within the city walls it would cost over £200,000.

The University of Kent, built in the Sixties high on a windy hill just outside the city, attracts a lot of students to the **St Stephen's** area. Many of the bay-windowed Thirties semis here are rented – some are bought by the parents of wealthier students. A three-bedroom house in need of maintenance would cost around £95,000; one in good condition would be nearer £110,000. Students also buy in the area around St Peter's Place, where a flat-fronted turn-of-the-century house may be picked up for around £70,000 to £75,000.

North of the city the landscape becomes flat and dull, so people prefer to look to the south. Two-and-a-half miles south-east is the village of **Bridge**, which is extremely pretty and commensurately expensive. It offers a mix of thatched cottages and turn-of-the-century and modern houses, but remains very compact. A small thatched cottage might cost £185,000; a five-bedroom neo-Georgian house on the outskirts £265,000. Further east is **Patrixbourne**, which is very tiny but also very pretty and so popular that half-timbered houses and thatched cottages often sell by word of mouth. A four-bedroom oast conversion might cost around £325,000. The Nail Bourne river runs through it, though it fills only after heavy down-pours. For most of the year it is dry.

Looking north-east you find **Wickhambreaux** – a typical Kentish village with a green and an old church on one side, the Little Stour running through it with a watermill now turned into flats, and a manor house. It once formed part of the Kentish estates of Joan Plantagenet, the Fair Maid of Kent, wife of the Black Prince. There are no shops and a minimal bus service, but the village does have a pub and a flourishing Church of England primary school. Two summer fêtes on the green bring the villagers together. There has been little new development for 40 years. A large village house with river frontage would cost £500,000. One way of telling old villagers from new is by the name they give to the main street. Incomers rather grandly call it The Street. To old villagers it is known as Gutter Street.

At **Stodmarsh**, slightly to the north, the landscape becomes very rural, with good views across the Stour valley. Stodmarsh itself is a small village with one pub, and very little ever comes on to the market. If you were lucky, you might pay £70,000 for an unmodernised two-up-two-down cottage; £350,000 or more for a converted oast house. The old coal-mining area has been turned into a nature reserve with man-made lakes to attract birds and wildlife.

Index of stations, towns and villages

Stations are in **bold type**

M

N

Y